Experiencing the Afterlife

The William and Katherine Devers Series in Dante Studies

Theodore J. Cachey, Jr., and Christian Moevs, editors
Simone Marchesi, associate editor
Ilaria Marchesi, assistant editor

Manuele Gragnolati

Experiencing the Afterlife

SOUL AND BODY IN DANTE AND MEDIEVAL CULTURE

University of Notre Dame Press

Notre Dame, Indiana

Manufactured in the United States of America

Library of Congress Cataloging-in-Publication Data

Gragnolati, Manuele.
Experiencing the afterlife : soul and body in Dante
and medieval culture / Manuele Gragnolati.
p. cm. — (The William and Katherine Devers series in Dante studies)
Includes bibliographical references and index.
ISBN 0-268-02964-4 (cloth : alk. paper)
ISBN 0-268-02965-2 (pbk. : alk. paper)
1. Dante Alighieri, 1265–1321—Criticism and interpretation.
2. Italian literature—To 1400—History and criticism.
3. Future life in literature.   4. Future life—History of doctrines—
Middle Ages, 600–1500.   5. Civilization, Medieval, in literature.
I. Title.   II. Series.
PQ4419.F87G73   2005
851'.1—dc22
2005016275

∞ *This book was printed on acid free paper.*

Contents

About the William and Katherine Devers Series in Dante Studies

The William and Katherine Devers Program in Dante Studies at the University of Notre Dame supports rare book acquisitions in the university's John A. Zahm Dante collections, funds an annual visiting professorship in Dante studies, and supports electronic and print publication of scholarly research in the field. In collaboration with the Medieval Institute at the university, the Devers program has initiated a series dedicated to the publication of the most significant current scholarship in the field of Dante Studies.

In keeping with the spirit that inspired the creation of the Devers program, the series takes Dante as a focal point that draws together the many disciplines and lines of inquiry that constitute a cultural tradition without fixed boundaries. Accordingly, the series hopes to illuminate Dante's position at the center of contemporary critical debates in the humanities by reflecting both the highest quality of scholarly achievement and the greatest diversity of critical perspectives.

The series publishes works on Dante from a wide variety of disciplinary viewpoints and in diverse scholarly genres, including critical studies, commentaries, editions, translations, and conference proceedings of exceptional importance. The series is supervised by an international advisory board composed of distinguished Dante scholars and is published regularly by the University of Notre Dame Press. The Dolphin and Anchor device that appears on publications of the Devers series was used by the great humanist, grammarian, editor, and typographer Aldus Manutius (1449–1515), in whose 1502 edition of Dante (second issue) and all subsequent editions it appeared. The device illustrates the ancient proverb *Festina lente,* "Hurry up slowly."

Theodore J. Cachey, Jr., and Christian Moevs, *editors*
Simone Marchesi, *associate editor*
Ilaria Marchesi, *assistant editor*

Advisory Board

Acknowledgments

Several people have helped and supported me in the different stages of this book, and I would like to thank them most sincerely: Zygmunt Barański, Teodolinda Barolini, Caroline Walker Bynum, Anna Maria Digirolamo, Lisa Gourd, Barbara Hanrahan, Anna Harrison, Amy Hollywood, Elena Lombardi, Ilaria and Simone Marchesi, my brother Mici, Christian Moevs, Monika Otter, Piergiacomo Petrioli, John Rassias, Andrea Tarnowski, Peter Travis, and Keith Walker. I would also like to thank Dartmouth College for granting me the sabbatical leave that allowed me to complete the book.

Finally, I would like to thank Christoph Holzhey for his generosity and intelligence. This book is dedicated to him.

Some of the work on Bonvesin da la Riva in chapters 1 and 3 appeared in "From Decay to Splendor: Body and Pain in Bonvesin da la Riva's *Book of the Three Scriptures*," in *Last Things: Death and Apocalypse in the Middle Ages,* edited by Caroline Walker Bynum and Paul Freedman (Philadelphia: University of Pennsylvania Press, 1999), 83–97. Portions of the material in chapter 2 appeared in "From Plurality to (Near) Unicity of Forms: Embryology in *Purgatorio* 25," in *Dante for the New Millennium,* edited by Teodolinda Barolini and Wayne Storey (New York: Fordham University Press, 2003), 192–210.

Preface

According to a famous statement made by Erich Auerbach and endorsed by subsequent critics, "Dante discovered the European representation (Gestalt) of man."[1] For the first time in medieval literature, the reader meets "man not as a remote legendary hero, not as an abstract or anecdotal representation of an ethical type, but man as we know him in historical reality, the concrete individual in his unity and wholeness."[2] In this respect, Dante's *Divine Comedy* is the culmination of the "discovery of the individual," which Colin Morris has linked to an eschatological development that began in the twelfth century and progressively changed its focus from the Last Judgment and the bodily reconstitution of the person to the time in the afterlife in which the soul remains separated from its body.[3] This development is best symbolized by the emergence of the doctrine of purgatory, and it is therefore not surprising that the *Divine Comedy* should also represent, in Jacques Le Goff's formulation, the "poetic triumph" of the newly established dogma of purgatory.[4]

The connection in Dante between the triumph of purgatory and the triumph of the individual would seem to emphasize the soul rather than the body, and to suggest that, contrary to twenty-first-century understandings, body plays no important role in Dante's concept of personal identity. This book questions this line of thought and explores the significant role that the body plays in Dante's understanding of the human being and the way in which Dante negotiates this role with an eschatological concept that focuses on the destiny of the soul when it is severed from its body. I place the *Comedy* in its broad cultural context and engage the specialized field of Dante studies in a dialogue with recent scholarship from other disciplines that has mapped out the richness of the eschatological thought in the Middle Ages and its anthropological implications. This larger perspective, which explores the *Comedy* in relation to not only learned but also popular and noncanonical texts, sheds new light on some of the most vigorously debated questions raised by the *Comedy*, such as the embryological account of *Purgatorio* 25 and the crux of the pilgrim's body in the *Paradiso*. It also makes visible issues that are otherwise difficult to discern: the tension between the representation of a fully embodied soul and the expectation of the resurrection of the body; the relation between the soul's experience in purgatory and the devotion that thirteenth-century culture began to express toward Christ's humanity and suffering; and the significance of the audacious vision of resurrected bodies that Dante the pilgrim enjoys at the end of his journey. At the same time, my analysis brings these questions and issues back into contemporary discussion of Christian eschatology in the thirteenth and early fourteenth centuries, opening new perspectives on the way in which its evolution was shaped by an embodied concept of identity and by the new, positive attitude toward pain's potential that Esther Cohen has named "philopassianism."[5]

In the central Middle Ages, assumptions regarding the experience of the person in the afterlife underwent a significant transformation. The traditional eschatological emphasis lay on bodily return at the end of time and the material reconstitution of the person. It was centered on the collective scenario of the Last Judgment (when humankind as a whole was divided into the wicked and the just), and the subsequent, fully embodied experience of heaven or hell. The new sense of eschatological experience that emerged in the twelfth century and developed thereafter concerns, on the contrary, the individual destiny of the separated soul and is closely related to the emergence of a new attitude toward physical death. As Philippe Ariès has shown, apart from the traditional notion of death as something for which one prepares and which one experiences in community ("tamed death"), in the eleventh and twelfth centuries a new focus on the individual's physical death arose ("my own death"). Personal death began to be considered the decisive moment of the individual's existence, when the actual judgment of his or her life takes place, and after which the separated soul's distinct experience either of pain (in hell and purgatory), or of joy (in heaven) begins immediately, even without the body.[6] The emphasis shifts, therefore, from the end of time to the eschatological time between one's death and resurrection.

This shift is best illustrated by the development of the doctrine of purgatory in the late twelfth and thirteenth centuries. It is further confirmed by the 1336 promulgation of the bull *Benedictus Deus,* with which Pope Benedict XII officially stated that the saintly soul enjoys the full beatific vision and consequent repose as soon as it reaches heaven (either after death or after the purification in purgatory). Recent scholarship, however, has highlighted the complexity of this eschatological transformation, suggesting that different eschatological emphases coexisted throughout the Middle Ages. In particular, Aron Gurevich's analysis of Christian visionary literature has identified a certain focus on the experience of the separated soul since the sixth century. On the other hand, Caroline Walker Bynum's study of textual metaphors, burial customs, and relic piety has pointed out the continuing importance of the doctrine of resurrection from late antiquity to the early fourteenth century.[7]

Gurevich's and Bynum's investigations make clear how much can be gained by crossing the boundaries between high and low culture and by opening up the study of learned medieval thought to aspects of medieval culture that do not necessarily suppose the same degree of reflection and education, including spirituality, religion, devotional and cult practices, and social context. Within Dante studies, Alison Morgan's 1990 monograph *Dante and the Medieval Other World* reopened the exploration of the relationship between the *Comedy* and previous popular eschatological literature. As Morgan pointed out, Ernst Robert Curtius's statement that "Dante stands within the learned tradition of the Middle Ages" marked the attitude of Dante criticism toward popular culture in the twentieth century, so that, by the 1930s, the study of the relationship between the *Comedy* and popular tradition was virtually abandoned.[8] While Morgan explored more than a hundred popular documents dating from the third century and considered six different aspects of the portrayal of the otherworld (ranging from topographical motifs to the representation of paradise), this book focuses on a single topic—the notion of experience in the afterlife and the concept of personal identity it expresses—and on a selection of documents that includes both learned and popular texts from the thirteenth and early fourteenth centuries.

The popular poems I consider are associated with the figures of Uguccione da Lodi (who worked in the Cremona area in the first half of the thirteenth century), Giacomino da Verona (who wrote texts in the Veronese vernacular around the middle of the same century), and Bonvesin da la Riva (who wrote texts in Milanese in the late thirteenth and early fourteenth centuries). These texts belong to a didactic tradition that flourished in Northern Italy and was characterized by what Francesco Zambon has defined as "a veritable obsession with the afterlife."[9] They were often meant to be sung and recited orally, serving the practical goal of strengthening popular religious beliefs. Since the second half of the nineteenth century, these poems have been acknowledged as important records of the old vernaculars of Italy and have been carefully edited. At the same time, they have often been dismissed as primitive and popular, and their intellectual significance has never been granted rigorous investigation. In particular, the earlier poems have not been deemed worthy of association with Dante's master-piece. Such an oversight is particularly striking in the case of Bonvesin da la Riva, whose *Book of the Three Scriptures*, written just a few decades before the *Comedy*, presents remarkable parallels with it. Just as the *Comedy* is divided into the *Inferno*, *Purgatorio*, and *Paradiso*, Bonvesin's poem is divided into the *Black Scripture* (describing hell), the *Red Scripture* (narrating Christ's Passion), and the *Golden Scripture* (describing heaven). Both the *Book of the Three Scriptures* and the *Comedy* are, therefore, tripartite in structure; at the same time, they are unitary poems that, beginning with hell and ending with heaven, describe the condition of the separated soul in the afterlife.

The texts of Northern Italian didactic poetry are interesting as docu-ments of the culture and spirituality that surrounded and informed all intel-lectual productions of the time, including complex poems such as Dante's *Comedy*. I do not look for direct sources that Dante might have found in the popular material. Rather, I take this material, which is now acknowledged to be the expression of widespread and orthodox beliefs, as a document of the general cultural assumptions of the time. A sustained analysis of these poems allows for a more nuanced and thorough understanding of both the literary tradition to which they belong and the eschatological tenets they express. It also allows for subsequent study of the *Comedy* within its historical and cul-tural context. In particular, a "deghettoized reading" of Dante's poem (as Teodolinda Barolini has put it)[10] shows that medieval culture considered the body's materiality and concreteness to be fundamental components of a human being, and physical pain to be a locus of identity and meaning. Such a reading suggests that limiting oneself to high art, theology, or intellectual history risks eclipsing a concern for corporeal identity that is more apparent in popular culture and spirituality but still essential for high culture. The popular texts are perhaps less attuned to and even unaware of contradictions, but they are also less willing to compromise the concrete materiality of the body, which always seems to resist theorization. If my analysis of the earlier poems shows the benefits of going beyond strict boundaries of discipline and genre, however, it also points to the particular subtlety and sophistication with which Dante mastered these issues. Creatively negotiating between Vergilian antecedents and the most recent Scholastic theories, Dante's poem expresses an original concept of personhood that allows for the perseverance of embodied identity in the afterlife and, at the same time, affirms the significance of the body's materiality.

Chapter 1, "Eschatological Poems and Debates between Body and Soul in Thirteenth-Century Popular Culture," studies the works of Uguccione da Lodi, Giacomino da Verona, and Bonvesin da la Riva, which combine a great emphasis on the afterlife with a profound interest in the body. This chapter examines a widespread cultural tradition that contrasts the idea of the body as ephemeral and negative with an understanding of it as a crucial component of the person that must be cherished and loved. It also investigates the complexity of the eschatological transition I have described above, showing that this transition struggles to maintain a corporeal understanding of experience and incorporates different emphases even when these emphases are not fully compatible with each other. In particular, this chapter demonstrates that the change of emphasis toward the time between physical death and resurrection corresponds to an increasing somatization of the soul, yet, at the same time, never entirely eclipses the significance of bodily return.

Chapter 2, "Embryology and Aerial Bodies in Dante's *Comedy,*" shows how Dante negotiates between different concepts of body and soul in order both to express the fullness of the separated soul's experience in the afterlife and to justify the embodiment connected with it. I study how Dante reelaborates the classical concept of "shades" through an original appropriation of some principles that were circulating in contemporary philosophical discussions. My analysis begins by focusing on *Purgatorio* 25, which gives a detailed account of the formation of the human soul in the fetus. I contextualize Dante's embryological explanation, which has long been the object of debate in Dante studies, within the thirteenth-century Scholastic controversy between the traditional doctrine of plurality of forms and the newer, exciting, but dangerous principle of unicity of form proposed by Thomas Aquinas and developed by his followers. I argue that Dante's original and ambivalent theory begins by following the empirical tenets of plurality (which maintain the concreteness of the body and clearly distinguish it from the soul) but ends up being close to the idea of unicity of form (which considers the rational soul to be the full carrier of the self, including the body). Then, I discuss how Dante uses this innovative conception of the soul to imagine that as soon as the soul separates from its earthly body and reaches the otherworld, it radiates a body of air and thus becomes a shade, which is capable of carrying identity and expressing sensitive faculties. I explore the concept of the aerial body as the expression of the soul, showing how the shades' features in the three realms (deformed in hell, distorted but fully human in purgatory, and perfected in heaven) are altered according to the different condition of the souls' intellectual faculties.

Chapter 3, "Productive Pain: The *Red Scripture,* the *Purgatorio,* and a New Hypothesis on the 'Birth of Purgatory,'" enters the debate that has followed Le Goff's study and its emphasis on the transformation of the eschatological landscape from two-part to three-part. Le Goff connects the emergence of purgatory primarily to the changes in the social and economic structures of the time. I argue that this development is also tightly linked to the positive understanding of physical pain as an opportunity for improvement and knowledge which began in the twelfth and thirteenth centuries and developed subsequently. This chapter reads Bonvesin's *Red Scripture* and Dante's *Purgatorio* against each other, focusing on the significance of physicality for the process of purification that the soul, with its aerial body, undergoes in purgatory. According to Dante, the pain that the damned experience in hell is no more than an eternal and sterile punishment that keeps them trapped in a continual state of perversion; yet at the same time, the pain of purgatory is a fruitful opportunity for true growth and change. It is here that the structural similarity between the middle sections of the *Book of the Three Scriptures* and the *Comedy* offers a new perspective on the connection between the suffering body of Christ and the transformative power of pain in purgatory. I argue that on the one hand, purgatory, which is absent as a place in Bonvesin's poem, is reflected in the power granted to physical suffering in the *Red Scripture;* on the other hand, Dante imagines purgatory not only as a place but also as the soul's experience of physical pain, through which it learns to assimilate to the suffering Christ.

Chapter 4, "Now, Then, and Beyond: Air, Flesh, and Fullness in the *Comedy,*" shows Dante's original solution to the tension between the power of the somatized soul and the significance of the resurrected body that, as in the *Book of the Three Scriptures,* informs the otherworldly panorama in the *Comedy.* I first argue that though Dante uses the concept of shade to stress the fullness of the separated soul's experience, he simultaneously highlights the inadequacy of the aerial body unfolded by the soul; ultimately, a shade is merely a surrogate for a fullness and a perfection that are only possible at the Resurrection, when the soul reunites with its fleshly body and the person is reconstituted in his or her corporeal wholeness. In the final part of the chapter, I propose that we read the *Comedy* as a "journey of the body," in the sense that, in structuring the transformation of the pilgrim's body in the afterlife, Dante keeps in mind the paradigm of Beatrice's account of salvation history in *Paradiso* 7, which indicates that the first human being was created immortal and that only the resurrection of the body will conclude and bring to a closure the experience of humankind. In particular, I study the transformation of Dante the pilgrim in heaven, asserting that although the pilgrim's journey takes place in 1300 (i.e., before the end of time), his body progressively acquires the qualities of a resurrected body. In this transformation lies Dante's ultimate attempt to combine the two eschatological emphases—before and after the Resurrection—that I have outlined for the *Comedy* and the previous eschatological tradition. When, in the final cantos of the *Paradiso*, the pilgrim is granted first the sight of the blessed with their resurrected bodies, and then the ultimate beatific vision with his own resurrection body, Dante's poetry creates an eschatological dimension—of fleshly fullness even before the Resurrection—that theologically does not exist, but for which the poem has carefully prepared its reader from the beginning.

Chapter 1

Eschatological Poems and Debates between Body and Soul in Thirteenth-Century Popular Culture

A deep ambivalence runs through thirteenth-century beliefs about body and soul, their nature, relationship, and destiny in the afterlife. This ambivalence is widespread and concerns both Scholastic discourse and popular culture. Focusing on poems associated with the figures of Uguccione da Lodi, Giacomino da Verona, and Bonvesin da la Riva, this chapter approaches the complexity of late-medieval beliefs about the body from the perspective of popular texts that have received little critical attention, except as documents of Northern Italian vernaculars. I will investigate these relatively unknown texts in order to identify and make more concrete the tensions resulting from the change of eschatological emphasis sketched in the preface. On the one hand, these poems show considerable traces of the doctrine of *contemptus mundi*, which associates the body with evil and, often in a very bleak way, stresses its fragility on earth and its decay in the grave. Through the imagery of the rotting corpse, they insist in particular on the motif of personal death, which participates in the change of the eschatological focus in the high Middle Ages. The individual's physical death appears increasingly as the decisive moment of existence, fixing the fate of the separated soul in the afterlife well before the Last Judgment. On the other hand, these poems attest to a pervasive positive sense of the body as a crucial, beloved, and beautiful component of the person. They demonstrate that despite the change of emphasis toward the experience of the separated soul, eschatology in the thirteenth century effaces neither the significance of the body nor the doctrine of the Resurrection.

The Last Judgment and Bodily Return: Uguccione da Lodi and Giacomino da Verona

Uguccione da Lodi

Philological research associates four poems with the figure of Uguccione, who was active in the first half of the thirteenth century and probably belonged to the noble family "da Lodi" of Cremona: the *Libro,* the *Istoria,* the so-called *Contemplazione della morte* (hereafter *Contemplazione*), and a fragment to which I will refer as *Contrasto.*[1] The *Libro,* written by Uguccione in the early thirteenth century, is a long sermon on the danger of sin and combines a description of the corruption of contemporary society with other moral observations and eschatological motifs. The *Istoria* is a slightly later, more didactic rewriting of the *Libro;* it is contained in the same manuscript as the *Libro* and was long attributed to Uguccione, but there is now general consensus that it was written by another author, usually referred to as Pseudo-Uguccione. The *Contemplazione* is inserted within a Tuscan re-adaptation of passages from the *Libro* and *Istoria* and focuses on the motif of death's inevitability. Finally, the *Contrasto* is a section of a debate between body and soul that was traditionally considered among the rewritings of the *Libro* or the *Istoria;* Claudio Ciociola has recently shown that it was written by Uguccione himself and was originally part of the *Libro.*[2] All these four texts express widely held medieval beliefs and belong to the same tradition, which was influenced by the genre of debate between body and soul and showed a strong interest in death and the afterlife.[3] They are therefore a good indication of the eschatological assumptions in Northern Italy in the first half of the thirteenth century.[4]

Like sermons in prose, Uguccione's poems are composed for the improvement of the public's behavior and are full of long passages listing bad deeds to avoid and good deeds to pursue.[5] In order to achieve their practical aim, they deploy a particularly dark vision of life, which is similar to the doctrine of *contemptus mundi* and stresses the fragility of the body and the worthlessness of everything on earth.[6] The *Libro,* in particular, veritably constitutes what Jean Delumeau calls an "evangelism of fear" and contains a constant, almost obsessive emphasis on the ineluctable and unforeseeable nature of death.[7] After an initial description of hell, the remainder of the poem's first part is dedicated to underscoring the unpredictability of death and urging people to repent. The numerous passages on death also function to emphasize the weakness of the human body, highlighting in particular its wretchedness after death and the decomposition of the corpse:

> Quig qe no cré morire,   sì à molto faladho:
> de quel penser q' ig' fai,   cascun à radegadho,
> c' ancoi è l' om alegro,   doman è traversadho
> de questo mond' al' altro,   sì com' è destinadho.
> En molto poco d'ora   dac' à perdud lo fladho,
> no par qe sia con lui   né specie né moscado,
> anci pue plui tosto   de can mort en fossadho;
> de quig qe plui l' amava   è feramen scivadho,
> serore né cosino   no i· pò durar daladho,
> né 'l pare né la mare   qe lo· à norigadho;
> d' una vil vestimenta   alo ven adobadho,
> en un poco de drapo   sì fi avolupadho,
> delo peçor q' ig' pò   s'el dé esser compradho,
> molto viaçamentre   ala glesia portadho;
> d' un palio fi coverto   qe i· vien poco lassadho.
> Deu!, con' freçosamente   lo mestier fi cantadho!
> Porta ·l al molimento   lao' el fi colegadho,
> de malta e de calcina   ferament sofrenadho;
> a tal percurator   eli l'à delivradho
> qe li ·mança la boca,   le brac' e lo costadho.
>
> (*Libro* 447–66)[8]

Those who think they won't die are very wrong: everyone is wrong about that thought they have, for today man is happy and tomorrow he is gone from this world to the other one, as he is doomed. In much less than an hour after he loses his breath, it does not seem that spices or musk are with him; rather, he stinks just like a dog that died in a ditch; he is fiercely avoided by those who loved him the most, and neither sister nor cousin can bear to stay close to him, nor can the mother and the father who have nourished him. He is immediately covered with a vile garment and wrapped in a little piece of fabric, of the worst possible kind if it needs to be bought. He is taken hastily to the church and covered with a cloth that is given to him for just a short time. My lord, how hastily the service is sung! They take him to the tomb and there he is placed, fiercely sealed with lime and cement. They have entrusted him to such guardians as those who eat his mouth, arms, and chest.

If this is the wretched destiny awaiting the body after death, however, the soul in hell fares no better:

> Vole' audir del' anema   com' ela è guiaa?
> Plui nigri è de carbone   quili qe l' à portaa;
> en le pene grandisseme   del' Infern l' à çitaa,
> en quel pessimo fogo   q' è de sì grand duraa
> qe, se tuta la mar   entro fos' enviaa,
> altresì arderia   como cera colaa.
> Quand' è molto destruta,   rostia e brusaa,
> poi fi çetaa en un' aqua   q' è sì freda e çelaa,
> se la maior montagna   q' en questo mond' è naa
> fosse del nostro fogo   enpresa et abrasaa,
> per art' e per ençegno   entro fos' enviaa,
> en un solo momento   seria tuta glaçaa.
>
>   (*Libro* 474–85)[9]

Do you want to know how the soul is taken? Those who seized it are blacker than coal. They threw it into the very great pains of hell, into that evil fire that lasts so long that, if one put all the sea in there, it would burn anyway like melted wax. When the soul is much destroyed, roasted and burned, it is then thrown into some water that is so cold and icy that if the biggest mountain in this world were lighted and burning with our fire and then by art and ingenuity thrown into [that water], in just one instant it would be all frozen.

These descriptions of the body's and soul's fate after death are but the last instance in the repetitive pattern of Uguccione's evangelism of fear, which is evident throughout the first part of the *Libro*. They seek to convey the urgent need for repentance and insist on the fragility of the body, the inescapable character of death, and the imminent misery awaiting body and soul thereafter. Therefore they also attest to the increasing significance of death as the decisive moment of the individual's existence and indicate the emergence of an eschatological emphasis on the individual fate of the separated soul, which does not seem to need the body in order to have experience of the afterlife.

In this final instance, the *Libro* also invokes another motif discrediting the body. The damned soul curses the body for the body's past behavior and holds it responsible for the soul's own suffering in hell:

> Oi corpo maladheto,   con' tu m'ài enganaa!
> Tu no às mal né ben,   pena no t' è livraa.
> L'asio qe te· faseve   m' à molto desertaa;
> la gola maladeta   qe fo tant' asiaa,
> la devicia q' el àve   molto i· è dalonçaa;
> kiqe ll' abia vendua,   eu l' ài' cara conpraa.
>
> (488–93)

Cursed body, to what extent you have deceived me! You have neither joy nor pain, and no suffering is given you. The luxury you granted yourself has utterly ruined me; as for the cursed gluttony, which was so luxurious, the abundance of it is far away; whoever sold it, I have bought it at a high price.

Here, the poem seems to express a preoccupation with the separated soul's experience after death, in addition to an attitude toward the body as vain and sinful. However, both the eschatological emphasis and this attitude toward the body are complicated by the poem's abrupt shift to the long prayer that concludes the *Libro*. In this prayer Uguccione begs that on Judgment Day he might not be damned to hell but saved in heaven. Unlike the first part of the *Libro*, which focuses on death as the pivotal event, this last section is entirely dominated by the idea of the Last Judgment and the embodied experience following it at the end of time. In Uguccione's final prayer, moreover, the Last Judgment takes the place of the body's response to the soul which in the medieval tradition of the debates between body and soul usually followed the soul's accusation of the body. Such a response of the body is attested by the *Contrasto*, which was arguably part of the *Libro* and to which I will now turn.

Although the *Contrasto* is only transmitted as a fragment, it develops further the motifs that I have thus far discussed in the *Libro* and, at the same time, takes them in a different direction. While the *Libro* simply mentions the fragility of the human body and the decomposition of the cadaver, the damned soul in the *Contrasto* lingers on them:

> . . . 'l viso
> [*k*]i solea esser sì assisso
> [*e*] bello e colorì:
> [*o*]r è' −l tut' ascurì
> [*e*] nigro devenù
> [*e*]t in pulver rendù.
> [*L*]a testa avivi b[*a*]da,
> [*n*]eta, lavadh' e rada
> [*e*] crespa caviludha
> [*e*] ben acercenudha;
> [*o*]r è −lla soça e bruta
> [*e*] scura fata tuta;
> . . . .
> . . . è<*t*> or le gotte
> n.. trasmortidh' e morte,
> ch[*e*] [*no*] *d*uravan miga
> de[*sasio*] ni fadigha,
> ma [*eran*] grasse e drudhe
> c[*omo*] pome madhure,
> e s[*empr*]e stavan rosse
> c[*omo*] 'n pintura fossen.
> . . . .
> Le [*bra*]çe colle man'
> a[*viv'*] intere e sanne,
> e dentro pelle e osse
> eran le polpe gross[*e*];
> le ungle cole did*h*[*e*]
> e bianche e color[*idhe*]
> or èn dadh' a desfar,
> no se 'n pon p[*ur*] aid[*ar*];
> èn seche como scorç[*a*],

no àn vigor ni força;
tut' èn abandonadhe,
no seran più lavad*h*[*e*];
no avran ma' anell[*o*]
ni guanti con orpell*o*.
De'!, com' e' m' è fadigh[*a*]
mo' questo ch' e' te· dig[*o*];
tu l' intendi ben tut[*o*],
an' tu st[i]a ·n sì muto.

       (*Contrasto* 153–218)[10]

_____

[Your] face, which used to be so firm, beautiful, and colorful, has now darkened, become black, and turned into dust. You had a brown head, clean, washed and shaved, full of curly hair and well dressed; now it has become all dirty and ugly and dark. . . . The cheeks are now torpid and dead, while before they did not have any discomfort or problem but were fat and strong like ripe apples, and were always red as if painted. . . . You had arms and hands that were whole and healthy, and thick flesh within skin and bones. The nails and the fingers that were white and colorful are now decomposing and cannot be helped; they are dry as bark and have neither vigor nor strength; they are all neglected and won't be washed anymore; they will never have a ring nor gloves with tinsel. Alas! how tiresome is all I am telling you; you understand it very well even though you remain silent.

In addition to highlighting the contrast between the beauty of the living body and the filthiness of the rotting corpse, the *Contrasto* also develops the motif of the body's guilt. As in the *Libro,* the soul addresses its dead body and blames it for the body's past behavior on earth, which is presented by the soul as the cause of its own—the soul's—damnation:

E s' tu ghe fussi stà,
per mendar gi peccà
e' sereve guaridha
ki fi arsa e rustidha;
ma no te· piaque miga
durar per me fadigha,

ni de reçever dano
pur un sol dì del' anno.
　　　(*Contrasto* 1–8)

———

> And if you had agreed to seek amendment of your sins, I would be
> saved instead of being burned and roasted; but you did not want to
> undertake any hard toil for me or to accept any suffering, not even
> for just one day in the year.

These lines of the *Contrasto* seem to reinforce and even enlarge the
negative image of the body that was first developed in the *Libro*. According
to the soul, the body refused to do the deeds that are repeatedly presented
in the *Libro* and *Istoria* as leading to salvation. While this critical perspective on the body might seem to absolve the soul from any responsibility and
make the body solely culpable, the last lines of the *Contrasto* challenge the
soul's claim to innocence. After the soul's long speech, the body defends
itself ("dis soa raxon" [244]) and explains to the "anima cativa" (245) that
the soul is actually responsible for all the charges that it had leveled against
the body: "S' tu vò pur ascoltar / e tu ·l vò' guarentar, / e' t'ò dir e proare /
ke tuti quigi peccà / che à' qui recordà / fon tratti a ffinimento / per to com-
mandamento" (If you want to listen and to confess it, I will tell you and
prove that all the sins that you have mentioned so far were enacted upon
your order [260–66]). The body's counteraccusation refutes the soul's equation of body with evil and soul with good, attesting to a cultural tradition
that encompasses a complex understanding of the relationship between
body and soul.
　　Although in the manuscript of the *Contrasto* the passage abruptly
breaks off just a few lines after the body begins its defense, a version of the
body's full speech can be found in the Old French *Desputeison de l'âme et du
corps*, which Ciociola has shown to be an important source of the *Contrasto*
and *Libro*.[11] In this text, the body argues that while body and soul are both
guilty for their damnation, the soul is more guilty, because it did not use
properly the control it was given over the body: "Andoi somes copable, /
*Qua*nt nos pour le deable / Deg*ue*rpimes l'amor / De nostre creator. / La
toie coupe est maire, / *Que* tu me faisis faire" (We are both guilty, as we de-
serted the love of our creator for the devil. Your fault is the greater because
you made me act [669–74]). By having the body continue to affirm the
soul's responsibility in a variety of ways for more than two hundred lines,

the *Desputeison de l'âme et du corps* shows that the body's self-defense was an important element of the debate between body and soul. Moreover, the same self-defense is also present in the *Visio Philiberti*, another well-known debate between body and soul, in which the body replies to the damned soul's accusation with the claim that as the body is the maid and the soul is the lady, the soul is fully responsible for whatever action is taken.[12]

Like the *Contrasto,* the *Istoria* participates in this tradition of debates between soul and body by beginning with a negative vision of the body but then moving on to a more nuanced position. After a celebration of God, the poem opens with the bleak image we have already encountered in the *Libro* (and expanded in the *Contrasto*); it stresses the transitory nature of earthly life, the constant, ineluctable threat of death, and the absurd fate of both body and soul after physical death (113–61). However, instead of developing these motifs further, the *Istoria* focuses on an argument that—despite being frequently interrupted by passages devoted to the familiar themes of repentance, Adam and Eve, the advent of the Antichrist, the parable of Lazarus and the rich man, and the Last Judgment—valorizes the body as an integral part of the human being.

While the *Contrasto* presents the opposition of body and soul from the perspective of the damned soul after death, the *Istoria* stages a debate on earth. Body and soul first appear as two belligerent enemies in contest with one another, mirroring the discord expressed by the damned soul in the *Contrasto* (373–406). When later the soul speaks to the body and tries to convince it to behave according to God's teachings, however, the soul's words offer a different perspective on the body, suggesting that both body and soul are essential components of the person and that both are responsible for the person's destiny. The soul begins to address the body with the argument that the body should not be proud because it is doomed to die and to rot in the grave (933–54), but then the soul introduces a new argument, namely, that the body will resurrect and thus will also be punished or rewarded after the Last Judgment:

> E ancor devem ad un tornar,
> çamai no se· devem sevrar.
> Stratuto sì com' tu èi,
> testa e busto e man' e pèi,
> no serà men cavel né dente,
> qé 'l santo Vagnelio no mente.
> Questo serà al dì çuisio:

là recevrà lo beneficio
qi avrà fato mal o ben,
tut' avrà çò qe se· covien.
                    (*Istoria* 959–68)

———

And we must come back together again and we will never separate
anymore. You will be completely whole the way you are now, head
and torso and hands and feet; not one hair or a tooth will be miss-
ing, for the holy Gospel does not lie. This will happen on Judgment Day: then whoever has done bad or good will receive his
reward, and everybody will have what is just.

This passage not only reminds the audience that the body will eventually be resurrected after decomposing in the grave, but also asserts that the
risen body will be "stratuto" (where the prefix "stra" enforces the concept of
wholeness) as it is now—that is, with all its parts, from head to foot. This
hyperwholeness of the resurrected body and its perpetual union with the
soul thus appear as the re-solution to the fragility of the earthly body and
the fear of death, which were commonplace in the culture of the time.
Moreover, the soul indicates that at the end of time, the body will also be
judged and subsequently rewarded or punished.

Further evidence that the roles of body and soul are being recast is the
change in the tone of the soul's words to the body. While the damned soul
in hell addresses the body as "maladheto" (*Contrasto* 87, and *Libro* 488), here
the soul portrays the body not as an enemy to hate and curse, but as a dear
and beloved companion to cherish, as "qarissimo" (971) and "amigo" (985):

Pregar te· voig per caritate
e per la vera Maiestate,
qarissimo, qe tu me· cre',
q' eu t' ài' aidar a bona fe':
qe tu lasse le vanitate,
e torna ad umilitate
e penetencia toi' verasia
e qe sea ferma né no frasia.
. . . .
Amigo meu, no te· recrer
per cobiticia del' aver:

s' tu dài a Deu, Deu te· dà
e mai no te· 'bandonarà.
. . . .
E, se faràs co· mi concordia,
de nui avrà misericordia.
Servemo molto ben a Deu
comunalmentre tu et eu,
qé molt' è bon lassar lo mal
per lo regno celestial.

(Istoria 969–98)

———

> I want to beg you, my dearest, with love and for the true Majesty,
> that you believe me that I will help you in good faith; [I want to
> beg] you to abandon vanities and go back to humility and to a pen-
> ance that is true, firm, and not fragile. . . . My friend, do not
> change your mind for cupidity of possessions: if you give some-
> thing to God, God will give back to you and will never abandon
> you. . . . And, if you remain in concord with me, he will be merci-
> ful toward us. Let us serve God very well, you and I together, for
> it is very good to abandon what is bad for the celestial realm.

When the interaction between body and soul is set on earth, the soul does
not accuse the body. Rather, the soul addresses the body as a partner sharing the responsibility of a common destiny and indicates that human experience is complete only when it involves both body and soul.

Unlike the first part of the *Libro,* the *Istoria* does not develop the theme
of death as a pivotal event. Ultimately, the soul's separation from the body
appears only as an interlude, and the *Istoria* concludes with a grandiose depiction of the Last Judgment that underscores the ways in which the doctrines of Resurrection and Last Judgment are tightly linked to one another.[13]
When the poem describes the anguish of the wicked and the joy of the just,
or when it depicts Christ the judge speaking to the saved and to the damned,
it implies that judgment and subsequent joy or pain occur not after physical death but only at the end of time (1023–35). Christ's words to the saved
about their reward, for instance, do not mention or even imply that they
will go back to a heaven where their souls have already been. Rather, they
express the novelty and the beginning of the experience of bliss: "Voi
benedheti, a mi vegni', / lo regno meu possederi' / q' eu v' ài prestad' e pre-
parato / sì com' a voi è nonciato" (O blessed, come to me; you will own my

kingdom that I have arranged and prepared for you, as it is announced to you [*Istoria* 1037–40]). Moreover, when Christ explains how the blessed have deserved heaven, he stresses that the moment for the beginning of their reward has finally come: "Mo' è vegnua la sasone / qe voi n' avre' bon gueerdone" (Now the moment has come when you will have good reward [1059–60]). Christ's words to the wicked also state that the moment is coming when they will be punished in hell for their sins on earth:

> Lo merito qe devi' aver,
> en pro[s]eman l' avri' veer.
> Voi brusare' en fogo ardente
> cruel e pessimo e buiente,
> en grieve puça et en calor
> et en trement' et en dolor,
> en fumo grand' e tenebros
> molto fort' et angostios;
> et aprof dela grand calura
> avre' sì pessima fredura,
> qe tuti criari' al fuogo;
> çamai no trovari' bon luogo
> e fam' e sed' avre' crudel,
> mai no avre' late né miel,
> enanci avre' diverse pene
> de cruelissime cadene:
> a dui a dui sere' ligai,
> molto sere' marturiai
> de scorpioni e de serpenti
> e de dragoni fier' e mordenti
> qe v' à percore e devorar,
> mai sì no ve· porà livrar.
> E quili marturii serà tanti,
> duol et angustie e crid' e planti,
> q' el ve· parrà mil' agni l' ora,
> e plui serà nigri qe' mora
> quig qe ve· dé marturiar:
> çamai no devi' requiar.
> (*Istoria* 1105–32)

Very soon you will see the recompense that you must have. You will burn in ardent fire, which is cruel and very bad and hot, in harsh stench and in heat and quivering and in pain, within great and dark smoke that is harsh and painful; and after the great heat you will suffer such a terrible cold that you will all ask for fire; you will never find a good place and you will suffer cruel hunger and thirst but you will never have milk or honey. Rather you will suffer several pains inflicted with very cruel chains: you will be tied two by two and you will be much tormented by scorpions and snakes and fierce and biting dragons that will hit and devour you, and nobody will ever be able to rescue you. And those tortures will be so numerous, pains and sufferings and cries and tears, that every hour will seem like a thousand years, and those who torment you will be blacker than a blackberry: you will never have any repose.

The *Istoria* hints at what happens to the separated soul, but focuses mainly on the Last Judgment and the end of time. Likewise, all the texts in the Uguccione tradition share this eschatological focus, even those that deal with the experience of the soul after death more than the *Istoria* does. The *Libro*, for instance, which often mentions the soul's fate in hell, makes significant reference to the Last Judgment and ends with Uguccione's long and fervent prayer that on Judgment Day he may be placed among the just.[14] Even the *Contemplazione,* with its descriptions of the body's decay in the grave and the soul's pains in hell (69–72 and 153–54), ends with a reference to the Last Judgment (171–74) that serves as an introduction to the grandiose scene that, in the Campori manuscript, follows the *Contemplazione.*[15] Moreover, given that the Last Judgment and the Resurrection were an integral part of the *Desputeison de l'âme et du corps* (the *Contrasto*'s model), it seems likely that the fragmentary *Contrasto,* which mentions the experience of the separated soul in hell, also contained references to the end of time.[16]

In spite of their gloomy perspective on life, the texts associated with Uguccione attest to the existence of a positive sense of the body in the thirteenth century. The body is not simply criticized for its fragility but is also cherished as an essential component of the person who will be resurrected in his or her entirety to be rewarded or punished. Through their focus on the Resurrection and the Last Judgment, these texts also illustrate the complexity of eschatology during Uguccione's time.

Aron Gurevich has drawn a distinction between medieval Christian iconography (which was closer to the theologians' teaching and the official dogma of the Church) and the literary genre of the visions in Latin (which were intended for the "widest audience" and were therefore expressions of "the fundamental views of the people").[17] He has argued that in the vision literature, the idea of the soul's individual judgment and its subsequent experience after death is attested as early as the sixth century, and furthermore, that the "interest in the last judgment is highly restricted."[18] Although not visions written in Latin, the texts related to Uguccione are likewise an expression of popular culture and, in particular, common assumptions about the afterlife.[19] Close reading of Uguccione's poems, however, allows for an argument that is complementary to Gurevich's idea that the interest in the separated soul already existed when the eschatological emphasis focused mainly on the end of time: the *Libro, Contrasto, Istoria,* and *Contemplazione* reveal that different eschatological perspectives continued to coexist in the first half of the thirteenth century, that is, when the eschatological focus has shifted toward the time between death and resurrection. On the one hand, Uguccione's poems combine Ariès's idea of personal death as the pivotal event of one's life with a sense of the immediacy of the separated soul's experience thereafter. They thereby reflect the eschatological emphasis that is gradually taking hold in the high Middle Ages. Yet, on the other hand, the poems show that the beliefs in the Last Judgment and the Resurrection remain important. If anything, the *Libro* and its rewritings reaffirm these doctrines, demonstrating that the eschatological conception of the high Middle Ages does not evolve linearly but combines different emphases in a rich and not always consistent way.

Giacomino da Verona

Around the middle of the thirteenth century, the Franciscan minorite Giacomino da Verona wrote two short poems that describe heaven *(De Jerusalem celesti)* and hell *(De Babilonia civitate).*[20] The *De Jerusalem* and the *De Babilonia* were written in the vernacular of Verona, and the meter employed is the monorhymed alexandrine quatrain *(aaaa, bbbb,* etc.) typical of thirteenth-century didactic poetry from Northern Italy.[21] Giacomino's poems were intended, like Uguccione's sermons, as oral preachings for a wide public and express common beliefs about the afterlife.[22] The two most important manuscripts containing the *De Jerusalem* and the *De Babilonia* also transmit two other works from the same cultural milieu as Giacomino's texts.[23] The first is *Della caducità della vita umana* (hereafter *Caducità*), "un sermon / de la vita e del sta' del miser om" (a sermon on the life and condition of the miserable man [5–6]), composed of 328 lines and organized in monorhymed hendecasyllabic quatrains; the second is *Del giudizio universale* (hereafter *Giudizio*), which consists of 402 hendecasyllables organized in rhyming or assonantic couplets and contains a long speech that the soul gives to the body about the Last Judgment.[24] Taken together, the four Veronese vernacular poems provide further evidence that in the mid-thirteenth century, eschatology and common notions of death are inextricably bound up with the Last Judgment and the Resurrection. The poems furthermore explicitly express a positive sense of the body as a crucial component of the person and the person's experience.

As the title given by Mussafia clearly indicates, the *Caducità* proposes to describe "la fragilità de l'om cativo" (the fragility of the miserable man [4]). Like Uguccione's *Libro*, it is heavily influenced by the doctrine of *contemptus mundi* and offers a pitiless description of the wretchedness of human life from the moment of conception to the moment of death. The most recurrent motifs of the *Caducità* are the fragility of the human body, the instability of life on earth, and the inevitability of death: "Né pur un sol dì tu non ài pax perfecta: / ancoi tu e' san, doman te dol la testa; / una vil fevra en lo leto te çeta, / de dì en dì la morto sì t'aspeta" (You do not have perfect peace, not even for one single day: even if you are healthy, tomorrow your head hurts; a vile fever forces you to bed, and thus every day death awaits you [137–40]).

This insistence on "l'emprovisa subitana morto," "the unexpected and sudden death" (196), is part of the *Caducità*'s evangelism of fear and is meant to urge people not to delay repentance. It is accompanied, as in the first part of the *Libro*, by the idea that while the body rots in the grave, the soul gets what it deserves in the afterlife. After the satirical description of ser Çoanno's funeral (213–96), for instance, the poem describes the decay awaiting the corpse in the grave: "Tu, miser hom, sol romani en la fossa; / li vermi manja la carno a gran força" (You, miserable man, remain alone in the ditch while the worms eat your flesh with all their strength [297–98]).[25] It would be better, the text continues, if the dead person were like a dead worm and had no experience after death (305–8); unfortunately, however, it is not so, and the sinner's soul goes to hell as soon as it separates from the body:

Mo en questo çogọ sì pendo un grevo fato,
ke tu no fai segundo Deo bon trato:
lo dïavolọ ven, sì te diso "Scacho",
né tu no'l pòi mendar, k'el è çà mato.

Dond el sença demora el te ne mena
cum lọ col ligà cun una gran caëna,
e poi te çeta entro l'enfernal pena
k'è de grameça e d'ogna dolor plena.
                              (*Caducità* 309–16)

—————

But in this matter a serious fate awaits, if you do not follow the
right path according to God: the devil comes and tells you "check,"
and you cannot defend yourself because it is already checkmate.
Then without delay, he places a chain around your neck and takes
you and throws you into infernal torment, which is full of every
sorrow and suffering.

The *Caducità* ends with the short, final remark that everyone should try to
avoid hell and gain heaven (321–28). The final section of the poem makes
clear the association between personal death and the subsequent separation
of the soul from the body during the afterlife. Until this final point, however, the graphic descriptions of the *Caducità* focus not on the independent
experience of the soul in heaven or hell but, rather, on the body's fragility
on earth.

The *Giudizio*, which is likewise concerned with the period of time that
the body and soul are united (on earth, but especially after the Resurrection), complicates the *Caducità*'s eschatological emphasis and negative perception of the body. Like the *Caducità*, the *Giudizio* states its practical aim
from the very beginning, urging those who have hard minds and hard
hearts to listen carefully to its narration so that they might be softened
and induced to sorrowful tears and sighs (1–6). Despite this programmatic
evangelism of fear, however, the *Giudizio* not only expresses a positive concept of the body but also makes explicit the important role the body plays
in a person's fate.

As in the *Istoria*, the soul in the *Giudizio* speaks to the body while they
"live together" on earth ("abitando ensenbra" [19]) in order to convince its

companion to serve Christ (25). Although the author announces at the beginning that he will narrate a "tençon, / Ke l'anema à col corpo," "a debate that the soul has with the body" (9–10), there is no sign of hatred or even of tension in the soul's words to the body. The soul repeatedly addresses the body with gentle expressions, which underscore the affection that the soul feels for its partner, such as "bel dolç' amigo" (beautiful, sweet friend [28 and 175]), "bel compagnon me" (my beautiful companion [41]), "bel dolço conpagnon" (beautiful, sweet companion [75]), and "dolçe compagnon" (sweet companion [92]). Throughout the poem, the soul stresses its union with the body, repeating that body and soul share the same destiny, that their separation at death will only be temporary, and that they will eventually reunite and undergo a common trial at the Last Judgment. Even the theme of personal death, usually connected with the idea of the separated soul's experience, is here inserted within the larger context of the Resurrection and Last Judgment, during which body and soul are reunited. These crucial events are portrayed as the beginning of the person's full and final experience, for not only does the soul present its separation at death from the body as a painful moment—"Et e' mesim' ò, bel dolço conpagnon, / Da ti partir cun granda afliction" (And I myself will leave you, my beautiful and sweet companion, with great affliction" [75–76])—but it also points to the Resurrection as the pivotal moment of its own existence.

The soul states that after the separation from its body, it will go alone to a place where the body will not be able to be of any help, and about which the soul knows nothing, not even whether it will be a place of joy or pain (78–90). Yet, the soul does not linger on its own experience in the afterlife, simply mentioning that it will be rewarded according to its deeds and that this experience will be temporary. Furthermore, although the soul hints at the body's fragility and warns it of its mortality (predicting that the corpse will be covered with the worst piece of cloth and placed in a ditch [50–72]), the author does not go on to develop the motif of the rotting corpse. Instead, the soul assures the body that it will resurrect: "el dì tu ài resusitar, / Quando le tube del cel à sonar" (you will resurrect that day when the trumpet of heaven will sound [73–74]). As the soul describes their eventual reunification on Judgment Day, when a never-ending experience will begin, it is clear that soul and body are both considered crucial components of the person, that they are co-responsible for the eschatological fate of that person, and that the moment of resurrection represents the beginning of an experience that, whether joyful or painful, will be communal and eternal:

Pur eo no poso staro k'eo no tel diga
A que porto eo e ti veremo
De l'ovre le quale nui fate averemo,
Dond' eo en verità sì tel prometo
Segundo el mal e 'l ben k' e' ò comesso
K'en quella terra e l'istà e l' inverno
El serà presta la ca' e l'albergo,
De qui k' e' ò tornar a stà cun ti
En quel fer e tanto forto dì,
Quando verà çò dal cel Jesù Cristo
Per çuigar segundo k'el è scrito,
E li serà li libri averti tuti
De l'ovre de li boni e de li justi
Davanço l'alto Deo omnipotento,
De qual si à tremar tuta la çento;
Dond' en quell'ora nui sì trovaremo
Logo [en] lo qual nui sempro staremo,
Mo o de ben o de mal k'el ne deba esro
Li libri ben 'l à diro en manefesto,
Li quali nui avremo en quel ponto
Scripti e rubicai per meço el fronto
E ben da lì enanço te so dir
Como no s' à çamai plu da nu partir,
Siando tuto 'l tempo comunal
D'enfra mi e ti lo ben e 'l mal;
Dond' eo te prego molto, s' el te plas,
Ke tu devotamente entende en pas
Zo ke de quel çorno te dirò
Per lo me ben gra[n]mente e per lo to,
E sì te prego ke queste parole
Ke tu le tegne en ti e sápiate bone,
K'eo to prometo ben, s' tu le terae,
Ke çà pena d'inferno tu non avrai.

      (*Giudizio* 94–126)

———

I cannot stay without telling you in which port you and I will end up according to the deeds that we will have done. Therefore truly I promise you that in that land in summer and in winter the house and the hostel will be equipped [for me] according to the good and evil that I have committed, and that from there I will return to be with you in that fierce and so forceful day when Jesus Christ will descend from heaven to judge according to what is written. Then the books of the deeds of the just and wicked will all be opened in front of high omnipotent God, and all people will tremble. Therefore, in that moment we will find a place where we will stay forever, and the books, which we will have by then written and inscribed in red in the middle of the frontispiece, will clearly tell whether what must happen to us will be good or bad. And I can tell you with certainty that from that moment we will not separate anymore and the good and the bad will be communal between you and me for all the time. Therefore I pray you much to listen devoutly and peacefully to what I will tell you about that day for it greatly matters to my and your own sake. And thus I pray you that you keep these words within yourself and that you consider them true, and I promise you with certainty that, if you keep them, you will not suffer any infernal pain.

The rest of the *Giudizio* is a grandiose, cosmic depiction of the Last Judgment, which confirms its connection with the doctrine of Resurrection. The poem first explains that a series of natural phenomena will anticipate the judgment (127–62). Secondly, it indicates that when the Resurrection takes place, the reconstituted persons will assemble in the Jehoshaphat Valley (163–202). Then it indicates that Christ will appear on the cross in the aspect that he had at the Crucifixion, judging humankind and separating the good from the wicked (203–76). Finally, the poem describes the spiritual and physical pain and joy that the damned and the blessed will respectively begin to experience (277–390). The damned will curse their parents for having given birth to them and will be led by the devils to hell, where they will be placed in an eternal fire and devoured by fierce worms. The saved, on the contrary, will bless their parents and will go to heaven, where they will be joyously received by God, Mary, and all the saints. The description of the blessed's joy after the Resurrection ends with another reference to the reunification of body and soul, which focuses on their respective bliss in the beatific vision: "E po serà en anima et en corpo / Tuti glorificai dal Segnor nostro, / Contemplando la soa figura, / La quala resplendo plui ke sol nè luna" (And then they will all be glorified by our Lord in soul and body, while they contemplate his figure, which shines more than sun and moon [385–88]). The *Giudizio* here clearly diverges from the *Caducità* by highlighting not the wretchedness of the earthly body but once more the reunion of body and soul at the Resurrection and their joint experience thereafter.

It is precisely this postresurrection experience that Giacomino describes in the *De Babilonia* and the *De Jerusalem,* which are the first extended descriptions of heaven and hell in the vernacular of Italy, and are the basis for considering Giacomino, along with Bonvesin da la Riva, as a precursor of Dante. However, my analysis will show that Giacomino's poems differ considerably from the *Book of the Three Scriptures* and the *Comedy* with respect to their eschatological emphasis.

The tone of Giacomino's account of the infernal Babylon is fixed from its beginning, where he writes that "La città è granda   et alta e longa e spessa, / plena d'ogna mal   e d'ognunca grameça" (The city is big and high and long and deep and full of every evil and every wretchedness [29–30]). Giacomino wants to frighten his popular audience, and his depiction of hell, which is not structured in any precise way but is a rather confused accumulation of punishments, is fully corporeal, expressing a sense of experience that requires full embodiment: sickening stench, dragons and snakes ceaselessly biting the sinners, horrible devils breaking their "ossi,   le spalle e li galoni" (bones, shoulders and thighbones [98]), icy water and fire. The scene of Balçabù roasting the sinner for Lucifer is representative of the lively and effective images used by Giacomino and exemplifies the extent to which the body is part of his description of the infernal torments:

Staganto en quel tormento, sovra ge ven un cogo,
  çoè Balçabù, de li peçor del logo,
ke lo meto a rostir com'un bel porco, al fogo,
en un gran spe' de fer per farlo tosto cosro.

E po' prendo aqua e sal e caluçen e vin
e fel e fort aseo e tosego e venin
e sì ne faso un solso ke tant è bon e fin
ca ognunca cristïan sì 'n guardo el Re divin.

A lo re de l'Inferno per gran don lo trameto,
et el lo guarda dentro e molto cria al messo:

"E' no ge daria   – ço diso – un figo seco,
ké la carno è crua   e 'l sango è bel e fresco.

Mo tornagel endreo   vïaçament e tosto,
e dige a quel fel cogo   k'el no me par ben coto,
e k'el lo debia metro   col cavo en çó stravolto
entro quel fogo ch'ardo   sempromai çorno e noito".
                                         (*De Babilonia* 117–32)

While he is tormented in that way, a cook supervenes, that is, Balçabù, one of the most evil fellows of that place, who puts him to roast, like a beautiful pig, in the fire, on a big spit made of iron so that he will cook faster. And then he takes water and salt and soot and wine and gall and strong vinegar and venom and poison, and out of all that he makes a sauce that is so good and fine! May God spare any good Christian from it. He sends him as a big gift to the king of hell, who checks him inside and yells at the messenger: "I do not give a dried fig—this is what he says—for him, because the flesh is raw and the blood is still cool. Take him back quick and fast and tell the cook that he does not seem well done and that he must put him upside-down into that fire that always burns night and day."

The sinners' pain is always portrayed as physical, and when Giacomino lingers on the torments inflicted by the devils, he enumerates the several parts of the sinners' bodies: "Altri ge dà per braçi,   altri ge dà per gambe, / altri ge speça li ossi   cun baston e cun stang[h]e, / cun çape e cun baìli,   cun manare e cun vang[h]e: / lo corpo g'emplo tuto   de plag[h]e molto grande" (One hits him in the arms, another hits him in the legs, another breaks his bones with sticks, bars, hoes, shovels, axes, and spades: they fill his body with very big wounds [213–16]).

In itself, the embodied portrayal of experience in the afterlife would not be quite sufficient to determine whether the described action takes place before or after the Resurrection. It would be possible to ascribe the pain and physical torment depicted by Giacomino to the separated soul, for, as several scholars have pointed out, the representation of souls as bodies afflicted by physical punishments is attested in several medieval otherworldly journeys and visions.[26] A closer examination of the *De Babilonia*, however, demonstrates that Giacomino is actually portraying the experience that takes place after the reunification of body and soul at the end of time. First, Giacomino never uses the word "soul" ("anema" or "anima") to refer to the embodied being he portrays. Second, the presence of a debate between father and son in the *De Babilonia* aligns it with other eschatological texts describing the Last Judgment.

This debate between father and son, situated in the last part of the *De Babilonia*, is placed after the depiction of infernal pains and the anguish of the damned in hell. It is a brutal description of despair and degradation: the son curses his father, insisting that the father is responsible for the son's damnation, while the father curses his son and argues that his own love for his son made him forget about God (285–316). As May has shown, the source for this contrast is Saint Anthony of Padua's sermon on the Last Judgment, which was well known throughout Northern Italy; the debate between father and son there is inserted after the description of the infernal pains that follow the proper scene of the Last Judgment.[27] The presence of this debate, which is also found in other poems on the Last Judgment (such as Bonvesin's *De die Iudicii* and the *Libro de la sentencia*), suggests that the *De Babilonia* either describes the experience of reconstituted persons after resurrection or—in a somewhat inconsistent way that aims at touching the emotions and the feelings of the listeners—anticipates this embodied experience in order to describe what happens in the afterlife.[28] The same ambiguity, which confirms the significance of the body in the commonplace understanding of the person, characterizes Giacomino's depiction of heaven.

While the *De Babilonia* aims at pushing its public to repent out of fear, the *De Jerusalem* seeks to convert its listeners by showing what awaits them if they behave well. In other words, it is conducted according to what Delumeau terms the "evangelism of seduction."[29] The poem begins with a description of the heavenly city that is modeled, according to the author, on the account in John's Apocalypse (32). Morgan argues that in following closely the account of the Apocalypse, Giacomino's depiction "belongs with the early visions rather than with those of the twelfth and thirteenth centuries," which place more emphasis on the Last Judgment at the expense of the depiction of the heavenly Jerusalem.[30] In fact, Giacomino passes over the Last Judgment and chooses instead to describe the experience following it.

Much like the *De Babilonia*, the *De Jerusalem* describes an embodied experience that is modeled upon the eschatological time after the reunification of soul and body. Not only are the heavenly joys described in a way that implies the presence of senses, but when Giacomino states that the confessors are "en anima et in corpo   tuti glorificai" (all glorified in soul and body [138]), it is clear that he is referring to heaven after the resurrection of the body. Moreover, Giacomino portrays the resurrected body of the blessed in such an attractive way that this description must have been very appealing to an audience constantly reminded of the fragility of their own bodies by the doctrine of the *contemptus mundi*. The streams flowing in the heavenly Jerusalem confer not only eternal satisfaction to the blessed, but also everlasting life: "quelor ke ne bevrà / çamai no à morir,   né seo plui no avrà" (the one who drinks from it will never die nor will feel thirst anymore [87–88]). Giacomino also describes the power of the heavenly waters even to rejuvenate the body that has been lying in the tomb for more than a thousand years:

Clare è le soe unde	plui de lo sol lucento,
menando margarite	[e]d or fin ed arçento,
e prëe precïose	sempromai tuto 'l tempo,
someiente a stelle	k'è poste êl fermamento.
De le quale çascauna	sì à tanta vertù
k'ele fa retornar	l'omo veclo en çoventù,
e l'omo k'è mil' agni	êl monumento çasù
a lo so tocamento	vivo e san leva su.
Ancora: li fruiti	de li albori e de li prai
li quali da pe' del flumo	per la riva è plantai,
a lo so gustamento	se sana li amalai;
e plu è dulçi ke mel	né altra consa mai.

(*De Jerusalem* 93–104)[31]

Its waters are more clear and luminous than the sun, carrying always pearls and pure gold and silver and precious gems that are similar to the stars in the sky. Each of them has so much power that the old man returns to his youth, and if he touches it, the man who has lain in the grave for one thousand years gets up alive and healthy. Moreover: when they are eaten, the fruits of the trees and meadows that are planted along the shore of the river heal the sick; they taste sweeter than honey and any other thing.

When Giacomino speaks of the joy the blessed feel in contemplating the face of God, he describes the experience of people who express that joy through beautiful bodies that have finally overcome the limitations and the fear of death characterizing their existence on earth:

> Perçò quigi cantaturi   tanto se resbaldisso,
> ke le man ge ne balla,   lo cor ge'n reverdisso,
> li pei ge ne saio,   li ocli ge'n resclarisso,
> e quanto igi plui Lo guarda,   tanto plui g'abelisso.
>
> E tant è entra si   pleni de fin amor,
> ke çascaun ten   l'un l'altro per segnor,
> e plui de seto tanto   ke no fa lo sol
> lo corpo ge luso   a çascaun de lor.
>
> D'oro è embrostae   le söe vestimente,
> blançe plui ke nevo   e plui de rose aolente,
> e tant' à setille   le veçue e le mente
> ke de celo en terra   cognoxo e vé la çente.
>
> Ferma segurtà   sì à tuti del so corpo
> k'el no dé mai morir   unca d'alguna morto,
> mo sempre aver vita,   reqüia e reponso
> e gaudio e solaço   e pax de gran conforto.
>   (*De Jerusalem* 185–200)

Therefore those singers rejoice so much that their hands dance, their heart is happy again. Their feet jump, and their eyes shine; and the more they look at Him, the more beautiful they become. And they are so full of pure love within themselves that one considers the other as his own lord, and the body of everyone shines seven times more brightly than the sun. Their clothes are embroidered with gold, whiter than snow and perfumed more sweetly than roses. Their sights and minds are so subtle that from heaven they know and see people on earth. They all have firm certainty that their body will never die any death but it will always have life, quiet and repose and joy and solace and the peace that comes from a great comfort.

This description of the splendor of the resurrection body in heaven alludes to the doctrine of the dowries that the body receives at Resurrection. After appearing in Scholastic discussions in the late twelfth century, these *dotes* progressively decrease from seven to four: *impassibilitas* (i.e., inability to suffer), *claritas* (i.e., beauty), *subtilitas* (i.e., lightness), and *agilitas* (i.e., a sort of weightlessness that enabled the body to move with the speed of light).[32] The heavenly body described in the *De Jerusalem* has acquired these gifts and shines forth as an attractive resolution to the fragility of the body on earth (which is fundamental to the doctrine of *contemptus mundi* and is stressed in the *Caducità*). Expressing an understanding of the person (and his or her experience) who is emphatically embodied, this description in the *De Jerusalem* brings home the importance of the body as the soul's beloved and indispensable companion and represents the apex of the trend in the Veronese tradition that offers a positive perspective on the body.

Giacomino's *De Babilonia* and *De Jerusalem*, along with the *Giudizio*, make many concepts explicit that were only implied in Uguccione's texts. The significance in the Veronese texts of the body, which appears as the soul's precious companion and is considered a crucial component of the person, is reflected in the eschatological assumptions of the poems, which express an embodied concept of experience. While the *Giudizio* explicitly focuses on the Last Judgment and the Resurrection as the expected moment for the reunification of soul and body, *De Babilonia* and *De Jerusalem* seem to stage their representation of hell and heaven after the Resurrection. We will see now that even when Bonvesin da la Riva writes a poem that programmatically focuses on the condition of the separated soul, both the body and the eschatological emphasis connected to it remain significant.

From the Resurrection to the Separated Soul: Bonvesin da la Riva

Bonvesin da la Riva was born in Milan before 1250 and died between 1313 and 1315.[33] He wrote both prose and verse in Latin, as well as several poems in the vernacular of Milan. Like Giacomino's *De Babilonia* and *De Jerusalem*, Bonvesin's poems are in monorhymed alexandrine quatrain and were intended to be recited orally in front of a large, popular public with the practical goal of improving their listeners' behavior.[34] As Gianfranco Contini has observed, Bonvesin's devotion is "mite e ordinaria" (mild and ordinary), and he is an ideal representative of contemporary culture and spirituality.[35] His poems, therefore, can be taken as documents of eschatological assumptions in the late thirteenth century.

Bonvesin's most famous work in the vernacular, and the one that has secured his status as a precursor of Dante, is the *Book of the Three Scriptures.* Written in Milanese dialect in the last decades of the thirteenth century, this poem is divided into three parts: the *Black Scripture,* the *Red Scripture,* and the *Golden Scripture.* After a general introduction to the whole poem, the *Black Scripture* opens with a *contemptus mundi,* and describes the death of the sinner and the twelve punishments of hell. The *Red Scripture* is a description of Christ's Passion and Mary's compassion; and the *Golden Scripture* describes the death of the just man and the twelve glories of heaven. While the poems in the Uguccione and Giacomino tradition only hint at the experience of the separated soul and are representative of a culture that in the thirteenth century continues to grant the greatest significance to bodily return at the end of time, Bonvesin's *Black Scripture* and *Golden Scripture* focus precisely on the soul's experience in heaven and hell before the Resurrection. Among the texts of Northern Italian didactic poetry, the *Book of the Three Scriptures* is thus the first poem fully attesting to the increasing emphasis on the eschatological time between death and resurrection. In this respect, Bonvesin's threefold poem is closer to Dante's *Comedy* than to Giacomino's poems, with which it has typically been associated.

During the same period when he was exploring the experience of the separated soul in the *Book of the Three Scriptures,* Bonvesin wrote other poems that continued to focus on bodily return and the experience of the reconstituted person: the *De die Iudicii,* a description of the Last Judgment; and the *De anima cum corpore,* a debate between body and soul. In order not to lose sight of the complex eschatological context within which the *Book of the Three Scriptures* must be read, I will first consider these lesser-known texts.

De die Iudicii and *De anima cum corpore*

Just like the end of Pseudo-Uguccione's *Istoria* and the Veronese *Giudizio,* Bonvesin's *De die Iudicii* is apocalyptic in tone. It depicts the Last Judgment as the collective event during which the reconstituted person will be judged for his or her deeds and subsequently granted eternal reward of joy or of pain. After the description of the natural signs anticipating Judgment Day, Bonvesin mentions, as a sort of prelude to the actual account of the judgment, that everyone will get his or her body back: "Li corpi d'omï-homo   resustaran illora, / E tugi s'an conzonzer   illò senza demora" (Then the bodies of everyone will resurrect, and they will all get together there [in the Jehoshaphat Valley] without delay [29–30]).[36] When Bonvesin then describes the events following Christ's descent from heaven and his judgment, he elaborates on two elements that were not fully developed in the depictions of the Last Judgment in the Uguccione and Giacomino tradition, namely, the qualities of the resurrected body and the sociability of the experience of heaven and hell after the Resurrection.

Bonvesin states that both the suffering of the damned and the joy of the blessed will redouble when the resurrected body takes part in infernal pain or heavenly bliss (169, 243–44, 327, and 330). Furthermore, he lingers on an elaborate description of the resurrected body in heaven and hell: in hell, Bonvesin explains, the bodies of the damned will be "desformai, / Infirmi, nigri e grevi   e spagurus e inflai, / Plu grossi ka karrere,   plu ka montagn gravai" (deformed, weak, black, heavy, frightful, inflated, bigger than a barrel and heavier than a mountain [174–76]). Later he specifies that "Li corp de quatro cosse   seran vituperai: / Plu gross ka sax ke sia   seran e plu inflai, / Plu pigri ka montanie,   plu ka nog obscurai, / E tant cativ e fragili   per poc firan dagnai" (The bodies will be disfigured with four defects: they will be bigger and more swollen than any rock, lazier than mountains, darker than the night, and so wretched and fragile that they will be easily harmed [*De die Iudicii* 237–40]). The four defects of the resurrected bodies of the damned are the counterpart *in malo* of the four dowries of impassibility, clarity, subtility, and agility, which will beautify the resurrected body of the blessed.[37] While Giacomino's *De Jerusalem* only alludes to these gifts, Bonvesin refers explicitly to them: "Li corp de quatro cosse   seran glorificai: / Plu firm ka adamanta   e plu ka 'l sol smerrai / E plu ka omnia vox   setí seran formai, / Plu prist han ess ka l'ogio   e plu avïazai" (The bodies will be glorified with four gifts: they will be formed harder than diamonds, more shining than the sun and thinner than any sound, and they will be faster and quicker than the eye [373–76]).

The theme of interaction among reconstituted persons is another new element that characterizes Bonvesin's *De die Iudicii*. After pointing to the wretchedness of the resurrected bodies of the damned, Bonvesin asserts that after the Last Judgment everyone will find her or his companion(s): "Lo patre col so fio   sí s'an conzonz insema / E l'un fraël co l'oltro   entr' infernal blastema, / L'un ivrïard co l'oltro,   l'adoltro con la femna, / Azò k'i fian punidhi   d'una medhesma pena" (The father will be in infernal misery with his son, and the brother with his brother. The drunkard will be with the drunkard and the adulterer with his woman, so that they will be tormented by the same punishment [177–80]). Bonvesin exemplifies the mutual hatred among those in hell with the dialogue between a father and his son. This dialogue, as in Giacomino's *De Babilonia* and in the *Libro de la sentencia,* most probably derives from Anthony of Padua's well-known sermon on the Last Judgment: "Lo patre col so fio,   dolent e angoxusi, / Se roëran entrambi   com hav fá can rabiusi, / Blastemaran l'un l'oltro   con homni manïusi: / Quellor k'il mond se amavano   seran fag odïusi" (The father and the son, sorrowful and miserable, will gnaw at each other, like rabid dogs. They will curse each other like mad people: those who loved each other in the world will hate each other [205–8]).[38] In heaven, the mutual hatred of the damned is replaced by the communal love of the blessed:

> Con grand honor mirabile,   con solazos conforto
> I andaran con Criste   in l'eternal deporto,
> Staran in dobia gloria   in anima e in corpo;
> Oi De, com quel è savio   ke sta per temp acorto.
>
> In l'alto paradiso   quand i seran volai,
> Illora dobiamente   seran glorificai,
> I han benedexir   l'ora quand i fon nai:
> Nixú porrïa dir   quant i seran beai.
>
> Lo bon fio col bon patre   e li bon companion,
> Cusin seror fraëi,   k'en stai fedhí baron,
> Tug s'an conzonz insema   in la regal mason
> E tug se abrazaran   per grand dilectïon.
>   (*De die Iudicii* 325–36)

They will go with Christ to eternal bliss with great and wonderful honor and with peaceful comfort; and they will be in double glory, in soul and in body. Oh God, what a wise man is he who sees the light in time. When they will fly to high paradise, then they will receive double glory. They must bless the hour of their birth: no one may say how much they shall be blessed. The good son shall be with the good father, and the good friends, cousins, sisters, brothers, who were loyal assistants, will all be together in the royal house, and they will all embrace one another with great pleasure.

Bonvesin imagines that the reassembled persons will finally be able to embrace again ("abrazaran") those they once loved. The idea of heaven as a social place where happiness is shared with others was rare among medieval theologians, who tended to conceive of heavenly bliss and its intensification at resurrection as concerning only the self and its individual relation to God. Even those who drew attention to the significance of the community of saints spoke of a general love that all the blessed feel toward one another, not of an individualized friendship in the beyond.[39] The *De die Iudicii,* in contrast, depicts resurrection as an opportunity for reconstituted persons to reunite with their relatives and other specific individuals dear to them in life. By stressing the body's dowries and reunification with one's beloveds after the Resurrection, Bonvesin effectively illustrates the emotional power that the doctrine of bodily return could have on a personal level as a victory over physical death and loss.

The *De anima cum corpore* places a similarly strong emphasis on the Resurrection, but it also demonstrates the complexity of contemporary eschatological assumptions. It describes several interactions between body and soul and stages them at different moments: on earth, after physical death, and at the Resurrection. Like Uguccione's fragmentary *Contrasto,* the *De anima cum corpore* belongs to the genre of the debate between body and soul—a genre that could also be traced in Pseudo-Uguccione's *Istoria* and the Veronese *Giudizio.* However, Bonvesin's poem testifies in a more extended way than either the *Giudizio* or the *Istoria* to a positive sense of the body as a beloved companion, praised for its goodness and missed by the soul when the soul is left alone after death.

The first part of the *De anima cum corpore* takes place while body and soul are alive. It is composed of three sections: a dialogue between God and the soul; a series of dialogues between the soul and the body; and a dialogue between the several parts of the body. In the initial dialogue between God and the soul (1–60), the soul expresses the common argument that the body is a "re companio," an evil companion (17), who does not allow the soul to serve God in the way it would like.[40] Beginning with God's reply to the soul, the whole poem aims at complicating the soul's simple argument by showing that the soul is at least as responsible as the body for the person's eschatological destiny. As mentioned in the discussion of Uguccione's *Contrasto,* the motif of the soul's co-responsibility with the body was common in debates between body and soul. Bonvesin highlights the soul's responsibility by having God himself tell the soul that it is granted "forza e libertà," "power and freedom" (26), over the body. If the soul manages to exercise this power and to control the body, it will be greatly rewarded in heaven; otherwise, it will be punished in hell. The soul should therefore try to warn its body, but if words are not enough, it should fight with the body until the soul prevails.

When the soul interacts with the body according to God's teachings, it addresses the body as "companio" (68) and "bon companio" (117) (as in the *Istoria* and the *Giudizio*). The soul tries to convince the body that they should serve God in harmony, "concordïevremente" (64), so that they can attain salvation together: "Sta' ben con meg insema,   sta' meg in grand careza, / Azò k'entramb meriscamo   sempiternal richeza" (Stay close beside me, stay dear to me, and we will both earn everlasting wealth [67–68]). Although the soul asserts that if the body behaves well, the soul will enjoy great glory in heaven, its speech centers on the Resurrection as the moment in which body and soul will be reunited and will share a communal experience of joy and splendor:

> Se tu havré ben fagio   segond la mia doctrina,
> Per ti havró gran gloria,   per ti seró regina,
> Per ti eo godheró   li ben dra cort divina,
> O è confort mirabele   e alegreza fina.
>
> A mi e anc a ti   el ha venir pur ben.
> Se tu 't rez al me' senno   teniand le membre in fren,
> Grand glorïa n'avró   pox questa vita almen,
> E tu il di novissimo   seré richism' e plen.
>
> Commeg il di novissimo   firé conzong anchora:
> Plu he lusir ka 'l sol   quand ha venir quel'ora;
> Comeg faré tal festa,   se tu' g pensass ben sovra,
> Ke fora 'd penitentia   tu no stariss un' hora.
>
> Il toe membre bellisseme   no ha ess magia alcuna:
> Plu he resplend ka 'l sol,   e plu ka stel ni luna.

In grand splendor entrambi   seram conzong in una:
Mai no firé plu toco   d'infirmità alcuna.
                           (*De anima cum corpore* 77–92)

_____

If you truly act in accord with my teaching, I will have great glory
through you, I will be queen through you, and through you I will
enjoy the good things of the divine Court where there is wonderful pleasure and joy unalloyed. To me and to you as well only good
will come. If you behave according to my advice and keep your
members in harness, I will have great glory for it after this life, and
on the Last Day you will enjoy abundance and fulfillment. On the
Last Day you will be joined to me again. You will shine brighter
than the sun when that hour comes. With me you will hold such
festival that if you now thought about it, you wouldn't pause in
your penance for a single hour. Upon the beauty of your members
there will be no stain. You will outshine sun and star and moon.
We will both share as one in great splendor. Never again will you
be touched by any infirmity.

After appealing to the body with a description of the bliss that, if they
merit it, body and soul will enjoy together at resurrection (93–120), the
soul turns to what will happen if they misbehave, meriting damnation.
Once more, the soul merely mentions its separated experience (129), instead
stressing resurrection as the moment in which the body will also undergo
punishment (121–56).

Despite the arguments of the soul, the body is not convinced, and its
response represents another negative view of the body (a view that will be
refuted later in the poem). The body argues that it was made of earth, and
that its nature is to enjoy earthly pleasures, such as drinking, eating, and
sleeping (157–92). Moreover, the body claims that, although the soul is immortal, the body itself eventually will die: "Tu 't partirai da mi   il temp
k'eo moriró, / Tu 't partirai da mi   e eo permaniró. / De terra fu creao   e
in terra tornaró. / Long temp staró sot terra,   nixun bon temp havró"
(You'll leave me when I die, you'll leave me and I will stay behind. Of earth
I was made and to earth I will return. I will be under the earth a long time,
and no good times will I have [193–96]).

The body's argument gives the soul (and thus also Bonvesin) the opportunity to offer again and again the doctrine of the resurrection of the

body as the ultimate answer to the body's mortality: "Anc sii tu fag de terra   e in terra tornaré, / El venirá po tempo   ke tu resustaré. / Se tu havré ben fagio,   glorificao firé; / Se tu havré mal fagio,   omiunca mal havré" (Albeit you are made of earth and to earth will return, a time will come afterwards when you will rise again; if you have done well, you will be glorified; if you have done evil, every evil will you endure [221–24]). And when the body reiterates its previous argument (that, since it will be buried under the earth, all it desires is to seek pleasure while alive on earth [233–44]), the soul begins by responding that it has power over the body and that the body must therefore obey it. The soul then introduces a new motif and claims that, in contrast with beasts, which think only of eating (263–64), the human body is noble and created to aim at heavenly pleasures: "Ma tu, k'e' corp human,   sí e' fag in statura / E drig e aslevao   e nobel per natura: / Invers lo ce è volta   la töa guardatura / Azò k' il coss ce- leste   tu dibili havé grand cura" (But you, who are a human body, you were created standing and straight and tall and noble in your nature. Your countenance was set toward heaven so that you would set great store by heavenly things [265–68]). At this point the soul wins over the body, and the following section of the poem concerns the summit the body organizes among all its parts, in order to determine which one is responsible for its bad behavior (273–388).[41]

The poem's second part is set in the time between physical death and resurrection. It is composed of the speeches that the damned soul and the blessed soul address to their respective bodies. The third part of the poem narrates first the dialogue between the damned body and soul and then the dialogue between the blessed body and soul, both of which take place at the Resurrection. In its speeches to the body both after death and at resurrec- tion, the damned soul holds the body wholly responsible for its damnation. If the body remains silent while dead, its reply at resurrection indicates once more that the soul is actually as responsible for the damnation as the body. Had the soul been a good leader, they would both be saved: "Mal vi e mal cognovi   la töa segnoria, / mal vi quand tu intrassi   in mia alber- garia, / Mal vi la toa reeza,   la töa traitoria, / Per ti sont pres e morto   in questa presonia" (To my sorrow I beheld, to my sorrow I knew your rule, to my sorrow I beheld the hour when you entered my lodgings, to my sorrow I beheld your wickedness, your treachery—because of you I am imprisoned and ruined in this prison house [493–96]).

The interaction between the blessed soul and its body is more interest- ing and develops the idea of the body as something dear to and cherished by the soul. When the blessed soul, enjoying the glory of heaven, goes to visit its dead body in the grave, it speaks to the body with expressions that underline the soul's love for its partner, such as "companion amao" (427), "companio dilecto" (429), and "bon companion dilecto" (432). The soul praises the body for its obedience and assures the body that although it lies now in the grave, it will be resurrected, and body and soul will again be together:

> Per ti eo sont scampadha   da l'infernal tormento,
> Eo sont venudha in gloria,   in grand confortamento,
> Eo ho festa compia   a tut lo me' talento:
> Ben habli tu, companio,   per omïunca tempo.
>
> Tu gias in questa tomba,   bon companion verax:
> Repossa fin a tempo   e sta' segur in pax.
> No t'art haver plu tema   ke l'inimig ravax
> Te possa mai comprende   entr'infernal fornax.
>
> Tost ha venir quel tempo   ke tu havré bon stao,
> Ke tu commeg insema   devré ess resustao:
> Dri toi bon ovramenti   comeg firé pagao,
> Zo è il di novissimo   ke tu seré beao.
>
> (*De anima cum corpore* 449–60)

Because of you, I escaped the torments of hell, I came to glory, to great consolation; I enjoy a perfect feast wholly after my desire; may you thrive, companion, for all time. You lie in this tomb, companion good and true. Rest securely, at peace, till the time comes. You need fear no more that the ravening Enemy can ever hold you in the infernal furnace. Soon the hour must come when you will enjoy a state of happiness and resurrection along with me. For your good deeds, you will be repaid with me, on the Last Day, when you will be made blessed.

As the damned soul spoke about its intense sufferings in hell, so does the blessed soul mention its profound joy in heaven. Bonvesin thus clearly grants each separated soul in *De anima cum corpore* a profound experience of pain or joy immediately following death. The entire dialogue, however, is a celebration of resurrection as the moment in which the body will finally be rewarded and the union of body and soul will be reconstituted. When the blessed soul speaks to its resurrected body on Judgment Day, it rejoices in the reconstitution of its union with the body: "Bon temp è k'eo t'aspegio   ke tu fuss qui venudho / A star comeg insema   in quest log benestrudho; / Ben te diseva al mondo   de zo ke t' è avenudho; / Conforta' t e alegrate,   sta' san e verd e drudho" (Long time I waited for you to come here and join me in this happy place. I told you clearly on earth about what has happened to you. Be of good heart and rejoice, stay hale and young and joyful [513–16]). By describing the saintly soul waiting for the body's return at the end of a poem that has celebrated the significance of resurrection, Bonvesin not only implies that resurrection is a guarantee of the body's eventual reward, but also draws attention to resurrection as that which ensures that the soul's separation from its body is temporary, and thereby allows the soul's full happiness in heaven.

The *Book of the Three Scriptures*

While the *De die Iudicii* and the *De anima cum corpore* focus on the end of time, the *Black Scripture* and the *Golden Scripture*—the first and third sections of the *Book of the Three Scriptures*—describe what happens to the separated soul in hell and heaven, shifting the focus toward the eschatological time between physical death and resurrection. In chapter 3, I will analyze the *Red Scripture*—the midsection of the poem—and show that the three-fold character of the *Book of the Three Scriptures* is connected with the emergence of the notion of purgatory and the increasing emphasis granted to the productive power of physical pain. Here, I will focus on the *Black Scripture* and the *Golden Scripture,* showing that the body continues to play a fundamental role in late thirteenth-century spirituality and conceptions of the person.

Although Bonvesin focuses on the separated soul in the *Book of the Three Scriptures,* he gives enormous attention to the body within the text as a whole: he opens by displaying contempt for the decay of the earthly body, describes the somatized experience of the soul in hell and heaven, and ends with an emphasis on the splendid body of resurrection and the subsequent redoubling of bliss.[42] Furthermore, a constant tension between the notion of a fully embodied soul (able to experience the punishment of hell or the joy of heaven before the Resurrection) and the expectation of the end of time (with the subsequent return of the body and a concomitant increase of pain or bliss) is present throughout the poem. In this way, the *Book of the Three Scriptures* illustrates the complexity of contemporary eschatology and its urge to incorporate the (somatomorphic) soul's experience between death and Last Judgment on the one hand, and the necessity of the (real) body of resurrection on the other.

Like all the poems explored so far, the *Book of the Three Scriptures* was composed for the spiritual improvement of its audience. The author announces this expectation at the beginning of the work, where he stresses that while understanding the poem is necessary, putting such understanding into action is absolutely essential:

> Odir e no intende   negota zovarave,
> E ki ben intendesse   anc negota farave,
> Ki no metess in ovra   zo k'el intenderave:
> O l'om no mett lo cor   e l'ingegn, nïent vare.
>
> In questo nostro libro   de tre guis è scrigiura:
> La prima sí è negra   e è de grand pagura,
> La segonda è rossa,   la terza è bella e pura,
> Pur lavoradha a oro,   ke dis de gran dolzura.
>
> De la scrigiura negra   de dir sí ven la sorte:
> Dra nassïon de l'omo,   dra vita e dra morte,
> Dre dodex pen dr' inferno,   o è grameza forte.
> De faza ke no intramo   dentro da quelle porte.
>
> La rossa sí determina   dra passïon divina,
> Dra mort de Iesú Criste   fïol de la regina.
> La lettera doradha   sí dis dra cort divina,
> Zoè dre dodex glorie   de quella terra fina.
> (*Black Scripture* 5–20)[43]

Listening without understanding would have no effect, and the person who understood quite well would still accomplish nothing if he failed to put into action what he had understood. That to which man fails to commit his intellect and energy is of no avail. In this book of ours, there are three sorts of script. The first is black and full of fear; the second is red; the third is fair and pure, wrought in gold only, speaking of great sweetness. Thus, the time comes for speaking of the black script, of the birth of man, of life and death, of the twelve pains of hell, where there is great woe. May God keep us from entering its doors! The red is concerned with the divine Passion, with the death of Jesus Christ, the queen's son. The Golden script speaks of the divine Court, namely, of the twelve glories of that excellent city.

Expressions like "grand pagura" and "gran dolzura" indicate the emotional way the listeners are supposed to respond to the poem. This expected emotional response is exemplified in the introductory lines of the *Black Scripture,* which insist that "ki la lezesse   col cor e co la mente, / E sospirar e planze   devrav amaramente" (anyone who reads it with heart and mind should sigh and weep bitterly [23–24]). Bonvesin's aim is to provoke in his audience what Sixten Ringbom, in his discussion of different attitudes toward art images, defines as the "empathic approach" of the beholder, which developed in the late Middle Ages.[44] While listening to the poem, the public was expected to feel a deep and powerful pull, which would produce strong empathy involving both heart and intellect. The *Black Scripture* and the *Golden Scripture* are constructed in order both to mirror and to contrast with each other. This opposition is designed to provoke opposing but complementary emotions; Bonvesin's evangelism of fear is followed by an evangelism of seduction.

The *Black Scripture* opens with the doctrine of contempt for the world, elaborated in two parts concerning, respectively, the birth and life of man (25–124) and his death (125–88). Bonvesin's description derives from Lotario da Segni's *De contemptu mundi* and develops many of the elements that we have already encountered in the texts of the Uguccione and Giacomino tradition. Bonvesin repeatedly underscores the miserable condition of the human body, which is characterized as weak, slack, and liable to continuous rot and decay (29–40). Even those men and women who exhibit external beauty are always ugly and filthy on the inside:

> Da po k'el è cresudho,   k'el è bel in persona,
> Voia k'el sïa masgio,   voia zentil garzona,
> Ben pò aver de fora   parudha bella e bona,
> Bel è nixun de dentro   ni cavalé ni dona.

No è masgio ni femena   ke sia de tal belleza,
Ni pizeno ni grande,   regina ni contessa,
Ke bella sia de dentro,   zo dig a grand boldeza,
Anz è vaxel de puza,   vaxel de grand bruteza.
(Black Scripture 41–48)

After he is grown up and fully formed, whether he be a male or a
fine girl, he may be of a fair and excellent appearance outside, but
no one, either knight or lady, is fair inside. There is no male or
female of such beauty, whether small or great, queen or countess,
that they are fair inside—this I boldly affirm. Instead, they are
vessels of filth, vessels of great nastiness.

The tone of Bonvesin's *contemptus mundi* becomes even darker when he
moves to deal with the dead and decomposing body:

Le braze e le gambe,   k'eran formae e grosse,
Sì bel e sí fidante,   mo en pur pel e osse:
Za marciran in proximo   entra terra il brut fosse,
Proëza on baronia   mai no faran in oste.

Oi De, oi carne misera,   com ste tu lassa e trista:
Com e't desfigurao,   com he tu soza vista.
No's pò trovar pro homo   ni medic ni legista
Ke possa le defende   ked ella no marcisca.

O è li toi parenti,   li amis e i casamenti,
Muié, fioi, nevodhi,   ke 's mostran sí dolenti,
L'aver e la grandisia?   Oi De, com mal te senti:
La fossa è to albergo,   li vermni en toi parenti.
(Black Scripture 149–60)

The arms and legs, which were well-formed and fleshy, so fair and
strong, are nothing but skin and bones now. Truly, they will
quickly rot underground in the ugly ditch; they will perform no
valiant or noble deeds in battle anymore. O God, O wretched

flesh, how slack and ugly you are, how disfigured you are, how vile you look. No champion or doctor or lawyer can be found to defend it from rotting. Where are your relatives, your friends and in-laws, wife, sons, nephews, who seemed so grief-stricken, property and grandeur? Oh God, how bad you feel! The ditch is your lodging place, the worms your relatives.

Decomposition and physical decay in the *Black Scripture* are not restricted to the postmortem condition but begin "intra vitam": corruption was also in the midst of life.[45] This is evident in Bonvesin's expression of *contemptus mundi*, where the putrefaction of the corpse is only one, if perhaps the most striking, among the several weaknesses of the earthly body. Immediately following the detailed description of the decomposing corpse, Bonvesin attributes the cause of its decay to original sin: "Le doie e li tormenti   e mort e sedhe e fame, / Tut queste coss avemo   per lo peccao de Adame: / La nostra vita fragele   orzem per quel forame / Ke plaza a De, ke certo   de nu firá levame" (Pains and torments and death and thirst and hunger—all these things we endure because of Adam's sin. Let us direct our lives along that narrow path that is pleasing to God, who will raise us up without fail, and so we shall certainly be counted as His "leaven"[*Black Scripture* 165–68]). Here Bonvesin refers to the doctrine that man was originally created perfect—body and soul—and his current imperfections are a consequence of sin. The Veronese *Caducità*, considered earlier, makes clear what Bonvesin takes for granted—that is, that sin has contaminated the original purity of the human condition and made it wretched and miserable:

Ma emprimament Deo a la Soa figura
sì te creà e fe' de terra pura,
poi tu peccasi, fragel creatura,
dond è corrota ognunca toa natura.

Fora del paraìs delicïal
tu fusi caçà per quel peccà mortal,
né mai no g'ài tornar plui sença fal
se no cun gran faìga e cun gran mal.

De dì en dì poi da quel tempo en ça
sempro [è] cresua la toa fragilità,

dal cò a li pei tuto ei plen de peccà,
né 'n ti no è né fe né lïaltà.

(Caducità 21–32)

———

Originally, God created you from his likeness and made you out of
pure earth. Then you sinned, fragile creature, hence all your nature
is corrupted. Because of that mortal sin, you were expelled from
the paradise of delights, and you cannot go back to it with ease but
only with great labor and pain. Since then, your fragility has increased more and more, and you are full of sin from head to foot,
and there is no faith or loyalty in you.

According to these passages, corruptibility, fragmentation, and decay—but
notably not the body itself—are negative results of the Fall. This enables
Bonvesin to hold out the promise that if men behave properly, they will find
the "salutary wealth" of heaven where, as we will see, they will eventually
regain the very same body that was theirs on earth but will now be redeemed from all its earthly defects. Only then will glory be complete.[46]

Before moving to his description of the twelve punishments of hell,
Bonvesin narrates the moment of the sinner's death (193–272), showing that
the soul's destiny is fixed at physical death and that the sinner's soul will be
punished in hell as soon as it separates from its body.[47] The devils surrounding the dying sinner look forward to his death, so that they can take
his soul to hell: "Quest'arma maledegia   ke le a tuta fiadha / Dal corpo se
partisca,   e po fia tormentadha" (So let his wicked soul be shaken out
without delay, let it immediately depart from his body and go into torment
[203–4]). When the sinner manifests his fear at the sight of the devils, they
show no pity and tell him that his suffering in hell will soon begin:

Za tost te portaram   il nostro fogo ardente,
O doia e grand pagura   zamai no dessomente.

  Denanz dal Belzebub,   il pozo profundao,
Lo qual è nostro prencepo,   za tost firé portao,
O't converrá sofrer   tremor dexmesurao:
Segond le toe ree ovre   za tost firé pagao.

(Black Scripture 211–16)

———

Very soon we will carry you into our burning fire, where anguish and great fear never fail. Before Beelzebub, in the deep well, before him who is our prince, very soon you will be conveyed, where you will have to submit to immeasurable trembling. According to your evil deeds, very soon you will be repaid.

As soon as the sinner dies, in fact, his soul goes to hell: "Quam tost el è perio,   senza nexuna triga, / El caz entro inferno" (As soon as he has perished, without any respite he falls into hell [229–30]). When the soul in hell then claims that the body is responsible for its damnation (238–40), however, the devils make it clear that both body and soul are responsible for the destiny of each person and both will eventually be punished: "Perzò ke l'arma e 'l corpo   entrambi en colpivri, / Il di dra gran sententia,   ke i pe seran delivri, / Lo corpo e l'arma á arde   in quist fog tormentivri" (Because both soul and body are guilty together, on the great Judgment Day, when feet will be free [i.e., when you can walk about again], body and soul will burn in this tormenting fire [*Black Scripture* 242–44]).

In this section, Bonvesin makes unequivocally clear that he is portraying the experience of the separated soul and not that of the body—unlike Giacomino, who, though describing a fully embodied experience in heaven and hell, did not state overtly in what eschatological time his poems were set. Bonvesin's focus on the separated soul notwithstanding, however, a limitless physicality characterizes the infernal punishments of the hell of the *Black Scripture,* and the presence of the body is constantly implied. The first pain, for instance, is the "dark fire that burns in that pit" (298). How the separated soul could be tormented by corporeal fire was amply discussed by medieval theologians, and the proposition that the separated soul cannot be tormented by material fire was condemned in Paris in 1277.[48] In the *Black Scripture,* however, Bonvesin goes further than affirming the corporeality of infernal fire and, in the description of infernal sufferings, continuously implies the senses and faculties of the body.[49] One of the most vivid examples of the physical pain of hell is the seventh punishment, the longest of hell (537–652), where the devils torture and slaughter the sinners' bodies with great cruelty:

> A membro a membro i scarpano   col gramp e coi denton,
> Li biassan e i seguiano   e i nizan coi baston,
> Con forc e cortelazi   li fan pur in bocon,
> Com fa i beché mondani   dri porc e dri molton.
>
> . . . .

Ancora li tormentano   d'un oltro grand dolor:
Le membre gh'incaënano   a ira e a furor;
Con tang mortai peccai   com mor lo peccaor,
Con tant cadhen ge ligano   le membre con dolor.

Le bog e le cadhene   pesant e trop ardente
Le membre sí ge guerzano   e 'l fan star trop dolente:
Le doi de tut lo mondo   le plu straveninente
Apress de quel marturio   pariraven nïente.

. . . .

Sor quel montagn li erpegan   mintro a la colmegna,
Zos per quii spinz ponzenti,   ke illó no è gramegna:
Li spin ge scarpa 'l membre,   dre que no'g par insegna
Ke tut no sïan guaste,   nïent se 'n ten insema.

Quand li han erpegai   in cima ai mont adolti,
Per quella istexa via   li erpegan pez ka morti,
O sí i reversan zoso   da quii sopran aspolti:
I flum ardent i cazeno   con dexorivri solti.

(*Black Scripture* 557–616)

They tear them limb from limb with tooth and talon, they worry them and jab them and bruise them with sticks, with fork and knife they cut them up bite-sized, just as butchers do on earth with pigs and sheep. . . . Yet they torment them with another great torture. In wrath and rage they fetter their limbs. In however many mortal sins the sinner dies, in so many fetters they bind his limbs painfully. The heavy, white-hot manacles and chains wrench their limbs and make them suffer excessively. The bitterest agonies in the whole world would seem as nothing beside that torture. . . . Up this mountain to the very top they harrow them right over the piercing thorns—no weed grows there. The thorns rend their limbs until there is no vestige left intact, nothing that still holds together. When they have harrowed them to the crown of those lofty mountains, along the same route they harrow them worse than corpses, when they tumble them down from those high bastions. They fall into the blazing rivers with shameful boundings.

The separated soul described by Bonvesin here is fully somatomorphic, even if it is not completely individualized as in Dante's *Comedy*.[50] In particular, Bonvesin lingers on its detailed description in the tenth pain, which consists of diseases of every sort harrowing and disfiguring all parts of the sinners' bodies:

> D'omïa guisa morbo   sí è 'l miser tormentoso:
> Tut è infistolao,   malsan e smanïoso,
> Febros e paraletico,   dal có tro ai pei ronioso,
> Cretic e ingotao,   inflao e pelagroso;
>
> E losc e zop, il dosso   sidrao e vermenoso;
> Lo có ge dol per tuto,   k'è brut e ascaroso,
> Entramb li og en marci,   lo collo screvoroso,
> Li ding ge dol, el cria,   bastass k'el foss rabioso.
>
> Le braze deslongae,   le golte g'en cazudhe,
> La lengua besinfladha,   le faze desveniudhe,
> E cancro e orbexie,   le spalle pendorudhe,
> La puza dre oregie   horribelment ge pudhe.
>
> Le membre en per intrego   inflae e veninente,
> Le interïor k'en dentro   en marz e puzolente,
> Lo peg è pur pusteme,   ke 'l fan star molt dolente:
> Nexun dolor k'el abia   zamai no dessomente.
>
> (*Black Scripture* 749–64)

The wretch is afflicted with every sort of disease; he is full of fistulas, morbid, delirious, feverish and paralytic, scabby from head to foot, malarial and gouty, bloated and pellagrous. Squinty and lame, his back crooked and verminous; his hideous and repulsive head hurts all over; the eyes are both rotten, the neck scrofulous; his teeth hurt him, and he cries out as if he were rabid. His arms are dislocated, his cheeks sunken, his tongue all swollen, his face emaciated. He is cancerous and half-blind, his shoulders slump, the stench of his ears stinks horribly. His limbs are swollen and gangrenous through and through, his inward parts are rotten and noisome, his chest is one (big) abscess, which keeps him in great pain. No suffering he endures ever decreases.

According to this description, the sort of defects that *De die Iudicii* attributes to the resurrected bodies of the damned (237–40 and 173–76) torment the soul's body in hell even before the Resurrection. In fact, the resemblance between the soul's body and the resurrected body is so striking in the first ten pains of hell that one may wonder what significance bodily return can hold. For Bonvesin, however, the soul's somatomorphism does not seem to represent a problem for the continued relevance of the Resurrection and the change it will entail. The final affliction of the *Black Scripture* consists of the sinner's knowledge that the Last Judgment will bring not a cessation of suffering but its increase. This is because, Bonvesin tells us, all the punishments of hell that have been described will redouble when the soul reunites with the body it had on earth. In other words, if punishment of the somatomorphic soul is painful, punishment of body and soul together is far worse:

> No spera 'l trist d'aver   alcun meioramento,
> Ma sí spera pur sempre   del so pezoramento,
> Zoè d'aver angustia   con dobio pagamento
> Al di de la sententia   ke 'l corp avrá tormento.
>
> Oi De, quent grand angustia   aver cotal speranza,
> Com pò ess gram lo misero   ke apena in grand turbanza
> E zamai no aspegia   alcuna consolanza,
> Ma pur pezoramento,   zoè dobia pesanza.
>
>   (*Black Scripture* 845–52)

The unhappy man hopes for no improvement but always expects nothing but worse, namely, to be paid anguish twice over on the Day of Sentencing, when the body (too) will have its torment. Dear God, what great anguish to endure such expectation! How woeful the wretch must be who suffers in great turmoil and expects no consolation ever, but only worse, namely, a double burden.

Despite the many graphic corporeal descriptions of infernal pain that have gone before, Bonvesin restates at the end of the *Black Scripture* that the punishment of the body will occur only at the end of time and that only then will infernal suffering be complete and definitive. The damned soul concludes by pointing to the Last Judgment and the resurrection of the body:

> Zamai no plu aspegio   k'eo debia ess consolao,
> Aspeg lo di novissimo   ke 'l corp firá pagao.
>
>   Lo di de la sententia   con grand tremor aspegio,
> Ke 'l corp firá punio,   mi miser maledegio.
> No m'á valer illora   a darme per lo pegio
> Ni a dir mëa colpa: con grand pagura aspegio.
>   (*Black Scripture* 871–76)

————

Nevermore do I expect to be consoled; I await the Last Day, when the body will be paid. I await the Day of Sentencing with great trepidation, when the body will be punished, miserable accursed me. It will be no use then for me to beat my breast or to say *mea culpa;* I await in great fear.

Like the *Black Scripture,* the *Golden Scripture* focuses on the experience of the separated soul. The *Golden Scripture* begins with a short introduction of the sweetness to come (1–24), followed by the description of the just man's death. As in the case of the sinner's death in the *Black Scripture,* this description indicates that the soul will be rewarded in the afterlife as soon as it leaves the body. As the angels surrounding the dying man promise, the good soul will be taken to heaven and will enjoy beatific vision and great bliss:

> Za tost portaramo   dnanz da l'Omnipoënte,
> O tu porré veder   la faza relucente,
> La faza stradulcissima   de quel segnor poënte.
>
>   Tu vedheré za tosto   richeza precïosa
> E glorïa dolcissima,   dolceza glorïosa,
> Confort e alegreza   e festa confortosa.
>   (*Golden Scripture* 38–43)

————

Truly, soon now we will carry you before the Almighty where you will be able to see His shining countenance, the sweet, sweet face of that mighty Lord. Soon now you will see precious riches and sweetest glory, glorious sweetness, comfort and rejoicing and festival full of comfort.

At the same time that they extol the joys of heaven, however, the angels also point to the Last Judgment and the beauty of the resurrected body, thus indicating that like Bonvesin's depiction of hell, his depiction of heaven is informed by the dialectic between the experience of the somatomorphic soul and the importance of the resurrected body: "Lo corp il di novissimo   serà in grand verdor, / Quilò starà co l'anima   in zoia e in splendor" (On the Last Day, your body will greatly thrive; here it will stand with the soul in joy and splendor [71–72]).

The description of the just man's death is followed by the description of heaven. The twelve glories are presented as the opposite of the twelve punishments of hell, although the contrast between them is often inconsistent.[51] The most striking feature of the twelve glories is that they describe the celestial realm as a place in which the defects of the earthly world are cured. This celestial reality has attained the purity that existed before the Fall, as if the world of Satan with its decay, sin, and pain had been overcome. The contrast emphasized in the *Golden Scripture* is thus not so much between hell and heaven as it is between the imperfect earthly condition (described at the beginning of the poem) and the regained perfection of the celestial condition. In heaven everything is the same as on earth, but the essential transition is from decay to incorruptibility, from continuous change to stability.

The description of the first glory (81–184) is the longest and gives a summary of the following ones. It portrays the physical land of heaven, which consists of buildings of gold and gemstone, gardens, flowers, and birds, which all delight the blessed. Heaven is explicitly described as the counterpart of the earthly condition that is portrayed in the beginning of the *Black Scripture:*

> Illó no è trop caldo   ni freg ni conturbanza,
> No'g floca ni 'g tempesta   ni g'è desconsoranza
> Ni nuvol ni cigera   ni tema ni pesanza.
> . . . .
>
> Ma el g'è strabel temporio,   mirabel temperanza,
> Dolcez e alegreze,   segura consolanza
> E sanitá con gaudio,   drüeza, delectanza,
> Richeza abundïevre,   aver senza temanza.
>
> Illó negota 's perde,   negota g'invedrisce,
> Negota se stramudha   ni 's guasta ni marcisce:

No g'è recrescimento,   nexun illó perisce,
No g'è sozor ni vermini   ni scorpion ni bisce.

  Tut coss en salv illoga   e fresc e reverdie
E sempre intreg e stavre,   godhevre e ben polie;
Le voluntá dri iusti   in tut coss en compie,
Le fest k'illó fin fagie   mai no seran finie.
                    (*Golden Scripture* 117–32)

There is never too much heat or cold or any bad weather in that place, neither snow nor thunderstorm nor any gloom nor cloud nor fog nor fear nor heaviness. . . . Instead, there is the finest weather, wonderful mildness, sweetness and rejoicing, the certainty of pleasure, health and joy, abundance, delight overflowing wealth, possession without fear. There nothing is lost, nothing grows old, nothing changes or spoils or decays; there is no subject of regret there; no one dies there; there is neither filth nor vermin nor scorpions nor snakes. All things are safe there, fresh and youthful, always whole and lasting, enjoyable and neat. The will of the just is fulfilled in everything; the festivals held there will never end.

Apart from the fifth glory (the great joy that the blessed feel in the contemplation of the beautiful faces of the angels, Mary, and Christ), the glories describe heavenly pleasures and delights that are similar to earthly ones—such as perfumes, riches, servants, food, songs, and precious garments. The difference is that these pleasures are now redeemed of their mutability, ephemerality, and decay. More importantly, these descriptions of the soul in heaven are—like the representations of the soul in hell—embodied.[52] The tenth glory, for instance, is "la grand beltae, / la specïa del iusto, la pura claritae" (the great beauty, the fine appearance of the just man, his pure clarity [601–2]). Although Bonvesin is still considering the separated soul, he describes a somatomorphic soul whose body has resolved all the limitations and defects of the earthly body:

  La faza stralucente   resplend a tal color
Ke 'l sol apress a quella   no g'av haver valor;
La lengua per parlar   trop è de grand dolzor,
Li ogi delectivri   trop en de grand splendor.

Li soi caví en d'oro,   lucent e affaitai,
Li dingi strablanchissimi,   li vulti colorai,
Le man en strabellissime,   li pei stradelicai,
Li membri tugi quangi   strabei e ben formai.

No g'è alcun infermo   ni gram ni rancuroso
Ni grepo ni trop grande   ni manco ni ernioso
Ni veg ni desformao   ni mudho ni levroso
Ni zopo ni sidrao   ni ceg ni lentigioso;

Ma el g'è zascun illoga   e san e alegroso,
De temperadha forma   intreg e specïoso
E fresc e ben formao,   facent e gratïoso,
Adrig e mond e zovene,   compio e solazoso.

Illó nexun è pegero   ni mat ni dexdesevre
Ni magro ni stragrasso   ni puzolent ni flevre:
Nexun è dentro marzo   ni brut ni dexdesevre,
Ni 'g sa de re lo flao   ni è za descordevre;

Ma el g'è zascun adorno,   vïaz e intendevre,
Cortes e temperao   e lev e ben desevre:
De fora e 'd dentro è bello,   olent e resplendevre;
De bon ge sa lo flao,   d'odor meraveievre.

La somma si è questa: k'eo parlo quas nïente
Dra gran beltae de iusto   ke mai no dessomente.
(*Golden Scripture* 609–34)

The resplendent face sheds such light that beside it the sun would be worthless. The tongue is of surpassingly sweet speech, the delightful eyes of surpassing splendor. The hair is of gold, shining and fair, the teeth of whitest white, the complexion brilliant, the hands very lovely, the feet very finely molded, every limb very fair and well formed. In that place, there is no man sick or ailing or in pain or too short or too tall or crippled or ruptured or old or misshapen or mute or leprous or lame or crooked or blind or freckled.

Instead, each one there is healthy and lively, of middling size, whole and beautiful and fresh and well formed, active and graceful, straight and clean and young, perfect and joyous. There no one is slothful or foolish or unseemly or thin or fat or smelly or feeble; no one is rotten inside or ugly or unseemly, nor does their breath smell bad, nor are they repulsive in any way. Rather, everyone there is fine looking, lively and quick, well behaved and temperate and nimble and very seemly; everyone is fine inside and out, sweet smelling and gleaming; their breath smells good, marvelously fragrant. In sum, what I am saying is nothing compared to the great beauty of the just man which never fails.

This portrayal of the soul's body contrasts sharply with the limitations of the earthly body described in the *contemptus mundi*.[53] Notably, it is also reminiscent of contemporary descriptions of the resurrected body. As we have seen, Bonvesin's *De die Iudicii* invokes the four qualities that will characterize the resurrected bodies in heaven: impassibility, clarity, subtility, and agility. In the *Golden Scripture,* Bonvesin shows us how theological discussions on the resurrected body could be understood by a more popular imagination. The celestial person he describes keeps all the parts he or she had on earth—face, tongue, eyes, hair, teeth, complexion, hands, and feet—but in heaven everyone is young, and the imperfections of the earthly body are cured.[54] Moreover, this flourishing perfection will never fade. In what looks like euphoric praise for the splendor of the resurrected body— although what is described is a separated soul before the Last Judgment!— Bonvesin places emphasis on both integrity and the lack of change. He wants to involve the emotions of his listeners and to seduce them with the idea of maintaining their own body, of continuing to be the same but in a new, purified way.

The poem places such importance on the body that the body appears everywhere, even when the author is focusing explicitly on the separated soul. In order to describe the experience of the separated soul, Bonvesin exploits—and pushes to its extreme possibilities—the potential of the somatomorphic soul progressively developed by a long tradition of otherworldly journeys and visions. Bonvesin in fact describes an embodied soul that is remarkably similar to his conception of the person after the Resurrection. At the same time, however, Bonvesin maintains the significance of bodily return at the end of time, and implies throughout the poem that the soul's somatomorphism is not enough. We have seen that the twelfth torment of hell consists of the soul's awareness that suffering will increase with the resurrection of the body. The twelfth joy of heaven is the corresponding knowledge that glory will endure, or rather be amplified, after the Last Judgment. In other words, despite the splendor of the separated soul in heaven, complete bliss and "true sweetness" will be possible only with the eventual resumption of the resurrected body:

> Zamai no tem lo iusto   d'aver alcun tormento,
> Ma spera il di novissimo   d'aver meioramento,
> Ke 'l corp será in gloria   e in grand alegramento:
> Illora será 'l iusto   in dobio pagamento.
>
> Per grand amor aspegia   d'aver dolzor verax,
> Ke 'l corp il di novissimo   resustará in pax
> Per la virtú dr'Altissimo,   ke pò zo ke ie plax,
> E odirá la vox   de quel Segnor verax.
>
> . . . .
>
> Per questa vox dolcissima   illora l'arma e 'l corpo
> Seran in dobia gloria,   in zog e in conforto.
> Oi De, quam bel serave   venir a quel deporto,
> A prender tanta gloria,   ki foss per temp acorto.
>
> Perzò stragoe lo iusto   e tuto se consora,
> Perzò ked el aspegia   k'el ha venir quella hora
> Ke 'l corp in tanta gloria   resustará anchora:
> El se conforta tuto   quand el ge pensa sovra.
>
> (*Golden Scripture* 689–708)

The just man never fears he will suffer any torment—rather, he expects to see improvement on the Last Day, for his body will be in glory and great rejoicing. Then the just man will be doubly repaid. In his great love he expects to have true sweetness, for the body will rise in peace on the Last Day through the power of the Most High, Who can do whatever He wishes, and hear the voice of that true Lord. . . . Through that sweetest of voices, soul and body will be in double glory then, in disport and in comfort. Dear God, how fine it would be to come to that bliss, to receive such glory, once one has seen the light in time! Therefore the just man overflows with joy and is all delight, because he expects that that hour will come when his body will rise again to such glory. He is all delight when he reflects on this.

By indicating that the soul in heaven, in spite of its embodiment, is still waiting for the moment in which it will be reunited to its body, the *Golden Scripture* underscores the necessity of the Resurrection for the fullness of glory.

The emphasis that Bonvesin places on the changes brought about at the Last Judgment at the end of both the *Black Scripture* and *Golden Scripture* relates to the importance that resurrection continued to have in contemporary medieval culture. As we have seen, there was an extensive poetic tradition in the vernacular of the Italian peninsula that conceived of resurrection as the moment in which heavenly bliss and infernal pain become full and complete. Bonvesin's *De die Iudicii* and *De anima cum corpore* in particular are witness to the significance that bodily return had both as the reconstitution of the unity of the person and as the victory over death and loss. We must read Bonvesin's references in the *Book of the Three Scriptures* to the reconstitution of the whole person against the background of the power the doctrine of the Resurrection retained throughout the thirteenth century. Significantly, just before he concludes the poem, Bonvesin shows that in heaven the blessed soul is still waiting for the Resurrection and the amplification of bliss that will also affect the body: "Aspeg lo di novissi- mo   ke 'l corp ha resustar, / Lo qual sí s' á quiloga   godher e alegrar / E in splendor purissimo   resplend e confortar: / Lo godhio k'eo aspe- gio   no se porav cuintar" (I await the Last Day when my body will rise again and have pleasure and joy here and shine and delight in the purest splendor. The enjoyment I await cannot be told [*Golden Scripture* 729–32]).

Close analysis of the *Black Scripture* and the *Golden Scripture* reveals the complexity of Bonvesin's thirteenth-century eschatological conception, which brought together different emphases but continued to uphold the importance of the body. On the one hand, the *Book of the Three Scriptures* portrays death as the decisive moment of one's existence on earth; Bonve- sin's descriptions of hell and heaven focus on the experience of a separated soul that encapsulates many physical characteristics, to the extent that it is sometimes described as a sort of resurrected person. Moreover, the human body itself gives structure to the whole poem, which opens with an account of the imperfection of the earthly body. On the other hand, Bonvesin shows that the separated soul, no matter how somatomorphic, is not enough: resurrection remains the ultimate moment of existence. It guarantees the expected reconstitution of the human person, and, for Bonvesin and his audience, it provides a comforting response to the tragedy of decay, death, and loss that torments earthly life.

Chapter 2

Embryology and Aerial Bodies in Dante's *Comedy*

Individual Judgment, Experience, and Embodiment

As the *Epistle to Cangrande* states succinctly, the literal subject of the *Divine Comedy* "around which the movement of the whole poem turns" is "the condition of the souls after death" ("status animarum post mortem").[1] The *Comedy* thus shares its eschatological emphasis with the *Book of the Three Scriptures*. It stresses the significance of personal death, describes the experience of the separated souls in the eschatological time between death and resurrection, and imagines that this experience is embodied. Yet, unlike Bonvesin, Dante engages openly with contemporary theoretical and theological discourse about the afterlife, showing more awareness than Bonvesin of the complexity and implications of an eschatological conception that somatizes the separated soul and stresses its experience after physical death but simultaneously maintains the significance of the resurrection of the body.

The Book of the Three Scriptures tells us that when the person is about to die, devils and angels eagerly wait to take the soul either to the pains of hell or to the joys of heaven as soon as it separates from its body. Like Bonvesin's poem, the *Comedy* also highlights the significance of personal death as the moment in which the individual destiny of the person is fixed once and for all. We are told, for instance, that when Guido da Montefeltro died,

Saint Francis came down from heaven to take his soul but was halted by a devil showing that, as Guido's repentance was not sincere, his soul deserved to be taken to hell (*Inf.* 27.112–23).[2] By contrast, when Guido's son Buonconte died, an angel came down from heaven and took his soul away from a devil who wanted to take it to hell, because Buonconte had sincerely repented of his sins just before dying. The comparison of Guido's and Buonconte's fates is meant to stress God's mercy and illustrate the difference between the efficacy of true repentance and the uselessness of the priest's absolution without the sinner's sincere contrition. But it also makes it clear that, as in the *Book of the Three Scriptures,* death is the exact moment in which the damned souls are separated from the saved ones.[3]

Like the *Book of the Three Scriptures,* the *Comedy* does not focus on a future, final trial at the end of time which will determine everyone's ultimate punishment or reward in the collective scenario of the Last Judgment. Rather, Dante's poem underscores that an individual's destiny is determined at the very instant of death. Moreover, Dante's work shows the extent to which the concept of individual judgment had developed in the early fourteenth century, and imagines that as soon as the damned soul separates from its body, it undergoes a personal trial that specifies the modality of its experience in the afterlife. Immediately after death, the damned souls go to the shores of the river Acheron (*Inf.* 3.122–26) and, after crossing it on Charon's boat, assemble in front of Minos, who judges them and assigns them to the proper circle of hell:

> Stavvi Minòs orribilmente, e ringhia:
> essamina le colpe ne l'intrata;
> giudica e manda secondo ch'avvinghia.
>   Dico che quando l'anima mal nata
> li vien dinanzi, tutta si confessa;
> e quel conoscitor de le peccata
>   vede qual loco d'inferno è da essa;
> cignesi con la coda tante volte
> quantunque gradi vuol che giù sia messa.
>   Sempre dinanzi a lui ne stanno molte:
> vanno a vicenda ciascuna al giudizio,
> dicono e odono e poi son giù volte.
>   (*Inf.* 5.4–15)[4]

> There stands Minos, horrible and snarling: upon the entrance he examines their offenses, and judges and dispatches them according as he entwines. I mean that when the ill-begotten soul comes before him, it confesses all; and that discerner of sins sees which shall be its place in Hell, then girds himself with his tail as many times as the grades he wills that it be sent down. Always before him stands a crowd of them; they go, each on his turn, to the judgment; they tell, and hear, and then are hurled below.

All the souls that do not go to the shore of the Acheron (i.e., all the saved souls) go to the shore of the Tiber.[5] From there they will either be carried to the mountain of purgatory or go to heaven.

As I have argued in the previous chapter, Bonvesin's focus on the condition of the separated souls in the time between death and resurrection did not imply dismissal of the body, but implied a somatomorphization of the soul that conveyed the physicality of the soul's experience in the afterlife. In the *Comedy* as well, the soul's experience, which begins immediately after physical death, is imagined as embodied, and the first thing that actually happens to the soul in the afterlife is that it becomes somatomorphic. Bonvesin (and medieval eschatological authors in general) seemed to be at ease in representing the separated soul—which, according to the theologians, is a completely spiritual being—with a strong insistence on its physical and corporeal dimension; yet Dante in contrast does not disregard the problems that arise in conceptualizing the soul's somatomorphism in more rigorous terms. With his usual boldness, Dante confronts the issue directly. In *Purgatorio* 25 he has Statius explain that as soon as the soul separates from its earthly body and lands on the shores of the Acheron (if it is damned) or the Tiber (if it is saved), it radiates a body of air that gives it an appearance and allows it to express sensitive faculties.[6] The union of a soul and the aerial body it radiates in the afterlife is called an "ombra," a shade, and it is shades—beings with an appearance but no substantiality—who inhabit the eschatological realms visited by the pilgrim.

As we will see, the shades' incorporeality (which Dante calls "vanità") is mentioned in the *Inferno* as early as the episode involving the pilgrim's encounter with the gluttons; but it is then not really emphasized, so that most of the time infernal shades are presented as corporeal and tangible. As soon as *Purgatorio* begins, however, things change radically. The shades' lack of corporeality becomes such an important issue of the entire canticle that the pilgrim (and the reader) begins to wonder what a shade really is and how it can feel physical torment. The nature of the shades is addressed directly for the first time right after the encounter with Casella, when the pilgrim is astonished to realize that unlike his (fleshly) body, Virgil's (aerial) body does not cast a shadow. Virgil does not know how that is possible, and can say only that God provides the separated souls with some sort of body that can experience physical pain. Human beings, Virgil adds, must not try to understand that and other divine mysteries but should be satisfied with the fact that they occur:

> A sofferir tormenti, caldi e geli
> simili corpi la Virtù dispone
> che, come fa, non vuol ch'a noi si sveli.
> . . . .
> State contenta, umana gente, al *quia;*
> ché, se potuto aveste veder tutto,
> mestier non era parturir Maria.
> (Purg. 3.31–39)

To suffer torments, heat, and frost, bodies such as these that Power ordains, which wills not that the way of Its working be revealed to us. . . . Be content, human race, with the *quia;* for if you had been able to see everything, no need was there for Mary to give birth.

The pilgrim obeys Virgil's advice not to investigate that which cannot be known until he arrives with Virgil and Statius at the terrace of lust, which is the last terrace of purgatory. Having just left the terrace of gluttony, where the contrapasso consists in the souls' continual thinning, the pilgrim is so shocked by the distortion and emaciation of the gluttons' features that he wants to know more about purgatorial suffering. He seems to be aware of the contemporary doctrine that the fire tormenting the separated souls in hell or purgatory is not metaphorical but real, and is now wondering how that is possible if, as he has been continuously reminded, the beings he encounters have shape but lack corporeality. With the confidence of asking something crucial ("sicuramente" [19]), the pilgrim inquires how a soul can get thinner if it does not need food: "Come si può far magro / là dove l'uopo di nodrir non tocca?" (*Purg.* 25.20–21). Virgil, who cannot answer any more precisely at the top of purgatory than he could at its bottom, asks Statius to answer the pilgrim's doubt. Statius's very long reply, which uses technical philosophical language, is divided into two parts: lines 37–78 relay the origin of the human soul, while lines 79–109 explain that in the afterlife the soul unfolds an aerial body and becomes a shade. Etienne Gilson has shown that for the conception of the shades that inhabit his poem, Dante borrows the classical concept of "shades" that inhabited the underworld and, in particular, the *umbrae* encountered by Aeneas in his descent to the underworld in *Aeneid* 6.[7] By having the Christian Statius explain what the pagan Virgil does not know, Dante at the same time emphasizes that his use of the Virgilian concept of shades is informed by Scholastic philosophy and transcends classical culture.[8] Critics have nonetheless long debated about how precisely Dante situates himself within Scholastic discussion.

The first part of Statius's speech generated a harsh debate in the 1920s between Giovanni Busnelli and Bruno Nardi.[9] Busnelli, who considered Dante a faithful disciple of Thomas Aquinas, wanted to show that Statius's account of the generation of the soul is fully Thomistic and follows Aquinas's doctrine of unicity of form. Nardi, on the other hand, tried to show Dante's freedom in following several doctrines. Dante's account of the origin of the soul, according to him, is much less close to Aquinas than Busnelli claimed, and Dante never explicitly asserted Aquinas's principle of unicity of form, according to which the rational soul is the only form of the person, including the body.[10] Subsequent critics have either sided with Nardi or equivocated. In the 1960s and 1970s Etienne Gilson, for instance, restated Dante's full adherence to the Thomistic doctrine, while Kenelm Foster stressed Dante's ambivalence and was ambivalent himself. Foster agreed with Nardi's interpretation but also stated that it is not possible fully to reject the Thomistic sense that Busnelli claims: "E, tutto considerato, l'interpretazione di Nardi è forse quella che meglio risponde al senso del passo, senza tuttavia escludere del tutto che D. abbia voluto attribuirgli quel senso tomista che G. Busnelli vi scorge."[11]

In this chapter, I will show that the embryological account of *Purgatorio* 25 indeed manifests the ambiguity that is reflected by the scholarly debate about it. In particular, the section begins by following the more traditional doctrine of plurality of forms but ends with an original appropriation of some principles of the doctrine of unicity. I will first consider the late thirteenth-century philosophical controversy between the doctrines of plurality and unicity of form, concentrating upon the different anthropological conceptions that these doctrines imply. I will then analyze the initial section of Statius's speech and contextualize it within the terms of this controversy, explaining thus the reasons for and the implications of its ambiguity between the two doctrines. I will then show how Dante exploits the embryological principles of *Purgatorio* 25 to create the theory of the soul's aerial body. Finally, I will discuss the anthropological model that is expressed by the concept of shade as Dante reinterprets it, and how Dante uses this concept to grant the soul a full experience even before the reunification with its body, which will take place only at the end of time.

Competing Anthropological Models in Late Thirteenth-Century Scholastics

The nature of the soul was one of the most debated topics in thirteenth- and fourteenth-century philosophy.[12] While Scholastic theologians had agreed on the unity of the human soul since the mid-thirteenth century, they differed on how to conceive of this unity.[13] During the second half of the thirteenth century, Bonaventure and Thomas Aquinas imposed a "polarization of views" upon the Scholastic discourse of the rational soul which would eventually lead to the controversy between the doctrines of plurality and unicity of forms.[14] The discussion focused on the question of whether the soul was composed of different forms having different properties or whether it was just one single form possessing all the faculties. Those who assumed or asserted plurality stressed that the human soul is one but at the same time composed of several forms, while the doctrine of unicity conceives of the rational soul as a "forma simplex"—a simple, single form.

The controversy between plurality and unicity of form was a metaphysical controversy that, as Daniel Callus has pointed out, hinged on three sets of alternatives: first, whether prime matter is absolutely passive potency or contains some actuality of its own, no matter how incomplete or imperfect it may be; second, whether privation is the disappearance of all the previous forms or not, so that matter is not deprived of all precedent forms in the process of becoming; and third, whether substantial form, including virtually all preceding forms, confers on prime matter its complete and specific determination, and alone actualizes all its perfections and activities or imparts one perfection only. If one takes as true the first hypothesis of each of these three sets, one advocates unicity of form; if one defends the second hypothesis, one advocates plurality of forms.[15] Although strictly speaking the controversy was about the human soul, the terms of the controversy show that the two philosophical positions also had implications for the way in which the body and its union with the soul were understood—that is, for what today we call "anthropology."

With the increasing assimilation of Aristotelian philosophy, Scholastic thinkers progressively strengthened the unitary character of the person as a composite of body and soul.[16] While they therefore agreed that the body was an essential part of the human person, they differed in how they conceived of body and soul and the relation between them. Theologians such as Bonaventure, Roger Bacon, John Peckham, and Richard of Middleton assumed a plurality of forms and also claimed that body and soul are each composed of their own form and matter.[17] By contrast, the partisans of unicity, such as Albert the Great, Thomas Aquinas, and Giles of Rome, maintained that the rational soul is the only form of the person, including the body. In this section, I will sketch the anthropologies of Bonaventure and Aquinas, whom Dante acknowledges as his complementary sources when he grants them the status of representative contemporary philosophers in the heaven of wisdom. Both anthropologies had advantages and disadvantages for Dante's purposes: since it was difficult for him to espouse either doctrine in an entirely consistent manner, I will show that he made a bold attempt to combine them.

Bonaventure assumes the more traditional doctrine of plurality of forms. He follows the principle of universal hylomorphism, which conceives of any subsisting entity, including body and soul, as composed of its own form and matter.[18] As Bonnie Kent summarizes the concept of plurality of forms in the human being, "Bonaventure and most Franciscans argued that the body has existence through its own form. The rational soul does indeed make the body-soul composite a person, just as it makes the body be alive and capable of sensation, but it does not make the body a body" (as the doctrine of unicity of form maintains).[19] By assuming that body and soul are two different entities with their own form and matter, the concept of plurality of forms has the advantage of both granting the body a concrete existence of its own and not threatening the immortality of the soul, thus avoiding two sets of problems that arise from the doctrine of unicity of form.[20] On the other hand, the principle of plurality has some serious problems in accounting for the unity of any compound. In particular, it raises the major problem of the unity of the soul.[21] Moreover, it threatens the unity of the person, which could be understood as a sort of partnership between two members—body and soul—rather than a unity.[22]

One of the problems with plurality of forms is in fact that it does not necessitate a soul-body union. If both body and soul are form-matter combinations, it is hard to see what keeps them together. Bonaventure tried to solve this problem by connecting body and soul through a mutual desire that each has for the other and by suggesting that one is incomplete without the other. The body needs the soul because the soul has the function of administering and perfecting the body. The union with the soul keeps the body alive and capable of sensation; when the soul separates from the body, the body remains lifeless and deficient. At the same time, the soul is equally incomplete without the body. The soul longs for its body and is fully happy only when it is united to it: "When God created the body, He joined it to the soul; He united the two in a natural and mutual desire; . . . this natural desire does not allow the soul to be fully happy unless the body is restored to it, for to regain the body the soul has a natural inclination" (*Breviloquium* part 7, chap. 7, par. 4).[23]

The soul's desire for its body creates some tensions with respect to the concept of the separated soul's experience in the afterlife. Like the majority of theologians in the second half of the thirteenth century, Bonaventure argued that the saintly soul does not need to wait for resurrection in order to attain the beatific vision. Instead, the separated soul can enjoy the *visio Dei* as soon as it gets to heaven, either right after leaving its body or after completing purgation.[24] Since Bonaventure considered happiness to be the cessation of any desire, the soul's desire for its body, which is necessary for the union of the person, also prevents the separated soul from fully enjoying the beatific vision before the Resurrection.[25] Bonaventure returned (through Peter Lombard) to Augustine's concept of *desiderium* and *retardatio,* arguing that the soul alone cannot enjoy full vision of God because it is distracted by its natural inclination toward its body.[26] A case in point is Bonaventure's defense of Mary's assumption to heaven:

> Her happiness would not be complete unless she were there personally [i.e., bodily assumed into heaven]. The person is not the soul; it is a composite. Thus it is established that she must be there as a composite, that is, of soul and body. Otherwise she would not be there in perfect joy; for (as Augustine says) the minds of the saints [before their resurrections] are hindered, because of their natural inclination for their bodies, from being totally borne into God.
>
> (*De assumptione Beatae Virginis Mariae,* sermon 1, sect. 2)[27]

Bonaventure's understanding of body and soul as two separate entities united through desire implies that before the reunification with its body at the end of time, the saintly soul, even when it is enjoying the beatific vision, still feels the lack of its body and is distracted from fullness of glory by this unfulfilled desire. Bonaventure thereby places emphasis on the necessity of resurrection and the improvement that it will bring to bliss. While the *visio Dei* will not increase "substantially" with the resumption of the body, Bonaventure argues, it will nonetheless increase both "extensively" and "intensively": extensively, because the body, as the second component of the person, will finally enjoy it; and intensively, because the desire of the soul to administer the body will be removed.[28]

While Bonaventure assumes that both body and soul are two distinct entities, each with its own form and matter, the position of unicity of form (already adumbrated by Albert the Great and perfected by Thomas Aquinas) rejects universal hylomorphism, asserting instead that the human being is composed of a substantial form—the rational soul—and the matter that it activates—its body.[29] Aquinas therefore considered the rational soul as the only form of the person, and the body as the matter of the person. The rational soul, which also has vegetative and sensitive powers, is the only substantial form of man: "We must affirm that the intellective soul alone informs man so as to give him existence, no other form does so. And just as it contains within its capacities all that the sense-soul and the nutritive soul contain, so it contains all the more elementary forms and of itself effects what they effect in other cases" (*Summa theologiae* 1a, q. 76, a. 4, resp.).[30] In the *De spiritualibus creaturis*, Aquinas can therefore state that "in man there is no other substantial form than the rational soul, and it is due to it alone that a man is not only a human being, but also animal, living, body, substance, 'something'" (a. 1, resp.).[31] According to Aquinas, it is better to say that the soul contains the body and makes it to be one rather than the opposite: "magis anima continet corpus et facit ipsum esse unum, quam e converso" (ST 1a, q. 76, a. 3, ad 1).[32] As Sofia Vanni Rovighi explains, the doctrine of unicity of form conceives of the rational soul not only as the principle of intellectual knowledge, but also as that which determines the human body in all its specificity, including, for instance, the color of the eyes.[33]

The doctrine of unicity of form thus granted enormous power to the soul, which continues also in the afterlife. In the *Summa contra gentiles*, for example, Aquinas emphasizes the plenitude of the soul's bliss even without the body, stating that the saintly soul sees God as soon as it separates from its body, and that this is the ultimate beatitude: "Statim igitur cum anima sancta a corpore separatur, Deum per speciem videt; quod est ultima beatitudo" (bk. 4, chap. 91).[34] And in the *Summa theologiae,* his response to the question of whether the body is required for man's beatitude ("Utrum ad beatitudinem hominis requiratur corpus") is negative for what concerns essential beatitude: "It is evident that the souls of the saints, separated from their bodies, walk by sight in the vision of God's essence, which is true happiness" (ST 1a2ae, q. 4, a. 5, resp.).[35]

Aquinas does not emphasize the separated soul's desire for its body, which for Bonaventure is essential to the union of person. As Simon Tugwell points out, "Thomas's basic conviction remains that, once beatitude is reached . . . there is nothing more to be desired," and his "basic instinct manifestly favours a two-stage rather than a three-stage eschatology. There is this life and the hereafter, not this life, the hereafter and then, as it were, the thereafter."[36] In other words, the importance of resurrection seems limited when Aquinas places emphasis on the perfection of the beatific vision before the Resurrection. Bliss no doubt increases with resurrection, but Aquinas stresses, especially in his mature works, that it increases not intensively and extensively (as Bonaventure claims) but only extensively: "corpore resumpto, beatitudo crescit non intensive, sed extensive" (ST 1a2ae, q. 4, a. 5, ad 5).[37] Nonetheless the body and the Resurrection remain important for Aquinas. Because within the anthropology of unicity the body is ontologically necessary for the person—rather than (merely) desired by the soul—Aquinas can accord both a fuller beatitude to the separated soul and a stronger sense of necessity to the Resurrection.

By considering the rational soul as the only substantial form of the person, the doctrine of unicity of form links body and soul very tightly and emphasizes the psychosomatic wholeness of the human being to the extent that it is often characterized by scholars as a victory over dualism.[38] However, the very success of the doctrine of unicity in guaranteeing the unity of the person and securing a tight connection between body and soul engenders two opposing problems: on the one hand, the doctrine of unicity threatens the soul's immortality, and, on the other hand, risks compromising the concreteness of the body.

On a philosophical level, the notion of a form (the soul) that separates even temporarily from its matter (the body) is problematic, and it even threatens the soul's immortality because, in Aristotelian terms, form and matter cannot be separated.[39] Aquinas tried to ensure the soul's immortality by positing the soul as a substantial form—that is, as a form that has and bestows substantiality and can therefore subsist without matter.[40] Nonetheless, the soul without body is a form without matter—and therefore by definition, incomplete. Aquinas accordingly stressed the doctrine of the resurrection of the body, affirming that the soul will eventually be reunited with its body, and the whole *homo*, not the soul alone, will enjoy beatitude:

> Si negetur resurrectio corporis, non de facili, imo difficile est sustinere immortalitatem animae. Constat enim quod anima naturaliter unitur corpori. . . . Unde anima exuta corpore, quamdiu est sine corpore, est imperfecta. . . . anima autem . . . non est totus homo, et anima mea non est ego; unde, licet anima consequatur salutem in alia vita, non tamen ego vel quilibet homo. (*On I Cor.*, chap. 15, lectio 2)[41]

> If one denies the resurrection of the body, it is not easy but, rather, difficult to defend the immortality of the soul. We know that the soul unites to the body naturally. . . . The soul that has separated from its body is therefore imperfect as long as it remains without its body. . . . The soul . . . is not the whole human being, and my soul is not I; therefore, even if the soul attains salvation in the afterlife, this is not to say that I do or that the human being does.

Paradoxically, emphasizing the importance of the body ensures the immortality of the soul. The partisans of unicity of form stress that it is important that the soul be united with the body because of the ontological completeness of the person: without its body, the soul is imperfect, like a fragment of a unity that has been broken at physical death and will be reconstituted only with bodily return. In this sense, those who assume unicity often argue that neither body nor soul alone is the full human being; each is only an incomplete part. Thomas Aquinas, for instance, argued that the body takes part in any action of man, implying precisely that soul alone is not *homo*, a human being.[42] In the *Summa theologiae* when he discusses "utrum anima sit homo," whether soul is man, he stresses that the human being is composed of both body and soul: "For as it belongs to the very conception of 'this man' that he have this soul and this flesh and bone, so it belongs to the very conception of 'man' that he have soul, flesh and bone . . . and hence it is plain that man is no mere soul, but a compound of soul and body" (1a, q. 75, a. 4, resp.).[43]

If the tight union of body and soul threatens the immortality of the soul and reasserts the significance of resurrection, the principle that the rational soul is the only form of the person could also offer a solution to the much discussed question of the identity of the resurrected body. The belief in the resurrection of the body, according to which the soul must be reunited with its same body as on earth at the Last Judgment, became part of Christian doctrine in the early third century. This doctrine required the identity of the earthly body with the resurrection body. The earthly body, however, not only decays but might also be eaten by animals and even by other human beings. This meant a possible problem in accounting for the earthly body's identity with the resurrected body. Almost every theologian assumed the importance of material continuity for the identity of the two bodies and therefore had to acknowledge the necessity of the resurrection of the material parts that lay in the tomb. In order to account for material continuity, each of these theologians was then forced to invent very complicated theories that inevitably underscored the problem even more.[44]

The principle of unicity of form could lead to the idea of formal identity, which stresses the Aristotelian principle that it is the form of something that accounts for its being the same thing. Formal identity could therefore dispense with the necessity of material continuity: if prime matter is pure potentiality—as a rigorous understanding of the doctrine of unicity would imply—and the rational soul is the only substantial form in man, what a self is (including what body is) is thus fully packed into the soul. Hence theoretically any matter the soul activates at resurrection could be considered its body.[45]

Aquinas seems to go in this direction when he rejects the idea that bovine flesh ("caro bovis") will be resurrected as such in the human body that once ate it. He stresses in fact that something is such because of its form and not because of its matter, and therefore, if the matter that was once bovine flesh resurrects under the form of human flesh, it will be human flesh.[46] However, Aquinas never pushed the implications of unicity of form to the extent of maintaining formal identity, as some of his contemporaries and followers did. Giles of Rome says that it is the form that guarantees numerical identity (i.e., being the same over time and space), and therefore no matter how greatly the matter of something changes, its numerical identity remains as long as its formal element remains.[47] Giles highlights the importance that this concept could have for the doctrine of the resurrected body, because it is the soul, and not the matter, that guarantees the numerical identity of the risen body with the earthly body.[48] Kieran Nolan points out that this concept implies the possibility that God can make the risen body out of matter other than the matter it originally had, or that he can make it out of entirely new matter.[49] Durand of St. Pourçain affirms this idea explicitly when he argues that one should not wonder whether at the Resurrection God can make the body of Peter with the body of Paul. This question, he argues, does not make any sense, since the body of Paul can only be the body of Paul. But to make the body of Peter, God can use the dust that was once the body of Paul.[50] Durand also reformulates the idea of formal identity when he avows that whatever matter unites with the soul of Peter, Peter will be the same numerically because the form is the same: "Cuicumque materiae uniatur anima Petri in resurrectione, ex quo est eadem forma secundum numerum, per consequens erit idem Petrus secundum numerum."[51]

Despite the potential of formal identity to solve the problem of how the resurrected body can be identical with the living body without the problematic assumption of material continuity, something was perceived as bothersome in the principle of unicity of form. Not only did the theologians who implied or defended formal identity not follow it consistently, stressing sometimes the importance of material continuity or implying some sense of actuality in prime matter, but the doctrine of unicity itself encountered opposition and several condemnations. Even though unicity of form was not directly condemned in Paris in 1277, some Thomistic notions that implied it were.[52] It even seems that the archbishop of Paris himself, Etienne Tempier and his collaborators asked Henry of Ghent to promote the position of plurality of forms in the human being.[53] Spared in Paris, the doctrine of unicity of form was condemned at Oxford by the archbishop of Canterbury, Robert Kilwardby, in March 1277; the condemnation was then ratified by his successor, John Peckham, in October 1284.[54] The objections that were made to unicity of form suggest that it is the sense of body as real and concrete that was lost. In his letter to Peter of Conflans about the problems of Aquinas's doctrine, Robert Kilwardby stresses the absurdity of the idea of unicity of form, which could theoretically imply that the soul unites with prime matter rather than with body. Kilwardby argues that if there were no forms of bodiliness ("formam corpoream"), sensation, and life, then body could not exist; the intellectual faculty would unite to mere matter ("intellectiva potentia nude materie uniretur"); and man would be only a sort of composite of rational soul and prime matter ("non esset homo aliud, nisi quoddam compositum ex intelligibili et materia aliis formis nudata"). Moreover, the rational faculty would have sensitive powers in a literal sense, and the activity of the eyes, ears, and all the senses would be (absurdly) connected with the rational soul.[55]

Those who rejected the doctrine of unicity of form accused it of giving absolute primacy to the rational soul as the only form of the body. According to their interpretation, the principle of unicity of form endangered the commonsense notion of body as something material and present—a sense that, in contrast, was well maintained by the idea of plurality, which conceived of the body as an entity composed of its own form and matter.[56] Unicity of form thereby threatened both theological principles and devotional practices. If it is the rational soul that makes a human body be a body, in the case of relics, for instance, what would be the point of venerating something that is not the body of the saint anymore?[57] It no longer contains the soul of the saint (i.e., it does not have the same form as before) and is not necessarily going to be resurrected (because what matters for identity is not matter but form). Moreover, several theologians argued that plurality of forms was required for several Christian doctrines, such as the Incarnation or the identity of Christ's body in the *triduum* (the three days between his death and resurrection).[58] It is not difficult to see how, if its presuppositions are stressed and pushed further than its partisans actually did, the doctrine of unicity of form could disturb a spirituality in which a concrete sense of the body was essential to self—a spirituality that was centered on the doctrine of the Incarnation, venerated relics and saints, and took great care in burying corpses because they were thought to be an important part of the loved ones who passed away.[59]

Dante wrote the *Comedy* in the first decades of the fourteenth century, when the controversy over the two doctrines had fully shown the strengths and disadvantages of the anthropological conceptions that they imply. Both Bonaventure and Aquinas stress that a person is composed of body and soul, with a substantial soul that survives after death and a body that adds something at resurrection. Bonaventure's conception of the person had the advantage of maintaining the importance and concreteness of the body, which was fundamental in contemporary spirituality and devotion, but threatened the unity of both the soul and the person—and could neither guarantee the person's identity in the afterlife nor allow the soul fully to enjoy the beatific vision before being reunited to its body. By conceiving of the rational soul as the only form of the person, Aquinas's doctrine of unicity of form solves all these problems. It secures the unicity of the soul and its union with the body; moreover, it grants full happiness to the soul even before bodily return and provides an avenue for solving the issue of the person's identity in the afterlife. However, at the same time, it threatens both the body's materiality and the soul's immortality. Ultimately, therefore, unicity's tight connection between body and soul is ambivalent with respect to the emphasis it places upon them as constituents of the person.[60] On the one hand, the soul is conceived of as the carrier of the whole self including the body. On the other hand, body is ontologically necessary to the person, and the separated soul is no more than the imperfect fragment of a psychosomatic unity that needs body for expression. In the following section, I will first discuss how the principles of plurality and unicity of forms lead to different understandings of the formation of the human soul in the fetus. I will then explain how Dante invents an original theory of embryology that begins with the tenets of plurality of forms but ends up being similar to the idea of unicity, thus allowing the separated soul to radiate a body of air and have full experience as soon as it gets to the afterlife.

From Plurality of Forms to (Near) Unicity of Form: Embryology in *Purgatorio* 25

The way in which the human soul develops in the fetus has crucial consequences for the understanding of the soul and its relation to the body. Embryology was therefore one of the most debated topics in thirteenth- and early fourteenth-century Scholastic philosophy. It was also at the core of the differences between the doctrines of plurality and unicity of forms. Dante deals with embryology at length in *Purgatorio* 25, where Statius addresses the pilgrim's question about how the separated soul can experience corporeal pain. While the second part of Statius's long speech explains that in the afterlife the separated soul radiates a body of air that allows it to express feelings and sensations (*Purg.* 25.79–109), Dante confronts the origin of the human soul in the first part of Statius's explanation and invents an original account that combines the principles of both plurality and unicity (37–78).

As discussed above, a strict version of the doctrine of unicity of form is based on the tenets that prime matter is pure potency, that privation is the disappearance of all the previous forms, and that substantial form confers on prime matter all its complete determination. With respect to embryology, the partisans of unicity of form, who believed that no substance can have two substantial forms at the same time, thought that the evolution of the embryo is a discontinuous process in which a series of various generations and corruptions occur. Aquinas in particular conceived of the process of human generation according to two principles that Robert Zavalloni and Bernardo Bazán define as the principle of "hiérarchie des formes" (according to which a more perfect form can confer a less perfect determination, as well as the determination proper to it) and the principle of "succession des formes" (according to which each time one new form appears, any other preceding substantial form passes away).[61] Aquinas states that whenever something changes, its preceding substantial form must disappear and be replaced by a new form:

> We must say then that, since the coming into existence of a being involves the dissolution of another being, it must be held that, both in the case of man and of other animals, when a more perfect form supervenes this brings about the dissolution of the preceding one. However, it does so in such a way that the second form possesses whatever the first one does and something more into the bargain. And thus in man, as in the other animals, the final substantial form comes about through many comings-into-being and dissolutions. (ST 1a, q. 118, a. 2, ad 2)[62]

The formation of the soul is explained as a discontinuous succession of forms in which each time a new and more perfect form appears, the old one corrupts itself. When the sensitive soul appears, it also contains the faculties of the vegetative soul, which passes away. Similarly, when the rational soul is created by God, the sensitive soul disappears. What remains is the rational soul alone, which is created as already having both vegetative and sensitive faculties and is the only substantial form of man: "Therefore it must be said that the intellective soul is created by God at the completion of man's coming-into-being. This soul is at one and the same time both a sensitive and nutritive life-principle, the preceding forms having been dissolved" (ST 1a, q. 118, a. 2, ad 2).[63] According to the principles of unicity of form, the soul is created by God as a "forma simplex," a simple, single rational form that contains all faculties, from the simplest to the intellectual, and is therefore fully immortal. This is why Aquinas can assume that, when the soul separates from its body, it keeps all its powers—the intellectual ones in act, and the sensitive and nutritive ones in potency; and the latter will be reactivated when the soul is reunited with its body at resurrection.[64]

Those who assert plurality of forms imply a different conception of prime matter—as something that is not completely passive potency but has a sort of imperfect actuality that is progressively perfected. They stress the empirical sense of change as a continuous process in which something evolves on the basis of the concept of act and potency. When the vegetative soul of an embryo is in an active state, the sensitive soul is in a state of potency, and when the sensitive soul is active, the rational soul is in potency.[65] The human soul is one, but composed of different forms that have different properties and that are added one onto the other: the vegetative soul becomes a sensitive soul (that is, a soul that has vegetative and sensitive forms) and the sensitive soul becomes—through God's intervention—a rational soul (that is, a soul that has vegetative, sensitive, and rational forms). Only the form that is created directly by God is immortal. All the other ones, which are educed from matter, are assumed to pass away with the soul's separation from the body.[66] While the theories that explain the formation of the human soul in the embryo according to the principles of plurality of forms succeed in accounting for the development from embryo into human body before the infusion of the rational soul, they all share the problem of accounting for the unity of a human soul that is partly corruptible and partly incorruptible.[67]

For reasons that I will discuss in what follows, I will argue that the account of the formation of the human soul in *Purgatorio* 25 combines both these accounts of embryology. More precisely, Statius's embryological account starts by following the more empirical theory of the continual evolution from one soul to the other, which Aquinas rejects, but ends up presenting a very powerful and unitary soul that possesses some important similarities with the soul as presented by the doctrine of unicity of form.

Statius begins his speech with the explanation of the formation of the human seed in men (*Purg.* 25.37–43). As Patrick Boyde has shown, Statius's explanation follows what Aristotle says in his *De generatione animalium* as commented on by thirteenth-century Christian philosophers using Galen and Avicenna.[68] Perfect blood, which is the final result of food processed through three digestions (in the stomach, in the liver, and in the heart), is imbued with what Statius calls "a tutte membra umane / virtute informativa" (*Purg.* 25.40–41)—that is, the power to give form to all the limbs of the human body. Most of this perfect blood goes to nourish the body through veins and arteries, while some of it remains in the heart and is transformed, through another digestion, into the sperm that goes to the genital organs (*Purg.* 25.37–45). When man's semen, which contains the formative power, unites to woman's blood, generation begins (*Purg.* 25.46–51). Statius continues to describe the formation of the embryo, and, in the first part of his account, we find the idea of change as an evolution from potency to act so that the very formative power of the semen becomes a vegetative soul. This vegetative soul then becomes a sensitive soul and develops the bodily organs that allow it to express the sensitive faculties that it already had in potency:

> Anima fatta la virtute attiva
> qual d'una pianta, in tanto differente,
> che questa è in via e quella è già a riva,
>   tanto ovra poi, che già si move e sente,
> come spungo marino; e indi imprende
> ad organar le posse ond' è semente.
>   (*Purg.* 25.52–57)

―――――

The active virtue having become a soul, like that of a plant (but in so far different that this is on the way, and that has already arrived), so works then that now it moves and feels, like a sea-fungus; then it proceeds to develop organs for the powers of which it is the germ.

Statius's account presupposes continuity until the formation of the sensitive soul. As Nardi emphasizes in his polemics with Busnelli, the continuous process described by Statius in lines 52–57 differs from Aquinas's theory of a discontinuous process in which the new form replaces the old one, which passes away when the new one supervenes.[69] However, when Statius arrives at the formation of the soul's rational powers, his argument shifts toward Aquinas. Statius has to explain the most controversial point, namely "come d'animal divegna fante" (61), that is, how the embryo, gifted with vegetative and sensitive powers, becomes endowed with intellective faculties, which Dante encapsulates in the ability to speak. Regarding the formation of the rational soul, Aristotle simply said that the intellect is created from the exterior, without giving any further specification.[70] This passage could be—and indeed was—interpreted in many different ways. First, Statius warns the pilgrim about the danger of Averroës' interpretation—which was understood by Christian theologians to argue that the possible intellect is a completely separate substance and hence to affirm that there is just one for all humankind.[71] Then, Statius moves to the crucial point of God's creation of the rational soul:

> Apri a la verità che viene il petto;
> e sappi che, sì tosto come al feto
> l'articular del cerebro è perfetto,
> lo motor primo a lui si volge lieto
> sovra tant' arte di natura, e spira
> spirito novo, di vertù repleto,
> che ciò che trova attivo quivi, tira
> in sua sustanzia, e fassi un'alma sola,
> che vive e sente e sé in sé rigira.
> <div align="right">(<i>Purg.</i> 25.67–75)</div>

___

Open your breast to the truth which is coming, and know that, so soon as in the foetus the articulation of the brain is perfect, the First Mover turns to it with joy over such art of nature, and breathes into it a new spirit replete with virtue, which absorbs that which is active there into its own substance, and makes one single soul which lives and feels and circles on itself.

When the brain has completely developed, the intellectual soul is created by God. God breathes forth the rational soul, which absorbs what it finds active in the fetus into its own substance, and becomes one single soul endowed with three different powers: vegetative, sensitive, and rational. It is here that the move from plurality to (near) unicity occurs.

As we have already seen, Busnelli is wrong in referring only to Aquinas's doctrine.[72] Aquinas states that the rational soul is created as already having vegetative/sensitive faculties and that the sensitive soul passes away with the creation of the rational soul. Statius, on the contrary, says that the rational soul absorbs the sensitive soul into its substance. Nevertheless, I want to argue against Nardi's fully anti-Thomistic interpretation of Statius's discourse. Nardi argues that Statius's account is close to the one described by Albert the Great in his *De natura et origine animae.* In this text, on the basis of the doctrine of *inchoatio formae,* which presupposes a sense of primary matter not as mere potentiality but as containing a sort of virtual or imperfect actuality, Albert describes the formation of the human soul, saying that it is a substance that comes partly from the inside and partly from the outside.[73] Nardi also quotes three passages by Thomas Aquinas, which offer an explanation of the formation of the human soul that is rejected by Aquinas but that is, Nardi argues, followed by Dante in the embryological account of *Purgatorio* 25.[74] While these passages agree with Statius's explanation of the continuous evolution that leads to the formation of the sensitive soul, I would argue that they differ from Statius's account in a significant way when they move to consider the formation of the rational soul. According to the passages quoted by Nardi as expressing an embryological doctrine similar to Statius's, the vegetative soul acquires first sensitive faculties, and then—with the direct intervention of God—rational powers. Statius's emphasis is different: he does not say that the sensitive soul becomes the rational soul because God irradiates the intellect into it; rather, he says that the rational soul created by God is the active and surviving agent, which absorbs in its substance the sensitive soul, thus acquiring vegetative and sensitive powers.[75]

Until he portrays the formation of the sensitive soul, Dante follows some tenets that differ from the principles of Thomism, but the move into the emphatically discontinuous process that is implied by the creation of the rational soul suggests a movement toward the Thomistic concept. When Etienne Gilson says that Dante "has here taken sides with Thomas Aquinas in the . . . famous discussion on the unity of the substantial form in the composite, including man," he may be overstating the case.[76] At the same time, I would stress that the text is ambiguous and indeed suggests the sort of Thomistic sense that Gilson and other critics perceive.

Other passages of the *Comedy* underline the discontinuity of the process that gives origin to the human soul. While Nardi says that Dante affirms only occasionally that the human soul is created by God in its entirety, and explains these passages on the basis of his interpretation of *Purgatorio* 25, I would maintain rather that these passages help to clarify Statius's explanation and confirm my hypothesis that the rational form is the active and surviving agent of the last process in the formation of the human soul.[77] When in the terrace of wrath Marco Lombardo describes God's creation of the soul, for instance, he identifies the human soul with the rational soul created by God and thus emphasizes the discontinuous moment of its divine creation: "Esce di mano a lui che la vagheggia / prima che sia, a guisa di fanciulla / che piangendo e ridendo pargoleggia, / l'anima semplicetta che sa nulla, / salvo che, mossa da lieto fattore, / volentier torna a ciò che la trastulla" (From His hands, who fondly loves it before it exists, comes forth after the fashion of a child that sports, now weeping, now laughing, the simple little soul, which knows nothing, save that, proceeding from a glad Maker, it turns eagerly to what delights it [*Purg.* 16.85–90]).

When Robert Kilwardby—whose views can be taken as representative of the anxieties that the doctrine of unicity awakened—rejected Aquinas's theory of the soul, he condemned two propositions: that the vegetative and sensitive souls pass away when the rational soul is introduced; and that vegetative, sensitive, and rational souls are "una forma simplex," just one simple form.[78] In the account of *Purgatorio* 25, the rational soul does not come from the potency of the vegetative-sensitive soul but is created discontinuously by God; when it is infused into the body, the vegetative-sensitive soul does not pass away completely, because it is drawn up by the rational soul into its substance, so that the result is an "alma sola"—one single soul that is fully incorruptible. Therefore Dante's soul, even though created in a different way from the soul of the Thomistic conception, could be a "forma simplex." It is difficult therefore to resist the temptation of associating the concept of the rational soul as a "forma simplex" to "l'anima semplicetta" of *Purgatorio* 16.88, where "semplicetta" is, as Bosco says in his commentary, "intensivo e non diminutivo" (280).[79]

As some critics have recently pointed out, an ideological syncretism often characterizes Dante's poem, insofar as its intellectual basis is not limited to Scholastic philosophy but also includes other epistemologies. My analysis of the embryological doctrine of *Purgatorio* 25 shows that by combining some principles of the doctrines of unicity and plurality of forms, Dante's syncretism can be just as bold when he constructs passages with a predominant Scholastic-Aristotelian basis.[80] Dante's account is different from Aquinas's series of discontinuous changes and successions of new forms replacing the old ones. At the moment of its creation, the rational soul does not contain the formative virtue and does not have vegetative and sensitive powers—as it would according to Aquinas. Rather, only subsequently does the rational soul "pull into its substance," as Dante writes, "that which is active" in the fetus. The difference from Aquinas is that the rational soul is not created as already possessing all its powers, but rather it absorbs the formative virtue and vegetative and sensitive faculties from the embryo to which it unites. By absorbing all these other faculties, the rational soul makes them immortal so that they do not disappear when it separates from the body at physical death. Thus, on the one hand, Dante's theory presents the evolution of the soul as a continuous process that takes place according to the more empirical and commonsense understanding of change presented by the tenets of plurality of forms.[81] On the other hand, it also manages to justify the unity of the soul, which is fully immortal and, even when it separates from the body, keeps all its powers, remaining the same as when it was united to the earthly body. Dante's "alma sola" can thus work in the same way as the one described by the doctrine of unicity of form. After the account of the origin of the soul, Statius explains that the separated soul carries with it both what is human (the formative virtue and vegetative-sensitive powers) and what is divine (the intellectual ones created by God):

> Quando Làchesis non ha più del lino,
> solvesi da la carne, e in virtute
> ne porta seco e l'umano e 'l divino:
>   l'altre potenze tutte quante mute;
> memoria, intelligenza e volontade
> in atto molto più che prima agute.
>   (*Purg.* 25.79–84)[82]

And when Lachesis has no more thread, the soul is loosed from the flesh and carries with it as faculties both the human and the divine; the other faculties all of them mute, but memory, intellect, and will far more acute in action than before.

With Statius's account, Dante grants the same unity to the soul as Aquinas did, and, like Aquinas, he imagines that when the soul separates from the body, it is fully immortal and keeps all its powers—the intellectual ones in act ("in atto") and all the others in potency ("mute").[83] However, while Aquinas maintained that the rational soul will reactivate all its other powers only when it reunites to the body at the end of time, Dante does not wait for the Resurrection in order to reactivate the "human" part of the person. In Dante's world the separated soul has the immediate opportunity to create a body of air that allows it to have a shape and to express all its powers—not only the rational ones—in the eschatological time between physical death and the Last Judgment. As soon as it has the opportunity, the formative virtue contained in the soul radiates forth in the very same way as it did with respect to the earthly living limbs: "Tosto che loco lì la circunscrive, / la virtù formativa raggia intorno / così e quanto ne le membra vive" (As soon as space encompasses it there, the formative virtue radiates around, in form and quantity as in the living members [*Purg.* 25.88–90]). The air that surrounds the soul is shaped "virtually"—that is, by virtue of the formative power that was in the semen and that the rational soul absorbed and made immortal when it united to the embryo:

> E come l'aere, quand'è ben pïorno,
> per l'altrui raggio che 'n sé si reflette,
> di diversi color diventa addorno;
>   così l'aere vicin quivi si mette
> e in quella forma che in lui suggella
> virtüalmente l'alma che ristette.
>
>   (*Purg.* 25.91–96)[84]

———

And as the air, when it is full of moisture, becomes adorned with various colors by another's rays, which are reflected in it, so here the neighboring air shapes itself in that form which is virtually imprinted in it by the soul that stopped there.

With the theory of the soul's aerial body, Statius can finally solve the pilgrim's doubt about how a separated soul can suffer corporeal punishment:

> Però che quindi ha poscia sua paruta,
> è chiamata ombra; e quindi organa poi
> ciascun sentire infino a la veduta.
>   Quindi parliamo e quindi ridiam noi;
> quindi facciam le lagrime e ' sospiri
> che per lo monte aver sentiti puoi.
>   Secondo che ci affliggono i disiri
> e li altri affetti, l'ombra si figura;
> e quest' è la cagion di che tu miri.
>
>   (*Purg.* 25.100–108)

———

Inasmuch as therefrom it has its semblance, it is called a shade, and therefrom it forms the organs of every sense, even to the sight. By this we speak and by this we laugh, by this we make the tears and sighs which you may have heard about the mountain. According as the desires and the other affections prick us, the shade takes its form; and this is the cause of that at which you marvel.

It is because shades are provided with every organ of sensation—"ciascun sentire" (*Purg.* 25.102)—from the simplest one to the most complex, that they are able to express the sensitive faculties that allow for the feeling of pain. The description of Muhammad among the sowers of scandal and schism shows the extent to which Dante imagines that in the afterlife shades have all the same organs as the bodies on earth, including the ones for digestion:

> Già veggia, per mezzul perdere o lulla,
> com' io vidi un, così non si pertugia,
> rotto dal mento infin dove si trulla.
> Tra le gambe pendevan le minugia;
> la corata pareva e 'l tristo sacco
> che merda fa di quel che si trangugia.
> (*Inf.* 28.22–27)

> Truly a cask, through loss of mid-board or side-piece, gapes not so wide as one I saw, cleft from the chin to the part that breaks wind; his entrails were hanging between his legs, and the vitals could be seen and the foul sack that makes ordure of what is swallowed.

Moreover, the shades that the pilgrim encounters in the course of his journey not only have all the organs that human bodies have on earth but are also fully individuated: the aerial body is not only the instrument of physical experience in the afterlife but also the vehicle for the expression of the eschatological self before the Resurrection, in heaven, as well as in hell and purgatory. Together with memory, desire, and character, the persistence of the earthly body's features is an important component of the much-celebrated individuality that shades have in the *Comedy*.[85]

The theoretical justification for this persistence is also given by Statius's account, which in fact ends by insisting that shades have an appearance ("paruta") that is the same as the one the body had on earth (*Purg.* 25.90), and changes according to how the soul is pierced by "desires" and "other affections" (*Purg.* 25.106–7). That the rational soul draws into its substance the formative virtue that, via the vegetative soul, had become part of the sensitive soul, allows the resultant soul to contain the physical structure of the living person and to express it in the aerial body that it unfolds in the other world. Yet if on earth too the expressions and the gestures of the body reflect the dispositions of the soul, Dante imagines much greater transformations for the afterlife. The representation of shades in the whole *Comedy* is constructed upon the idea—implicit in the doctrine of unicity of form and pushed to its extremes by those who asserted formal identity—that the soul contains and expresses the structure of the body. Now we shall see that this concept of soul allows the soul not only to create a body of air in the otherworld but also to alter its features drastically.

The Power of the Soul: Aerial Bodies in Hell and Heaven

The shades of hell are generally individualized through the physical particularities they had as living persons. In the circle of violence against others, for example, Azzolino da Romano and Opizzo d'Este are differentiated from each other because the hair of one is dark ("ha 'l pel così nero" [*Inf.* 12.109]), while the other is blond ("è biondo" [110]). As Piero Boitani has shown, however, pain or punishment generally distorts the features of the damned shades, often to the extent that recognition becomes "a difficult, agonizing process" and even "tends towards its negation."[86] The pilgrim sometimes manages to recognize the identity of the shades only after great effort, while at other times the shades' features are too altered for recognition to take place. The first encounter in hell between the pilgrim and one of his fellow citizens, for instance, is a case of failed recognition. When, in the circle of gluttony, the Florentine Ciacco asks the pilgrim whether he is able to recognize him, the pilgrim answers that his suffering makes him unrecognizable:

> "O tu che se' per questo 'nferno tratto",
> mi disse, "riconoscimi, se sai:
> tu fosti, prima ch'io disfatto, fatto".
> E io a lui: "L'angoscia che tu hai
> forse ti tira fuor de la mia mente,
> sì che non par ch'i' ti vedessi mai".
> (*Inf.* 6.40–45)

"O you that are led through this Hell," he said to me, "recognize me if you can: you were made before I was unmade." And I to him,

"The anguish you endure perhaps takes you from my memory, so
that I do not seem ever to have seen you."

While it is not surprising that pain and punishment may alter the features
of a tortured person, the power Statius's embryology grants to the soul accounts for far greater distortions (and, as we will see in the last chapter,
thereby ultimately engenders a tension between earthly and aerial appearances). More specifically, I will focus on how sin contaminates the soul's
intellectual faculties and is responsible for the deformation of the shades'
features in hell.

One of the major themes of Dante's work is that human beings are free
and therefore responsible agents because the souls' intellectual faculties of
reason and will distinguish them from other animals and allow them to
exert control over their appetites.[87] Moreover, it is through its intellectual
powers that the human soul takes part in God's divine nature.[88] In the
heaven of Mercury, Beatrice explains that sin deprives the human soul—
which is created by God with the gifts of immortality, freedom, and conformity to him—of its freedom, making it dissimilar to God: "Solo il
peccato è quel che la disfranca / e falla dissimìle al sommo bene, / per che
del lume suo poco s'imbianca" (Sin alone is that which disfranchises it
and makes it unlike the Supreme Good, so that it is little illumined by Its
light [*Par.* 7.79–81]). By depriving the human being of its rational and free
nature, sin, as Thomas Aquinas explains, also makes it fall into a beastly
state: "Homo peccando ab ordine rationis recedit; et ideo decidit a digni-
tate humana, prout scilicet homo est naturaliter liber, et propter seipsum
existens; et incidit quodammodo in servitutem bestiarum" (A man who
sins deviates from the rational order, and so loses his human dignity in so
far as a man is naturally free and an end to himself. To that extent, then, he
lapses into the subjection of the beasts [ST 2a2ae, q. 64, a. 2, ad 3]).

Although on earth a human being can repent and get rid of sin (through
a process of expiation that can eventually be completed in purgatory), sin
continues to contaminate souls that have been damned to hell.[89] The implications of this contamination become clear in the passage that Charles
Singleton has used to explain the whole moment of purgatory as a process
of "justification":

O superbi cristian, miseri lassi,
che, de la vista de la mente infermi,
fidanza avete ne' retrosi passi,

non v'accorgete voi che noi siam vermi
nati a formar l'angelica farfalla,
che vola a la giustizia sanza schermi?
  Di che l'animo vostro in alto galla,
poi siete quasi antomata in difetto,
sì come vermo in cui formazion falla?
(Purg. 10.121–29)

O proud Christians, wretched and weary, who, sick in mental vision, put trust in backward steps: are you not aware that we are worms, born to form the angelic butterfly that flies unto judgment without defenses? Why does your mind soar up aloft, since you are as it were imperfect insects, even as the worm in which full form is wanting?

According to Singleton, the justice recovered by the soul through the terraces of purgatory is "original justice," which Adam and Eve possessed before the Fall and which consists of the right order within the soul—that is, the dominion of the reason over the other faculties.[90] Other scholars have developed Singleton's idea and suggested (with a definition taken from Thomas Aquinas) that if the process of justification is a *motus ad formam*, a movement toward form (which, in this case, is order of the soul's faculties), then what the damned souls experience is a parody of the process of justification—that is, a *motus a forma*, a movement away from form and order.[91]

In hell, sin inalterably damages reason and will, which are the faculties that define the souls as human and grant them the possibility to be free. Hence, the damned souls have lost the good of the intellect ("le genti dolorose / c'hanno perduto il ben de l'intelletto" [*Inf.* 3.17–18]), and hell is the place where it is impossible to return to good will ("lo 'nferno, u' non si riede / già mai a buon volere" [*Par.* 20.106–7]).[92] The perverse will, which was in life the result of free decision and the cause of damnation, continues in hell, where it becomes an unchangeable state of being. Capaneus is the character who best exemplifies the psychological condition of the damned as the never-ending perpetuation of their sin. As he was a blasphemer against God, in hell he lies supine while being tormented by a rain of fire. In spite of the punishment that clearly shows his ultimate defeat, however, Capaneus not only says proudly that in hell he is precisely the same as he was on earth ("Qual io fui vivo, tal son morto" [*Inf.* 14.51]), but also confirms that his statement is true by continuing to challenge God and claim that God will never be able to punish him.[93] Like Capaneus, all the damned souls are forever stuck in the same sinful condition they had in life, without any possibility of repentance, change, or improvement.[94] By inalterably impairing the intellectual faculties of the souls in hell, sin forbids them to attain original justice and to become angelic butterflies that fly to God. Sin therefore condemns them to remain forever a "vermo in cui formazion falla," a worm in which full form is wanting, a monstrous being that corrupts the essence of what it was created to be.[95]

While the condition of original justice to be attained by the soul in purgatory is the right order within its several faculties, what distinguishes the soul in hell is precisely its disorder. This disorder is then reflected in the aerial body that the damned soul expresses.[96] Here, I would like to propose that the move of the embryological explanation in *Purgatorio* 25 from the principles of plurality toward those of unicity accounts for the connection between the deformation of the shades' features in hell and the corruption of the intellectual faculties of the souls unfolding them. By having the rational soul absorb what it finds in the body to which it unites, Dante imagines that even when it separates from the body, the rational soul contains the physical characteristics of the person. His account thereby reflects the principle of unicity of form, which could be understood as making the body fully depend on the rational soul, even to the degree of particulars like the color of the eyes. Since sin permanently disrupts the order within the rational faculties of the damned soul, the aerial body that the soul radiates in hell can be greatly distorted and altered—as in the case of the diviners (who wanted to see too much ahead and have their heads twisted the other way around) or the sowers of discord and schism (who are endlessly mutilated).[97] If at other times the shades of hell even appear metamorphosed into different bodies, it is because what the soul expresses is so corrupted by sin that it can even cease to look like a human body. This is the case of the suicides, who are transformed into bushes, and the thieves, who are punished with continuous metamorphoses into snakes and whose contrapasso makes them lose the ownership of their own features.[98]

Sin transforms the damned souls into monstrous hybrids that are both bestial and reminiscent of the humanity that they rejected on earth. Moreover, sin is also responsible for the heaviness and tangibility that often characterizes the shades in hell, especially in the second part of the *Inferno*.[99] The comparison between the incorporeality of shades in purgatory and the pilgrim's body, which becomes faster and more agile when the seven *P*'s are erased from his forehead, makes clear that the thickness of the shades in hell represents the burden of sin, which makes any real progress within the soul impossible and keeps it stuck in hell.[100] The infernal souls' heaviness is a sign that they are not only unglorified but also unglorifiable: it represents both the lack of desire to move toward God and the impossibility of doing so.

One of the most interesting examples of both deformation and heaviness is the shade of Master Adam, a falsifier of coins whose limbs are completely distorted by dropsy:

> Io vidi un fatto a guisa di lëuto,
> pur ch'elli avesse avuta l'anguinaia
> tronca da l'altro che l'uomo ha forcuto.
>   La grave idropesì, che sì dispaia
> le membra con l'omor che mal converte,
> che 'l viso non risponde a la ventraia,
>   faceva lui tener le labbra aperte
> come l'etico fa, che per la sete
> l'un verso 'l mento e l'altro in sù rinverte.
>
> (*Inf.* 30.49–57)

I saw one shaped like a lute, if only he had been cut short at the groin from the part where a man is forked. The heavy dropsy which, with its ill-digested humor, so unmates the members that the face does not answer to the paunch, made him hold his lips apart, like the hectic who, for thirst, curls the one lip toward his chin and the other upwards.

As is typical of the sinners, Master Adam does not blame himself for his damnation and seek repentance; rather, his concern is to take revenge on those who asked him to falsify the coins. One of these persons is in the same pouch, but, as Master Adam says, he is so heavy that he cannot move to seek him out:

> ma che mi val, c'ho le membra legate?
>   S'io fossi pur di tanto ancor leggero
> ch'i' potessi in cent' anni andare un'oncia,

io sarei messo già per lo sentiero,
  cercando lui tra questa gente sconcia,
con tutto ch'ella volge undici miglia,
e men d'un mezzo di traverso non ci ha.
(Inf. 30.81–87)

———

But what does it avail me whose limbs are tied? If I were only still so light that I could move one inch in a hundred years, I would have set out already on the road to seek him among this disfigured people, for all it is eleven miles around and not less than half a mile across.

With his heavy limbs ("le membra che son gravi" [30.107]) and distorted shape, Master Adam is a good example of a soul in hell—that is, a monstrous being prevented by its own sin from flying toward God like an angelic butterfly.

Not only in hell, but also in purgatory, the soul carries and expresses the features of the body even in the absence of the body. As we will see in the next chapter, there a shade's shape might be altered by pain and punishment, but it always keeps the same appearance as on earth and never changes to the extent of being unrecognizable. While in hell the aerial body allows the soul to experience pain and to express its perverted self in a never-ending, repetitive way, there is a dynamic relationship between soul and aerial body in purgatory: the soul expresses and shapes the body, but at the same time the body changes the soul through pain. The deformation of the shades' features in purgatory is hence not due to the souls' contamination with evil but is the sign that the souls are experiencing their pain in a productive way that conforms them to the suffering Christ.

While the eventual distortion of the shades' features in hell and purgatory is an indication that the souls' intellectual faculties are, respectively, unalterably contaminated by sin or learning to assimilate to Christ's exemplar, the features that the souls express in heaven are enhanced and perfected. The first souls that the pilgrim meets in paradise are the ones in the heaven of the Moon. They are still shades, but so pale that he mistakes them as "specchiati sembianti" or reflected images (*Par.* 3.19). After Beatrice tells the pilgrim that he is encountering real souls, he bends toward the shade who looks most eager to talk, "l'ombra che parea più vaga / di ragionar" (34–35), and asks its name and condition. The shade replies that she is Piccarda Donati and that though she is now more beautiful than when he had known her on earth, it should not be difficult for him to recognize her: "I' fui nel mondo vergine sorella; / e se la mente tua ben sé riguarda, / non mi ti celerà l'esser più bella, / ma riconoscerai ch'i' son Piccarda" (In the world I was a virgin sister, and if your memory be searched well, my being more beautiful will not conceal me from you, but you will recognize that I am Piccarda [*Par.* 3.45–48]). The pilgrim looks more carefully and acknowledges that in the appearance of these shades, something divine makes them different from their earthly figures, but they are nonetheless recognizable:

> Ne' mirabili aspetti
> vostri risplende non so che divino
> che vi trasmuta da' primi concetti:
>   però non fui a rimembrar festino;
> ma or m'aiuta ciò che tu mi dici,
> sì che raffigurar m'è più latino.
> (*Par.* 3.58–63)

In your wondrous aspects a something divine shines forth that transmutes you from recollection of former times; therefore I was not quick in calling you to mind, but now that which you tell me helps me so that I more clearly recall your features.

In heaven, Piccarda's shade maintains an appearance similar to that on earth, but it is more beautiful because her features are radiated by a separated soul that has attained permanent perfection.

Unlike the damned souls, whose intellectual faculties are inalterably corrupted and perverted by sin, the blessed souls are characterized not only by perfect order within their faculties but also, as the souls constantly stress throughout the *Paradiso*, by their perfect conformity to God's will: "Li nostri affetti, che solo infiammati / son nel piacer de lo Spirito Santo, / letizian del suo ordine formati" (Our affections, which are kindled solely in the pleasure of the Holy Ghost, rejoice in being conformed to His order [*Par.* 3.52–54]). As a passage from the *Monarchia* makes clear, it is precisely because the saintly souls cannot alter their permanent control over their appetites that they enjoy the maximum and most perfect freedom, which is a sign that the souls' intellectual faculties are working at their best:

Si ergo iudicium moveat omnino appetitum et nullo modo preveniatur ab eo, liberum est; si vero ab appetitu quocunque modo preveniente iudicium moveatur, liberum esse non potest. . . . Et hinc est quod bruta iudicium liberum habere non possunt, quia eorum iudicia semper ab appetitu preveniuntur. Et hinc etiam patere enim potest quod substantiae intellectuales, quarum sunt inmutabiles voluntates, necnon anime separate bene hic abeuntes, libertatem arbitrii ob inmutabilitatem voluntatis non amictunt, sed perfectissime atque potissime hoc retinent. Hoc viso, iterum manifestum esse potest quod hec libertas sive principium hoc totius nostre libertatis est maximum donum humane nature a Deo collatum—sicut in Paradiso *Comedie* iam dixi—quia per ipsum hic felicitamur ut homines, per ipsum alibi felicitamur ut dii. (*Mon.* 1.12.4–6)[101]

If the judgment completely directs the appetite and is in no way deflected by it, then it is free; but if the judgment is in any way deflected or influenced by the appetite it cannot be free. . . . And this is why the brute beasts cannot enjoy free judgment: because their judgments always follow their appetites. It also explains how intellectual substances, whose wills are immutable, and disembodied souls who depart this life in a state of grace, do not lose their free choice on accounts of their will being immutable but rather enjoy it in its highest perfection. Once this is realized, it becomes equally clear that this liberty, or this principle of all our liberty, is God's most precious gift to human nature—as I have already said in the *Paradiso* of the *Comedy*—for by it we are made happy here as men, and happy as gods in the beyond.

The pilgrim's encounter with Piccarda in the heaven of the Moon shows that the perfected, almost divine way in which the intellectual powers of the souls work in heaven is reflected in the more beautiful features they express.

In the heaven of Mercury, which follows the heaven of the Moon, an important transition occurs. While at first the pilgrim still sees shades and can perceive their features, at a certain point the light that surrounds them begins to increase and hide them: "E sì come ciascuno a noi venìa, / vedeasi l'ombra piena di letizia / nel folgór chiaro che di lei uscia" (And, as each came up to us, the shade was seen full of joy, by the bright effulgence that issued from it [*Par.* 5.106–8]). After the pilgrim's words, the light surrounding Justinian's soul becomes so strong that the pilgrim cannot see the shade's features anymore:

> Questo diss' io diritto a la lumera
> che pria m'avea parlato; ond' ella fessi
> lucente più assai di quel ch'ell' era.
>   Sì come il sol che si cela elli stessi
> per troppa luce, come 'l caldo ha róse
>   le temperanze d'i vapori spessi,
> per più letizia sì mi si nascose
> dentro al suo raggio la figura santa.
> (Par. 5.130–37)[102]

———

This I said, turned toward the light which first had spoken to me; whereon it glowed far brighter than before. Even as the sun, which, when the heat has consumed the tempering of the dense vapors, conceals itself by excess of light, so, by reason of more joy, the holy figure hid itself from me within its own radiance.

In the remaining heavens, the pilgrim will not encounter shades anymore but only lights that cover the shades' features. This light that surrounds the souls' aerial bodies in heaven is a manifestation of the souls' intellectual joy: "Per letiziar là sù fulgor s'acquista, / sì come riso qui; ma giù s'abbuia / l'ombra di fuor, come la mente è trista" (Through rejoicing, effulgence is gained there on high, even as a smile here; but below, the shade darkens outwardly as the mind is sad [*Par.* 9.70–72]). In the heaven of Saturn, Peter Damian explains more thoroughly that the light that surrounds the souls in heaven is a consequence of the beatific vision that the *lumen gloriae* enables them to attain:

> Luce divina sopra me s'appunta,
> penetrando per questa in ch'io m'inventro,
>   la cui virtù, col mio veder congiunta,
> mi leva sopra me tanto, ch'i' veggio
> la somma essenza de la quale è munta.
>   Quinci vien l'allegrezza ond' io fiammeggio;

per ch'a la vista mia, quant' ella è chiara,
la chiarità de la fiamma pareggio.

(*Par.* 21.83–90)[103]

———

A divine light is directed on me, penetrating through this wherein
I embosom myself, the virtue of which, conjoined with my vision,
lifts me above myself so far that I see the Supreme Essence from
which it is drawn. From this comes the joy with which I am aflame,
for to my sight, in the measure of its clearness, I match the clearness of my flame.

We can see the contrast between the condition of the soul in hell and
that in heaven, between the "worm in which true formation is failing" and
the "angelic butterfly that flies towards God with no defense." Infernal disorder, heaviness, and darkness are replaced by celestial order, lightness, and
clarity. From the third heaven up to the Empyrean, the pilgrim will not see
human features because the light of blessedness is stronger than their features. Before moving to the heavens in which the pilgrim will meet lights
in lieu of shades, however, the episodes of Piccarda and Justinian make
clear that human features do not actually disappear from heaven; they are
simply hidden by light, which represents the glory of beatitude. The presence of each soul's human features expresses the individuality that is a fundamental component even of heavenly experience.[104]

Not only in hell but also in heaven the soul carries the structure of the
person in the afterlife and, even before the Resurrection, can express its self
in an aerial body having individual features that reflect the soul's eschatological condition—be it perversion or perfection. Dante's concept of shade
therefore reflects the power that Statius's embryological account confers to
the separated soul as the guarantor of identity. The next two chapters will
show the ways in which Dante's representation of aerial bodies exemplifies
the early fourteenth-century eschatological emphasis on the destiny of the
separated soul in the afterlife. The otherworldly realm that is most connected with the eschatological change of emphasis toward the time between physical death and resurrection is purgatory, and it is here, as the
following chapter argues, that the concept of the aerial body reveals its
greatest potential for meaningful experience. The last chapter shows the
complex and creative way in which Dante's concept of aerial body provides
a theory not only for the full experience of the separated soul, but also for

its imperfection and temporariness, thereby pointing to the changes that the resurrection of the flesh will entail with respect to both the person's identity and his or her experience. Significantly, while Dante's discourse of embryology ends up sharing important characteristics with Aquinas's conception of the soul, it begins with the more traditional tenets of plurality of forms. We shall see, in fact, not only that Dante plays with the ambiguity within unicity of form's understanding of the soul, but also that he vacillates between the principles of unicity and plurality, arriving at his own original position on personhood, which allows for the perseverance of identity in the afterlife and at the same time maintains the significance of the body's materiality.

Chapter 3

Productive Pain: The *Red Scripture,* the *Purgatorio,* and a New Hypothesis on the "Birth of Purgatory"

Òtti mostrato, carissima figliola, come la colpa non si punisce in questo tempo finito per veruna pena che si sostenga, puramente per pena. E dico che si punisce con la pena che si sostiene col desiderio, amore e contrizione del cuore, non per virtù della pena, ma per la virtù del desiderio dell'anima, siccome il desiderio ed ogni virtù vale ed à in sé vita per Cristo crocefisso unigenito mio Figliuolo, in quanto l'anima à tratto l'amore da lui e con virtù seguita le vestigia sue. Per questo modo vagliono e non per altro; e così le pene satisfanno alla colpa col dolce e unitivo amore, acquistato nel cognoscimento dolce della mia bontà, e amaritudine e contrizione di cuore, cognoscendo sé medesimo e le proprie colpe sue.

—Catherine of Siena[1]

Puzzling Similarities

The *Book of the Three Scriptures* and the *Divine Comedy* are two eschatological poems that were written in Italy within a few decades of one another and that describe the experience of the separated soul in the afterlife. Both begin with hell and end with heaven, and both are threefold. Yet these structural similarities only serve to highlight a startling difference in the middle segment of these poems. Bonvesin's second section, the *Red Scripture,* offers a detailed account of Christ's Passion that aptly represents contemporary spirituality's new emphasis on Christ's humanity and his physical suffering. The central section of the *Divine Comedy,* by contrast, offers the first thorough and systematic representation of purgatory after the definition of the dogma at the second Council of Lyons in 1274. The absence of purgatory in the *Book of the Three Scriptures* as a third place between hell and heaven is all the more striking when we consider that it was written around the time when purgatory was ubiquitous and mentioned in all types of texts.[2]

Scholars have tended to overlook this puzzle by giving it an easy solution. As I have discussed in the introduction, Bonvesin has been acknowledged as one of Dante's precursors, but his eschatological poem has generally been labeled as popular and therefore unworthy of comparison to Dante's highly sophisticated masterpiece. The fact that its midsection describes Christ's Passion rather than purgatory only served to confirm its distance from Dante's poem. The historian Jacques Le Goff, for instance, first associates Bonvesin with Giacomino da Verona, placing both among the "conservatives and traditionalists who preferred to stick to the old couple, Heaven and Hell, and to close their eyes to the newer Purgatory, the brainchild of theologian-intellectuals."[3] Then he proceeds by drawing attention to the difference between these poets and Dante: "Bonvesino dalla Riva and Giacomino da Verona have been regarded as precursors of Dante. The comparison only serves to accentuate the audacious genius of the *Divine Comedy.*"[4] Similarly, literary critics Giorgio Bárberi Squarotti, Francesco Bruni, and Ugo Dotti have considered the difference between the account of Christ's Passion in the *Book of the Three Scriptures* and of purgatory in the *Divine Comedy* as further proof of the abyss that separates the "art and thought" of these texts: "basta riflettere al fatto che la posizione centrale è occupata dalla crocefissione, e non dal Purgatorio, per rendere improponibile quel confronto con la *Commedia* che è poco proficuo già per le ovvie differenze di arte e di pensiero."[5]

Nonetheless, (undeniable) artistic and intellectual differences do not exclude the possibility of a fruitful comparison of the *Divine Comedy* and the *Book of the Three Scriptures,* and my analysis of Giacomino's and Bonvesin's poems in chapter 1 shows that Le Goff's brief mention of Bonvesin does not acknowledge the novelty of his eschatological poem. Le Goff is certainly right to distinguish Bonvesin's and Giacomino's works from the theoretical and doctrinal concerns that led theologians to the formulation of the dogma of purgatory. However, Bonvesin's eschatological poem is the first extant poem within the poetic tradition of Italy to be threefold and to focus explicitly upon what happens to the separated soul in the afterlife. It thereby expresses the new emphasis on the eschatological time between physical death and resurrection which is tightly connected with the emergence of purgatory. When the *Book of the Three Scriptures* is studied against its intellectual background, it becomes apparent that its eschatological perspective represents both a departure from the depictions of the afterlife offered by Giacomino (and the previous poets of Northern Italy) and a bridge toward Dante's *Comedy*. Bonvesin's poem therefore deserves further consideration. Going further, I will argue that its importance lies precisely in the fact that it inserts Christ's Passion in an eschatological context between the description of hell and heaven—that is, at the place that could be occupied by purgatory. Bonvesin thereby helps us to understand how closely purgatory and Christ's Passion could be associated with each other. If in the *Book of the Three Scriptures* Christ's Passion takes the place that one would expect to be held by purgatory, Dante's *Purgatorio* is emphatically Christological and, as Kenelm Foster points out, Christ is ubiquitous in the *Comedy*'s second canticle.[6]

It is on the basis of the similarities between the structures of the two poems and between their eschatological emphases that, despite the different genres to which the *Book of the Three Scriptures* and the *Divine Comedy* belong and the resultant differences between them, I will offer a comparative analysis of their central parts. Starting with the *Red Scripture* and continuing with the *Purgatorio,* this chapter will highlight important connections between them and stress in particular the relation between Bonvesin's emphasis on Christ's Passion (and Mary's compassion) and Dante's emphasis on the physical pain of purgatory. The comparison is fruitful in several senses: for Dante studies, because it will allow us to look at the *Purgatorio* from a new perspective and to situate purgatorial suffering within the spiritual milieu of the time; for a better understanding of the *Book of the Three Scriptures,* because showing the connections between Christ's Passion and the soul's experience in purgatory will help to define better the meaning and position of the *Red Scripture* within Bonvesin's poem; and also for a more general understanding of the significance that physical pain had in the emergence of purgatory in the thirteenth and early fourteenth centuries.

My analysis in this chapter thereby continues to enlarge Le Goff's perspective on the emergence of purgatory. Recent scholarship has in fact distanced itself from Le Goff's study, arguing that it gives too much importance to the concept of purgatory as a place, to its connection with the emergence of the bourgeoisie, and to the appearance of the noun "purgatorium" around 1170. Among the scholars who have enriched Le Goff's perspective, Barbara Newman, for instance, has pointed out that as a concept, purgatory had existed in "a more or less rationalized form" since Augustine and that, even later, it was not necessarily conceived of as a third place with a local habitation and a name but could be understood as a condition of suffering both punitive and redemptive, which, especially in the case of female piety, could also be experienced on earth.[7] My analysis moves in a similar direction and goes further. By showing that a similar emphasis on pain informs the accounts of both Bonvesin's *Red Scripture* and Dante's *Purgatorio*, I argue that the development of purgatory is tightly connected with the emergence of a new, positive understanding of the productive potential of physical suffering to forge identity and meaning.

Redemptive Suffering: Pain, Blood, and the *Red Scripture*

The opening lines of the *Red Scripture* announce the contents and the mode of the description that will follow:

> De la scrigiura rossa   quiló si segu' a dire,
> Dra passïon de Criste   a ki'n plasess odire,
> La qual per nu cativi   ge plaqu' de sostenire:
> Quest en parol mirabile   da planz e da stremire.
>
> Quiló ve dig del passio   del fio de la regina,
> La qual me dïa gratia   e alegreza fina
> Ke parle drigiamente   dra passïon divina;
> Apress zo sí ne scampe   da l'infernal ruïna.
> (*Red Scripture* 1–8)[8]

_____

Now I shall go on to speak of the red scripture, of the passion of Christ, to whoever would like to listen. It pleased him to bear it for us wicked men. These are wonderful words of weeping and fear. Now I shall tell you about the passion of the Son of the Queen— may she give me grace and excelling joy to speak properly of the divine passion, and save us thereafter from ruin in hell.

Bonvesin equates the red scripture with Christ's Passion and suggests that the red words are written with Christ's blood. He thereby shows that he is about to stress the physical sufferings of Christ, and he expects from his public a strong emotional reaction to them.[9] However, the tone is ambivalent, and if Bonvesin announces that his account will be written with "words of weeping and fear," he also invokes Mary as a sacred muse and asks for her "grace and excelling joy." As becomes clear in the course of the poem, this fluctuation between sorrow and joy informs the whole account of Christ's Passion. My analysis will show that the *Red Scripture*, situated as a turning point between the infernal horror of the *Black Scripture* and the heavenly splendor of the *Golden Scripture*, confronts us through the figures of Christ and Mary with a different kind of pain from the one encountered in hell—a pain that liberates from sin and gives access to heaven.[10]

The *Red Scripture* is part of a very well developed genre of late medieval devotional literature, both in Latin and in the vernacular, which consists of descriptions of Christ's Passion that are more detailed and specific than the sober accounts of the Gospels. This genre emphasizes Christ's physical sufferings and humiliations and is connected with the emotional religiosity of the period and with the rise of devotion to Christ's crucifixion.[11] In the eleventh and twelfth centuries, Christian spirituality began to shift from a concentration on Christ's divinity to a strong focus on his humanity. Beginning with Anselm's prayers (or perhaps with those of John of Fécamp), a new appreciation of the human sufferings of the Redeemer arose; and by the time the *Book of the Three Scriptures* was composed at the end of the thirteenth century, the pain of Christ's suffering flesh was deemed responsible for paying the ransom for original sin, and Christ's crucifixion rather than his incarnation or resurrection was stressed as the saving moment of Christian history. The most evident indication of this shift toward Christ's humanity concerns the visual representation of Christ, where the majestic and triumphant depiction of the divine and victorious savior is progressively replaced by the image of the tormented and agonized body of the suffering man on the cross.[12]

Bonvesin's description of Christ's Passion in the *Red Scripture* well exemplifies the emphasis that the spirituality and devotion of his time placed upon Christ's physical sufferings and their salvific potential. When Christ on the cross speaks to Mary, he explains that the reason for God's incarnation is the possibility of suffering—a concept that began to be common in twelfth- and thirteenth-century texts:

Oi dolce matre,   ke tant e' suspirando,
Tu sai k'eo vign il mondo,   lo patre me' voiando,
Per prender questo passio,   sul legn dra crox moirando.

Il mond, oi dolce matre,   tu sai ke sont veniudho,
Da ti recever carne   tu sai ke ho voiudho
Perzò ke per la croxe,   o eo sont mo methudo,
Salvao debia ess lo mondo,   lo qual era perdudho.
(*Red Scripture* 346–52)[13]

————

O sweet mother, who is groaning so, you know that I came into
the world, as my father wished, to accept this Passion, dying on the
wood of the cross. O sweet mother, you know that I came into
the world, you know that I wished to take flesh from you so that
the world which was lost might be saved through the cross on
which I have now been set.

Bonvesin makes clear not only that Christ's suffering on the cross is
what "saved the world which was lost" and redeemed humankind, but
also that God took human flesh from Mary precisely to gain the capacity
of feeling corporeal pain. It is not surprising therefore that the *Red Scripture* concentrates upon the moments in which Christ's body is most torn
and tormented. Bonvesin displays several strategies in order to express the
extent of Christ's suffering during the Passion and to touch the emotions
of the listeners, but what most vividly conveys the incredible acuity of the
pain that Christ's body experienced is bleeding, which was closely associated with pain and was the most powerful symbol for cleansing and expiation:[14]

Doe die in pertraverso   in tut lo corp no era
Ke tut no'g foss guastao   e niz per tal mainera
Ke 'l carne quas parivano   sí negre com coldera:
Mercé de lu no'g fiva,   sì'g devan i vontera.

La zente dri Zudé   sì fortment lo bateva
Ke tut ge maxaravano   le membre k'el haveva:
Lo corpo tut pariva   k'el foss covert de levra
E 'l sangu' da tut le parte   in terra ge cadeva.

La carne per afagio   borniosa e implagadha,
Lo sangu' da le soe membre   in terra ge gotava;
Compassïon no have   quella zent renegadha,
Ma pur sempre ge devano   e tut lo maxarava.
                      (*Red Scripture* 53–64)

There was no spot two fingers broad on His entire body that was not broken and bruised to such a degree that the flesh looked almost as black as a kettle. They had no mercy on Him but laid it on with a will. The race of the Jews beat Him so violently that all His limbs were lacerated. His whole body seemed to be leprous, and His blood fell to the ground on every side. His flesh was everywhere battered and torn. The blood dripped down from His limbs to the ground. That renegade race had no pity but only kept laying it on and lacerating Him all over.

On the cross, Christ's body becomes a piece of bleeding flesh and his four wounds are described as a "living fountain" that spills blood incessantly. Christ's blood flows like a river; the image of blood is so prevalent in the text that it is easy to visualize the script as red:

Intramb li pei e 'l man   coi gioi ge fon passai,
Dond el ne sosteniva   dolur dexmesurai:
Sí fort e sí fidanti,   trop eran tormentai,
Li membri vigorusi   ge fivan ingioai.

Perzò ke i soi membri erano   e fort e vigorusi
Intant i sostenivano   dolur plu angustïusi,
Le man ge stradolevano,   li pei eran nervusi,
Lo sangu' da quatro parte   g'insiva dai pertusi.

Li du latron da parte   fon sor la crox ligai;
Il membre del segnor   li gioi fon inficai,
Li pei l'un sover l'oltro   pur d'un gioo fon passai:
Sentiva grand angustia   li membri delicai.

Lo sangue precïoso   da la fontana viva,
Dal man e da li pei   a moho de flum insiva;

Dal có mintro ai pei   tuta la carne viva
Guastadha e sanguanenta   da tute part pariva.

   Dal có mintro ai pei   no hav el membro il corpo
Dond no gotass lo sangue   e ke no'g foss bestorto.
                     (*Red Scripture* 153–70)

———

Both His feet and His hands were pierced with nails, from which He bore enormous suffering. So strong and sturdy, they were greatly tormented, the vigorous limbs nailed up there. Because His limbs were strong and vigorous, they bore all the more agonizing suffering, His hands hurt Him dreadfully, His feet were wracked, blood flowed out of the holes at four points. To crosses on either side, the two thieves were bound. Nails were driven into the limbs of the Lord, the feet, laid one atop the other, were pierced with a single nail. His sensitive limbs felt great anguish. From the living fountain, His precious blood flowed like a river from hands and feet; from the head to the feet, all the living flesh was seen to be torn and bloody. From His head to His feet, there wasn't a limb in His body from which blood did not drip and which was not twisted.

By connecting the extreme harshness of Christ's suffering with the vigor of his body, Bonvesin refers to the concept, common in thirteenth-century Scholastic analysis, that Christ's body on the cross suffered more intense pain than any other body because it was the most perfect of all the bodies.[15] The notion that the body's susceptibility to pain increases with its perfection not only functions as a rhetorical strategy to highlight the intensity of Christ's suffering; it also confronts us with a different conception of pain from that of the *Black Scripture*. While the *contemptus mundi* of the *Black Scripture* highlighted the suffering of the human body made imperfect and subject to decay through sin, the bodies of hell were subject to endless torments without hope for relief. Christ, by contrast, employs his perfect body for a generous sacrifice that saves the world. His Passion is as productive as it is painful and therefore it induces not only sorrow but also joy.[16] It is indeed by insisting on the product of his temporary pain that Christ seeks to console his afflicted mother:

Anc sïa zo k'eo moira   a quest crutïamento,
Lo terzo di á esse   lo me' resustamento:
Illora 'm vedheré   con grand alegramento,
A ti e ai discipuli   apparíró in quel tempo.

Denanz da ti illora   eo m'ó manifestar.
Oi matre, k'e' sí molle   a planz e contristar,
Demet lo to dolor   e lo to suspirar,
A prender l'alta gloria   dal patre voi andar.

Inanz te di' alegrar,   oi dolce matre mia,
K'eo ho trovao la pegora   la qua era peria:
Per questa passïon   k'eo port a tuta via,
Se salva tut lo mondo,   pur zo conven ke sia.

Oi matre stradulcissima,   a ti per que desplax
Se questa mort eo fazo   k'al patre me' complax?
Lo calex k'el m'á dao   no vo't ke 'l beva im pax,
Azò ked eo desfaza   l'ovra del Satanax?

(Red Scripture 357–72*)*

———

Although I die under this torture, the third day will be my resurrection; you will see me then with great rejoicing; I will appear to you and to the disciples at that time. I will reveal myself before you then, O mother, you who are so prone to lament and grieve—dismiss your sorrow and your groaning; I will go and receive the high glory of the Father. You should rejoice, instead, O sweet mother mine, because I have found the sheep that was lost. Through this passion that I now bear the whole world will be saved, and so this must be. O sweet sweet mother, why are you upset if I die the death my Father wishes? Don't you want me to drink the cup that he has given me in peace, so that I may undo the work of Satan?

Christ's physical suffering on the cross rescues humankind from the "work of Satan." If we remember that in *Black Scripture* the "sin of Adam" was the cause of the painful limitations and decay of the human body (165–66), we can see how pain can be conquered through pain. By undoing original sin, the agony of Christ's tormented limbs attains the possibility for human-kind to attain the glory of heaven, the culmination of which will take place at the end of time when (as the *Golden Scripture* makes clear) the resur-rected body will shine in its splendor and finally overcome all the limita-tions of the earthly condition.

Bonvesin exemplifies the redeeming power of physical pain not only through Christ's Passion but also through Mary's compassion—her "suf-fering with" Christ. The great attention given to Mary's sufferings in the *Red Scripture* is common in contemporary accounts of the Passion or of the Deposition, both in literary works and iconographic representations. First appearing in the twelfth century, this new attitude toward Mary's com-passion is defined more explicitly in the thirteenth century through the af-fective mysticism of Saint Francis and his followers, especially Bonaven-ture, and progressively increases until the role of *co-redemptrix* is attributed to Mary herself.[17] Since Mary's first appearance on Calvary, Bonvesin asso-ciates her enormous anguish in seeing Christ's Passion with the pain of her body:

> Lo so fïol sí conzo   da po k'ella lo vie,
> Ell'av le doi tamagne,   sí dur e sí compie
> K'ell'era sí com morta,   col membre sí stremie
> Ke mai no è hom vivo   ke lo poëss descrive.
>
> Del so fïol portava   angoxa tormentevre,
> Angustïosa doia,   dolor angustïevre;
> Planzeva e suspirava,   tant era lagrimevre
> Ke tut ge delenguava   lo so cor angoxevre.
> *(Red Scripture* 137–48)

When she had seen her Son in such a sorry plight, she felt over-whelming sorrow, so intense and so absolute that she was as if dead, her limbs so lifeless that no man alive could describe it. She bore tormenting anguish for her Son, agonized sorrow, sorrowful agony. She wept and groaned, she was so full of tears that her anguished heart swooned.

When Christ's limbs are in agony on the cross, Mary's sorrow becomes physical and her limbs express her pain:

Vezand lo so fiol   col membre sí guastae,
Malconz e sanguanente   e sí desfigurae,
Dal có mintro ai pei   bornios e implagae,
Del strag e dra brutura   e soz e desorae;

Tuta se condoleva   dre doi dexmesurae,
D'angustïos angustie,   stradur e strafondae:
le membra soe tut erano   per gran dolor gravae,
Le doi k'ella portava   no haven fí cuintae.
(*Red Scripture* 221–28)

———

Seeing her Son's limbs so torn, battered and bloody and so disfigured, bruised and wounded from head to foot, filthy and defiled
with abuse and garbage, she was afflicted with immeasurable af-
flictions, with agonizing anguish, very harsh and profound. Her
limbs were all weighed down with great sorrow, the sorrows she
bore will never be counted.

While the idea of Mary's suffering not only in her soul but also in her flesh
was common in sermons and literature of the late Middle Ages, in the *Red
Scripture* Mary's own suffering moves closer and closer to that of her son
and ends in an identification with it.[18]

Like Christ's, Mary's suffering is limitless. To express its harshness,
Bonvesin creates rhetorically elaborate expressions, such as the double chiasmus in lines 242–43: "Plurando se torzeva,   torzandose plurava / Planzeva suspirando,   planzando suspirava" (she writhed and lamented and
lamented and writhed, she sighed and wept, she wept and sighed). In Bonvesin's account, Mary's agony is described as strikingly similar to Christ's.
In the same way as in the expressions referring to Christ's pain (70, 159, 179,
189), the prefix "stra-" for the superlative suggests the intensity of her love
for Christ (269, 333–34) and of her pain (226, 252, 282, 290). In line 230 her
"doler" is even "stradurissimo": not only is the prefix "stra-" ungrammati-
cally added to the superlative "durissimo," but the same expression "strado-
lere" defines the pain of Christ's hands when they are nailed to the cross
(159: "le man ge stradolevano") and his suffering limbs (179: "In si no ha el
membro   ke tut no ge stradoia"). The same terms ("doia," "angustia,"
"angoxa," "pena," "dolor") refer to both Christ's and Mary's sufferings.
Often the very same phrases define both Mary and Christ, such as Christ's

"dolur dexmesurai," his enormous suffering for the nailing of his feet and hands in line 154, and Mary's "doi dexmesurae" and "dolor dexmesurao" in lines 225 and 248; or Christ's "dolur angustïusi" in line 158 and Mary's "dolor angustievre" in line 142. In line 177 the expression "Oi tormentosa angustia, oi doia sover doia," which was recurrent in the description of the infernal pains in the *Black Scripture,* refers to Christ's crucified body, while in line 289 "Oi dolorosa angustia, oi doia sover doia" defines Mary's agonizing body.[19]

Since Christ's and Mary's sufferings are described in the same words, when the *Red Scripture* was recited orally, it must have been difficult to distinguish the two figures. Mary's compassion blends with Christ's Passion, and she becomes her son through her pain. Bonvesin thus conveys through words the concept that in painting is expressed through the representation of Mary's body posed in the same attitude as Christ's.[20] Mary's love for Christ makes his suffering hers. Through her empathic participation in Christ's agony, she unites with him. An earlier text makes the assumption behind such *imitatio,* or identification, clear. In explaining that Mary was "transformed into the likeness of Christ," Bonaventure quotes Hugh of St. Victor that "vis amoris amantem in amati similitudinem transformat," "the power of love transforms the lover into an image of the beloved."[21] In the *Red Scripture* Mary's love ("inama" in line 283) for Christ moves her to ask not only for death but also for the opportunity to take part in the physical passion of her son. She begs the Jews to crucify her as well:

> Oi De, fio precïoso, ke'l me' cor tant inama,
> Receve 'm il to passio, k'eo sont dolent e grama.
>
> Oi miseri Zudé, e mi olcir debiei
> Perfin ke'l me fïol sor la crox ingioei;
> La matre seg insema vení e crucifichei;
> Mi grama a qualke morte col me fïol svengei.
> (*Red Scripture* 283–88)

O God, precious son, whom my heart loves so, may you receive me into your Passion in my suffering and woe. O miserable Jews, you should kill me too, seeing that you nail my Son to the cross. Come and crucify the mother along with Him. Take vengeance on woeful me along with my Son by any death you wish.

Even though Mary is not physically on the cross, she suffers as if she were. Her pain is the same as her crucified son's. Indeed, through compassion, she suffers the Crucifixion. The almost contemporary *Meditations on the Life of Christ* of the Pseudo-Bonaventure likewise greatly highlights Mary's compassion under the cross (chaps. 74–80). In chapter 78, Christ himself acknowledges the identification of his Passion with Mary's compassion as he speaks to his Father and says that Mary too is on the cross with him:

> Pater mi, vides quomodo affligitur mater mea. Ego debeo crucifigi, non ipsa; sed mecum est in cruce. Sufficit crucifixio mea, qui totius populi porto peccata; ipsa nihil tale meretur.[22]

> My father, see how afflicted my mother is. I ought to be crucified, not she, but she is with me on the cross. It is enough that I, who bear the sins of all the people, am crucified; she does not deserve the same.

In the *Red Scripture*, the boundaries between Mary and Christ are so confused that she can even ask to have his compassion (319).[23] During the description of Mary's immeasurable suffering, the physicality of which is underlined by the summarizing expression "portar stradura disciplina" (to take very harsh discipline) in line 252, Bonvesin suggests that this suffering, like that of her son's, attains salvation and glory:

> La söa dolce matre, vezand li convenenti,
> Lo so fiol vezando ke steva in grang tormenti,
> Desnor e vituperio e grang desoramenti
> Ke'g fiva sor la crox e strag e schernimenti;
>
> Ella se torze tuta, tant è 'l so cor dolento,
> E planze lagremando con grand suspiramento,
> Delengua pur d'angustia, tant era 'l so lomento
> No s'av poër descrive lo so contristamento.
>
> . . . .
>
> Apena ke 'l dolor in lé poëss caver,
> Tant era stradurissimo egrand lo so doler;

Maior grameza al mondo   'la no poëva aver
Com era 'l so fïol   passïonao vedher.

   Le membre soe parivano,   tant era suspirando,
Ke tut se resolvesseno   in lagrem lagremando,
E molto s'ingramiva   lo sol fïol vezando
Sì guast e sí malconzo   a poc a poc moirando.

   Ni favellar poëva,   sí fort angustïava;
Ma quand la lengua soa   a dir sí se sforzava,
Lo so dolor grevissimo   la lengua g'imbregava,
Torzeva's e ingramiva   e molt se cordoiava.

   Perdudha la favella,   la vox sí ge mancava,
Plurando se torzeva,   torzandose plurava,
Planzeva suspirando,   planzando suspirava:
No è hom ke pensasse   le doi k'ella mostrava.

   Tant'era 'l so dolor   ke mai no fo hom nao
Ke tant angustïasse,   ke tant foss apenao:
Per li contegn dra matre   fiva denuntïao
Ke dentro permaniva   dolor dexmesurao.

   Oi grand compassïon   dra nostra grand regina,
De quella dolce matre   k'è nostra medicina,
Ke tanto suspirava   planzand a tal rüina,
Portand per lo so fio   stradura disciplina.
            (*Red Scripture* 213–53; my emphasis)[24]

His sweet mother, seeing these events, seeing her son lingering in great torments, and the dishonor, invective, and great abuse, and slander and mockery done to Him on the cross, writhed to and fro, so sorrowful was her heart, and wept with tears and great groaning, collapsing from anguish. Her lamentation was such that her grief cannot be described. [. . .] She could scarcely contain the suffering in her, so very harsh and great was her suffering. No greater woe could she have on earth than to see her Son's passion.

She was groaning so, her limbs seemed to be dissolved in tears on tears, and she was stricken with much woe seeing her Son so torn and abused, dying little by little. She felt such anguish, she could not speak. But when her tongue tried to speak, her crushing suffering blocked her tongue, she writhed full of woe and sorrow. She could not speak, her voice failed her, she writhed and lamented and lamented and writhed, she sighed and wept, she wept and sighed—no one could have imagined the suffering she displayed. Such was her suffering that no man born ever felt equal anguish, felt equal pain. Through the mother's demeanor it was revealed that immeasurable suffering dwelt within. Oh the great compassion of our great Queen, of that sweet mother who is our remedy, who groaned and lamented so at such destruction, *taking for her Son very harsh discipline.*

When Bonvesin exclaims "Oi grand compassïon   dra nostra grand regina," he highlights the connection between Mary's compassion and her status as queen. Through her "stradura disciplina," Mary gains glory. Not only do Christ's words to his mother in line 385—"you will come with me in time"—affirm that Mary will go to heaven after death, but the emphasis on the splendor of Mary's "faza strabellissima,   plena de gran dolzura" (her fair fair face, full of great sweetness) in the fifth glory of the *Golden Scripture* implies her bodily assumption to heaven (352–72; quote on l. 360). In the thirteenth century, belief in Mary's bodily assumption was commonly held and was followed by Bonaventure in his sermon *De assumptione B. Virginis Mariae.* Bonvesin explicitly refers to it in two passages, to which I will return later, where he says that Mary is in the court of heaven "co la nostra carne," "with our flesh" (*De peccatore cum Virgine* 114–15, and *Rationes quare Virgo tenetur diligere peccatores* 32).[25] Like Christ's body, therefore, Mary's body has already attained all the gifts of clarity, impassibility, subtlety, and agility that, as we have seen in chapter 1, characterize the resurrected body. As in all the passages that refer to Mary's bodily assumption to heaven, in this passage from the *Red Scripture,* "regina" (queen) is the term that defines Mary and refers to her glory, which is complete because she is in heaven with her body. Bonvesin thereby suggests that through compassion, Mary identifies with Christ to the extent that she attains the privilege of being bodily assumed to heaven even before the general resurrection taking place at the end of time.

Both Christ represented in his suffering humanity and Mary represented as the model of compassion are examples for the rest of humankind.[26] With his writing and the emotions that it elicits, Bonvesin hopes to reform the behavior of his public. As he says in the opening of the poem, his aim is that the public use "heart and mind" (*Black Scripture* 23–24). At the end of the fifth glory, which consists of the contemplation of the face of Christ and of Mary, merit is attributed to attending masses and giving alms to the poor, but also to the fact that love for Christ makes the just man call up Christ's image in his heart and in his mind (*Golden Scripture* 401–2: "Perzò k'in mia vita   lo me' Segnor amava, / Col core co la mente   sovenz l'imaginava"). The reference is to the contemporary, well-developed cult of the Veronica: the material image of God was understood as a mediator between Creator and creature, and the very act of viewing implied the desire of viewers to resemble the One they had in view.[27] Bonvesin's poem is a sort of "verbal Veronica." About the same time that the Veronica begins to be conceived not as a portrait but as the imprint of the very suffering face of Christ on a piece of cloth, Bonvesin suggests that the account of the Passion is written by the very blood of Christ. The poem aspires to the same goal as the Veronica: to mediate between Christ and man and to induce in its audience the desire to resemble Christ.

What enables this mediation is the fact that if Christ's and Mary's suffering flesh gave them the site in which redemption can take place, their flesh is also shared by the rest of humankind, which can therefore suffer in the same way. Two passages from other poems by Bonvesin stress that Christ's and Mary's flesh and blood are what connects the rest of humankind to them. In the *De peccatore cum Virgine*, the sinner talks to Mary and says that Christ's and Mary's flesh is the same flesh as ours, and, as they are in heaven with their flesh, Mary must continue to help the human beings on earth:

Nu sem conteg insema   per generation
D'una medhesma massa   de sangu' e'd carnason.

 E tu e lo to fio   viviss in carne humana,
E co la nostra carne   voi sij in cort soprana.
Grand amistá è questa,   regina premerana,
La qual tu di' haver   con tuta zent mondana.
(III–16)

By birth we are together with you, made of the same stuff of blood and flesh. And you and your Son lived with human flesh, and with our flesh you are now in the supreme court. This is a great friendship, supreme queen, that you must have with all the people of the world.

Bonvesin expresses the same concept in the *Rattiones quare Virgo tenetur diligere peccatores:*

Anchora la Regina   sí ha molt grand rason
D'aiar nu peccaor   con grand compassïon:
Elle è nostra parente   per generatïon,
Ella è c' la nostra carne   in l'eternal mason.

La Vergen glorïosa,   e 'l so fio oltresí,
La nostra carne e 'l sangue   sí ha portao da qui:
Nostra parent è donca,   ni altrament pò dí,
Ni se'n porrav lavar   con quant purrav pur fí.
                    (29–36)[28]

———

Furthermore, the Queen has an excellent reason to help us sinners with great compassion: she is our kinswoman through her engendering, she dwells with our flesh in the eternal mansion. The glorious Virgin, and her Son as well, carried our flesh and blood hence. So she is our kin, nor can she say otherwise, nor can she wash it off herself whatever she does.

Through Mary, Christ's body is made of the same flesh and blood as every other human being—the same blood and flesh that were despised in the *contemptus mundi* at the beginning of the poem.[29] But like Christ's flesh (which he took from Mary precisely so that he could have the experience of physical pain), the decaying body of humankind can suffer and can be, paradoxically, the instrument of salvation.

The capacity to suffer bodily is what human beings have in common with Christ, and suffering is what they can use to move toward him. After reminding his listeners at the beginning of the poem that their beloved bodies are decaying and rotting, Bonvesin indicates to them—through the example of Christ and especially of Mary—the way to redemption, the sweetness of which he goes on to describe in the *Golden Scripture*. Just after the description of Mary's compassion, Bonvesin asks for her help in weeping for his sin in the same way she wept during Christ's Passion: "Oi precïosa dama,   oi stella matutina, / A planz li mei peccai   lo me' cor tu degina,   / Azò ke lagremar   poëss a tal rüina, / sì com tu fiv in l'ora   dra passïon divina" (O precious Lady, O morning star, induce my heart to lament for my sins, so that it can weep for such devastation, just as you did in the hour of the divine Passion [*Red Scripture* 253–56]). Following the description of Christ's Passion, Mary's compassion, and the anticipation of their glory attained through suffering, the final passage of the *Red Scripture* is a synthesis of the several practical suggestions that are found throughout the whole poem, especially in the *Golden Scripture*.[30] Just before the narration of the heavenly glories, which will entice the listeners, the central section of the *Book of the Three Scriptures* ends with an invitation to the audience's compassion:

> Aregordado hablemo   dra dura passïon,
> La qua Iesú sostenne   senza remissïon.
> Ki sover zo pensasse,   il mondo no è baron
> Ke no's devess comove   a grand compassïon.

> Ki ben odiss la passio   de quel Segnor lodhao
> E com el fo tradhio   e fo passïonao,
> Mai no è hom il mondo   sí ardio ni sí indurao
> Ke no devess ess tuto   stremio e amaricao.

> Mai no devrav ess homo   ke no portass in pax

> . . . .

> Quand el odiss cuintar   la passïon malvax
> La qual per nu sostenne   Iesú segnor verax.

> No ge devrav ess greve   d'inverno ni de stae,
> Portar per De desaxio,   vergonza e povertae,
> E fam e sedhe e fregio,   desnor e infirmitae,
> Offensïon e iniurie   ke ge fissen portae.

No ge devrav ess greve   la tribulatïon
Ni a perdonar a quii   ke'g fan offensïon
E star in penitentia   con grand afflictïon
E planz li soi peccai   con grand contritïon.

No ge devrav far pro   lo bever ni 'l condugio,
Pensand ke'l rex de gloria   sí fo per nu destrugio,
Ke mai no fé peccao   ni casonevre frugio:
El fo per nu cativi   a tal desnor redugio.

(Red Scripture 425–48)

———

We have related the harsh Passion which Jesus bore unremittingly. There is no man of worth who could reflect on this without giving himself up to great *compassion*. There is no one on earth, once he has properly listened to the Passion of that admirable Lord and how He was betrayed and tormented, no one so impudent or so hardened that he ought not to be filled with fear and affliction. There ought to be no one who would not bear in peace . . . when he heard the dreadful Passion which Jesus our true Lord bore for us. It should be no burden to him to bear deprivation, shame, and poverty through winter and summer, and hunger and thirst and cold, disgrace and sickness, affronts and wrongs of all sorts inflicted upon him. Tribulation should be no burden to him, nor forgiving those who affront him, nor living in penitence with great affliction, nor mourning for his sins with great contrition. Food and drink should give him no pleasure when he reflects that the King of Glory was slain thus for our sakes yet had never committed sin or culpable action. For the sake of us wretches, He was reduced to such degradation.

In the *Red Scripture*, suffering indicates, especially through the exemplary figure of Mary, a path to union with Christ, and Mary's compassion can be viewed as the exemplar of the empathic reactions that the poet is attempting to instigate in his public. *Con-passio*, "suffering with," is the means by which we can conform to Christ and attain redemption: through patience, humility, penitence, and ascetic practices, our ability to accept and to experience suffering in body and in soul gives us access to salvation and to the wonderful fullness of glory.

Bonvesin's *Red Scripture* thus expresses the new attitude toward pain that develops in the late Middle Ages, which Esther Cohen labels "philopassianism." This new attitude contrasts with the previous rejection of pain and demand for impassivity, endorsing the experience of physical pain as a positive tool of redemption and improvement.[31] In particular, imitation of Christ was considered an important way to move toward him, and pain was often experienced as a way of uniting with (or even becoming) Christ on the cross. To regain the lost image of God, man could conform to his humanity and earthly experiences, among which pain on the cross was one of (if not the) most important: suffering was viewed, as Richard Kieckhefer points out, as "the specific means God had chosen both for Christ's redemptive work and the sanctification of those who imitate Christ."[32] Union with the suffering Christ was experienced as a way of both taking part in his pain and sharing his divinity. *Imitatio Christi* became more and more literal, and stigmata, as a case in point, became the most evident sign of the desire to experience Christ's sufferings. The highest model of this identification is Francis of Assisi, who, as Dante writes, in 1224, "da Cristo prese l'ultimo sigillo," received the actual wounds of Christ on his body as the ultimate sign of his conformity with him (*Par.* 11.107).

At the very end of the *Book of the Three Scriptures,* after the explicit description of glory as integrity of the person, soul and body, without the fear of decay, Bonvesin stresses again that humankind gains glory through penitence and love:

> Aregordado hablemo   dra lettera doradha,
> La qual è dolz da lezere,   plasevre e delicadha.
> Ki lez in questa lettera,   no è persona nadha
> Ke d'acatar tal gloria   devess ess fadigadha.
>
> S'el foss ki questa lettera   per grand amor lezesse,
> Mai no è hom al mondo   k'infenzer se devesse
> De star in penitentia,   azò ked el poësse
> Aguadhaniar tal vita   ke mai no g'av incresce.
> (*Golden Scripture* 741–48)

———

We have told of the golden script, which is sweet to read, agreeable and refined. There is no person born who reads this script that should weary of winning such glory. If the script were only read with great love, there is no one in the world who would hesitate to live in penitence, so that he might gain such a life that he would never tire.

Our ability to express love for Christ with our suffering body allows us to avert the corruption of the earthly body and the useless torments of hell, and to gain the glory of heaven and the eventual splendor of the resurrected body described in the *Golden Scripture*. Or, to use the images of the book and its three scriptures, we can move from the fear of black to the seduction of gold through the cleansing power of blood. We will see now that the same concept informs the structure of Dante's eschatological poem: after the horror of the *Inferno* and before the splendor of the *Paradiso*, the *Purgatorio* focuses upon a productive experience of physical pain that is embraced as the opportunity to conform to the suffering Christ and attain heavenly glory.

Passion, Purgatory, and Pain

Dante wrote his account of purgatory in the second decade of the fourteenth century, that is, about forty years after purgatory was officially defined at the Second Council of Lyons. The extant text of the 1274 promulgation is as follows:

> [The Roman Church] states and proclaims that those who fall into sin after baptism must not be rebaptized, but that through a genuine penitence they obtain pardon for their sins. That if, truly penitent, they die in charity before having, by worthy fruits of penance, rendered satisfaction for what they have done by commission or omission, their souls . . . are purged after their death, by purgatorial or purificatory penalties, and that, for the alleviation of these penalties, they are served by the suffrages of the living faithful, to wit, the sacrifice of the mass, prayers, alms, and other works of piety that the faithful customarily offer on behalf of others of the faithful according to the institutions of the Church. The souls of those who, after receiving baptism, have contracted absolutely no taint of sin, as well as those who, after contracting the taint of sin, have been purified either while they remained in their bodies or after being stripped of their bodies are, as was stated above, immediately received into heaven.[33]

Purgatory is the state in which the baptized souls that have been dis-charged—through contrition or through confession—from the guilt of sin *(culpa)* can complete the process of satisfaction for it *(poena)* in the afterlife. Guilt is the most serious consequence of sin because it makes the sinner fall from grace, lose heaven, and become susceptible to eternal punishment. *Poena* is the temporal penance that the repentant sinner has to carry out be-fore the absolution from guilt can become fully effective. In case satisfac-tion is not completed on earth, purgatory offers the opportunity to expiate and erase the stain of *culpa* after death.[34]

The 1274 official formulation of the Church stated the essence of the dogma of purgatory but also left many possible interpretations open to the sensibility, spirituality, and imagination of individuals.[35] Dante's poem of-fers the first extensive representation of purgatory and has been defined by Jacques Le Goff as the "poetic triumph" of the new doctrine. The con-ceptualization of purgatory in the *Divine Comedy* is in general accordance with the principles expressed in the Lyons statement. At the same time it constitutes a personal interpretation of these principles based upon many original choices that therefore deserve particular attention.

Several important interpretations have been given about the results that are attained by the soul through the purification process in Dante's purgatory. Charles Singleton, for instance, has explained the soul's journey of purgatory as the journey of "justification" toward the condition of origi-nal justice that was lost through Adam's sin: the inalterable freedom that the soul attains at the end of its purgation in the garden of Eden is the prelapsarian condition of justice, which consists of the right order within the several parts of the soul.[36] More recently, Teodolinda Barolini has shown that the aim of purgatory is "not the cessation of desire but the mas-tery of an infallible desire": the journey of purging souls can be considered as an Augustinian pilgrimage, through which they learn to devalue their affective inclinations toward the not-necessarily-wrong goods of Earth and to exchange such goods for God, to whom they are returning.[37] Lately, Marc Cogan, who has focused upon the Scholastic distinction between sin and vice, has argued that the goal of purgatory is to purge souls of bad hab-its that still prevent them from getting rid of the stain of sin: through the cure of purgatory, the souls heal from the capital vices from which they suffered on earth, transforming them into the otherworldly virtues that perfect the souls' powers and allow full happiness in heaven.[38]

My analysis of Dante's purgatory takes a different track that is in-formed by the eschatological discussion begun in the previous chapters.

The 1274 definition of purgatory testifies that the change of emphasis toward the full experience of the separated soul has taken place. In a way, the concept of purgatory symbolizes the complexity of the new emphasis on the eschatological time before resurrection. While it presupposes that after physical death the separated soul undergoes an individual judgment that fixes its destiny in the afterlife, it also highlights the possibility of important developments after death. On the one hand, once a soul has reached purgatory, it will eventually go to heaven. As Dante stresses while describing the harshness of the pain in the terrace of pride, purgatorial punishment is not permanent; in the worst case, it will last from the moment of one's death to the Last Judgment, when the purging process will necessarily finish and all the saved souls will ascend to heaven:

> Non vo' però, lettor, che tu ti smaghi
> di buon proponimento per udire
> come Dio vuol che 'l debito si paghi.
>   Non attender la forma del martìre:
> pensa la succession; pensa ch'al peggio
> oltre la gran sentenza non può ire.
>   (*Purg.* 10.106–11)[39]

> But, reader, I would not have you turned from good resolution for hearing how God wills the debt shall be paid. Heed not the form of the pain: think what follows, think that at the worst beyond the great Judgment it cannot go.

In most cases, by implication, the soul reaches heaven and there its ultimate goal—the beatific vision—before the Last Judgment. On the other hand, if purgatory is temporary and does not represent the soul's ultimate goal, Dante's poem makes it also clear that the soul's journey through purgatory is in itself a full, meaningful process. The soul's experience of purgatory is not merely a punishment or a waiting for something else but also a development that entails real growth and change even in the afterlife. It is a curative process of improvement through suffering for which the aerial body is crucial.

As we have seen in the previous chapters, both contemporary theology and popular culture stressed the materiality of otherworldly punishment, and through Statius's long speech on embryology and formation of the aerial body, Dante aimed to explain how the separated soul can keep sensitive faculties and experience corporeal pain. While this is also true for hell, I will show below that it is particularly important in purgatory. While thirteenth-century theologians usually agreed that the saintly soul goes to heaven as soon as it is ready (i.e., either after completing purgation in purgatory or after physical death if it does not need any purgation), Dante deals at length with the case of a soul (Statius) who completes purgation and moves toward heaven, but he does not mention any soul going directly to heaven. He thereby emphasizes the significance of the process that the soul undergoes in purgatory.

Focusing on purgatory as an experience of pain that is temporary because it effects change, my main argument is that Christ's Passion plays a decisive role in Dante's idiosyncratic conception and representation of purgatory. In the remaining part of this section, I will explore how Dante's personal choices in interpreting the Lyons formulation of the dogma align purgatory with Christ's Passion both topographically and conceptually as the model for purgation through physical pain. In the next section, I will look closely at some passages of Dante's *Comedy* to show how the soul's physical pain in purgatory relates to the salvific potential of Christ's Passion which I have explored in my analysis of Bonvesin's *Red Scripture*. I will thus suggest that the soul's suffering in purgatory is conceived of as an opportunity to conform to the suffering Christ.

Two questions that were amply discussed but left open by the theologians of Dante's time concerned the location of purgatory and its relation to Eden. Dante answers these questions with an original and eclectic reappropriation of beliefs and ideas first elaborated in the patristic times and then reinterpreted by theologians in the thirteenth century.[40] In the *Divine Comedy*, purgatory has the shape of a prodigiously high mountain with the garden of Eden on its summit. Through this topography, Dante symbolizes that man, having sinned, regains his prelapsarian purity through arduous expiation. The precondition for such a return to perfection is, however, the sacrament of baptism, through which man is freed from the original sin thanks to Christ's Passion. Dante associates purgatory with Christ's Passion not only by placing the garden of Eden on top of purgatory, but also by situating both on an island in the southern hemisphere in the middle of the ocean, which is located exactly at the antipodes to Jerusalem. Bruno Nardi has pointed out that in locating Eden at the exact antipodes to Jerusalem,

Dante was not led by scientific concerns but by the desire to symbolize the Pauline opposition between ancient guilt and redemption, between Adam, the man-sinner, and Christ, the man-savior.[41] Dante's invention of purgatory's physical situation thus closely aligns purgatory with Christ's Passion. If Christ's Passion redeemed humankind from Adam's sin and gave it the possibility of regaining the prelapsarian perfection of Eden, the passion of purgatory redeems the sinner's sins and allows him or her a (temporary) return to Adam's condition.[42]

To be sure, such a topographical arrangement does not clarify why pain, in particular physical pain, should be necessary for redemption. Yet the very structure of purgatory highlights this necessity, and Beatrice will explain it as she answers the pilgrim's question about the necessity of Christ's crucifixion. Before showing how Dante's invention of ante-purgatory gives profile to the kind of pain that is redemptive, I would like to highlight a most elementary decision about purgatory, namely Dante's placement of it on earth. This decision underscores the conceptual connection between earth and purgatory: purgatory continues the process of giving satisfaction for the debt of punishment that was not completed on earth.[43] It should therefore not be surprising that Dante transposes into the afterlife the conception—also shared by theologians, as I will show—that the process through which one atones for one's own sins relies on Christ's Passion.

Dante imagines that the mountain of purgatory is divided in three parts: below Eden and the seven terraces of purgatory proper, the bottom of the mountain is occupied by a place that is invented by Dante—the so-called ante-purgatory, where the souls of those who have delayed repentance until the end of their lives must wait before being allowed into purgatory proper. In ante-purgatory the pilgrim meets the excommunicate, the negligent, those who died a violent death, and finally, the princes who cared too much for earthly things. The first cantos of the *Purgatorio* are meant to highlight God's mercy and stress that sincere contrition and late repentance, even a last-minute one, are enough to save even the worst sinners. At the same time, however, Dante also makes clear that late repentance delays the beginning of expiation in purgatory.[44] If not helped by the prayers of the living faithful, those who have died excommunicated must wait in ante-purgatory thirty times the number of days they have been excommunicated.[45] Likewise, the souls who have delayed repentance until the last moment of their lives must wait, as Belacqua explains, in ante-purgatory for the same amount of time as the duration of their lives:

O frate, andar in sù che porta?
ché non mi lascerebbe ire a' martiri
l'angel di Dio che siede in su la porta.
    Prima convien che tanto il ciel m'aggiri
di fuor da essa, quanto fece in vita,
    per ch'io 'ndugiai al fine i buon sospiri,
se orazïone in prima non m'aita
che surga sù di cuor che in grazia viva.
                    (*Purg.* 4.127–34)[46]

O brother, what's the use of going up? For God's angel who sits at
the gate would not let me pass to the torments. First must the
heavens revolve around me outside it, so long as they did during
my life, because I delayed good sighs until the end—unless prayer
first aid me which rises from a heart that lives in grace.

According to theologians, purgatorial punishment is twofold and consists of the delay in attaining the beatific vision *(poena damni)* and of the
physical sufferings of the torments *(poena sensus).*[47] Placed among those
who died a violent death and delayed repentance until the very end of their
lives, Iacopo del Cassero clarifies that the sorrow of the souls of ante-
purgatory is due to their unsatisfied desire to see God:

Noi fummo tutti già per forza morti,
e peccatori infino a l'ultima ora;
quivi lume del ciel ne fece accorti,
    sì che, pentendo e perdonando, fora
di vita uscimmo a Dio pacificati,
che del desio di sé veder n'accora.
                    (*Purg.* 5.52–57)

We were all done to death by violence, and sinners up to the last
hours. Then light from heaven made us mindful, so that, repenting and pardoning, we came forth from life at peace with God,
who fills our hearts with sad longing to see Him.

Not subject to any corporeal punishment, these souls experience only the *poena damni,* the unfulfilled longing to see God. Ante-purgatory is "la costa ove s'aspetta," the slope where one waits (*Purg.* 23.89), the place where time is repaid for time ("dove tempo per tempo si ristora" [*Purg.* 23.84]). Before entering purgatory proper, punishment consists "only" of the delay of beginning the process of purgation and, therefore, enjoying the vision of God. Through their wait, the souls of ante-purgatory are punished for delaying repentance until the end of their life on earth but do not experience any of the interior evolution that occurs through the curative and productive suffering of purgatory, which is physical. Significantly, then, the *poena damni* is not enough: the *poena sensus,* the experience of pain inflicted by the punishment of purgatory, is required for redemption and improvement.[48]

Dante's invention of ante-purgatory indicates that interior grief does not cause any real progression of the soul and that the experience of physical suffering is necessary for the soul's expiation and healing. At the same time, Dante's poem makes it clear that pain per se is not enough to allow evolution: not every kind of pain is effective. The pain that the souls experience through their aerial bodies in both hell and purgatory is physical, but Dante insists on the productivity of suffering in purgatory, categorically contrasting it with the sterility of suffering in hell. While purgatory is the realm of improvement, hell is the realm of stasis. The damned are stuck in the same psychological condition they had in life, without any possibility of repentance or change. Infernal souls are so contaminated by sin that their intellectual faculties are inalterably perverted and corrupted: Dante's hell is "lo mondo senza fine amaro," "the world endlessly bitter" (*Par.* 17.112), where the perverted souls of the sinners are not only unglorified but also unglorifiable.[49] The sterility of the contrapasso in the *Inferno* is reflected in the fact that it is often both a fitting punishment for sin and a continual manifestation of evil. It is this idea of a pain that will never cease or allow any release or improvement that makes the condition of the souls of hell most unbearable and hopeless.[50]

The clearest evidence that the harshness of infernal punishment consists precisely of its interminable and useless character is represented by Capaneus, whose statement about his absolute lack of change can be considered as the blueprint of the psychological situation of hell: "Qual io fui vivo, tal son morto" (What I was living, that I am dead [14.51]). The Capaneus episode is particularly relevant to my argument because in addition to pointing out the eternal duration of the punishment of hell ("l'etternale ardore" [*Inf.* 14.37]), it associates the atrocity of this punishment with its uselessness. Like all those who have been violent against God, Capaneus lies supine and is tormented by the fiery rain (*Inf.* 14.22).[51] When the pilgrim sees Capaneus, he wonders who could be so spiteful that he is unsoftened by the punishment: "chi è quel grande che non par che curi / lo 'ncendio e giace dispettoso e torto, / sì che la pioggia non par che 'l maturi?" (Who is that great one who seems not to heed the fire, and lies disdainful and scowling, so that the rain seems not to ripen him? [*Inf.* 14.46–48]).[52] At this point, Capaneus proudly declares his lack of change. His reply shows that he is still the same as he was on earth and, like many other souls in hell, still perpetuating his curses and challenges to God (*Inf.* 14.51–60). As Virgil explains to him, Capaneus's punishment is made harsher precisely by the fact that it does not help him change his proud disposition: "O Capaneo, in ciò che non s'ammorza / la tua superbia, se' tu più punito; / nullo martiro, fuor che la tua rabbia, / sarebbe al tuo furor dolor compito" (O Capaneus! In that your pride remains unquenched you are punished the more: no torment save your own raging would be pain to match your fury [*Inf.* 14.63–66]). In the stasis of hell, the perverted soul is stuck in its sin and is never able to change or to improve.[53] "Pianti" are "vani," tears are useless in hell (*Inf.* 21.5), which is "la valle ove mai non si scolpa," the valley where it is impossible to get rid of the guilt of sin (*Purg.* 24.84). With an expression that defines the pain in the city of Dis, where the heretics are punished, one can say that pain and punishment are evil (*Inf.* 9.110: "duolo e . . . tormento rio") in all of hell, in the sense that, as the Ottimo commentary explains, they are not productive of any purgation or improvement.[54] Hell is sin and stasis, and infernal suffering is eternal, merely punitive, and completely sterile.

If hell is the realm of inalterable despair, purgatory is quite the opposite: the realm of hope, evolution, and improvement. While the tears of hell are useless, those of purgatory are, as the pilgrim's words to Hadrian V in the terrace of avarice make explicit, productive and ripening: "Spirto in cui pianger matura / quel sanza 'l quale a Dio tornar non possi, / sosta un poco per me tua maggior cura" (Spirit in whom weeping matures that without which there is no returning to God, suspend a little for me your greater care [*Purg.* 19.91–93]).[55] A comparative analysis of ante-purgatory and hell shows that neither the desire to suffer nor physical pain is in itself enough to heal the soul. I will argue that purgatory "works" precisely because it combines the physical pain of hell with the desire of expiation of ante-purgatory. The

purging spirits are happy in the fire—"contenti nel foco" (*Inf.* 1.118–19)—
and know that through their temporary suffering along "lo monte che
salendo altrui dismala," the mountain whose ascent delivers from evil
(*Purg.* 13.3), they make themselves ready for heaven. Furthermore, Dante's
original conception of the topography of purgatory reveals not only that
physical pain is necessary for atonement but also that purgatory is associated with Christ's Passion.[56] Before showing that Dante conceives of the
soul's experience of pain in purgatory precisely as an opportunity to train
the will to love like the suffering Christ, I will show that conceptually as
well, the importance granted by Dante to the role of purgatorial pain and
the reason for its efficacy are connected with Christ's Passion.

Like Bonvesin, Dante considers the Crucifixion to be the central moment of salvation history and holds that the pain of Christ's body on the
cross paid the ransom for Adam's sin. Although Dante does not linger on
the details of Christ's agonizing body the way Bonvesin does, he places the
same importance as the *Red Scripture* on Christ's salvific suffering when
he says that Christ freed us with his blood on the cross ("ne liberò con la
sua vena" [*Purg.* 23.75]); that Christ's high victory was gained with both
his palms ("l'alta vittoria / che s'acquistò con l'una e l'altra palma" [*Par.*
9.122–23]); and that it was Christ's wounded breast that paid the ransom for
original sin ("in quel che, forato da la lancia, / e prima e poscia tanto sodisfece, / che d'ogne colpa vince la bilancia" [*Par.* 13.40–42]).[57] Moreover,
Dante highlights the role of Christ's Passion by offering a theoretical justification for it in *Paradiso* 7. In the heaven of Mercury, the pilgrim does not
understand precisely why Christ's suffering was necessary for the atonement of Adam's sin and wonders why God demanded that the pain of
Christ's crucifixion ("La pena . . . che la croce porse" [*Par.* 7.40]) be the only
appropriate means of our redemption ("a nostra redenzion pur questo
modo" [7.57]). Beatrice perceives the pilgrim's doubt and answers with a detailed account of salvation history, which explains the reasons for Christ's
Passion within a more general discussion about sin, its consequences, and
the way to atone for it. Beatrice's speech starts with the claim that everything that is created directly by God is endowed by him with the three gifts
of immortality, freedom, and conformity with him:

> La divina bontà, che da sé sperne
> ogne livore, ardendo in sé, sfavilla
> sì che dispiega le bellezze eterne.
> Ciò che da lei sanza mezzo distilla

non ha poi fine, perché non si move
la sua imprenta quand' ella sigilla.
   Ciò che da essa sanza mezzo piove
libero è tutto, perché non soggiace
a la virtute de le cose nove.
   Più l'è conforme, e però più le piace;
ché l'ardor santo ch'ogne cosa raggia,
ne la più somigliante è più vivace.
                                  (*Par.* 7.64–75)

_____

The Divine Goodness, which spurns all envy from itself, burning within itself so sparkles that It displays the eternal beauties. That which immediately derives from it thereafter has no end, because when It seals, Its imprint may never be removed. That which rains down from It immediately is wholly free, because it is not subject to the power of the new things. It is the most conformed to It and therefore pleases It the most; for the Holy Ardor, which irradiates everything, is most living in what is most like Itself.

Among the things created directly by God is the "umana creatura," the human creature, which is therefore immortal, free, and in conformity with God. Sin is what takes its freedom away and makes it dissimilar to God. The only way that the human creature may regain its lost dignity and divine conformity is to expiate its bad behavior with just penalties:

   Di tutte queste dote s'avvantaggia
l'umana creatura, e s'una manca,
di sua nobilità convien che caggia.
   Solo il peccato è qual che la disfranca
e falla dissimìle al sommo bene,
per che del lume suo poco s'imbianca.
   e in sua dignità mai non rivene,
se non rïempie, dove colpa vòta,
contra mal dilettar con giuste pene.
                                  (*Par.* 7.76–84)

_____

With all these gifts the human creature is advantaged, and if one fails, it needs must fall from its nobility. Sin alone is that which

disfranchises it and makes it unlike the Supreme Good, so that it
is little illumined by Its light; and to Its dignity it never returns
unless, where fault has emptied, it fill up with just penalties against
evil delights.

In the subsequent lines, Beatrice interprets the human creature as Adam
(whose sin caused the loss of the three gifts of immortality, freedom, and
conformity with God) and proceeds to explain why God chose Christ's
Passion as the means for the atonement of humankind and the recovery of
its dignity that was lost with the Fall.[58]

In general terms, Beatrice's explanation follows the doctrine of Anselm of Bec, who argued in the *Cur Deus homo* that the Incarnation was
necessary because the Son of God's sacrifice of his human life would both
satisfy God's justice and preserve human responsibility. Not only did Anselm's doctrine have great success but it also prepared a theoretical justification for the new feeling about the humanity of the Savior and the
emphasis on Christ's sufferings that came with it (aptly represented by the
Red Scripture).[59] What is most relevant to my argument is that, as Bianca
Garavelli points out in her commentary, the "human creature" of Beatrice's
account is both Adam and man in general each time he commits sin.[60] Beatrice explains that Adam's sin had to be atoned for by Christ's Passion, but
her words about the consequences of sin also express a general statement
about the condition of man. As she says at the end of her speech, God
creates the human soul "sanza mezzo" and causes it to be enamored of himself so that the soul always desires him: "vostra vita sanza mezzo spira /
la somma beninanza, e la innamora / di sé sì che poi sempre la desira"
(*Par.* 7.139–44). As was Adam, the human soul is created with the three
gifts of immortality, freedom, and conformity with God; and, as Adam
did, so the human soul can sin, thereby losing freedom and its other gifts.[61]
At the same time, the soul always longs to go back to God.[62] As Beatrice
makes clear, the only way the human creature is able to regain its lost freedom and the subsequent conformity with God is to fill the void that guilt
has created with just penalties. Beatrice's words about sin and atonement
refer to a general case, and by inserting them in *Paradiso* 7, within her explanation of Christ's redeeming Passion, Dante suggests that man's way of
paying for his personal sins is connected with Christ's pain on the cross.

This connection between Chist's pain and general atonement of sin
was in fact common in the theology of Dante's time. When Thomas Aquinas deals with the results of Christ's Passion, for instance, he claims that it

is the cause of the deliverance from our sins, "vel praeterita vel praesentia vel futura," whether past, present, or future.[63] Aquinas explains that Christ's Passion rescued man from the debt of punishment in two ways: directly, because the Passion redeemed humankind from original sin, and, indirectly, because it is the cause of the forgiveness of sin.[64] In order to take advantage of Christ's Passion, men must conform to him. While baptism is the sacrament that communicates its effect to men and allows them to conform to Christ, men cannot be baptized twice, and if they sin again, they "should be made to conform to the suffering Christ by experiencing some penalty or suffering in their own persons" ("oportet quod . . . configurentur Christo patienti per aliquid poenalitatis vel passionis quam in seipsis sustineant").[65]

Like Aquinas, but in more forceful tones, Bonaventure stresses the same importance of conforming to the suffering Christ in order to regain what has been lost through sin. Both the *Lignum vitae* (a meditation on the life, death, and resurrection of Christ) and the *Vitis mystica* (or "Tractatus de passione Domini") stress the extraordinary intensity of Christ's pain during the Crucifixion, aim to enkindle love for the suffering Savior, and express the Franciscan ideal of conforming to him. The *Vitis mystica*, for instance, is organized around the image of Christ as the true vine (John 15:1) and focuses on the redeeming power of Christ's blood and sufferings. With his tormented and battered body, Christ not only pays the ransom for our freedom from sin but also offers a model to imitate:

> Venite, quaeso, et condolete mihi, omnes, qui gaudere desideratis in Domino. Attendite vestrum manu fortem, quomodo contritus est; desiderabilem vestrum, quam miserabiliter deformatum est; pacificum vestrum, quomodo in bello peremptus est. Ubi est ruber roseus, ubi candor niveus, ubi in corpore tam contrito decorem invenies? . . . et *ossa eius sicut cremium aruerunt, percussus* est *ut foenum, et aruit cor* eius, elevatus est, allisus est valde; sed in dedecore extrinseco decorem simul et decus retinebat intrinsecus.—Noli ergo deficere pro ipso in tribulationibus suis; quia hunc *speciosum forma prae filiis hominum* viderunt homines in cruce, qui tamen exteriora intuentur, et viderunt eum *non habentem speciem neque decorem*, sed facies eius quasi despecta et quasi deformis positio eius; de hac tamen deformitate Redemptoris nostri manavit pretium decoris nostri. Sed dedecoris extrinseci nigredinem corporis amantissimi Iesu pro parte exsecuti sumus; formositatem vero intrinsecam, *quia in ipso habitat omnis plenitudo Divinitatis,* quis enar-

rabit? Deformemur igitur et nos in corpore exterius cum deformato Iesu, ut reformemur interius cum formoso Iesu. Conformemur corpori vitis nostrae in corpore nostro, ut reformetur *Corpus humilitatis nostrae configuratum corpori claritatis suae.*

(Chap. 5; emphasis in the original text)[66]

Come, I pray, and share my sorrow, all of you who desire to rejoice in the Lord. Behold how your Strong One is broken, your Desirable One disfigured; behold your Peaceful One dying in battle. Where are now the cheeks flushed with life, the skin fair as snow? Where in this ravaged body will you find any beauty? . . . His *bones have been parched like firewood, His heart cut down* and *dried like grass;* He has been lifted up and cast down to the depths. Yet, throughout this external disgrace, He has kept all His inner beauty and honor. Do not then, despair for Him in His affliction. Those who are led only by appearances saw on the cross Him who is *fairer in beauty than the sons of men* deprived of beauty or human sightliness. They saw a disfigured face and a distorted body. Yet from this disfigurement of our Saviour flowed the price of our grace. We have seen, at least in part, the dark and outward ugliness of the body of our most loving Jesus. But who shall tell of the inner beauty of Him in whom *dwells all the fullness of the Godhead?* Let us, too, be deformed outwardly in our bodies, together with Jesus deformed, that we may be reformed internally, to companion Jesus most fair. Let us, in our own body, conform to the body of our Vine, so that *the body of our lowliness* may be reformed *through conformity to the body of His glory.*

The final words of the *Vitis mystica* in particular stress that to regain the image of Christ's divinity, which one has lost by sinning, it is necessary to conform to Christ's Passion:

Et qui dedisti te pro nobis in pretium, da, ut, licet tanto pretio minus digni simus, nos tuae gratiae tam integre et perfecte in toto reddamur, ut conformati imagini passionis tuae, ad eam quoque, quam peccando amisimus, Divinitatis tuae imaginem reformemur, praestante Domino nostro. (24.4)[67]

You gave yourself in payment for us; grant that, although we are little worthy of such a price, we may be so completely and fully restored to your favor that, conforming to the image of your passion, we may also be re-formed to the image of your divinity. May God grant it to us.

If Aquinas highlights that Christ's pain on the cross redeems men from original sin and continues to give them the chance to atone for their personal sins, Bonaventure stresses that man's potential to conform to the suffering Christ is his necessary tool to atone for his sin and recover the divine likeness that sin made him lose. The significance that both Aquinas and Bonaventure grant to Christ's Passion is another sign of the widespread devotion to Christ's suffering humanity and of the extensive philopassianism of the time which I have highlighted in my analysis of Bonvesin's *Red Scripture*. Dante's conceptualization of purgatory is an expression of the same culture and spirituality. Purgatory is the state in which the souls of repentant sinners, who have not completed the satisfaction of their *poena*, can finish atoning through their suffering. Through purgatory, the repented guilt is finally removed ("la pentuta colpa è rimossa" [*Inf.* 14.138]), and the soul finds again its sanctity and original resemblance to God ("si rifà santa" [*Purg.* 23.65]). To use Beatrice's words of *Paradiso 7*, the "just punishments" of purgatory fill the void that sin has created, and while paying for its debt, the soul moves not only away from sin but also toward the recovery of the freedom and the conformity with God that it lost due to bad behavior.

The original topography of the mountain of purgatory suggests the significance of physical pain. While the punishment of ante-purgatory does not purge one's sins and consists of the grief produced by the postponement of purgation, in purgatory proper the souls change through the *poena sensus*, the experience of physical pain that the punishment inflicts on them and that their aerial bodies allow them to feel. If hell shows that pain in itself is not enough for improvement and makes us wonder what makes pain productive, the topography of purgatory also suggests that Dante is transposing into purgatory the connection between Christ's Passion and man's way to atone for his sins which was common in the culture of his time. We will see now that the productivity of the shades' experience of pain in purgatory is connected with how they embrace it as an opportunity to conform to the suffering Christ and become like him.

The Pattern of Purgatory as a Journey to/as Christ

Dante imagines that purgatory proper is divided into seven terraces, each devoted to the soul's purification from a capital sin. In structuring the experience of the soul in purgatory, Dante uses a constant pattern; one could say that the narrative components of the seven terraces are "ritualized."[68] The components of the pattern are three: (1) each terrace is surrounded by two angels, and the angel at the threshold of the new circle sings a beatitude from Christ's Sermon on the Mount each time a soul moves from one terrace to the next; (2) two sets of examples are situated within each terrace (usually at the beginning and at the end of it), the first one showing examples of the virtue opposed to the sin that is purged, and the second one showing cases in which people have been punished for the sin that is purged; (3) the souls patiently bear the pain inflicted by their physical punishment while singing hymns and psalms. Given such a ritualized structure, my analysis will not focus on the differences between the terraces or the individual choices that Dante makes in each particular case. Instead, I will explore first the significance of the fixed pattern of purgatory and then the soul's experience within a single terrace.[69]

The result of each individual terrace is represented by the beatitude that the angel sings each time a soul moves from one terrace to the next.[70] In Christ's Sermon on the Mount (Matthew 5:3–10), the beatitudes are composed of two parts: the first starts with the word "Beati" and contains a praise in the present tense, while the second announces a reward of joy and glory for those who have just been proclaimed "blessed." The beatitudes of the *Purgatorio* represent the spiritual qualities that are necessary to attain God's kingdom, and their proclamation testifies that the purgation process of each terrace has been completed.[71] Dante's adaptation of the fourth beatitude shows, for instance, that after purgation in the terrace of gluttony, the souls now have learned not only to master their appetite but also to turn their love toward justice: "Beati cui alluma / tanto di grazia, che l'amor del gusto / nel petto lor troppo disir non fuma, / esurïendo sempre quanto è giusto" (Blessed are they who are so illumined by grace that the love of taste kindles not too great desire in their breasts, and who hunger always so far as is just [*Purg.* 24.151–54]).[72] The beatitude sung by the angel is a sign that by purging their excessive appetite, the gluttons have learned, like all the souls at the end of each terrace, to conform to Christ's teaching in the Gospel.

Anna Maria Chiavacci Leonardi has pointed out that the beatitudes are not a mere ornament of the moral structure of purgatory but rather its pillar and essence: while the *Inferno* is structured on the classical ideal of justice and retribution, the "spiritual virtues" of the *Purgatorio* go so far beyond this ideal that purgatory is the realm of gratuitous love, which does not calculate or measure but gives much more than is due or just. The ultimate model of purgatory is thus Christ in the Gospels, who praises those who are humble and meek, who rewards those who suffer and cry, and who offers his own tormented life and death as a model of limitless love.[73]

While the beatitudes at the end of each terrace indicate that Christ is the one to whom the souls have learned to conform, Mary is the model to be followed in order to accomplish this. In each terrace, the purging souls are confronted with *exempla* to be imitated and to be rejected. The presence of the *exempla* as an instrument for the souls' improvement is a further sign of the connection between earth and purgatory and of the souls' being in a process that is still to be completed: as people on earth were pushed toward conversion by the "practical" value of the *exempla* with which preachers enriched their sermons, so the purging souls are pushed to imitate the figures that are presented as their models.[74] These *exempla* are expressed in different media but have in common that the first model of the virtue contrasting the sin to be purged is always Mary. Mary is the only figure who appears in the *exempla* of all the terraces and therefore represents the ultimate model to be imitated through purgation.

The idea of contrasting each capital sin to an episode of Mary's life was already present in Conrad of Saxony's *Speculum Beatae Virginis Mariae*, which is now acknowledged as the main source for Mary's opposition to the seven deadly sins in the *Divine Comedy:*

> She is *Mary*, in whom there is no vice, and who is glorious in every virtue. She is Mary, who was entirely immune from the seven capital sins. She was most humble in opposition to pride; most loving by charity in opposition to envy; most meek against anger by her gentleness; indefatigable by her diligence against sloth; Mary by her poverty was detached against avarice; against gluttony she was most sober by her temperance; against lust she was most chaste by her virginity. We can gather all these things from the Scriptures, in which we find the name of Mary written. (*Speculum Beatae Virginis Mariae*, lectio 4)[75]

Samuele Girotto has offered a detailed analysis of the episodes of Mary's life that Dante takes or modifies from the *Speculum,* but a further study of the connections between the *Speculum* and the *Divine Comedy* is usually avoided.[76] A look at Conrad's spirituality, however, will provide a better understanding of Mary's prominent presence within the Christological ethics of the *Purgatorio* and her role as mediator toward Christ.[77]

Conrad was a Franciscan preacher and author of many sermons centered on Christ and Mary. The focus of his spirituality was the affective piety that stressed Christ as the man of sorrows, whose sufferings and enormous pain paid the price for our redemption. His devotion to Christ's Passion was such that Girotto has defined him as "truly in love with the Cross."[78] Like Bonvesin, Conrad called attention to all the elements and circumstances that made Christ's Passion more painful, associating the perfection of Christ's body with the intensity of his pain.[79] He manifested great affection for Christ's wounds and blood, which cleansed humankind from original sin: "Considerandum est ergo, quod Pontifex noster per sanguinem suum operatus est mundi purgationem."[80] While Conrad underscored the price that Christ had to pay to redeem humankind, he also presented Christ as the ultimate master and model of virtue and moral perfection. Even the *Speculum Beatae Virginis Mariae,* for instance, emphasizes Christ's bloody sacrifice and opposes Christ to the seven capital sins while elaborating its Marian doctrine, which is centered on Mary's divine maternity and similarity with Christ.[81]

Like Bonvesin, Conrad stresses that Mary and Christ share the same flesh and that Christ took from Mary the flesh and blood that he offered on the cross for our redemption.[82] And like Bonvesin, he stresses Mary's suffering under the cross and, after affirming that the name "Maria" means also "mare amarum," bitter sea, precisely for Mary's compassion ("Maria est amara, filio compatiendo"), he writes that "Maria in passione filii sui valde amara fuit, quando suam ipsius animam gladius pertransivit" (Mary in the Passion of her Son was filled with bitterness when the sword of sorrow passed through her soul).[83] Again like Bonvesin, Conrad affirms Mary's bodily assumption to heaven and highlights the splendor of her resurrected body.[84] The merits (and subsequent privileges) that Mary has within Conrad's teaching are connected to her similarity with Christ. Mary always conformed to Christ's exemplar, and to follow Mary is therefore a way to get closer to Christ. Mary is a sort of "alter Christus" and, as Christ mediated between man and God, so Mary is *mediatrix* between man and

Christ: "per Mariam ad Jesum," with Girotto's definition of Conrad's Marian doctrine, toward Christ through Mary.[85]

If in the *Divine Comedy* Mary is the mediator between man and God so that the pilgrim's journey starts and ends through her intercession, in purgatory she is more precisely the mediator between the purging souls and Christ. Mary is the "rosa in che 'l verbo divino / carne si fece," the rose in which the word became flesh (*Par.* 23.73–74), the one who so ennobled human nature that its creator did not disdain to become its creature (*Par.* 33.34–36: "Tu se' colei che l'umana natura / nobilitasti sì, che 'l suo fattore / non disdegnò di farsi sua fattura"). Not only does Dante take sides, like Bonvesin and Conrad, with those who affirmed Mary's bodily assumption, but he even imagines that he was asked to settle a question that was debated at the time, explicitly stating that Mary is the only human being to share the privilege of assumption with Christ.[86] It is because of Mary's conformity and similarity with Christ—even in her appearance, her face is the one that resembles Christ the most (*Par.* 32.85–86: "la faccia che a Cristo / più si somiglia")—that Dante contrasts her to the seven capital sins and makes her the first *exemplum* of all the terraces of purgatory. Like Christ, Mary is a model of extreme love and generosity, and her prominence in the *Purgatorio* shows that Dante considers her the best exemplar of closeness to Christ.[87]

By being the first *exemplum* of each terrace, Mary represents the conformity with Christ that is the goal of purgation, indicated by the beatitude that the angel sings when a soul moves from one terrace to the next. It is not surprising therefore that the *exemplum* of Mary is often followed by others that highlight the connection with Christ. In the terrace of gluttony, for instance, the *exempla* of temperance begin with the case of Mary (whose request of wine at the wedding in Cana was not motivated by her own thirst [*Purg.* 22.142–44]) and—passing through the ancient Roman women, Daniel in Babylon, and the golden age—end with the Christ figure of John the Baptist, whose greatness is connected with his starvation in the desert: "Mele e locuste furon le vivande / che nodriro il Batista nel diserto; / per ch'elli è glorïoso e tanto grande / quanto per lo Vangelio v'è aperto" (Honey and locusts were the viands that nourished the Baptist in the desert; wherefore he is in glory and so great, as in the Gospel is revealed to you [*Purg.* 22.151–54]). The *exempla* of charity (versus envy) are represented by Mary asking for the miracle of Cana, Orestes wanting to be killed in lieu of his friend Pilades (*Purg.* 13.32–33), and Christ inviting others to love those by whom they have been hurt (13.36: "Amate da cui male aveste"); and the *exempla* of meekness (versus wrath) start with Mary in the temple and end with the martyr Stephen, another Christ figure, praying for those who are killing him:

> Poi vidi genti accese in foco d'ira
> con pietre un giovinetto ancider, forte
> gridando a sé pur: "Martira, martira!".
> E lui vedea chinarsi, per la morte
> che l'aggravava già, inver' la terra,
> ma de li occhi facea sempre al ciel porte,
> orando a l'alto Sire, in tanta guerra,
> che perdonasse a' suoi persecutori,
> con quell'aspetto che pietà diserra.
>
> (*Purg.* 15.106–14)

_____

Then I saw people, kindled with the fire of anger, stoning a youth to death, and ever crying out loudly to each other, "Kill, Kill!" and him I saw sink to the ground, for already death was heavy upon him, but of his eyes he ever made gates unto heaven, praying to the high Lord in such torture, with that look which unlocks pity, that He would forgive his persecutors.

The aim of purgation is represented by Mary's similarity to Christ, and the result is precisely the soul's conformity with Christ as exemplar. As I have indicated throughout the chapter, the process of change from aim to result occurs through pain. By analyzing now the physical punishment of the souls, I will focus on the soul's experience in the terrace of gluttony and propose that we use it as a paradigm for what the soul goes through in all of the terraces. I have chosen the terrace of gluttony for several reasons. First, it is acknowledged to be the one that best expresses the nature of purgatorial punishment and its precise opposition to the sin to be purged.[88] Second, the terrace's importance is highlighted by the fact that, as we have seen, Statius's crucial explanation of the formation of the aerial body answers a question raised by the gluttons' condition. And finally, this terrace has been chosen because it deals with all the issues that we have encountered so far and offers the best evidence for interpreting all of purgatory as a pool of suffering.

As is often the case in purgatory, Dante depicts the physical punishment of the terrace of gluttony as a contrast to the sin that is to be purged:

the souls cleanse their immoderate desire for food and drink by experiencing an excruciating hunger and thirst. While walking along the terrace, the pious group of the purging souls ("d'anime turba tacita e devota" [*Purg.* 23.21]) weep and, at the same time, sing a line from the *Miserere:* "Ed ecco piangere e cantar s'udìe / '*Labïa mëa, Domine*' per modo / tal, che diletto e doglia parturìe" (In tears and song was heard: *"Labïa mëa, Domine,"* in such manner that it gave birth to joy and to grief [*Purg.* 23.10–12]).[89] Tormented by hunger and thirst, the souls are provoked by the sight of two trees full of fruit and two springs of fresh water. Dante stresses the acuteness of the souls' pain by lingering on their emaciated and tortured aspect:

> Ne li occhi era ciascuna oscura e cava,
> palida ne la faccia, e tanto scema
> che da l'ossa la pelle s'informava.
>   Non credo che così a buccia strema
> Erisittone fosse fatto secco,
> per digiunar, quando più n'ebbe tema.
>   Io dicea fra me stesso pensando: "*Ecco*
> la gente che perdé Ierusalemme,
> quando Maria nel figlio diè di becco!".
>   Parean l'occhiaie anella sanza gemme:
> chi nel viso de li uomini legge *"omo"*
> ben avria quivi conosciuta l'emme.
>   (*Purg.* 23.22–33; my emphasis)

————

Each was dark and hollow in the eyes, pallid in the face and so wasted that the skin took its shape from the bones. I do not believe that Erysichton became thus withered to the utter rind by hunger when he had most fear of it. I said to myself in thought, "*Behold* the people who lost Jerusalem, when Mary struck her beak into her son!" The sockets of their eyes seemed rings without gems: he who reads *omo* in the face of man would there surely have recognized the M.

The comparison of the souls' condition to two horrible cases of starvation—a man who ate himself and a woman who ate her son—emphasizes their suffering. But apart from these references to Ovid and Flavius Josephus usually noted by the commentators, I want to point out that the "omo" the pilgrim reads on the souls' faces is a reference to Christ, the "homo" whose bodily sufferings have redeemed humankind. The reference to the passage in the Gospel of John, where, during his Passion, the flagellated Christ was crowned with thorns and presented by Pilate to the Jews with the expression "Ecce homo," suggests that the souls are assimilating the suffering Christ through their pain and suffering.[90] Not only does the image of the body as a text inscribed by suffering recall the idea of Christ's Passion as a red scripture, but it seems no coincidence that "Ecce homo" sounds very similar to the Dantesque "legge omo" and that "Ecco" and "omo" are rhyme words only three lines distant from each other.[91] As Gertrud Schiller points out, "Western sermon writers of the second half of the twelfth century regarded Pilate's exhibition of Christ to the people as the nadir of his degradation."[92] While the iconography of the "Ecce homo" became important only toward the end of the Middle Ages and in the Renaissance, it is attested since the ninth century. Moreover, one of the earliest and most important manifestations is found among the scenes of the Passion that Duccio painted in the verso of his Sienese *Maestà* around 1311.[93] The "omo" that is written on the gluttons' faces is a sign that, as in the case of Mary in the *Red Scripture*, pain transforms them into an image of the suffering Christ.

If pain makes "omo" visible on the souls' faces, it also makes individual recognition more difficult. Dante points to the intensity of the purging souls' pain throughout the seven terraces of purgatory, and on the terrace of gluttony, he fully exploits the recognition motif. For the most part, the shades of purgatory have the same features and aspect as on earth. In purgatory recognition is therefore usually not problematic (and ultimately always possible). In ante-purgatory, where there is no physical suffering, the pilgrim has no trouble recognizing his old friends Casella, Belacqua, and Nino Visconti.[94] In purgatory proper, the experience of physical pain may distort the shades, but their features never change to the extent of being unrecognizable (as they do in hell). The features of the proud, for instance, are so distorted by their punishment in purgatory (which consists of being bent under the heavy rocks that they carry on their shoulders) that when the pilgrim first sees them from afar, he even fails to realize that they are human figures (*Purg.* 10.112–14). When he gets closer to the shades, however, he recognizes Oderisi of Gubbio without much trouble. Only in the encounter with Forese Donati among the gluttons does the pilgrim have some real problems recognizing his old friend, whose "body" is torn and emaciated by pain. As we have seen, he can easily read on the gluttons' faces that they express the core of humanity as they suffer in a way that is reminiscent of Christ, but he hardly distinguishes their original features. It is only after some hesitation, due to Forese's thinness and emaciation, that the pilgrim realizes that he is seeing his friend's face: "Questa favilla tutta mi raccese / mia conoscenza a la cangiata labbia, / e ravvisai la faccia di Forese" (This spark rekindled in me all my knowledge of the changed features, and I recognized the face of Forese [*Purg.* 23.46–48]).

As we have seen in the previous chapter, the infernal souls are so contaminated and corrupted by sin that the aerial bodies they express are deformed to the extent that they often are unrecognizable and, in the cases of the suicides and thieves, can even cease to have human shape. The shades of purgatory, on the other hand, are free from the guilt of sin, and the aerial bodies they unfold are always fully human and never liable to metamorphosis or parodic deformation. In purgatory, the distortion of the shades' features is not a manifestation of sin (as in hell) but rather the sign that the souls are experiencing their pain in a productive way that conforms them to Christ.

The reason for the productivity of pain is disclosed by Forese in the subsequent part of the episode. Forese's dried-out scabs, "asciutta scabbia" (51), and tortured aspect are a sign of such an intense suffering that the pilgrim feels like crying and wonders what causes such torment:

> "La faccia tua, ch'io lagrimai già morta,
> mi dà di pianger mo non minor doglia",
> rispuos' io lui, "veggendola sì torta.
>   Però mi dì, per Dio, che sì vi sfoglia;
> non mi far dir mentr' io mi maraviglio,
> ché mal può dir chi è pien d'altra voglia".
>
> (*Purg.* 23.55–60)

———

> "Your face, which once I wept for dead," I answered him, "now gives me no less cause for tears when I see it so disfigured. Therefore tell me, in God's name, what strips you so? Make me not talk while I am marveling, for ill can he speak who is full of other desire."

Forese's answer about the pain of the gluttons is the key to understanding the whole process of purgation. He first explains that the pain of purgatory, which in the case of the gluttons consists of their excruciating starvation, is due to God's intervention:

> De l'etterno consiglio
> cade vertù ne l'acqua e ne la pianta
> rimasa dietro, ond' io sì m'assottiglio.
>   Tutta esta gente che piangendo canta
> per seguitar la gola oltra misura,
> in fame e 'n sete qui si rifà santa.
>
> (Purg. 23.61–65)

———

From the eternal counsel virtue descends into the water and into the tree left behind, whereby I waste away thus. All these people who weeping sing, sanctify themselves again in hunger and thirst, for having followed appetite to excess.

The pain is a punishment for the sin of gluttony committed on earth ("per seguitar la gola oltra misura"), but it is also a way for improvement and growth. The excruciating intensity of the physical pain that makes the soul cry and sing at the same time is the real means of purification: it is only "in fame e 'n sete," through hunger and thirst, that the soul "si rifà santa," recovers the sanctity that it lost through sin.

After a brief explanation of the particular punishment in the terrace of gluttony (*Purg.* 23.67–69), Forese lays open the nature of purgatorial pain, confirming the affinity between the suffering souls and the suffering Christ that I identified in the "omo" passage:

> E non pur una volta, questo spazzo
> girando, si rinfresca nostra pena:
> io dico pena, e dovria dir sollazzo,
>   ché quella voglia a li alberi ci mena
> che menò Cristo lieto a dire *"Elì,"*
> quando ne liberò con la sua vena.
>
> (Purg. 23.70–75)

———

And not once only, as we circle this road, is our pain renewed—I say pain and ought to say solace: for that will leads us to the trees which led glad Christ to say *"Elì,"* when He delivered us with His blood.

In a paradoxical way that does not hide or mask the intensity of the suffering, the pain of purgatory is embraced, through identification with Christ on the cross, as a source of joy. Conversely, pain in purgatory is productive precisely because it allows the soul to conform to the crucified Christ, whose blood liberated (and still liberates) humankind from sin and who is the ultimate paradigm of redemptive suffering. Forese's identification of the soul's will with Christ's recalls Statius's explanation of the voluntary nature of purgatorial punishment. While illustrating the cause of an earthquake that has just occurred, Statius says that it is the sign that the purgation process of one soul is completed and that the soul is then free to go to heaven. He explains that before completing the satisfaction of the *poena,* the souls of purgatory are not yet free to move toward God. What keeps them in purgatory is the desire that led them to sin on earth and that divine justice turned toward the purging pain. Only when purgation is complete does the will become wholly free and the soul able to move forward:

> Tremaci quando alcuna anima monda
> sentesi, sì che surga o che si mova
> per salir sù; e tal grido seconda.
> De la mondizia sol voler fa prova,
> che, tutto libero a mutar convento,
> l'alma sorprende, e di voler le giova.
> Prima vuol ben, ma non lascia il talento
> che divina giustizia, contra voglia,
> come fu al peccar, pone al tormento.
> (*Purg.* 21.58–66)

It trembles here when some soul feels itself pure so that it may rise or set out for the ascent, and that shout follows. Of its purity the will alone gives proof, which takes by surprise the soul, wholly free now to change its convent, and avails it to will. It wills indeed before, but the desires consents not, which Divine Justice sets, counter to the will, toward the penalty, even as it was toward the sin.

Dante tries here to combine the soul's natural desire to move toward God with its willingness to accept the punishment of purgatory and therefore delay the enjoyment of the beatific vision.[95] Forese's words in *Purgatorio* 23.70–75 clarify Statius's speech of *Purgatorio* 21.58–69, as they stress that the purging souls embrace their punishment in the same manner as Christ his crucifixion.

Dante conceives of purgatory as the experience of pain through which the soul learns to conform with Christ and redeems itself. And, as Christ in the most tragic moment of his Passion—when on the cross he said, "Heli, Heli lema sabachtani" (My God, my God, why hast thou forsaken me?)—was nonetheless "lieto" (glad), so the incredible pain of purgatory is, at the same time, "sollazzo" (joy): like the Crucifixion, the soul's voluntary experience in purgatory is a combination of pain and pleasure, the state in which the soul drinks the sweet wormwood of martyrs, "lo dolce assenzo d'i martìri," as Forese himself defines it (*Purg.* 23.86).

The coexistence of incredible pain and joy is expressed by the association of tears and songs which is an insistent motif of the terrace of gluttony (*Purg.* 23.10 and 64) and characterizes all of purgatory. Already at the end of the first terrace, the pilgrim realizes the difference between the way pain is experienced in hell and in purgatory: "Ahi quanto son diverse quelle foci / da l'infernali! ché quivi per canti / s'entra, e là giù per lamenti feroci" (Ah, how different these passages from those of Hell, for here the entrance is with songs, and down there with fierce laments [*Purg.* 12.112–14]). While the infernal souls continue to curse divine justice and the punishment they are forced to endure, all the songs and psalms that the souls sing throughout purgatory are a sign of the way they experience their punishment and of their joy in accepting it.[96]

Although it is unclear whether joy is the result of the progress achieved through pain or the condition for pain to be productive, Dante's emphasis on the co-existence of pain and joy resonates with the doctrine of Mary's co-redemption in the theology contemporary to Dante. The doctrine of co-redemption started in the twelfth century with Arnauld of Bonneval and was progressively developed in the following centuries, especially the thirteenth and fourteenth, when it dominated the medieval attitude toward Marian studies.[97] Albert the Great had an important role in pointing out both the theological value of Mary's compassion and the fact that her participation in the suffering of Christ would have been useless if she had not agreed with the intentions and purpose of her Son in his redemptive sufferings.[98] Mary therefore experienced a natural sorrow ("dolorem") in the participation in her son's suffering and, at the same time, a supernatural joy ("gaudium") in her agreement with Christ's redeeming sacrifice.[99] For the Franciscan Peter Olivi, the participation of Mary in the redemptive sacrifice of Christ is based upon the consent of the Virgin to the Incarnation, since by accepting the physical motherhood of Christ, the Virgin consented internally and externally to the work of Redemption, even to embracing the crucifixion of her son.[100] Like Albert, Olivi affirms that Mary took active part in the Redemption, experiencing both sorrow and joy at Christ's sacrifice on the cross.[101]

Although Dante makes only implicit references to the doctrines of compassion and co-redemption, his obvious emphasis on the pain and joy that the souls feel in purgatory (and the way in which he links them to Christ on the cross) can be read with respect to the idea that Mary experienced both "dolor" and "gaudium" on Calvary.[102] The joy that the souls feel and incessantly express with their songs throughout purgatory is a sign that they are motivated by good will and right love ("cui buon volere e giusto amor cavalca" [*Purg.* 18.96]), as Dante defines the attitude of the slothful toward their punishment. While Infernal suffering is sterile because hell is the crystallization of the evil love of sin and the place where good will is impossible, purgatorial pain is productive precisely because it is experienced through the right love. The aim of purgatory is to attain the virtues that are represented by Christ and Mary-as-Christ, and the process through which the soul conforms to these figures involves not only enduring but also embracing the physical torment of punishment. To learn the radical love that is fundamental to the virtues of purgatory, the soul must experience the pain of the Crucifixion: by accepting it with patience and joy, and living it as a manifestation of love in the way Christ and Mary did, the soul becomes like Christ.

The souls' journey along purgatory is therefore a journey with and toward Christ. The beatitude sung by the angel at the end of each terrace shows that the purging soul has learned how to conform with Christ and that the purification of one particular sin is over. When the whole process of purification is complete, and the soul is ready to go to heaven, Dante gives three indications of the association between the by-then-sanctified soul and Christ himself. While the pilgrim and Virgil are walking along the terrace of avarice, they are frightened by the sudden occurrence of an earthquake.[103] Immediately afterward, they hear a very loud cry coming from everywhere and realize that everybody in purgatory is singing the *Gloria in excelsis Deo*.[104] Canto 20 ends with the pilgrim's urgent desire to know the meaning of the earthquake and the song (145–51), and canto 21 opens with the same troubling desire (1–4). Suddenly a shade appears, in the same way the newly risen Christ appeared to the two disciples on the road to Emmaus (Luke 24:13ff.): "Ed ecco, sì come ne scrive Luca / che Cristo apparve a' due ch'erano in via, / giù surto fuor de la sepulcral buca, / ci apparve un'ombra" (And lo, as Luke writes for us that Christ, new-risen from the sepulchral cave, appeared to the two who were on the way, a shade appeared to us [*Purg.* 21.7–10]). The shade of Statius, who has just completed the process of purgation, explains that the earthquake and the hymn are connected precisely with his recovered freedom: each time one soul is pure and ready to go to heaven, an earthquake occurs and all the souls of purgatory sing the *Gloria* (*Purg.* 21.58–72).

The earthquake is compared to the instability of the island of Delos before Latona gave birth to Apollo and Diana (*Purg.* 20.130–32), yet within a passage of such Christological insistence, it is also clearly reminiscent of the earthquake that occurred after Christ's death on the cross and is therefore a reference to the Crucifixion.[105] The *Gloria,* on the other hand, is the hymn that the angel sang when Jesus was born and is a reference to the Incarnation that made Christ's sacrifice possible.[106] Finally, the fact that the soul to whom these signs refer is explicitly compared to the resurrected Christ points to the Resurrection, which is the victory over death and the ultimate result of Christ's sacrifice. Incarnation, Crucifixion, and Resurrection are recapitulated and refer to the condition of the soul who has completed purgation. Physical suffering in purgatory is not merely punitive—it is also a curative process. Through pain, which the purging soul is able to experience through its aerial body, the soul has the opportunity to identify with the suffering Christ. Insofar as it does so with the right kind of will and love, the soul indeed assimilates to Christ on the cross and thereby recovers its lost conformity with him at the end of this process. It can now move to heaven where it will enjoy the beatific vision with the reassuring confidence that it will eventually recover its own flesh, which will be, as we will see in the next chapter, glorious and sanctified, "gloriosa e santa," in the splendor of the Resurrection.

Productive Pain

The *Red Scripture* and the *Purgatorio* have at first sight little more in common than being the midpoints of two eschatological poems differing notably in genre, style, and intended audience. While one is primarily dedicated to Christ's Passion, the other describes foremost the way in which individual souls complete the purification from their personal sins. But in spite of the apparent differences between the *Red Scripture* and the *Purgatorio,* a comparative analysis shows that they share concepts and issues representative of the moment in which they were written and that they illuminate one another. By reading the *Red Scripture* through the mirror of the *Purgatorio,* and vice versa, it is possible to acquire a better understanding of the connection between two important cultural transformations occurring at that time, namely between the increasing importance of a productive form of pain and the emerging emphasis on the eschatological time between death and resurrection.

My analysis in this chapter indicates on the one hand that purgatory, though absent as a place in Bonvesin's text, is reflected in the enormous power that is granted to physical suffering. While the *Black* and *Golden Scriptures* describe hell and heaven according to the logic of an evangelism of fear and seduction, which presupposes a clear opposition of pain and pleasure, the *Red Scripture* presents a different model of pain: a form of pain that is embraced as meaningful and productive. Focusing on the flesh that Christ shares with humankind, Bonvesin shows that the intensity of Christ's pain during the Passion frees the earthly body from its contamination with original sin and gives it the possibility of attaining the splendor of the resurrection. The blood that flows from Christ's body on the cross cleanses away sin and is the ultimate sign of his generosity and love. The power of pain is expressed primarily by Christ's Passion but also by the purifying and salvific power that, especially through the figure of Mary, is accorded to human suffering when it is experienced as a manifestation of love: through the experience of love and pain, Mary unites with the sufferings of her son and bespeaks a path of union with Christ for the rest of humankind. After the useless torments and punishments described in the *Black Scripture,* the *Red Scripture* is a pool of productive pain, the efficacy of which will appear evident from the subsequent description of heavenly glories in the *Golden Scripture.*

On the other hand, Dante also conceives and structures purgatory as the soul's journey toward Christ through pain. After the sterile suffering of the *Inferno,* the souls in purgatory proper experience pain as growth and change, through which they conform to the suffering Christ and learn how to become like him. If Bonvesin's *Red Scripture* presents a form of pain that is to be embraced and thereby escapes the opposition between the feared

pain of hell and the seductive bliss of heaven, Dante's *Purgatorio* emphasizes the joy that the purging souls experience in their suffering. Dante thus
transposes the philopassianism of his time into the otherworldly experience
of the separated soul in purgatory. Pain is an instrument of union with
Christ, and the souls of purgatory become like Christ through the pain
they experience with the sensitive faculties they keep and express with their
aerial body. While the infernal body is often the monstrous and not fully
human expression of a corrupted and sinful soul (which is like a worm in
which full formation is wanting: "vermo in cui formazion falla" [*Purg.*
10.129]), the soul casts off sin through the experience of purgatory, recovers
its original purity, and learns how to become an angelic butterfly that flies
freely toward God ("l' angelica farfalla, / che vola a la gustizia sanza
schermi" [10.125–26]): its regained beauty will shine—as the Piccarda episode shows—in the perfected features of heaven.[107] Like Christ's torn body,
the soul's body in purgatory is tortured and often distorted. But like Christ's
body, it is never liable to any grotesque or parodic caricature. Rather, it has
the dignity of productive suffering: the body of purgatory is always fully
human and reflects the process of purgation and assimilation with the
suffering Christ. Its deformation is never the monstrous expression of sin
but rather the sign that pain is working to transform the soul into an image
of Christ. The purifying blood that colored the *Red Scripture* continues to
flow in the *Purgatorio*.

Chapter 4

Now, Then, and Beyond: Air, Flesh, and Fullness in the *Comedy*

The thorough development of the concept of purgatory in the thirteenth and early fourteenth centuries shows that the new emphasis on the eschatological time between death and resurrection has taken place. Yet if purgatory can take place only during this eschatological time, the new focus also concerns the soul's experience in hell and heaven. Like Bonvesin in *Book of the Three Scriptures,* Dante in the *Comedy* represents this experience as embodied. Unlike Bonvesin, however, Dante offers a theoretical justification for this embodiment by imagining that the soul in the afterlife radiates an aerial body and becomes a shade. As we have seen in chapter 2, Dante accounts for this possibility with the embryological doctrine of *Purgatorio* 25, which begins with the traditional principles of plurality of forms but ends by suggesting a solution that is close to the newer doctrine of unicity and the idea that the soul is the single form of the person.

The relation between this understanding of identity and the shades of the *Comedy* has been acknowledged by John Bruce-Jones and Francesco Santi, the former proposing that the doctrine of unicity of form allows Dante to stage encounters with human souls that are substantial forms of real persons,[1] and the latter maintaining that Dante's notion of the person in the *Comedy* is a "very clear example of Thomism" because the soul contains the substance of its body before the Last Judgment.[2] While both Bruce-Jones's and Santi's suggestions confirm my reading of *Purgatorio* 25 and my emphasis on its significant move toward the principle of unicity of form, this chapter will show that Dante's position on personhood is more complex than either Bruce-Jones or Santi indicates.

As we have seen in chapter 2, the doctrine of unicity of form is ambiguous with respect to the soul, which can be understood either as the immortal carrier of the self or as just one component of a psychosomatic unit that is imperfect when separated from its body. We shall now see that the *Comedy*'s eschatological panorama illustrates this ambiguity: while the concept of shade reflects unicity's former understanding of the soul and symbolizes the fullness of the separated soul's experience before the Resurrection, it also expresses the imperfection of this experience and reflects the second way in which the doctrine of unicity conceived of the soul. In addition, it is significant that Dante's embryology is not fully Thomistic but starts with the traditional principle of plurality of forms. We shall see, in fact, that in a way that is at once inconsistent and illuminating, the *Comedy* often expresses a sense of the body (whether earthly or resurrected) similar to that presented by the doctrine of plurality of forms—that is, as a material and tangible entity with an existence independent of the soul. It will thus become apparent that Dante's concept of personhood creatively combines different philosophical doctrines.

Identity, Experience, and Eschatological Clashes

From the very beginning of the *Comedy,* a sense of strangeness and imperfection characterizes the shades inhabiting the poem. When at the outset of his journey the pilgrim sees Virgil, the first encounter with an otherworldly being, the Roman poet is described as someone who looks "faint for the long silence" ("chi per lungo silenzio parea fioco" [*Inf.* 1.63]). Critical debate about this peculiar expression has focused on whether "fioco" means faint to the eye or to the ear, and whether "silenzio" refers to space or to time.[3] Here, I would like to point out that the composite rhetorical trope of synesthesia expresses the hybrid nature of the being faced by the pilgrim and the cognitive confusion that it causes in him: "'*Miserere* di me', gridai a lui / 'qual che tu sii, od ombra od omo certo'" (I cried to him, "Have pity on me whatever you are, shade or real man" [*Inf.* 1.65–66]).[4]

Without entering the debate about the meaning of Virgil's long silence, I would also like to suggest that Virgil's strange aspect, which gives rise to the pilgrim's question, refers also to the way shades are described in the underworld of *Aeneid* 6, where they are said to fly here and there "with an empty appearance of shape" ("cava sub imagine formae") and defined as "thin lives without body" ("tenuis sine corpore vitas").[5] Virgil's dimness echoes the "tenuitas" of the shades in the *Aeneid,* and his answer to the pilgrim, "Non omo, omo già fui" (No, not a real man, though once I was [67]), suggests that, like the shades of his poem, Virgil in the *Comedy* might be "fioco" also because he is "sine corpore"—that is, lacking his body.

As Statius will explain later in the poem, in the afterlife souls have the opportunity to radiate a body of air, yet the initial scene of the *Comedy* warns the reader that to possess an aerial body is not the same as being a human being: in spite of the significance of shades, they should not be confused with real people. Dante's language in this section further accentuates this concept. Virgil's answer "Non omo, omo già fui" is in the vernacular, but has a very strong similarity to Latin: only "già" makes it Florentine. It is actually only the letter *g* (instead of *m*) that distinguishes the sentence from the sound of its Latin correlative, which would be "non omo, omo iam fui." By having Virgil's soul ("anima" in both Italian and Latin) repeat twice that it is not an "omo" in a sentence that is almost written in Latin, Dante not only recalls the incorporeality of the shades in the *Aeneid* but also underlines the same difference between separated soul and person as Thomas Aquinas's phrase "anima autem . . . non est totus homo, et anima mea non est ego."[6]

This first encounter between the pilgrim and an otherworldly shade anticipates the complex picture of personhood that the *Comedy* eventually maps out. Although the whole poem focuses on what happens to separated souls and imagines that they can radiate bodies of air, allowing identity and experience in the afterlife, Dante also distinguishes shades from real persons. This distinction underscores the imperfection of the separated soul and points to the changes that the resurrection of the flesh will entail with respect to both the person's identity and experience. This eschatological tension becomes explicit when the pilgrim arrives at the circle of gluttony, which is the third circle of hell but the first one in which Dante does not delay or mask the description of the harshness of infernal torments.[7] When, after the melancholic light of limbo and the dangerous attraction of Francesca's refinement, the pilgrim finally faces the crude reality of hell, the poem emphasizes the intensity of the gluttons' pain:

> Io sono al terzo cerchio, de la piova
> etterna, maladetta, fredda e greve;
> regola e qualità mai non l'è nova.

Grandine grossa, acqua tinta e neve
per l'aere tenebroso si riversa;
pute la terra che questo riceve.
　Cerbero, fiera crudele e diversa,
con tre gole caninamente latra
sova la gente che quivi è sommersa.
　Li occhi ha vermigli, la barba unta e atra,
e 'l ventre largo, e unghiate le mani;
graffia li spirti ed iscoia ed isquatra.
　Urlar li fa la pioggia come cani;
de l'un de' lati fanno a l'altro schermo;
volgonsi spesso i miseri profani.

(*Inf.* 6.7–21)

———

I am in the third circle of the eternal, accursed, cold and heavy rain; its measure and its quality are never new; huge hail, foul water, and snow pour down through the murky air; the ground that receives it stinks. Cerberus, monstrous beast and cruel, with three throats, barks dog-like over the people who are here submerged. His eyes are red, his beard greasy and black, his belly wide and his hands taloned; he claws the spirits, flays and quarters them. The rain makes them howl like dogs; the profane wretches often turn themselves, making of one side a screen for the other.

This passage stresses the physicality of the shades' punishment in hell: while the damned are submerged in mud and incessantly tormented by a filthy shower of dirty rain, their limbs are torn apart and quartered by Cerberus, who not only slaughters but also "'ntrona / l'anime sì, ch'esser vorrebber sorde" (so thunders on the souls that they would fain be deaf [*Inf.* 6.32–33]). Everything Dante describes seems to indicate that the punishment tormenting the damned is fully physical and will continue eternally like the cursed rain representing it. Yet, in this passage Dante also introduces the concept of the shades' "vanità"—their incorporeality—and indicates that aerial bodies only *look* like bodies: "Noi passavam su per l'ombre che adona / la greve pioggia, e ponavam le piante / sovra lor vanità che par persona" (We were passing over the shades whom the heavy rain subdues, and we were setting our feet upon their emptiness, which seems real bodies [*Inf.* 6.34–36]).

Dante continues to elaborate on the difference between aerial bodies and fleshly bodies by describing how the identity and experience of the reconstituted persons will change at the end of time. Right after the pilgrim's encounter with Ciacco, whom, as we saw in chapter 2, the pilgrim does not recognize because his features are distorted (ll. 40–45), Virgil states that the gluttons will lie under the rain until the Last Judgment, when they will go to their tomb and regain both their flesh ("carne") and shape ("figura"):

> Più non si desta
> di qua dal suon de l'angelica tromba,
> quando verrà la nimica podesta:
>   ciascun rivederà la trista tomba,
> ripiglierà sua carne e sua figura
> udirà quel ch'in etterno rimbomba.
>
> (*Inf.* 6.94–99)

He wakes no more until the angel's trumpet sounds and the hostile Power comes, when each shall find again his dismal tomb and take again his flesh and form, and hear that which resounds to all eternity.

Virgil's statement makes explicit, for the first time in the poem, the impermanence of the shades' "vanità" and the souls' eventual reunion with their flesh. The reference to the recovery of one's own "figura" contrasts with the pilgrim's failed attempt to recognize Ciacco and also indicates that while aerial bodies might be deformed because the souls radiating them are corrupted by sin (as we have seen), the resurrected bodies will regain their own shape. The concept of body that emerges from Virgil's statements in this passage about the Resurrection is therefore different from the aerial body of the soul that I have analyzed so far, which is aligned with the doctrine of unicity. It is not a body of air that is expressed by the soul and dependent on the soul's state, but rather a body of flesh that, like the one presented by the doctrine of plurality, has its own independent and material existence. In fact, the assertion that the souls will take their flesh back from their own tombs seems to imply that the resurrected body will be made of the same matter as the earthly body, thereby underscoring material continuity between them.

If the concept of resurrection leads to ambiguities, however, it none-theless remains central to the doctrine of unicity of form. While Virgil's words reflect the principle of plurality of forms when they refer to the changes that the Resurrection will entail with respect to the person's shape and corporeality, they recall the unicity of form when he replies to the pilgrim's question about whether the experience of pain in hell will also change after the Last Judgment ("Maestro, esti tormenti / crescerann' ei dopo la gran sentenza, / o fier minori, o saran sì cocenti?" [*Inf.* 6.103–5]):

> Ritorna a tua scïenza,
> che vuol, quanto la cosa è più perfetta,
> più senta il bene, e così la doglienza.
>   Tutto che questa gente maladetta
> in vera perfezion già mai non vada,
> di là più che di qua essere aspetta.
>   (*Inf.* 6.106–10)

————

Return to your science, which has it that the more a thing is perfect, the more it feels the good, and so the pain. Although this accursed folk can never come to true perfection, yet they look to be nearer it then than now.

By recalling Aristotelian philosophy and suggesting that the soul is more perfect when united with its body and can therefore feel more pain or joy than when separated from it, Virgil expresses a concept that is similar to what the partisans of unicity maintain when they emphasize the psychosomatic wholeness of the human being and the imperfection of the separated soul. In the *Summa theologiae*, for instance, Thomas Aquinas writes that the soul is part of human nature and is therefore imperfect unless it is united with its body: "Anima autem, cum sit pars humanae naturae, non habet naturalem perfectionem nisi secundum quod est corpori unita" (1a, q. 90, a. 4, resp.). In a passage of the *Summa contra gentiles*, Aquinas develops this concept further by stating explicitly that the soul is the form of the body and it is unnatural for the soul to be separated from it. Therefore, he continues, not only is resurrection necessary for the immortality of the soul and the separated soul somewhat imperfect, but the human being, which is composed of soul and body, cannot enjoy ultimate happiness or punishment unless the soul reunites with its body:

Anima corpori naturaliter unitur; est enim secundum suam essentiam corporis forma. Est igitur contra naturam animae absque corpore esse. Nihil autem quod est contra naturam, potest esse perpetuum. Non igitur perpetuo erit anima absque corpore. Cum igitur perpetuo maneat, oportet eam corpori iterato coniungi: quod est resurgere. Immortalitas igitur animarum exigere videtur resurrectionem corporum futuram . . . Anima autem a corpore separata est aliquo modo imperfecta, sicut omnis pars extra suum totum existens: anima est naturaliter pars humanae naturae. Non igitur potest homo ultimam felicitatem consequi nisi anima iterato corpori coniungatur. (*Summa contra gentiles*, bk. 4, chap. 79)[8]

———

The soul is naturally united to the body, for in its essence it is the form of the body. It is, then, contrary to the nature of the soul to be without the body. But nothing which is contrary to nature can be perpetual. Perpetually, then, the soul will not be without the body. Since, then, it persists perpetually, it must once again be united to the body; and this is to rise again. Therefore, the immortality of souls seems to demand a future resurrection of bodies. . . . The soul separated from the body is in a way imperfect, as is every part existing outside of its whole, for the soul is naturally a part of human nature. Therefore, man cannot achieve his ultimate happiness unless the soul be once again united to the body.

Like Aquinas, Virgil in *Inferno* 6 explains that the soul without its real body is imperfect. He thereby highlights that the aerial body is provisionary and less perfect than the final body of resurrection, and that complete reward and punishment are possible only after bodily return. Virgil even says that though the damned will never attain true perfection, they nonetheless will be "more perfect" when their bodies resurrect than they are now. In other words, he suggests that a damned person with his or her own body made of flesh is less imperfect (and can therefore experience more pain) than a damned shade.[9]

The eschatological dialectic between experience before and after bodily return, shown by the pilgrim's encounter with the gluttons, continues in the following cantos of the *Inferno*, which make further references to the shades' lack of corporeality (8.25–27 and 12.80–82) and insist on the changes that the resurrection of the body will effect.[10] In particular, the motif of resurrection is developed with respect to the concept of human identity in the episode of the suicides, where the pilgrim meets Pier della Vigna. The suicides, Pier says, were once men but are now turned to dry twigs ("Uomini fummo, e ora siam fatti sterpi" [*Inf.* 13.37]), which are condemned to remain bush-like shades and to be separated from their bodies even after the Resurrection:

> Quando si parte l'anima feroce
> dal corpo ond' ella stessa s'è disvelta,
> Minòs la manda a la settima foce.
> Cade in la selva, e non l'è parte scelta;
> ma là dove fortuna la balestra,
> quivi germoglia come gran di spelta.
> Surge in vermena e in pianta silvestra:
> l'Arpie, pascendo poi de le sue foglie,
> fanno dolore, e al dolor fenestra.
> Come l'altre verrem per nostre spoglie,
> ma non però ch'alcuna sen rivesta,
> ché non è giusto aver ciò ch'om si toglie.
> Qui le strascineremo, e per la mesta
> selva saranno i nostri corpi appesi,
> ciascuno al prun de l'ombra sua molesta.
> (*Inf.* 13.94–108)[11]

When the fierce soul quits the body from which it has uprooted itself, Minos sends it to the seventh gullet. It falls into the woods, and no part is chosen for it, but wherever fortune flings it, there it sprouts like a grain of spelt; it shoots up to a sapling, and to a wild growth; the Harpies, feeding then upon its leaves, give pain and to the pain an outlet. Like the rest we shall come, each for his cast-off body, but not, however, that any might wear it again; for it is not just that a man have what he robs himself of. Hither shall we drag them, and through the mournful wood our bodies will be hung, each on the thorn-bush of its nocuous shade.

Like the episode of the gluttons in hell, this passage reveals the complexity of the *Comedy*'s eschatological panorama and the concept of identity it indicates. On the one hand, the separated soul is able to create an aerial body in the afterlife that allows the feeling of physical pain in hell even before the Resurrection. The sin of separating body from soul is such an evil act that the damned souls, which continue to be contaminated by that sin, radiate a body of air that is deprived of a human shape. (As is often the case in hell, the monstrous shapes of the shades reflect the disorder of the sinful souls.) On the other hand, this episode also makes clear that the person is a tight union of soul and fleshly body; and in spite of the fullness and intensity of the shades' fate, it is only the soul's reunion with its resurrected body that entails the self's ultimate experience.[12] The image of the resurrected body as clothing to wear moreover suggests again that the separated soul is naked (and therefore incomplete) and that the resurrected body is something distinct and material that can be dragged and, eventually, worn. When Pier indicates that the souls will search not for any matter but specifically for their own earthly remains ("nostre spoglie" on line 103), he also highlights the material continuity between the earthly and the resurrected body.

After the episode of the suicides, the second part of the *Inferno* focuses mainly on the fullness of the damned souls' physical suffering and, as we have seen in chapter 2, represents shades that are so corporeal and tangible that the reader might forget that their bodies are made of air. As soon as the *Purgatorio* begins, however, Dante once more stresses the shades' incorporeality. In particular, the contrast between the pilgrim's body, which breathes and produces a shadow, and the insubstantiality of the shades is a leitmotif of the canticle and constantly reminds the reader of the distinction between a shade and a living person.[13]

The poem reiterates three times the difference between the shades' aerial body and the pilgrim's body, which is real and human because it is made of flesh. First, when the souls of the excommunicated wonder at seeing the shadow of the pilgrim's body, Virgil indicates that the pilgrim's body casts a shadow because it is still human: "questo è corpo uman che voi vedete; / per che 'l lume del sole in terra è fesso" (this is a human body which you see, whereby the light of the sun is cleft on the ground [*Purg.* 3.94–96]). When other souls feel the same wonder, Virgil even invites a comparison with Christ and tells them that the pilgrim's body is "true flesh" ("'l corpo di costui è vera carne" [5.33]).[14] The same expression is used by the pilgrim himself when he introduces Virgil to Forese: "costui per la profonda / notte menato m'ha d'i veri morti / con questa vera carne che 'l seconda" (He it is that has led me through the profound night of the truly dead, in this true flesh which follows him [*Purg.* 23.121–23]). Next, the souls in the terrace of lust indicate when they perceive the pilgrim's shadow that the shades' body is in contrast feigned ("fittizio" [26.12]) because it is not made of flesh.[15] The suggestion of these passages is made explicit in Statius's speech on the formation of the aerial body, when he states that a shade is such, rather than a person, precisely because its body is made out of air, rather than flesh: "Però che quindi ha poscia sua paruta, / è chiamata ombra" [*Purg.* 25.100–101]).

Thus, in purgatory, where the experience of pain is most meaningful and productive, the concept of the aerial body again exists in tension with the physical body. However, the tension here is not between the concept of aerial body and resurrected body, as it is in hell and (as we will see) heaven. Rather, the aerial body points back nostalgically to the earthly body. This nostalgia is expressed in the first encounter between the pilgrim and a penitent soul in the *Purgatorio*. When, on the shore of purgatory, Virgil and the pilgrim speak with some of the souls who have just arrived there, the souls show great bewilderment as the pilgrim's breathing makes them realize that he has a real body and is alive: "L'anime, che si fuor di me accorte, / per lo spirare, ch'i' era ancor vivo, / maravigliando diventaro smorte" (The souls, who had perceived from my breathing that I was yet alive, marveling grew pale [*Purg.* 2.67–69]). The initial curiosity of the shades, who stare at the pilgrim's face with such an intensity that they almost forget their task of purging themselves (*Purg.* 2.73–75), anticipates the difference between fleshly and aerial bodies that the following part of this episode highlights from an even more emotional perspective. When one shade leaves the group and moves toward the pilgrim to embrace him, words such as "abbracciarmi" and "affetto" charge the episode with a sense of intimacy and fondness: "Io vidi una di lor trarresi avante / per abbracciarmi, con sì grande affetto, / che mosse me a far lo simigliante" (I saw one of them with such great affection drawing forward to embrace me that he moved me to do the same [*Purg.* 2.76–78]). In response, the pilgrim tries to embrace the shade in front of him three times but fails each time because, as the poet regretfully states, shades are "vane"—that is, they have an appearance but no corporeality: "Ohi ombre vane, fuor che ne l'aspetto! / tre volte dietro a lei le mani avvinsi, / e tante mi tornai con esse al petto" (O empty shades except in aspect! Three times I clasped my hands behind him and as often brought them back to my breast [*Purg.* 2.79–81]).

The pilgrim's unsuccessful attempt to embrace the shade overtly recalls three other failed embraces—between Aeneas and Creusa, Aeneas and Anchises, and Orpheus and Eurydice—which Vergil celebrated in poignant passages about the death of one's beloved.[16] After the shade asks the pilgrim "sweetly" ("soavemente" [*Purg.* 2.84]) to stop, the pilgrim recognizes his old friend Casella. As the pilgrim is surprised by the incorporeality of the being that he has just tried to embrace, Casella's soul reminds him that although it is now deprived of its mortal body, it continues to love the old friend in the same way as when it was within that body: "Così com'io t'amai / nel mortal corpo, così t'amo sciolta" (*Purg.* 2.89–90). The use of the feminine past participle "sciolta" highlights that it is the separated soul of Casella that is speaking—"anima sciolta" from the mortal body is in fact the literal translation of the theological concept of *anima exuta*. Dante scholarship has widely acknowledged the focus on the mortality of the human, earthly body in the *Comedy*, yet in this encounter Dante does much more than this. By alluding to the Vergilian passages and emphasizing that the shades' incorporeality does not allow the embrace between friends, he also stresses the imperfect state of the soul that has separated from its body. The poem thereby suggests that although the separated soul is immortal and can unfold an aerial body, the fleshless shades lack something that is tightly connected to the intimate sphere of one's desires and affections.

The other failed embrace in purgatory—between Virgil and Statius in the terrace of avarice—also associates the lack of flesh with the difficulty of interacting with one's beloved in an affectionate way.[17] There are also other passages in the *Purgatorio* that share the idea of the imperfection of the shade's aerial body, and they associate this imperfection with the concept that the soul alone is not the person, which is composed of soul and body. At the very beginning of the journey up the mountain of purgatory, for instance, when the pilgrim sees only his own shadow, he fears he has been abandoned by Virgil:

> Lo sol, che dietro fiammeggiava roggio,
> rotto m'era dinanzi a la figura
> ch'avëa in me de' suoi raggi l'appoggio.
> Io mi volsi dallato con paura
> d'essere abbandonato, quand'io vidi
> solo dinanzi a me la terra oscura.
> (Purg. 3.16–21)

———

The sun, which was flaming red behind, was broken in front of me by the figure which was formed by the staying of its rays upon me. I turned to my side, fearing that I was abandoned, when I saw the ground darkened before me only.

As Virgil explains, he does not cast a shadow because he lacks his body, which is buried in Italy:

> Vespero è già colà dov' è sepolto
> lo corpo dentro al quale io facea ombra.
> Napoli l'ha, e da Brandizio è tolto.
>   Ora, se innanzi a me nulla s'aombra,
> non ti maravigliar più che d'i cieli
> che l'uno a l'altro raggio non ingombra.
> (*Purg.* 3.25–30)

———

> It is now evening in the place where the body is buried within which I made shadow: Naples has it, and it was taken from Brindisi. If in front of me now there is no shadow, do not marvel more than at the heavens, that one obstructs not the light from the other.

By highlighting that the pilgrim casts a shadow because he is traveling with his real body, while his own shade does not, Virgil explains more clearly what he had meant when he first acknowledged being an "ombra" (shade), and not an "omo certo" (veritable human being) (*Inf.* 1.65–67): a separated soul, which is provided with only an aerial body, cannot produce an "ombra" precisely because it *is* an "ombra" and not a real person.[18]

Virgil's words about his body, which underline the separated soul's significant lack of something, are in perfect concordance with the general atmosphere of the initial cantos of the *Purgatorio,* which, as is often pointed out, express a sense of the body as something dear and important.[19] After the dialogue with Virgil about the absence of his shadow, for instance, the pilgrim encounters the emperor Manfred, who asks the pilgrim to try to recognize him (*Purg.* 3.103–5). The pilgrim looks intensely and describes him as blond, beautiful, noble, and with a scar on the eyebrow ("biondo era e bello e di gentile aspetto, / ma l'un de' cigli un colpo avea diviso" [107–8]) but cannot identify him.[20] After revealing his identity, Manfred explains the fate of his earthly body, which was left unburied by the archbishop of Cosenza and is now disfigured by rain and wind:

> l'ossa del corpo mio sarieno ancora
> in co del ponte presso a Benevento,

sotto la guardia de la grave mora.
  Or le bagna la pioggia e move il vento
di fuor dal regno, quasi lungo 'l Verde,
dov' e' le trasmutò a lume spento.

(*Purg.* 3.127–32)

———

The bones of my body would yet be at the bridgehead near Benevento, under the guard of the heavy cairn. Now the rain washes
them and the wind stirs them, beyond the Kingdom, hard by the
Verde, whither he transported them with tapers quenched.

The same nostalgic affection that Virgil showed toward his body at the
beginning of this canto (25–30) here characterizes Manfred's words about
the savage treatment of his own body: although Manfred's soul radiates
an aerial body that keeps all the same physical particularities as on earth
(even the scar!), it still reveals attachment to the earthly body. Moreover,
the corpse seems to be an essential component of his identity and cannot
be dismissed—as the doctrine of unicity of form could be interpreted to
imply—simply because it is now deprived of its soul.[21]
    Most of the passages stressing the shades' fondness for their earthly
bodies belong to ante-purgatory, where the souls have not yet begun their
purification process. Several critics have shown that the souls' attachment
to their earthly affections, including the body and what is associated with
it, is precisely what the souls need to relinquish in order to become ready
for heaven.[22] While this is true, we shall also see that the souls' desire for
their own dead bodies and the association of this desire with the affection
for one's beloved are also present in heaven. In paradise, the souls' desire for
their bodies does not hinder their beatific vision or the bliss deriving from
it, but is, rather, the sign that further glory will come to the souls when they
reunite with their resurrected bodies. By stressing the insubstantiality of
the aerial body in purgatory, the poem therefore confirms the significance
of the fleshly body for the full expression of one's identity. Moreover, the
aerial body of the shade exemplifies the peculiarity of purgatory as the eschatological realm in which the separated soul's experience of pain is at once
quintessentially temporary (because it is a process of preparation for something else that will end on Judgment Day, if not before) and quintessentially
meaningful (because it allows the soul to improve in the afterlife).

As Dante stressed the separated soul's full experience of pain in hell and purgatory, so does he place a major emphasis on the perfection of the bliss that the saintly soul enjoys in heaven. Like Thomas Aquinas, Dante underscores the fullness of the souls' beatitude in heaven and has the pilgrim meet with souls that are perfectly satisfied by the beatific vision bestowed by the *lumen gloriae:* "Lume è là sù che visibile face / lo creatore a quella creatura / che solo in lui vedere ha la sua pace" (A light is there above which makes the Creator visible to every creature that has his peace only in beholding him [*Par.* 30.100–102]). When he writes about the angels, Dante makes clear that every intellect (both the angels' and ours) "si queta," finds satisfaction for all its desires and thereby attains full repose in the heavenly *visio Dei:*

> e dei sapere che tutti hanno diletto
> quanto la sua veduta si profonda
> nel vero in che si queta ogne intelletto.
>   Quinci si può veder come si fonda
> l'esser beato ne l'atto che vede,
> non in quel ch'ama, che poscia seconda;
>   e del vedere è misura mercede,
> che grazia partorisce e buona voglia.
>   (*Par.* 28.106–13)[23]

———

> And you should know that all have delight in the measure of the depth to which their sight penetrates the Truth in which every intellect finds rest; from which it may be seen that the state of blessedness is founded on the act of vision, not on that which loves, which follows after; and the merit, to which grace and good will give birth, is the measure of their vision.

Dante is as resolute as Aquinas in removing any sort of desire that might represent an obstacle for the soul or an impediment from God. Although the souls in heaven experience different degrees of bliss, Dante is always careful to highlight that all are completely satisfied by their vision of God; in Dante's heaven, as Marc Cogan has put it, "no soul is, or feels that it is, in any way deficient in its blessedness."[24] When the pilgrim encounters the souls experiencing the least amount of bliss in the heaven of the Moon and wonders whether they desire a higher degree of beatitude (*Par.* 3.63–65), Piccarda states that all the souls are perfectly satisfied with what they enjoy:

> Frate, la nostra volontà quïeta
> virtù di carità, che fa volerne
> sol quel ch'avemo, e d'altro non ci asseta.
>   Se disïassimo esser più superne,
> foran discordi li nostri disiri
> dal voler di colui che qui ne cerne;
>   che vedrai non capere in questi giri,
> s'essere in carità è qui *necesse*,
> e se la sua natura ben rimiri.
>   Anzi è formale ad esto beato *esse*
> tenersi dentro a la divina voglia,
> per ch'una fansi nostre voglie stesse;
>   sì che, come noi sem di soglia in soglia
> per questo regno, a tutto il regno piace
> com' a lo re che 'n suo voler ne 'nvoglia.
>   E 'n la sua volontade è nostra pace.
>   (*Par.* 3.70–84)[25]

_____

Brother, the power of love quiets our will and makes us wish only for that which we have and gives us no other thirst. Did we desire to be more aloft, our longings would be discordant with His will who assigns us here: which you will see is not possible in these circles if to exist in charity here is of necessity, and if you well consider what is love's nature. Nay, it is the essence of this blessed existence to keep itself within the divine will, whereby our wills themselves are made one; so that our being thus from threshold to threshold throughout this realm is a joy to all the realm as to the King, who draws our wills to what He wills; and His will is our peace.

Piccarda acknowledges here that although the souls' beatitude in heaven is not uniform, the blessed souls are all perfectly happy and do not desire anything other than what they have. The differences and gradation that characterize the heaven described in the *Paradiso* are due to the unique conditions of individual souls and will remain forever, even after resurrection. There is no desire in heaven that can hinder the beatific vision or distract a separated soul from God—notably, not even the mutual desire that, according to Bonaventure, cements soul and body and prevents the soul from being completely happy before resurrection.[26]

The dialectic between experience/identity before and after resurrection in fact complicates Dante's assertion throughout the *Paradiso* that all saintly souls are perfectly satisfied in heaven. The blessed souls' beatitude is symbolized by the brightness of the lights that, beginning with the heaven of Mercury, replace the shades in heaven. However, the *Comedy* also maintains that perfect happiness notwithstanding, the blessed souls are incomplete when they are separated from their bodies. This complication has its parallel in Dante's representation of hell. While the *Inferno* begins with an emphasis on this twofold eschatological perspective and after canto 13 focuses on the fullness of the soul's experience of pain, the movement of the *Paradiso* in this respect is exactly the opposite: it first indicates the fullness of the soul's glory in heaven, but after canto 13 begins to suggest that bodily return coincides with the fulfillment of one's identity and with the subsequent growth of one's beatitude.

Paradiso 14 is the heavenly counterpart of *Inferno* 6, which highlights at once the shades' physical suffering and their incorporeality, making explicit that the pains of hell will increase when at the end of time the person regains his or her flesh and shape.[27] After the encounter with Thomas Aquinas and Bonaventure in the heaven of the Sun, Beatrice anticipates the pilgrim's desire by addressing the question whether things in heaven will change when the body is resurrected and the person's features are discernible again. In particular, she asks whether the light surrounding the soul of the blessed will continue to shine forever, and, if it does, how the organs of the resurrected body will be able to bear it:

> Diteli se la luce onde s'infiora
> vostra sustanza, rimarrà con voi
> etternalmente sì com' ell' è ora;
>   e se rimane, dite come, poi
> che sarete visibili rifatti,
> esser porà ch'al veder non vi nòi.
>   (*Par.* 14.13–18)[28]

Tell him if the light wherewith your substance blooms will remain with you eternally even as it is now; and, if it does remain, tell how, after you are made visible again, it can be that it will not hurt your sight.

Merely by listening to this question, all the souls express new joy, "nova gioia" (23), through wonderful dances and songs, conveying once more the sublime happiness they enjoy in heaven: "Qual si lamenta perché qui si moia / per viver colà sù, non vide quive / lo refrigerio de l'etterna ploia" (Who so laments because we die here to live there on high has not seen the refreshment of the eternal rain [*Par.* 14.25–27]).

The soul of Solomon replies and first elucidates that the light surrounding the soul will continue eternally (*Par.* 14.37–39). Then, after explaining that this light is proportional to the degree of the souls' beatific vision and that the intensity of the beatific vision is a combination of merit and grace, he states that when the soul reunites with its resurrection body, the beatific vision of the reconstituted person will increase with respect to that enjoyed by the soul alone:

> La sua chiarezza séguita l'ardore;
> l'ardor la visïone, e quella è tanta,
> quant' ha di grazia sovra suo valore
>   Come la carne glorïosa e santa
> fia rivestita, la nostra persona
> più grata fia per esser tutta quanta:
>   per che s'accrescerà ciò che ne dona
> di gratüito lume il sommo bene
> lume ch'a lui veder ne condiziona;
>   onde la visïon crescer convene,
> crescer l'ardor che di quella s'accende,
> crescer lo raggio che da esso vene.
>   (*Par.* 14.40–51)

Its brightness follows our ardor, the ardor our vision, and that is in the measure which each has of grace beyond his merit. When the flesh, glorious and sanctified, shall be clothed on us again, our persons will be more acceptable for being all complete; wherefore whatever of gratuitous light the Supreme Good gives us will be increased, light which fits us to see Him; so that our vision needs must increase, our ardor increase which by that is kindled, our radiance increase which comes from this.

These lines reiterate that the resurrection of the body will finally make the person whole again ("tutta quanta"). The chiasmus of lines 40–42 with 49–51 with respect to light, love, and vision further enhances the sense of completion that characterizes the reconstituted human being. Notably, Dante's association of this completion with an increase in bliss deriving from the soul's reunification with the body is different from that of both Bonaventure and Thomas Aquinas. Bonaventure maintained that heavenly bliss will increase both in extension (because the body will also be in glory) and in intensity (because the soul's *desiderium,* the desire the separated soul feels for the body, distracts it from fully enjoying the beatific vision until the soul reunites with its body). Thomas Aquinas, by contrast, progressively defended the idea that the intensity of the soul's vision will not change, and that bliss will therefore increase only extensively inasmuch as the body will also be glorified.[29] By saying that the flesh will be "gloriosa e santa," Dante's Solomon indicates that the body will also be glorified and that bliss will therefore increase by extension. Like Bonaventure, Solomon suggests also that the intensity of the soul's vision of God will increase. Yet, unlike Bonaventure, Solomon does not base the growth of the soul's bliss upon the satisfaction of the desire it feels for the body—because, like Aquinas, Dante places emphasis on the fullness of the soul's bliss and does not mention any desire hindering it. Rather, Solomon argues that as the whole person will be more pleasing ("più grata") to God, God will bestow more "gratüito lume," that is, more "lumen gloriae," which enables the soul to attain the *visio Dei.* This is why the vision of God, and therefore also love and light, will increase.

Solomon's words reveal Dante's complex negotiation among different doctrines and emphases when dealing with human identity in the *Comedy.* Like *Inferno* 6, which stressed the harshness of the soul's experience of pain in hell and its increase with the soul's reunification with its body, *Paradiso* 14 expresses both the fullness of the souls' glory in heaven and its growth when the person is finally reconstituted in his or her fleshliness. On the one hand then, the ambivalence toward the separated soul that is expressed by the doctrine of unicity of form is also found in the *Comedy.* The concept of aerial body reflects the idea that the soul is the only carrier of the self and has full experience of the afterlife even when it is separated from the body; yet the poem also emphasizes the imperfection of the soul with respect to the whole person. This emphasis recalls the other possible understanding of the soul according to the principle of unicity of form, namely that the human being is a psychosomatic unit, with the separated soul only an incomplete part of it. Indeed, if we combine Solomon's premise that the whole person is more pleasing to God with Beatrice's affirmation that the more a thing is similar to God, the more he likes it ("Più l'è conforme, e però più le piace" [*Par.* 7.73]), we arrive at Thomas Aquinas's idea that "the soul united to a glorified body is more like to God than when separated therefrom, in so far as when united it has more perfect being" (*Supplementum* 93, a. 1).

On the other hand, the *Comedy* uses images that express a more conservative and concrete sense of body and reveal a sympathy with the principle of plurality of forms. Usually when it refers to the earthly and resurrected body, the *Comedy* presents the body as a cloth covering the soul and suggests that the separated soul is naked without it (*Par.* 14.43–44). In particular, the verb that Dante uses for having the earthly body is "vestire" (to clothe), and the one for the resurrected body is "rivestire" (to clothe again). Although the shade's aerial body is radiated by the soul, the images that Dante uses for the person's resurrected body throughout his poem reflect an emphasis on a material sense of body as something that is not expressed by the soul but added to it—a concept more closely related to the principle of plurality rather than unicity.[30]

The rest of Solomon's speech about the resurrection of the body makes explicit the connection between the concreteness expressed by the image of the body as a cloth and the principle of plurality of forms. As Solomon explains, not only will the soul put on its flesh again, but the flesh will be "gloriosa e santa"—that is, glorified with the four gifts of *impassibility, agility, subtlety,* and *clarity* that were usually referred to in contemporary discussions about the resurrected bodies.[31] In particular, Solomon refers to the gift of *clarity* and stresses that when the flesh resurrects, its appearance will be stronger than the light that now surrounds the soul:

> Ma sì come carbon che fiamma rende,
> e per vivo candor quella soverchia,
> sì che la sua parvenza si difende;
>   così questo folgór che già ne cerchia
> fia vinto in apparenza da la carne
> che tutto dì la terra ricoperchia;

né potrà tanta luce affaticarne:
ché li organi del corpo saran forti
a tutto ciò che potrà dilettarne.
                    (*Par.* 14.52–60)[32]

———

> But even as a coal which gives forth flame, and with its white
> glow outshines it, so that its visibility is maintained, so shall this
> effulgence which already surrounds us be surpassed in brightness
> by the flesh which the earth still covers; nor will such light have
> power to fatigue us, for the organs of the body will be strong for
> everything that can delight us.

In order to indicate that the features of the resurrected body will appear through the light of the soul's bliss, Dante uses an image that is also
used by Bonaventure in his *Sentence* commentary, where he describes the
clarity of the resurrected body. The resurrected body, Bonaventure says, is
like a brand that has a color by its nature, and when placed in fire, it bright-
ens but still retains its color. The resurrected body, therefore, will keep the
color that it possesses by its nature, and clarity will wrap it up as fire does
with a brand.[33] Chiavacci Leonardi has indicated that unlike Thomas Aquinas, who says that the clarity of the resurrected body will be produced
by the "redundantia gloriae animae," the overflowing of the soul's glory into
the body, here Dante suggests that the resurrected body will have by itself
the glow that surpasses the effulgence produced by the glory of the soul.[34]
In particular, when he celebrates bodily return and the dowries of the resurrected body, Dante once more steps back from the principle of unicity
and uses images that highlight the body's materiality and autonomy from
the soul (and which therefore express a sense of the body similar to the one
presented by the doctrine of plurality of forms).[35] Indeed, this passage not
only indicates that the dead body is a part of the self temporarily severed by
physical death, but also stresses material continuity (because the resurrected
body will be made of the same flesh that is now covered by earth).

Solomon's praise of the resurrected body is followed by the joyful response of all the blessed souls, who clearly indicate that they long for their
dead bodies. Moreover, the recovery of these tangible and visible bodies at
the end of time seems to coincide with the fulfillment of the self's most intimate affections:

Tanto mi parver sùbiti e accorti
e l'uno e l'altro coro a dicer "Amme!",
che ben mostrar disio d'i corpi morti:
  forse non pur per lor, ma per le mamme,
per li padri e per li altri che fuor cari
anzi che fosser sempiterne fiamme.

(Par. 14.62–66)

———

So sudden and eager both the one and the other chorus seemed to
me in saying "Amen," that truly they showed desire for their dead
bodies—perhaps not only for themselves, but also for their moth-
ers, for their fathers, and for the others who were dear before they
became eternal flames.

In contrast with the *desiderium* that, according to Augustine, Bernard, and
Bonaventure, distracts the separated souls from complete happiness in
heaven, the souls' longing for their bodies in the *Paradiso* does not hinder
their bliss (which, as is constantly repeated throughout the poem, is full
even before the Resurrection) but is rather a further expression of glory. At
the same time, however, this passage connects the souls' desire to reunite
with their bodies with their desire not only to become again full individuals (and therefore more similar and pleasing to God), but also to find again
the people they loved on earth.

Dante's originality with respect to this aspect of theology is significant.
As discussed in chapter 1, the idea of the sociability of the joys of resurrection (also found in Bonvesin's popular imagination) was rare among theologians, who insisted rather on the individual's relation with God and his
or her eventual improvement with the soul's reunification with its body.
Even those theologians acknowledging some relationship among the saints
rejected the idea that friendship and affection can be personal or exclusive
in heaven.[36] Bonaventure, for instance, writes that every saint is equally
close to all the other saints: with the resurrection of the body, one will rejoice in other people's happiness as much as in one's own; in fact, Peter will
rejoice in Linus's happiness even more than Linus does.[37] What Dante's
Solomon expresses is more intimate than Bonaventure because it is not
Peter rejoicing in Linus's and anyone else's glory, but each individual rejoicing at the idea of reunification with his or her dearest loved ones.

In the *Paradiso* passage quoted above, Dante uses the rhyme words "amme" / "mamme" / "fiamme" to indicate that with the revitalization of what now are dead bodies, the spiritual flames will again become corporeal and complete individuals. Moreover, the souls' desire for their bodies is, as Teodolinda Barolini has put it, the passionate "expression of their desire to love fully in heaven what they loved on earth."[38] The soul's recovery of its flesh entails, therefore, both an increase of the individual's bliss and the possibility of reuniting with his or her beloved. Moreover, if we remember that Bonvesin's *De die Iudicii* viewed the Resurrection as the moment in which the reconstituted persons will be able again to embrace the people they loved on earth, *Paradiso* 14's poignant connection of bodily return with the reunification with one's beloved appears as the solution to the failed embraces of the *Purgatorio* and of the epic tradition to which they refer. Like Bonvesin's popular poetry, Dante's *Comedy* not only indicates that personal desires for others continue to be part of one's identity in heaven, but also shows the importance that the doctrine of the resurrection of the body held at a human and personal level—as a victory over death and loss.

Dante's complex treatment of the resurrection of the body in *Paradiso* 14 evinces the same vacillation between the principles of plurality and unicity of form that characterizes Statius's embryological account in *Purgatorio* 25. In the *Comedy*, Dante emphatically focuses on the eschatological time before the Resurrection and is as insistent as Aquinas in stressing the fullness of the separated soul's experience in the afterlife. In the representation of this experience, Dante's poem refers to some principles of unicity of form allowing the soul to be the full container of the self, to the extent that the separated soul can unfold an aerial body immediately after physical death and have an embodied experience of pain (in hell and purgatory) and bliss (in heaven). At the same time, however, Dante's eschatological panorama reveals the same ambiguity that is present in Aquinas's anthropological system between packing the self into the soul and stressing the ontological incompleteness of the human being without its body. From the very beginning and throughout the poem, Dante underscores the shades' deficiency and the imperfection of the experience that aerial bodies allow them to have. The *Comedy* never mixes shades with real persons, but presents them as surrogates for a unity that has been disrupted by physical death and is going to be reassembled only with bodily return at the end of time.

As in the *Book of the Three Scriptures*, the soul's somatomorphism in the *Comedy* allows for full experience before the Resurrection but never replaces the traditional emphasis on the resurrection of the body as the necessary reconstitution of the person in his or her material wholeness. If the most meaningful experience of pain in purgatory is also a temporary preparation for something else, the separated soul's experience in hell and heaven is at once full and yet destined to increase with the soul's resumption of its resurrected body. In the passages dealing with bodily return, in particular, Dante uses images that stress both the body's fleshliness and a sense of the body as something independent of the soul, thereby reflecting the principle of plurality of forms with which he begins the embryological doctrine of *Purgatorio* 25. In celebrating the resurrection of the body in *Paradiso* 14, Dante, like Aquinas, removes any impediment from the separated souls' enjoyment of beatific vision and stresses its perfection and fullness even before the Resurrection; however, he also indicates poignantly that the separated souls still desire their body, and that bodily return entails an increase of happiness both in intensity and extension. Moreover, *Paradiso* 14 also reveals that the resurrection of the body represents the ultimate fulfillment with respect to what concerns both the individual's beatific vision and the expression of his or her personal affections. Thus, no matter how bright and luminous the blessed soul may be, only at the end of time will it stop being an incomplete fragment, because only then will it finally be reunited with its real body in the fleshly, tangible, embraceable perfection of the whole person, "la persona tutta quanta."

Epilogue: The Body's Journey and the Pilgrim in the *Paradiso*

The *Book of the Three Scriptures* and the *Comedy* illustrate that the focus of late thirteenth- and early fourteenth-century eschatology had shifted toward the experience between death and Last Judgment. Both poems show that this change coincides with a somatization of the separated soul but does not efface the significance of bodily return at the end of time. However, the two poems deal with this complex eschatology in very different ways. Whereas Bonvesin ignores the implications of an embodied representation of the soul, Dante clearly explores the complex dialectic between pre- and post-resurrection experience.

In the *Black Scripture and Golden Scripture*, Bonvesin announces that he will show the condition of the separated souls in hell and heaven, but then describes—without any explanation of how it is possible—an embodied soul that is hardly distinguishable from a person with a real body. With such a description, readers may often wonder whether Bonvesin is in fact already illustrating a post-resurrection reality. Bonvesin ultimately maintains, however, that his description is actually of the time before the Last Judgment, making the last pain of hell and the last glory of heaven consist of the separated souls' awareness that resurrection will entail the body's punishment and reward, respectively. In this way, Bonvesin simply juxtaposes, one after the other, two eschatological emphases that are not fully compatible with each other. He seems unaware of—or at least undisturbed by—the tension existing between the fully embodied representation of the separated soul and the idea that the whole person will be reconstituted only at the end of time.

By contrast, Dante's handling of the matter is more sophisticated. He uses the concept of shade to highlight the fullness of the separated soul's experience and, at the same time, to stress that the aerial body unfolded by the soul is not enough—that a shade is just a surrogate for a fullness and a perfection that are only possible when the soul reunites with its fleshly body and the person is reconstituted in his or her corporeal wholeness. Dante therefore not only justifies the separated soul's embodiment with the theory of the aerial body but also inextricably entwines the two different eschatological emphases: on experience before and after the Resurrection.

The *Comedy*, however, does more than master this eschatological tension. As I will show now, Dante first increases the eschatological tension in the second half of the *Paradiso* and then tries to resolve it in the representation of the pilgrim entering the Empyrean and completing his journey. Beginning with the heaven of Jupiter and continuing through the heaven of Saturn until the heaven of the Fixed Stars, *Paradiso* 19–25, without undermining the happiness of the blessed souls, nonetheless emphasizes the incompleteness of their experience and point to the resurrection of the body and the Last Judgment as the events perfecting this experience. When the souls in the heaven of justice are confronted with the question of the salvation of virtuous pagans, for instance, they admit that in spite of their vision of God, they do not know everything yet:

> O predestinazion, quanto remota
> è la radice tua da quegli aspetti
> che la prima cagion non veggion *tota!*
>   E voi, mortali, tenetevi stretti
> a giudicar: ché noi, che Dio vedemo,
> non conosciam ancora tutti gli eletti;
>   ed ènne dolce così fatto scemo,

perché il ben nostro in questo ben s'affina,
che quel che vole Iddio, e noi volemo.

(Par. 20.130–38)

_____

O predestination, how remote is thy root from the vision of those who see not the First Cause entire! And you mortals, keep yourselves restrained in judging; for we, who see God, know not yet all the elect. And to us such defect is sweet, because our good is refined, that what God wills we also will.

As Christian Trottmann has convincingly argued, the elect whom the blessed do not know yet include not only those to come but also some of those who were not baptized but have nonetheless been saved.[39] Although the blessed make sure to stress that their lack of knowledge does not harm their bliss but is rather a source of joy (because it conforms to God's desire), this passage ultimately corroborates Solomon's claim that the beatific vision will increase with the resurrection of the body. Together with the end of the previous canto, where the blessed give a long speech about the full knowledge and understanding that will finally be available at the Last Judgment (*Par.* 19.103–48), the souls' acknowledgment of their own ignorance highlights a sense of imperfection in their current condition which does not affect their bliss but nonetheless creates an expectation for the end of time and the completion it will bring about.

The same sense of imperfection and temporariness persists in the heaven of Saturn, where the pilgrim meets the souls with the highest degree of beatitude. This section concerns not the blessed souls' knowledge but rather their corporeal identity. In particular, the interaction between the pilgrim and Saint Benedict highlights the imperfect nature of the heavenly souls. When Saint Benedict describes the souls in the heaven of Saturn, he states, "Questi altri fuochi tutti contemplanti / *uomini fuoro*, accesi di quel caldo / che fa nascere i fiori e ' frutti santi" (These other fires were all contemplative men, kindled by that warmth which gives birth to holy flowers and fruits [*Par.* 22.46–48], my emphasis). "Uomini fuoro" is in the same initial position as "Uomini fummo, e or siam fatti sterpi," the line used by Pier della Vigna to refer to the condition of the suicides in hell (*Inf.* 13.37). Unlike the souls of the suicides, the souls in the heaven of Saturn are not damned bushes but blessed fires ("fuochi"); like the souls in hell, however, the souls in heaven are not human beings ("uomini") because they too are separated from their bodies. Likewise, the splendors in the highest heavens are imperfect creatures, and, in spite of the bliss that their luminosity represents, they express a sense of lack that will be fulfilled only with bodily return.

By suggesting that souls in paradise enjoy the vision of God and are perfectly content but are not human beings anymore, or yet, Dante reiterates that while the soul is the immortal carrier of the self which attains bliss as soon as it gets to heaven, it is not to be confused with the whole human being, which is composed of both soul and fleshly body. It is therefore significant that the pilgrim, right after seeing all the dazzling fires of the heaven of Saturn, finds the confidence to ask Benedict for the privilege to see him "con imagine scoverta," that is, with his human features:

> L'affetto che dimostri
> meco parlando, e la buona sembianza
> ch'io veggio e noto in tutti li ardor vostri,
>   così m'ha dilatata mia fidanza,
> come 'l sol fa la rosa quando aperta
> tanto divien quant' ell' ha di possanza.
>   Però ti priego, e tu, padre, m'accerta
> s'io posso prender tanta grazia, ch'io
> ti veggia con imagine scoverta.
> (Par. 22.52–60)

> The affection you show in speaking with me, and the good semblance which I see and note in all your ardors, have expanded my confidence as the sun does the rose when it opens to its fullest bloom. Therefore I pray you—and do, you, father, assure me if I am capable of receiving so great a grace, that I may behold you in your uncovered shape.

The pilgrim's desire to see Benedict's features emphasizes that, as Solomon had suggested in the heaven of the Sun, even in paradise, the soul alone is not the whole human being but just an incomplete part of it. Yet, for the first time, the poem does not point to the end of time as the moment for the material reconstitution of the person. Rather, Benedict replies that the pilgrim's "high"—and therefore not only understandable but also praiseworthy—desire to see the features of the blessed will be satisfied when he is in the Empyrean: "Frate, il tuo alto disio / s'adempierà in su l'ultima spera, / ove s'adempion tutti li altri e 'l mio" (Brother, your high desire shall be fulfilled up in the last sphere, where are fulfilled all others and mine [*Par.* 22.61–63]). Through the pilgrim's encounter with Benedict, Dante the poet highlights once more the sense of lack that the soul's separation from the body implies; more importantly, he also implicitly anticipates the original solution that he will give to that lack at the end of the poem.

The importance that Dante attributes to resurrection as the ultimate completion of beatitude is also dramatized in the pilgrim's examination on faith occurring in the heaven of the Fixed Stars after the encounter with Saint Benedict. When the pilgrim is asked by Saint James about hope, he gives the canonical answer, which he translates directly from Peter Lombard's *Sentences* ("Spes est certa expectatio futurae beatitudinis, veniens ex Dei gratia et ex meritis praecedentibus" [bk. 3, dist. 26]): "'Spene,' diss' io, 'è uno attender certo / de la gloria futura, il qual produce / grazia divina e precedente merto'" ("Hope," I said, "is a sure expectation of future glory, which divine grace produces, and preceding merit" [*Par.* 25.67–69]). Yet when the pilgrim is asked what hope precisely consists of ("quello che la speranza ti 'mpromette" [87]), he does not speak of bliss as vision or contemplation of God, nor as supreme peace or perfect love. The pilgrim's ultimate hope is the resurrection of the body, which is once more described with images of garment and clothing:

> Le nove e le scritture antiche
> pongon lo segno, ed esso lo mi addita,
> de l'anime che Dio s'ha fatte amiche.
>   Dice Isaia che ciascuna vestita
> ne la sua terra fia di doppia vesta:
> e la sua terra è questa dolce vita;
>   e 'l tuo fratello assai vie più digesta,
> la dove tratta de le bianche stole,
> questa revelazion ci manifesta.
> (Par. 25.88–96)

———

The new and the old Scriptures set up the token of the souls that God has made His friends, and this points it out to me. Isaiah says that each one shall be clothed in his own land with a double garment, and his own land is this sweet life; and your brother, where he treats of the white robes, makes manifest this revelation to us far more expressly.

The poem confirms the significance that these words place upon the resurrection of the body when, after the pilgrim pronounces them, a new splendor appears beside the lights in which Peter and James are hidden. As is usual in heaven, the pilgrim cannot recognize the identity of the soul because its features are hidden by too strong a light. As soon as Beatrice tells him that the light hides Saint John (*Par.* 25.112–14), however, the pilgrim immediately fixes on it and tries to distinguish something: "Qual è colui ch'adocchia e s'argomenta / di vedere eclissar lo sole un poco, / che, per veder, non vedente diventa; / tal mi fec' ïo a quell' ultimo foco" (As he who gazes and strains to see the sun a little eclipsed, and who through seeing becomes sightless, so did I become in respect to that last fire [*Par.* 25.118–21]). A medieval legend maintained that John had been assumed to heaven with his body, and the pilgrim is so concerned with seeing John's resurrected body that, as soon as he realizes John is in front of him, he tries impetuously to perceive it.[40] John tells the pilgrim that the only two persons assumed with their bodies are Christ and Mary, and that his own body will resurrect only at the Last Judgment:

> Perché t'abbagli
> per vedere cosa che qui non ha loco?
>   In terra è terra il mio corpo, e saragli
> tanto con li altri, che 'l numero nostro
> con l'etterno proposito s'agguagli.
>   Con le due stole nel beato chiostro
> son le due luci sole che saliro;
> e questo apporterai nel mondo vostro.
> (Par. 25.122–29)

Why do you dazzle yourself in order to see that which has here no place? On earth my body is earth, and there it shall be with the rest, until our number equals the eternal purpose. With the two robes in the blessed cloister are those two lights only which ascended; and this you shall carry back into your world.

John's words do not only emphasize a lack that will be filled only by the resurrection of the body, but also express a sense that the corpse is something
important and that, in spite of the soul's ability to unfold an aerial body, the
earthly remains are still part of the dead person's identity. One is even
tempted to feel in these lines some nostalgia for the dead body, the same
ambiguous and touching nostalgia of the first cantos of *Purgatorio*.[41]

Despite John's discouragement of seeing what "has no place," the pilgrim's desire to see the features of the blessed is fulfilled in the Empyrean.
On entering the last heaven, Beatrice makes clear what Benedict had antici-
pated but not explained. That is, when the pilgrim is allowed to see both
the angels and the blessed, he will see the blessed with the same aspect they
will have after resurrection: "Qui vederai l'una e l'altra milizia / di paradiso, e l'una in quelli aspetti / che tu vedrai a l'ultima giustizia" (Here you
shall see the one and the other soldiery of Paradise, and the one in those
aspects which you shall see at the Last Judgment [*Par.* 30.43–45]). In the
Empyrean, the pilgrim sees first the linear shape of a river of light and
then, when his sight has improved, a circle of light bounded by the blessed
sitting on innumerable steps (*Par.* 30.103–17). When Beatrice invites the
pilgrim to look at the blessed, she confirms that he is seeing them with
their resurrected bodies: "Mira / quanto è 'l convento de le bianche stole!"
(*Par.* 30.128–29). The luminous bodies of the blessed form the figure of a
"candida rosa," a white, glowing rose (*Par.* 31.1), and cantos 31 and 32 are devoted to descriptions of them and the pilgrim's joy in seeing the way they
will be after the Last Judgment. The desire that the pilgrim declared to
Saint Benedict and manifested with Saint John is finally fulfilled, and he
sees not the pale shades of the first heavens nor the bright lights of the last
ones but persons with the real aspect of the Resurrection: "Vedëa visi a carità
süadi, / d'altrui lume fregiati e di suo riso, / e atti ornati di tutte onestadi"
(I saw faces all given to love, adorned by the light of Another, and by their
own smile, and movements graced with every dignity [*Par.* 31.48–51]).

After a first, general overview of the blessed, the pilgrim turns to speak
to Beatrice, but instead, he meets Bernard of Clairvaux, who replaces her
in the same sudden and unexpected way she had replaced Virgil in the garden of Eden: "credea veder Beatrice e vidi un sene / vestito con le genti glo-
riose. / Diffuso era per li occhi e per le gene / di benigna letizia, in atto pio /
quale a tenero padre si convene" (I thought to see Beatrice, and I saw an
elder, clad like the folk in glory. His eyes and cheeks were suffused with be-
nign gladness, his mien kindly such as befits a tender father [*Par.* 31.59–63]).

As Boitani points out, this is the last encounter of the pilgrim in the poem and recalls the first in that the pilgrim's emotion is similar to that which he felt when he saw Virgil at the beginning of his journey.[42] In addition, by comparing the two encounters, Dante points out a significant difference between the characters the pilgrim meets: while Virgil, the pilgrim's initial guide, was not an "omo certo" but an "ombra"—a shade provided with a temporary body of air—Bernard appears to him like "a sene vestito con le genti glorïose," that is, like a real person after the resurrection of the body.[43] In its movement from the threshold of hell to the summit of heaven, the poem has therefore created an original eschatological dimension that goes beyond the inherent limitations of the eschatological time before the Resurrection.

Although temporarily and only for the pilgrim's sake, Dante's representation of the Empyrean has the Resurrection take place before the end of time. It thereby tries to overcome the sense of imperfection that increases in the second half of the *Paradiso*. However, Dante's audacity and novelty in the *Paradiso* go yet further than having the pilgrim see the blessed with the aspect they will have when their bodies are resurrected: he even imagines that the pilgrim's body progressively acquires the quality of a glorious body. In this respect, the pilgrim in the Empyrean would be similar to the other blessed, whom he sees with their resurrected bodies even though his journey takes place before the end of time. This glorification takes place, like the vision of the resurrected bodies in the Empyrean, as a foretaste of a future reality, experienced as already realized. With this subtle yet effective innovation, the last cantos of the *Paradiso* create a unique dimension combining the two eschatological emphases (before and after the Resurrection) that I have outlined for the *Comedy* and the previous eschatological tradition.

Scholars have generally acknowledged that the pilgrim's role as an individual and everyman is present from the very first line of the poem.[44] In the past the pilgrim's role has been read as referring to the journey of the soul to God, be it a specific or a general one (i.e., as an *itinerarium mentis in Deum*). I propose that the pilgrim's journey can also be read as a "journey of the body": in structuring the transformation of the pilgrim's body in the course of his journey through the afterlife, Dante keeps in mind the paradigm expressed by Beatrice's account of salvation history in *Paradiso 7*, which emphasizes that the first human being was created immortal, that Christ's pain on the cross redeemed humankind from the consequences of the Fall, and that only resurrection will conclude and bring to a closure the experience of humankind.[45]

As Beatrice explains in *Paradiso* 7, what is created directly ("sanza mezzo") by God is endowed with the three gifts of immortality, freedom, and conformity with him; sin takes freedom away and makes God's creature lose these privileges (67–81). Adam, who was created directly by God, was therefore immortal, free, and in conformity with God, but when he sinned, he (and all of humankind) was banished from these gifts and Eden: "Vostra natura, quando peccò *tota* / nel seme suo, da queste dignitadi, / come di paradiso, fu remota" (Your nature, when it sinned totally in its seed, was removed from these dignities, even as from Paradise [*Par.* 7.85–87]). After demonstrating that Christ's Passion was the only appropriate means to pay the ransom for Adam's sin and redeem humankind (88–120), Beatrice proceeds to explain that everything that is not created by God "sanza mezzo" is mortal and perishable and that, while the human soul is created directly by God, the souls of animals and plants are the product of generation and are therefore corruptible (*Par.* 7.124–44). Beatrice's long speech accounts not only for the soul's immortality (which is actually only implied by her words) but also, and especially, for the resurrection of the body: "E quinci puoi argomentare ancora / vostra resurrezion, se tu ripensi / come l'umana carne fessi allora / che li primi parenti intrambo fensi" (And hence you further can infer your resurrection, if you reflect how was the making of human flesh then when the first parents were both formed [*Par.* 7.145–48]). Beatrice's argument is that if every thing that is created "sanza mezzo" is immortal, and Adam and Eve were created "sanza mezzo" not only in their soul but also in their flesh, then the body was also created immortal and will therefore resurrect.[46]

As Bruno Nardi has pointed out, Beatrice's speech implies that death is natural only in the relative sense that it is a consequence of Adam's sin.[47] Nardi also makes a parallel between what Dante thinks would have happened to Christ's body if he had not accepted death and what some theologians (including Augustine and Peter Lombard) have argued would have happened to Adam if he had not sinned. Dante explains in the *Convivio* that if Christ—whose human nature was, like Adam's before the Fall, "sincera e buona," that is, uncontaminated by original sin (*Par.* 7.35–36)—had not died, his body would have been transformed at the age of eighty-one, from mortal to eternal: "E io credo che se Cristo fosse stato non crucifisso, e fosse vissuto lo spazio che la sua vita poteva secondo natura trapassare, elli

sarebbe a li ottantuno anni di mortale corpo in etternale trasmutato"
(4.24.6).[48] Dante therefore implies that before this final transformation,
both Adam and Christ had only the possibility of not dying. They were
thus in the condition that Augustine defines as "posse non mori." Adam
forwent this possibility when he fell: sin made the human body lose the gift
of immortality and become perishable. Christ's sacrifice—his choice to die
on the cross—redeemed humankind and gave it the possibility not only of
recovering Adam's prelapsarian condition, but of going where Adam could
have gone had he not sinned. The transformation from a "mortal" to an
"eternal body" suggests the Augustinian concept that in heaven the reconstituted person will enjoy not only the "posse non mori" (the possibility of
avoiding physical death) that Adam had in Eden, but also the "non posse
mori" (the impossibility of dying).[49]

The pilgrim's body goes through several stages of transformation as he
moves through the otherworld. When his journey begins in the dark wood,
the pilgrim stands for man in his fallen condition.[50] Along the infernal trip,
the pilgrim's body remains the heavy, mortal body that any other human
being has after the Fall. It begins to change in purgatory proper, at the
threshold of which the pilgrim's forehead is inscribed by the guardian angel
with seven *P*s representing the seven capital sins to be purged. When the
pilgrim moves from one terrace to the next, a *P* is canceled and, as a sign
that he has been freed from some burden of sin, his body becomes lighter.
Though the pilgrim usually does not take part in the physical punishment
tormenting the souls in purgatory, the experience of pain plays a significant
role in his purification at the summit of the mountain. The last *P* is in
fact erased from his forehead only when, in a moment full of Christological resonance, Virgil encourages him to cross a fiery barrier, which makes
him feel incredible pain and represents at once the punishment of lust
and a summary of all the punishments of purgatory: "Sì com' fui dentro, in
un bogliente vetro / gittato mi sarei per rinfrescarmi, / tant' era ivi lo 'ncendio sanza metro" (As soon as I was in it I would have flung myself into
molten glass to cool me, so without measure was the burning there [*Purg.*
27.49–51]).[51] After crossing the fire, the pilgrim arrives in Eden, where he
recovers the condition that Adam had before the Fall. Like all souls who
have completed purgation, however, the pilgrim does not remain in Eden
but instead proceeds to paradise, where his body continues to change.

At the beginning of the *Paradiso*, when he is still in Eden, the pilgrim
follows Beatrice's example and stares at the sun:

E sì come secondo raggio suole
uscir del primo e risalire in suso,
pur come pelegrin che tornar vuole,
  così de l'atto suo, per li occhi infuso
ne l'imagine mia, il mio si fece,
e fissi li occhi al sole oltre nostr' uso
  Molto è licito là, che qui non lece
a le nostre virtù, mercé del loco
fatto proprio de l'umana spece.
  Io nol soffersi molto, né sì poco,
ch'io nol vedessi sfavillar dintorno,
com' ferro che bogliente esce del foco.
(Par. 1.49–60)

———

And even as a second ray is wont to issue from the first, and mount
upwards again, like a pilgrim who would return home: thus of her
action, infused through the eyes into my imagination, mine was
made, and I fixed my eyes on the sun beyond our wont. Much is
granted to our faculties there that is not granted here, by virtue of
the place made for humankind as its proper abode. I did not endure
it long, nor so little that I did not see it sparkle round about, like
iron that comes molten from the fire.

This passage confirms the improvement of the pilgrim's physical faculties
("oltre nostr' uso") and associates it with the prelapsarian condition of Eden
that he has attained.[52] Still, while Beatrice keeps her eyes fixed on the sun,
the pilgrim cannot endure the intensity of the light—at least not yet—and
turns his eyes toward his guide. The first transformation of the *Paradiso*
occurs at this point:

Beatrice tutta ne l'etterne rote
fissa con li occhi stava; e io in lei
le luci fissi, di là sù rimote.
  Nel suo aspetto tal dentro mi fei,
qual si fé Glauco nel gustar de l'erba
che 'l fé consorto in mar de li altri dèi.
  Trasumanar significar *per verba*

non si poria; però l'essemplo basti
a cui esperïenza grazia serba.
  S'i' era sol di me quel che creasti
novellamente, amor che 'l ciel governi,
tu 'l sai, che col tuo lume mi levasti.

(Par. 1.64–75)

Beatrice was standing with her eyes all fixed upon the eternal
wheels, and I fixed mine on her, withdrawn from there above.
Gazing upon her I became within me such as Glaucus became on
tasting of the grass that made him sea-fellow of the other gods.
The passing beyond humanity may not be set forth in words:
therefore let the example suffice any for whom grace reserves that
experience. Whether I was but that part of me which Thou didst
create last, O Love that rulest the heavens, Thou knowest, who
with Thy light didst lift me.

Here Dante explicitly addresses the issue of the pilgrim's body in
heaven and rephrases the passage in which Paul wonders during his rapture
whether he ascended to heaven with or without his body: "Scio hominem,
sive in corpore sive extra corpus nescio, Deus scit, raptum usque ad ter-
tium coelum" (2 Corinthians 12:2–4). If the Pauline reference seems to leave
the question of the pilgrim's body open, I would argue that Dante's reference to the Ovidian episode of Glaucus works as a gloss to Paul and not
only affirms the presence of the pilgrim's body but also specifies what is
happening to it.[53] Ovid narrates that Glaucus was a Beotian fisherman who
ate a special herb and was transformed into a divinity of the sea:

Vix bene combiberant ignotos guttura sucos,
Cum subito trepidare intus praecordia sensi
Alteriusque rapi naturae pectus amore.
Nec potui restare diu: "repetenda" que "numquam
Terra, vale"; dixi corpusque sub aequora mersi.
Di maris exceptum socio dignantur honore,
Utque mihi quaecumque feram mortalia, demant,
Oceanum Tethynque rogant; ego lustror ab illis
Et, purgante nefas novies mihi carmine dicto,
Pectora fluminibus iubeor supponere centum.

(Metamorphoses 13.944–53)[54]

Scarce had I swallowed the strange juices when suddenly I felt my heart trembling within me, and my whole being yearned with desire for another element. Unable long to stand against it, I cried aloud: "Farewell, O Earth, to which I shall nevermore return!" and I plunged into the sea. The sea-divinities received me, deeming me worthy of a place with them, and called on Oceanus and Tethys to purge my mortal nature all away. And then they purged me, first with a magic song nine times repeated to wash all evil from me, and then they made me bathe my body in a hundred streams.

After eating the magical herb, Glaucus feels forced to abandon the earth and jumps into the sea. What is important here is that the sea-divinities ask Oceanus and Tethys to take away from Glaucus whatever trace of mortality he has: in becoming a god, therefore, he does not relinquish his body but has it purified from any mortal condition ("quaecumque mortalia"). In the same way, the pilgrim leaves the earth and, as Beatrice will explain to him, cannot help but move toward heaven, which now has become his natural place: "Tu non se' in terra, sì come tu credi; / ma folgore, fuggendo il proprio sito, / non corse come tu ch'ad esso riedi" (You are not on earth, as you believe; but lightning, fleeing its proper site, never darted so fast as you are returning to yours [*Par.* 1.91–93]). As Glaucus jumps into the sea with his body, so does the pilgrim enter heaven with his body. Moreover, the reference to Glaucus specifies that the pilgrim's "trasumanar" does not entail the quittance of his body but rather its improvement, suggesting that during his journey through the heavenly spheres, his body progressively puts off any remaining element of mortality. In other words, it changes from the condition of "posse non mori" of Eden to the condition of "non posse mori" of resurrection.

Dante continues to reflect on the pilgrim's corporeality as the pilgrim passes through paradise. After learning from Beatrice that he is entering heaven, the pilgrim wonders how he can pass through the spheres of heaven, which are lighter than his earthly body: "ora ammiro / com' io trascenda questi corpi levi" (now I marvel how it can be that I should pass through these light bodies [*Par.* 1.98–99]). In the following canto, he wonders how his body can be received by the Moon:

> Per entro sé l'eterna margarita
> ne ricevette, com' acqua recepe

raggio di luce permanendo unita.
　S'io era corpo, e qui non si concepe
com' una dimensione altra patio,
ch'esser convien se corpo in corpo repe,
　accender ne dovria più il disio
di veder quella essenza in che si vede
come nostra natura e Dio s'unio.
(Par. 2.34–42)

———

Within itself the eternal pearl received us, as water receives a ray of
light, itself remaining uncleft. If I was body (and if here we conceive
not how one bulk could brook another, which must be if body enters body), the more should longing enkindle us to see that Essence
wherein we behold how our nature and God united themselves.

Chiavacci Leonardi has pointed out in her commentary that theologians
commonly discussed the question of how the elect going to the Empyrean
at the Last Judgment could pass through the heavens with their resurrected
bodies. Both passages are hence further references to the qualities of the
resurrected body, which the pilgrim's body is acquiring. Indeed, the pilgrim's concerns about passing through "questi corpi levi" recall a passage
of the *Summa contra gentiles* in which Thomas Aquinas states that the
resurrected bodies of the blessed will occupy some space, but God's power
will allow them to pass through light elements—"supra elementa levia
elevari" (4.87).
　Acquiring the characteristics of a resurrected body is a gradual process
that begins in Eden in canto 1 and concludes only in canto 33. Throughout
the *Paradiso* many passages stress that the pilgrim cannot bear the intensity
of the light he faces, followed by other passages that describe the improvement of his condition. For example, when the pilgrim enters the heaven of
Saturn, for the first time Beatrice does not smile, explaining that if she
smiled, the pilgrim would be burned to ashes like Semele:

　Già eran li occhi miei rifissi al volto
de la mia donna, e l'animo con essi,
e da ogne altro intento s'era tolto.
　E quella non ridea; ma "S'io ridessi",
mi cominciò, "tu ti faresti quale
fu Semelé quando di cener fessi:

ché la bellezza mia, che per le scale
de l'etterno palazzo più s'accende,
com' hai veduto, quanto più si sale,
  se non si temperasse, tanto splende,
che 'l tuo mortal podere, al suo fulgore,
sarebbe fronda che trono scoscende".
(Par. 21.1–12)[55]

———

Already my eyes were fixed again on the face of my lady, and with them my mind, and from every other intent it was withdrawn; and she did not smile, but, "Were I to smile," she began to me, "you would become such as was Semele when she turned to ashes; for my beauty which, along the steps of the eternal palace, is kindled the more, as you have seen, the higher the ascent, were it not tempered, is so resplendent that your mortal powers at its flash would be like the bough shattered by a thunderbolt."

In this passage, Dante returns to Ovid to comment on the condition of the pilgrim's body. Ovid narrates that when Juno finds out that Semele, a Theban princess loved by Jove, is pregnant with Jove's child, she decides to take revenge on her. She takes the shape of Semele's old nurse and persuades her rival to convince Jove to swear to fulfill any wish she might have. And when Jove accepts, Semele asks him to show himself to her in the same way as with Juno. Unwillingly but forced by the promise, Jove reveals his divine nature to the woman, whose mortal body cannot bear such intensity and is reduced to ashes: "Corpus mortale tumultus / Non tulit aetherios donisque iugalibus arsit" (Her mortal body bore not the onrush of heavenly power, and by that gift of wedlock she was consumed [*Metamorphoses* 3.308–9]). Although the Ovidian allusion in *Paradiso* 21 has been interpreted as a way of presenting the pilgrim as a "corrected, Christian Semele,"[56] I suggest that, as in the case of Glaucus in *Paradiso* 1, Dante's reference to the *Metamorphoses* points also to the condition of the pilgrim's body: it has not fully completed its heavenly transformation but, like Semele, retains mortality.

In addition to his sight, the pilgrim's other faculties are likewise limited. Not only does Beatrice refrain from smiling, but there is no music in the heaven of Saturn. The pilgrim asks Peter Damian the reason for that silence (*Par.* 21.58–60), and the soul confirms that the pilgrim's body is still mortal and thus not yet ready for such an intensity: "'Tu hai l'udir mortal sì come il viso,' / rispuose a me; 'onde qui non si canta / per quel che Bëatrice non ha riso'" ("You have the hearing as the sight of mortals," it replied to me, "wherefore here is no song, for that same reason for which Beatrice has not smiled" [*Par.* 21.61–63]).

In the heaven of the Fixed Stars, the pilgrim's physical sight is once again challenged. He sees Christ's resurrected body but is not able to endure its intensity: "e per la viva luce trasparea / la lucente sustanza tanto chiara / nel viso mio, che non la sostenea" (And through its living light the lucent Substance outglowed so bright upon my vision that it endured it not [*Par.* 23.31–33]). However, he can now bear to look at Beatrice's smile: "Apri li occhi e riguarda qual son io; / tu hai vedute cose, che possente / se' fatto a sostener lo riso mio" (Open your eyes and look at what I am; you have seen things such that you are become able to sustain my smile [*Par.* 23.46–48]). This physical improvement relates to the pilgrim's earlier discussion with Solomon, who referred to the gift of impassibility when asked whether the eyes of the resurrected persons will be able to endure the sight of the other resurrected bodies. Solomon answers that the organs of the resurrected body will be so strong that they will bear the intensity of whatever can delight them ("li organi del corpo saran forti / a tutto ciò che potrà dilettarne" [*Par.* 14.59–60]). Thus, the mortality that the pilgrim progressively casts off during his heavenly journey seems to correspond to the transformation of his body into a resurrected body, which is able to endure whatever can please him.

The dialectic between improvement and deficiency continues throughout the following cantos until the arrival at the Empyrean,[57] where the pilgrim realizes that he is now ready to bear any light without being harmed: "io compresi / me sormontar di sopr' a mia virtute; / e di novella vista mi raccesi / tale, che nulla luce è tanto mera, / che li occhi miei non si fosser difesi" (I comprehended that I was surmounting beyond my own power, and such new vision was kindled in me that there is no light so bright that my eyes could not have withstood it [*Par.* 30.56–60]). The pilgrim is then shown the aspect that Beatrice and the other blessed within the "candida rosa" will have when their bodies are resurrected at the end of time. Finally, Bernard prays to Mary to grant a last privilege to the pilgrim so that he can enjoy the ultimate vision of God:

> Or questi, che da l'infima lacuna
> de l'universo infin qui ha vedute

le vite spiritali ad una ad una,
  supplica a te, per grazia, di virtute
tanto, che possa con li occhi levarsi
più alto verso l'ultima salute.
  E io, che mai per mio veder non arsi
più ch'i' fo per lo suo, tutti miei prieghi
ti porgo, e priego che non sieno scarsi,
  perché tu ogne nube li disleghi
di sua mortalità co' prieghi tuoi,
sì che 'l sommo piacer li si dispieghi.

(Par. 33.22–33)

Now this man, who from the lowest pit of the universe even to here has seen one by one the spiritual lives, implores thee of thy grace for power such that he may be able with his eyes to rise still higher toward the last salvation. And I, who never for my own vision burned more than I do for his, proffer to thee all my prayers, and pray that they be not scant, that with thy prayers thou wouldst dispel for him every cloud of his mortality, so that the Supreme Pleasure may be disclosed to him.

At the end of the pilgrim's journey in heaven, the text makes a reference to the Glaucus passage that marks its beginning: Bernard prays that Mary will free the pilgrim from any remaining mortality ("ogne nube . . . di sua mortalità") so that the transformation that began with the "trasumanar" of canto 1 can be completed, and his body can fully attain the "non posse mori" of resurrection. It is only now that the pilgrim's body is as strong as the resurrected body that Solomon first described, finally able to enjoy the beatific vision in its fullness.

Through the representation of the Empyrean, Dante creates a unique dimension that transcends the tension between experience before and after the Resurrection, which informs the whole *Comedy* and generally characterizes the eschatological imagination of its time. Although the pilgrim's journey is set in 1300 and therefore before bodily return at the end of time, the material body of the Resurrection triumphs in the last cantos of the *Paradiso*. Dante's poem thereby overcomes the anxiety concerning the soul's separation from the body, which threatens the perfection of experience in the eschatological time before the Resurrection. To the lights that had populated the previous heavens, Dante's poetry adds, in the depiction of

Empyrean, the splendid features that the blessed will have after the Resurrection, and also imagines that the pilgrim's body attains the same splendor. Only in this unexpected fullness is the pilgrim granted the vision of the mysteries of the universe and the Trinity (*Par.* 33.85–126). And only when the pilgrim, in possession of his resurrected body, sees the mystery of the Incarnation in the circle painted with our image—"la nostra effige" (*Par.* 33.131)—can his journey (and with it, the poem) finally reach a conclusion.[58]

Appendix

Figure 1.
Roger van der Weyden, *Descent from the Cross,* circa 1435. Oil on panel.
195 × 326 cm. Museo del Prado. Reproduced by permission.

Figure 2.
Duccio, *Flagellation* (back panel of the *Maestà*), 1308–11. Tempera on wood, 50 × 53.5 cm. Museo dell'Opera del Duomo, Siena. Opera della Metropolitana di Siena, aut. N. 1209/04. Photo by Foto Lensini, Siena. Reproduced by permission.

Figure 3.
Duccio, *Crown of Thorns* (back panel of the *Maestà*), 1308–11. Tempera on wood, 50 × 53.5 cm. Museo dell'Opera del Duomo, Siena. Opera della Metropolitana di Siena, aut. N. 1209/04. Photo by Foto Lensini, Siena. Reproduced by permission.

Notes

Preface

1. Erich Auerbach, *Dante, Poet of the Secular World* (Chicago: University of Chicago Press, 1961), 174.

2. Ibid., 174–75.

3. Colin Morris, *The Discovery of the Individual, 1050–1200* (New York: Harper and Row, 1972), 144–52.

4. "*Il Purgatorio* is the sublime product of a lengthy gestation. It is also the noblest representation of Purgatory ever conceived by the mind of man, an enduring selection from among the possible and at times competing images whose choice the Church, while affirming the essence of the dogma, left to the sensibility and imagination of individual Christians" (Jacques Le Goff, *The Birth of Purgatory*, trans. Arthur Goldhammer [Chicago: University of Chicago Press, 1984], 334).

5. Esther Cohen, "Towards a History of European Physical Sensibility: Pain in the Later Middle Ages," *Science in Context* 8 (1995): 47–74.

6. Philippe Ariès, *Western Attitudes toward Death: From the Middle Ages to the Present*, trans. Patricia Ranum (Baltimore: Johns Hopkins University Press, 1974), especially 27–52; idem, *L'homme devant la mort* (Paris: Editions du Seuil, 1977). See also Michel Vovelle, *La mort et l'Occident: De 1300 à nos jours* (Paris: Gallimard, 1983).

7. Aron Gurevich, "The *Divine Comedy* before Dante," in *Medieval Popular Culture: Problems of Belief and Perception*, trans. János M. Bak and Paul A. Hollingsworth (Cambridge: Cambridge University Press, 1988), 104–52; idem, "Perceptions of the Individual and the Hereafter in the Middle Ages," in *Historical Anthropology of the Middle Ages*, ed. Jana Howlett (Cambridge: Polity Press, 1992), 65–89; Caroline Walker Bynum, *The Resurrection of the Body in Western Christianity, 200–1336* (New York: Columbia University Press, 1995). On the complexity of Christian eschatology and its tensions in the high Middle Ages, see also Colomon Viola, "Jugements de Dieu et jugement dernier: Saint Augustin et la scolastique naissante (Fin Xi^e–milieu XIIIe siècles)," in *The Use and Abuse of Eschatology in the Middle Ages*, ed. Werner Verbeke, Daniel Verhelst, and Andries Welkenhuysen (Leuven: Leuven University Press, 1988), 242–98; Jérôme Baschet, "Jugement de l'âme, jugement dernier: Contradiction, complémentarité, chevauchement?," *Revue Mabillon* n.s. 6 (1995): 159–92; Caroline Walker Bynum and Paul Freedman, "Introduction"

in *Last Things: Death and Apocalypse in the Middle Ages,* ed. Caroline Walker Bynum and Paul Freedman (Philadelphia: University of Pennsylvania Press, 1999), 1–17.

8. Alison Morgan, *Dante and the Medieval Other World* (Cambridge: Cambridge University Press, 1990). On the attitude of Dante criticism toward popular culture, see 1–10. Curtius's statement (*European Literature and the Latin Middle Ages,* trans. W. R. Task [New York: Pantheon Books, 1953; 1st ed. 1948]) is quoted by Morgan on page 7. In a succinct article about the otherworldly journeys preceding the *Comedy,* Cesare Segre also points out that Dante's "superiority" with respect to most of the cultural material that could represent a source for his work should not hinder an exploration of his relation with such material: "Non facciamo più l'errore di trascurare le ricerche sulla cultura di Dante—i suoi affluenti si rivelano nella loro feconda eterogeneità—in base all'assioma immobilizzante che egli era troppo superiore alle sue eventuali fonti per aver potuto degnarle di uno sguardo" (Cesare Segre, *"L'itinerarium animae* nel Duecento e Dante," *Letture classensi* 13 [1984]: 18).

9. "Forse il tema più caratteristico di tutta la produzione didattica settentrionale è costituito da quella che si potrebbe definire come una vera e propria ossessione oltretombale" (Francesco Zambon, "Tradizione latina e tradizione romanza," in *Manuale di letteratura italiana: Storia per generi e problemi,* vol. 1, *Dalle origini alla fine del Quattrocento,* ed. Franco Brioschi and Costanzo Di Girolamo [Turin: Bollati Boringhieri, 1993], 477).

10. Teodolinda Barolini, *The Undivine "Comedy": Detheologizing Dante* (Princeton: Princeton University Press, 1992), 143.

CHAPTER 1 Eschatological Poems and Debates between Body and Soul in Thirteenth-Century Popular Culture

1. The name Uguccione is mentioned only in the rubric "Questo è lo començamento de lo libro de Uguçon de Laodho" (This is the beginning of the book of Uguccione of Lodi) which in ms. Saibante-Hamilton 390 precedes *Libro* and *Istoria.* The only monograph written on Uguccione is Ezio Levi, *Uguccione da Lodi e i primordi della poesia italiana,* 2nd ed. (Florence: La Nuova Italia, 1928; 1st ed., Florence: Battistelli, 1921). For a more recent overview of Uguccione's works, see Corrado Bologna, "La letteratura dell'Italia settentrionale nel Duecento," in *Letteratura italiana: Storia e geografia,* directed by Alberto Asor Rosa, vol. 1, *L'età medievale* (Turin: Einaudi, 1987), 144–48, which provides a helpful outline of the questions concerning Uguccione and the manuscript tradition of the texts attributed to him. See also Francesco De Sanctis, *Storia della letteratura italiana dai primi secoli agli albori del Trecento,* ed. Gerolamo Lazzeri (Milan: Hoepli, 1950), 127–29; and Aldo Rossi, "Poesia didattica del Nord," in *Storia della letteratura italiana,* directed by Emilio Cecchi and Natalino Sapegno, vol. 1, *Le origini e il Duecento* (Milan: Garzanti, 1965), 440–48.

2. The *Libro* (composed of monorhymed strophes of alexandrines and hendecasyllables) and the *Istoria* (written in couplets of assonantic nine-syllable lines) are contained, one after the other, in ms. Saibante-Hamilton, written in the second half of the thirteenth century and now in Berlin's Staatsbibliothek. (For the Saibante manuscript, see Renato Broggini, ed., "L'opera di Uguccione da Lodi," *Studi Romanzi* 32 [1956]: 8–12.) The *Contemplazione,* contained in ms. Campori of the Biblioteca Estense in Modena, is a section of 172 eight- and nine-syllable lines which is part of a Tuscan re-adaptation of passages from the *Libro* and *Istoria*: although all the other lines of the Tuscan re-adaptation are also attested in the *Libro* and *Istoria* as transmitted in the Saibante, the lines of the *Contemplazione* are attested only in the Campori manuscript, which was copied in Tuscany around 1265. (See Giulio Bertoni, "Un rimaneggiamento toscano del *Libro* di Uguçon da Laodho," *Studi medievali* 1 [1904–5]: 235–62, published with some changes as "Un rimaneggiamento fiorentino del *Libro* di Uguçon da Laodho," *Rendiconti della Reale Accademia dei Lincei* serie V, 21 [1912]: 607–85; and, more recently, D'Arco Silvio Avalle, "Introduzione," in *Concordanze della lingua poetica italiana delle Origini,* ed. D'Arco Silvio Avalle [Milan: Ricciardi, 1992], clvii–clviii.) The *Contrasto* is composed of seven-syllable lines and is contained in ms. 4251 of the Biblioteca Casanatese in Rome, which was copied in the last quarter of the thirteenth century. (See Giacinto Ciccone, "Un poemetto lombardo del secolo XIV inedito sul contrasto fra l'anima e il corpo," *Rivista Abruzzese di scienze, lettere ed arti* 23 [1908]: 223–33; and especially Claudio Ciociola, "Nominare gli anonimi [Per Uguccione]," *Filologia e critica* 15, 2–3 [May/Dec. 1990]: 419–33.)

3. The *Libro* and *Istoria* were first published as a single poem by Adolf Tobler in 1884 ("Das Buch des Uguçon da Laodho," *Abhandlungen der Preussischen Akademie der Wissenschaften zu Berlin* 18 [1884]: 53–94). Their unity was not questioned until 1901, when, on the basis of both meter and content, Vincenzo De Bartholomaeis suggested that these lines represent an amalgamation of two different poems (Bonvesin da Riva, *Il Libro delle Tre Scritture e il Volgare delle Vanità,* ed. V. De Bartholomaeis [Rome: Società Filologica Romana, 1901], 23–24, n. 4). In 1921, Ezio Levi distinguished two poems, calling them *Libro* and *Istoria,* but attributed them to the same author—the former would have been written by Uguccione in old age, the latter in his youth (*Uguccione da Lodi,* 5–25; and cf. Antonio Medin's critique of Levi's attribution of the poems to the same author in "L'opera poetica di Uguccione da Lodi," *Atti del Reale Istituto Veneto di scienze, lettere ed arti* 81 [1921–22]: 185–209, esp. 185–92). In 1956, Renato Broggini re-edited the two poems and definitively settled the question, citing not only the metrical differences between the two texts but also their phonetic, linguistic, and syntactic characteristics to show that they cannot be attributed to the same author ("L'opera di Uguccione da Lodi," 12–19). Since then, common consensus distinguishes two poems and two authors in the 1842 lines transmitted in the Saibante: lines 1–702 form Uguccione's *Libro* (called "Primo sermone" by Broggini), while the remaining ones

form the Pseudo-Uguccione's *Istoria* (called "Secondo sermone" by Broggini), which is a more popular version of the *Libro*. Gianfranco Contini uses Broggini's text for Uguccione's poem and calls it *Libro* in his edition of *Poeti del Duecento*, vol. 1 (Milan and Naples: Ricciardi, 1960), 597–624. Both poems have been recently re-edited in the *Concordanze della lingua poetica italiana delle Origini*, 54–68.

The *Contemplazione* and the *Contrasto* show that the 1842 lines attributed to Uguccione in the Saibante were originally part of a larger tradition. In 1929, Giulio Bertoni stressed that the two texts are related to each other but could not specify the terms of their relationship ("Intorno alla cosiddetta *Contemplazione della morte* attribuita a Uguccione," *Giornale storico della letteratura italiana* 94 [1929]: 197–200). In 1956, Broggini thought that the *Contemplazione* should be connected with the Pseudo-Uguccione (whose work would be more substantial than that attested in the Saibante) and that the *Contrasto* is an attempt to put this wider Pseudo-Uguccione into seven-syllable lines. He thereby republished the *Contemplazione* as *Frammento del Secondo Sermone* attributed to the Pseudo-Uguccione ("L'opera di Uguccione da Lodi," 19–21). More recently, Ciociola convincingly argued that the *Contrasto* is to be connected not with the Pseudo-Uguccione (as Broggini maintained), but with Uguccione ("Nominare gli anonimi"). Ciociola's hypothesis is convincing: in this case, *Libro* and *Contrasto* would have been written by Uguccione, while *Istoria* and the Tuscanized poem in ms. Campori would be rewritings of this material. Whichever thesis is correct, it is clear that *Libro, Istoria, Contemplazione,* and *Contrasto* are all part of a larger tradition that is connected to the figure of Uguccione da Lodi.

4. Ezio Levi, who brought Northern Italian didactic literature to scholarly attention in the 1920s, argued that its genesis was connected with heretical movements; see *Uguccione da Lodi* and *I poeti antichi lombardi* (Milan: Cogliati, 1921; anastatic facsimile reprint, Bologna: Forni, 1979). Levi's thesis has been subsequently rejected, and it is now commonly agreed that no heterodox element is present in any of the texts of this literary tradition.

5. For the genre of the sermon in verse (of which Uguccione is considered the most important Italian representative), see Cesare Segre, "Le forme e le tradizioni didattiche," in *Grundriss der romanischen Literaturen des Mittelalters*, directed by Hans Robert Jauss, vol. 6, *La littérature didactique, allégorique et satirique* (Heidelberg: Carl Winter and Universitätsverlag, 1968), part 1, 60–66; and Lino Leonardi and Francesco Santi, "La letteratura religiosa," in *Storia della letteratura italiana*, directed by Enrico Malato, vol. 1, *Dalle origini a Dante* (Rome: Salerno, 1995), 377–83.

6. The doctrine of *contemptus mundi* originated in monasteries and was further developed in the convents of mendicant orders. It was eventually transmitted to society as a whole as a self-evident truth and was expected to provoke in the public strong feelings of its own misery and insignificance. For an excellent and

concise study of the motifs of contempt for the world, see Jean Delumeau, *Sin and Fear: The Emergence of a Western Guilt Culture: 13th–18th Centuries,* trans. E. Nicholson (New York: St. Martin's Press, 1990), 9–34. For a more detailed monograph, see Robert Bultot, *Christianisme et valeurs humaines: La doctrine du mépris du monde en Occident, de S. Ambroise à Innocent III* (Louvain: Éditions Nauwelaerts; Paris: Béatrice-Nauwelaerts, 1963–64), esp. vol. 4, parts 1 and 2; and Francesco Lazzari, *Mistica e ideologia tra XI e XIII secolo* (Milan and Naples: Ricciardi, 1972), with ample bibliography on pp. 10–14.

7. It has been noted that an important source for Uguccione's many passages on death in the *Libro* is Helinant of Froidmont's *Vers de la Mort,* written in the last decade of the twelfth century. See, for instance, Leonardi and Santi, "La letteratura religiosa," 382. For the evangelism of fear, see Delumeau, *Sin and Fear,* 343.

8. Italian text is quoted from the *Concordanze della lingua poetica italiana delle Origini.* All English translations are mine. I have found the following helpful in understanding the difficult language of the texts associated with Uguccione: Giorgio Colussi, ed., *Glossario degli antichi volgari italiani* (Foligno: Editoriale Umbra, 1983–); and the glossary in Tobler, "Das Buch des Uguçon," 39–52.

9. The gloomy perspective on life on earth present in the *Libro, Istoria, Contrasto,* and *Contemplazione* carries over into the afterlife insofar as all these texts focus most of their attention on infernal pain and the sinner's fear of the Last Judgment. Heaven is barely described and remains largely implied as the alternative to suffering in hell and as the standard compared with which everything on earth is vain and "nothing."

10. I quote from the *Concordanze della lingua poetica italiana delle Origini* where the *Contrasto* is published on pp. 87–89. All translations are mine.

11. Ciociola considers the version of the *Desputeison* that is contained in the ms. 3516 of the Bibliothèque de l'Arsenal in Paris and that Hermann Varnhagen has indicated as P in his synoptic edition of it: "*The Desputisoun bitwen the Bodi and the Soule,* herausgegeben von Wilhelm Linow. Nebst der ältesten altfranzösischen Bearbeitung des Streites zwischen Leib und Seele, herausgegeben von Hermann Varnhagen," *Erlanger Beiträge zur englischen Philologie* 1 (1889): 113–96. The *Desputeison* was written in the twelfth century and is probably to be attributed to Philippe de Thaon: see the discussion and bibliographical information in Ciociola, "Nominare gli anonimi," 427. The model for the *Desputeison* is the Latin poem *Nuper huiuscemodi* (also know as *Royal Debate*), which is contained in a twelfth-century manuscript. Both the *Royal Debate* and *Desputeison* are composed of just two long speeches, one of the soul and one of the body. The *Royal Debate* was published by Eleonor Heningham, *An Early Latin Debate of the Body and the Soul Preserved in MS Royal 7 A III in the British Museum* (New York: privately printed, 1939), 54–81. The *Desputeison* has been translated into English by Mary Heyward Ferguson,

"The Debate between the Body and the Soul: A Study in the Relationship between Form and Content" (Ph.D. diss., Ohio State University, 1965), 146–67. For general overviews of the genre of the debate between body and soul, see Theodore Batiouchkof, "Le débat de l'âme et du corps," *Romania* 20 (1891): 1–55 and 513–78; Hans Walther, *Das Streitgedicht in der lateinischen Literatur des Mittelalters* (Munich: Beck, 1920), 53–64; Arnold Barel Van Os, *Religious Visions: The Development of the Eschatological Elements in Mediaeval English Religious Literature* (Amsterdam: H. J. Paris, 1932), 177–216; Segre, "Le forme e le tradizioni didattiche," 74–78. See also Robert Ackerman, "The Debate of the Body and the Soul and Parochial Christianity," *Speculum* 37 (1962): 541–65; and Michel-André Bossy, "Medieval Debates of Body and Soul," *Comparative Literature* 28 (1976): 144–63.

12. See, for instance, the body's words in ll. 104–15 of a Tuscan version of the *Visio Philiberti* in the vernacular (in Vincenzo De Bartholomaeis, "Due testi latini e una versione ritmica italiana della *Visio Philiberti*," *Studi medievali* n.s. 1 [1928]: 304):

> E sai che mi dicesti   che Dio sì te creò,
> Savia forma e nobile   et ragion ti donò,
> A sua similitudine   nel corpo ti formò,
> Et me siccome ancilla   ad te accompagnò.
> Dunque, se a tte fó dato   il sermo e la bontade
> E lla ragione ch'ensegna   quel che si debba fare,
> Se ttu mi seguitasti   in mala voluntade,
> Tutta è tua la colpa,   ché nol dovevi fare.
> Più si puote l'Anima   che lla Carne incolpare,
> Perciò che, essendo dopna,   consente a seguitare
> La Carne, ch'è ancilla   e devesi domare
> Di fame e sete et verghe,   ché non seguiti il male.

The Latin version of the *Visio Philiberti* can be read in Edelstand P. du Méril, ed., *Poésies populaires latines antérieures au douzième siècle* (Paris: Brockhaus et Avenarius, 1843), 217–30. While the Old French debate and the *Royal Debate* that is its model are composed of just two long speeches (one of the soul and one of the body), the *Visio Philiberti*, composed in Latin in the twelfth or early thirteenth century and subsequently translated or readapted in many vernaculars, is a veritable dialogue, where the soul speaks four times and the body three. In spite of their different structures, *Royal Debate* (and its rewriting in Old French) and *Visio Philiberti* share several motifs—among which is the body's reply that the soul is the guide and therefore responsible for the sins that are committed. Heningham even hypothesizes that the *Visio Philiberti* is a "free and talented reworking" of the *Royal Debate* (*An Early Latin Debate*, 42). See also the discussion in Ackerman, "The Debate of the Body and the Soul," 542–45; Ferguson, "The Debate between the Body and the Soul," 1–6; and Segre, "Le forme e le tradizioni didattiche," 75.

13. For the connection between the doctrines of Last Judgment and Resurrection, see Bernard McGinn, "The Last Judgment in the Christian Tradition," in *The Encyclopedia of Apocalypticism,* ed. Bernard McGinn (New York: Continuum, 1998), 2:361–401, esp. 362 and 369. The presence in the *Istoria* of a long section on the imminent coming of the Antichrist makes clear that the collective scenario of the Last Judgment is connected with the reemergence in the twelfth century of apocalyptic spirituality, which stresses the imminence of the end of the world.

The passage on the expected coming of the Antichrist is part of a long section that combines apocalyptic assumptions with the necessity of repentance (561–922) and precedes the soul's words to the body about its resurrection. The *Istoria*'s passage on the Antichrist shares many similarities with an anonymous thirteenth-century poem on the Antichrist that was written in Northern Italy in the vernacular and is contained in the thirteenth-century ms. D. IV. 32 of the library in the Escorial. Levi attributed it to Uguccione. It is published by Broggini, who entitles it *Liber Antichristi* and attributes it to an "Anonimo Euganeo" ("L'opera di Uguccione da Lodi," 105–18). It has been recently republished in *Concordanze della lingua poetica italiana delle Origini,* 43–46. Both texts derive from the treatise *De ortu et tempore Antichristi,* which Adso of Montier-en-Der addresses to Gerberga, wife of Louis IV, in the mid-tenth century.

In recent decades, scholars have paid particular attention to the reemergence of apocalyptic spirituality in the late twelfth century and, especially under the influence of the Franciscan Spirituals, in the following ones. See, for instance, Marjorie Reeves, *The Influence of Prophecy in the Later Middle Ages: A Study in Joachinism* (Oxford: Clarendon Press, 1969); eadem, "History and Prophecy in Medieval Thought," *Medievalia et Humanistica* n.s. 5 (1974): 51–75; Bernard McGinn, *Visions of the End: Apocalyptic Traditions in the Middle Ages* (New York: Columbia University Press, 1979); idem, "Introduction: Apocalyptic Spirituality," in *Apocalyptic Spirituality: Treatises and Letters of Lactantius, Adso of Montier-en-Der, Joachim of Fiore, the Franciscan Spirituals, Savonarola,* ed. Bernard McGinn (New York: Paulist Press, 1979), 1–16; Robert E. Lerner, "Millennialism," in *The Encyclopedia of Apocalypticism,* 2:326–60. For the Antichrist in particular, see Richard K. Emmerson, *Antichrist in the Middle Ages: A Study of Medieval Apocalypticism, Art, and Literature* (Seattle: University of Washington Press, 1981); Bernard McGinn, *Antichrist: Two Thousand Years of the Human Fascination with Evil* (San Francisco: Harper, 1994); Roberto Rusconi, "Antichrist and Antichrists," in *The Encyclopedia of Apocalypticism,* 2:287–325.

14. Although the Last Judgment and the experience thereafter dominate the final part of the *Libro,* they are also present in its first part, which often hints at the soul's fate in hell. Immediately after a long list of good and bad deeds leading to salvation or damnation, for instance, Uguccione states that on Judgment Day these deeds will be weighed, and the just will then be rewarded with a beatitude that will satiate any desire they might have (346–56). Furthermore, the only pas-

sage of the *Libro* that describes heavenly bliss at any length seems to place it after the Resurrection (*Libro* 403–20).

15. This passage is taken directly from the *Istoria* 1003–1132.

16. See especially lines 454–654. The Resurrection and the Last Judgment are also mentioned in the *Visio Philiberti,* in which the body, after mentioning that it is now rotting in the grave, hints at its own eventual resurrection and punishment on Judgment Day (206–13; De Bartholomaeis, "Due testi latini," 307):

> De' diversi mangiari   et vestimenti ornati
> Solo una fossa scura   et vermini affamati:
> Di tutte mie richezze   questi mi son rimasi
> Che sempre mi devorano   come cani arrabiati.
>
> Certo sono che techo   debbo resuscitare
> A quel dì del Giudicio,   che nci deve condampnare
> Quel che nci creò perché   habiamo facto male
> Di quella morte orribile   che deve sempre durare.

17. Aron Gurevich, "The *Divine Comedy* before Dante," in *Medieval Popular Culture: Problems of Belief and Perception,* trans. János M. Bak and Paul A. Hollingsworth (Cambridge: Cambridge University Press, 1988), 111. See also idem, "Perceptions of the Individual and the Hereafter in the Middle Ages," in *Historical Anthropology of the Middle Ages,* ed. Jana Howlett (Cambridge: Polity Press, 1992).

18. Gurevich, "The *Divine Comedy* before Dante," 136.

19. Uguccione's texts must have enjoyed a wide circulation, not only in the north but also in central Italy: Giacomino da Verona shows a familiarity with them; Pietro da Barsegapé takes the passages about the Last Judgment that are a major part of his *Sermone* (written probably in Milan in 1274) from them; and the readaptation of *Libro* and *Istoria* contained in ms. Campori was written in Tuscany. The text of Pietro da Barsegapé's *Sermone* can be read in Emil Keller, ed., *Die Reimpredigt des Pietro da Barsegapè. Kritischer Text mit Einleitung, Grammatik und Glossar* (Frauenfeld: Huber, 1901), 33–71.

20. The full titles of the poems are *De Jerusalem celesti et de pulchritudine eius et beatitudine et gaudia sanctorum* and *De Babilonia civitate infernali et eius turpitudine et quantis penis peccatorum puniantur incessanter.* May attempts a more precise date and suggests that Giacomino wrote the *De Babilonia* around 1230 and the *De Jerusalem* twenty or thirty years later (Esther I. May, *The "De Jerusalem celesti" and the "De Babilonia infernali" of Fra Giacomino da Verona* [Florence: Le Monnier, 1930], 24–29). Giacomino's poems are contained in four manuscripts: ms. Marciano it. 4744 of the Biblioteca Marciana in Venice (written in the late thirteenth century); ms. 7.1.52 of the Colombina Library in Seville (related to the Marciano and similar to it); ms. Lat. in quarto XIII of the Biblioteca Arcivescovile in Udine; and

ms. Canoniciano it. 48 of the Bodleian Library in Oxford (which contains only the *De Jerusalem*). The *De Jerusalem* and *De Babilonia* were edited on the basis of the Marciano by Frédéric Ozanam, *Documents inédits pour servir à l'histoire littéraire de l'Italie, depuis le VIIIe siècle jusqu'au XIIIe, avec des recherches sur le moyen âge italien* (Paris: Jacques Lecoffre, 1850), 291–312; and by Adolfo Mussafia, "Monumenti antichi di dialetti italiani," *Sitzungsberichte der Kaiserlichen Akademie der Wissenschaften. Philosophisch-Historische Classe* 46 (1864): 136–58 (anastatic facsimile reprint, Bologna: Forni, 1980). Emilio Barana published a diplomatic edition of the four manuscripts (Giacomino da Verona, *La Gerusalemme celeste e la Babilonia infernale* [Verona: La Tipografica Veronese, 1921]), which was used by May in her 1930 edition (*The "De Jerusalem celesti"*). Romano Broggini has prepared the edition published in *Poeti del Duecento*, ed. Contini, 1:625–52, from which I quote. For a description of the manuscripts with bibliography, see Mussafia, "Monumenti antichi," 113–20; May, *The "De Jerusalem celesti*," 9–15; Contini, ed., *Poeti del Duecento*, 1:842–43. For an overview of the bibliography on Giacomino, see Marco Schrage, *Giacomino da Verona: Himmel und Hölle in der frühen italienischen Literatur* (Frankfurt am Main: Lang, 2003), 17–27.

21. On the technical aspects of the meter, see D'Arco Silvio Avalle, "L'origine della quartina monorima di alessandrini," in *Saggi e ricerche in onore di Ettore Li Gotti* (Palermo: Centro di studi filologici e linguistici siciliani, 1962), 119–60. For information about the audience and the genre of this well-developed didactic literature, see May, *The "De Jerusalem*," 30; Umberto Cianciolo, "Contributo allo studio dei cantari di argomento sacro," *Archivium Romanicum* 30 (1938): 180–83.

22. Giacomino was not a learned man. As Esther May explains, "It would seem . . . that he gathered the thoughts and views of the people about the life after death" (*The "De Jerusalem*," 34). Giacomino shows an awareness of his lack of intellectual sophistication when, at the beginning of the *De Jerusalem*, he states that some passages are to be taken literally, others allegorically; and he urges the theologians who might read his poem not to despise it for its lack of ingenuity (13–20). For the use of allegory in Giacomino and Bonvesin, see Monica Cerroni, "Tipologia dell'allegoria e dinamiche del vero in Giacomino da Verona e Bonvesin da la Riva," *Strumenti critici* 92 (2000): 53–74. The most important sources are the Apocalypse and contemporary Franciscan literature and sermons. Giacomino also reveals some familiarity with Uguccione's writings. See May, *The "De Jerusalem*," 30–46.

23. The manuscripts of both the Marciana and Colombina libraries containing the *De Jerusalem* and the *De Babilonia* also contain other poems in old Veronese: *Dell'amore di Gesù, Del giudizio universale, Della caducità della vita umana, Lodi della Vergine, Preghiere.* These poems have been edited by Mussafia in his "Monumenti antichi" and attributed by him to Giacomino. It is now commonly accepted that they were not written by Giacomino.

24. Quotations of the *Giudizio* are from Mussafia's edition in his "Monumenti antichi." The *Caducità*, which Levi attributed to Uguccione, was reedited by Broggini, "L'opera di Uguccione," 93–103. Broggini's edition is then reproduced in Contini, ed., *Poeti del Duecento*, 1:653–66, which I use. All translations are mine. I have found the glossary that Mussafia places at the end of his edition helpful (pp. 215–35). See also the vocabulary in May, *The "De Jerusalem,"* 125–32; and Vittorina Cecchetto, "The Language of Giacomino da Verona and a Concordance of His Works" (Ph.D. diss., University of Toronto, 1982). Commenting upon the closeness of *Caducità* and Giacomino's poem, Bologna highlights the tight connection among the didactic poems that were written in Northern Italy and stresses "l'immagine d'un intreccio culturale solido e ramificato, che connette organicamente dall'interno la produzione letteraria lombardo-veneta del primo Duecento: non solo topico bensì concretamente testuale, tramato di richiami allusivi, ma anche di citazioni *ad litteram*" ("La letteratura dell'Italia settentrionale nel Duecento," 148–49). See also Contini, *Poeti del Duecento*, 1:624: "Indubbie affinità stilistiche congiungono ai versi certi di Giacomino, e fra loro, alcuni poemetti in vario metro . . . i quali tengono dietro al *De Babilonia* nei due codici Marciano e Sivigliano . . . e con Giacomino costituiscono il meglio della non ricchissima produzione in volgare veronese."

25. This scene is similar to the one described in the *Istoria*, 103–54.

26. See Peter Dinzelbacher, "Il corpo nelle visioni dell'aldilà," *Micrologus: Natura, scienze e società medievali* 1 (1993): 301–26; and Claude Carozzi, "Structure et fonction de la vision de Tnugdal," in *Faire Croire: Modalités de la diffusion e de la réception des messages réligieux du XIIe au XVe siècle: Table Ronde organisée par l'École française de Rome, en collaboration avec l'Institut d'Histoire Médiévale de l'Université de Padoue [Rome, 22–23 juin 1979]* (Rome: École française de Rome; Turin: Bottega d'Erasmo, 1981), 223–34; idem, *Le voyage de l'âme dans l'au-delà d'après la littérature latine* (Rome: École française de Rome; Paris: Diffusion de Boccard, 1994); Ronald Finucane, *Appearances of the Dead: A Cultural History of Ghosts* (London: Junction Books, 1982); Carol Zaleski, *Otherworld Journeys: Accounts of Near-Death Experience in Medieval and Modern Times* (New York: Oxford University Press, 1987), 45–52; Gurevich, "Perceptions of the Individual"; Jean-Claude Schmitt, *Les Revenants: Les vivants et les morts dans la société médiévale* (Paris: Gallimard, 1994); and Caroline Walker Bynum, *The Resurrection of the Body in Western Christianity: 200–1336*, (New York: Columbia University Press, 1995), 291–305.

27. May, *The "De Jerusalem,"* 36–37.

28. The *Libro de la sentencia* is a poem contained in ms. 381 of the Biblioteca Estense. It is described by Giulio Bertoni, "Una redazione tosco-veneta di un sermone in rima sul giudizio universale," in *Poeti e poesie del Medio Evo e del Rinascimento* (Modena: Orlandini, 1922), 213–26. Bertoni, who quotes the text of the contrast between father and son on pp. 222–24, also summarizes the content of the poem, which begins with a short prologue and ends with a prayer to God. It

describes the fifteen signs that anticipate Judgment Day, Christ's descent to judge good and wicked, the joys of the celestial Jerusalem, the pains of the infernal Babylon, and the contrast between father and son. As a further indication that also the debate in the *De Babilonia* is referring to the post-resurrection reality, the son states that the father is in hell with his body: "El fig de Deo   k'en cel porta corona / te maleìga, pare,   l'anema e la persona" (May the son of God who is crowned in heaven curse you, father, body and soul [287–88]). And the author's final comment on the contrast also presumes the presence of the body: "La pugna è entro lor   sì grana e sì forto / com'i s'aves çurà   entrambidu' la morto, / e s'el poëso l'un   a l'altro dar de morso, / el ge manjaria   lo cor dentro lo corpo" (The fight between them is as harsh and strong as though they had promised death to each other, and if one could bite the other one, he would eat the heart in his body [313–16]).

29. Delumeau, *Sin and Fear,* 343.

30. Alison Morgan, *Dante and the Medieval Other World* (Cambridge: Cambridge University Press, 1990), 180.

31. This passage refers to the doctrine, common in theological discussions about the Resurrection, that the person will resurrect at the approximate age of thirty.

32. For the evolution of the doctrine of the dowries, see Nikolaus Wicki, *Die Lehre von der himmlischen Seligkeit in der mittelalterlichen Scholastik von Petrus Lombardus bis Thomas von Aquin* (Freiburg: Universitätsverlag, 1954), 202–37; Joseph Goering, "The *De dotibus* of Robert Grosseteste," *Mediaeval Studies* 44 (1982): 83–101; and Bynum, *The Resurrection of the Body,* 131–32 and 335–37.

33. A layman who was married twice, he was a tertiary of the Humiliati and may also have been a third-order Franciscan. He was a successful and wealthy teacher of Latin in a private capacity in both Legnano and Milan, where he taught the sons of the Lombard high bourgeoisie, accumulating sufficient funds to allow him to become a public benefactor of various hospitals. For a summary of his life, see Bonvesin da la Riva, *Volgari scelti,* trans. P. Diehl and R. Stefanini, with commentary and notes by R. Stefanini and a biographical profile by P. Diehl (New York: Lang, 1987), 1–4. For more detailed information about Bonvesin's life, see Luigi Zanoni, "Fra Bonvesin della Riva fu Umiliato o Terziario Francescano?" *Il Libro e la Stampa* 8 (1914): 141–48; Pio Pecchiai, "I documenti sulla biografia di Bonvicino della Riva," *Giornale storico della letteratura italiana* 78 (1921): 96–127. For a general presentation of Bonvesin's work, see De Sanctis, *Storia della letteratura italiana,* 137–43 and 240–66; Rossi, "Poesia didattica e poesia popolare del Nord," 470–86; D'Arco Silvio Avalle, "Bonvesin da la Riva," in *Dizionario biografico degli Italiani* (Rome: Istituto della Enciclopedia Italiana, 1970), 12:465–69; Manuele Gragnolati, "Bonvesin da la Riva," in *Italian Literature of the Thirteenth Century,* ed. Zygmunt Barański and Theodore J. Cachey (Columbia, S.C.: Bruccoli Clark Layman, forthcoming).

34. The strong commitment in Bonvesin's vernacular poetry to moving the audience members to make changes in their lives may be connected with the kind of preaching typical of the Humiliati. Raoul Manselli, addressing the preaching of the Humiliati, writes that "tout en partant d'un passage de l'Evangile, on évitait les devéloppement théologiques pour se limiter à une exhortation à la pénitence, la prière, la vie de sainteté" ("Italie. Haut Moyen Age: Mouvements spirituels orthodoxes et hétérodoxes [11ᵉ et 12ᵉ siècles]," in *Dictionnaire de spiritualité, ascétique et mystique, doctrine et histoire* [Paris: Beauchesne, 1971], vol. 7, part 2, cols. 2184–93; quotation on col. 2190).

35. "[Bonvesin] È . . . rappresentativo e, se fosse possibile dire, riassuntivo quanto in Spagna un Gonzalo de Berceo, in Francia un Gautier de Coincy. La sua bonaria abilità retorica (collaudata in un repertorio più esteso di qualsiasi suo conterraneo), la sua cultura e atteggiamento mentale, la sua posizione verso la lingua (dialettale ma non vernacolore) coincidono, più vistosamente che mai, con una media e con un ideale" (Contini, ed. *Poeti del Duecento,* 1:667, first quotation on p. 668).

36. Resurrection is also stressed in the fifty-two lines of the *De quindecim miraculis que debent apparere ante diem iudicii,* a poem in which Bonvesin describes the fifteen marvels that will anticipate the day of Sentencing. First Bonvesin writes that resurrection will occur on the eleventh day: "L'undexen di apresso   tal segn se dé mostrar: / Le oss de tug li morti   devran tut resustar. / So le soe sepulture apparegiae den star / E l'ora dra sententia   illó den aspegiar" (37–40). Then he mentions it again at the end of the poem, when he speaks about the renewal of the world that will take place on the fifteenth day: "Lo quindesen di apresso,   segond ke fi cuintao, / Tuta la terra e l'airo   firá tut renovao, / Lo mond firá fag novo,   e zascun hom k'è nao / Col so proprïo corpo   devrá ess resustao" (49–52). The image of resurrection concludes the poem and is thus presented—as in the *De die Iudicii*—as a bridge between the signs preceding the judgment and the judgment proper. I quote the texts of the *De quindecim miraculis* and *De die Iudicii* from Gianfranco Contini, ed., *Le opere Volgari di Bonvesin da la Riva* (Rome: Società Filologica Romana, 1941), where they are found on pp. 192–94 and 195–210, respectively. Translations are mine. For making sense of Bonvesin's often obscure language, one work proves very useful: Fabio Marri, *Glossario al milanese di Bonvesin* (Bologna: Patron, 1977).

37. See note 32 above.

38. These lines are merely a summary of the dialogue, which is relayed in the preceding lines (185–204). Such mutual hatred will define the relations of all hell's sinners to one another. Brothers, Cathars, believers, heretics, innkeepers, adulterers, prostitutes, princes, nobles, and thieves will all be punished together and hate one another (209–16):

Entri fraëi ha esse   la semeiant rüina,
L'un se trará co l'oltro   entr' infernal sentina

E 'l gazar col credhente   plen de malvax doctrina,
E i compagnion dri vitii   staran in tal rüina.

Li taverné insema,   li gazar coi credhenti,
L'adoltro e la meltrix,   li princip coi poënti,
Li fuiri co le fuire,   tug peccaor nocenti
Firan punidhi insem   a semeiant tormenti.

39. See Colleen McDannell and Bernhard Lang, *Heaven: A History* (New Haven: Yale University Press, 1988), 90ff. For the individuality of Bernard of Clairvaux's heaven, see Anna Harrison, "Community Among the Saints in Heaven in Bernard of Clairvaux's *Sermons for the Feasts of All Saints*," in *Last Things: Death and Apocalyse in the Middle Ages,* ed. Caroline Walker Bynum and Paul Freedman (Philadelphia: University of Pennsylvania Press, 1991), 191–204; and Bynum, *The Resurrection of the Body,* 303.

40. I quote the text of the *De anima cum corpore* from Contini's edition, 54–76. The English translation of the *De anima cum corpore,* which I use with slight modifications, is found in Bonvesin, *Volgari scelti,* 133–202.

41. After a dialogue among the limbs, the heart, and the eyes, the heart is deemed responsible because it has power over all the other parts of the body.

42. For a reading of the poem as a whole, see my article "From Decay to Splendor: Body and Pain in Bonvesin da la Riva's *Book of the Three Scriptures*," in *Last Things,* 83–97. In the current book, where I connect Bonvesin to Dante, I have preferred to divide my analysis of the *Book of the Three Scriptures* into two parts: one concerning the dialectic between different eschatological emphases in the *Black* and *Golden Scriptures,* and one regarding the transforming power of pain and the relationship between the *Red Scripture* and the *Purgatorio.*

43. While Giacomino's *De Babilonia* and *De Jerusalem* were two separate poems, these lines make clear that the three sections of Bonvesin's poem, represented by the three scriptures, are not independent of one another but are, on the contrary, intimately connected: the opposition lies between the fear of black and the fair purity of gold, and the transition between the two is red. I quote from Contini's edition of the *Book of the Three Scriptures,* which is found on pp. 101–76. I use, with slight modifications, Diehl and Stefanini's translation in Bonvesin, *Volgari scelti,* 133–202.

44. Sixten Ringbom, *Icon to Narrative: The Rise of the Dramatic Close-up in Fifteenth-Century Devotional Painting* (Åbo: Åbo Akademi, 1965), 12–13.

45. Phillipe Ariès, *Western Attitudes toward Death: From the Middle Ages to the Present,* trans. Patricia Ranum (Baltimore: Johns Hopkins University Press, 1974), 39–46. See also Johan Huizinga, *The Waning of the Middle Ages: A Study of the Forms of Life, Thought, and Art in France and the Netherlands in the XIV and XV Centuries,* trans. F. Hopman (London: Arnold, 1924; reprint, Garden City, N.Y.: Doubleday, 1956); and Alberto Tenenti, *Il senso della morte e l'amore della vita nel Rinascimento* (Turin: Einaudi, 1957).

46. In this section of the poem, the contrast between earthly and heavenly elements remains implicit, and Bonvesin's way of arguing relies on a common background of emotions, images, fears, and hopes, which would have enabled the public to make connections that become explicit elsewhere in the poem. Listeners would have repeatedly heard the doctrine of the contempt for the world in sermons, and would also have expected to find discussions of the glory of creation and of man in the final part of the argument. (See Caroline Walker Bynum, "Why All the Fuss about the Body? A Medievalist's Perspective," *Critical Inquiry* 22 [Autumn 1995]: 14.) The doctrine of *contemptus mundi* was strongly connected with the ambiguity of the biblical term "world," which could indicate the reign of Satan—which had started with the Fall and is characterized by sin, death, and continuous corruption—but could at the same time designate both humanity and the earth in which men live as creations of God (Delumeau, *Sin and Fear*, 11–12). In spite of sin, the universe created by God continues to demonstrate the greatness and the goodness of the Creator and will be fully regenerated on the Last Day. The redemption of humanity began with Christ's Passion but will be completed only at the end of time, when the perfection and the purity of the original condition, which were lost because of Adam's sin, will be recovered. This is the mental frame that organizes not only the *De contemptu mundi* but also the whole *Book of the Three Scriptures*.

47. The idea of the soul's personal judgment after physical death was fully elaborated in the second half of the twelfth century and became widespread in the thirteenth century. See Santi, "Un nome di persona al corpo e la massa dei corpi gloriosi," *Micrologus* 1 (1993): 274. See also Philippe Ariès, *L'homme devant la mort* (Paris: Editions du Sevil, 1977), 109–12; and Colomon Viola, "Jugements de Dieu et jugement dernier," in *The Use and Abuse of Eschatology in the Middle Ages*, ed. Werner Verbeke et al. (Leuven: Leuven University Press, 1988), where the author argues that, even though Scholastic theologians affirmed the doctrine of individual judgment explicitly, some notions of it were already present in Augustine's philosophy.

48. One of the passages that illustrates most clearly the belief that the separated soul is tormented by material fire is Hugh of St. Victor's *De sacramentis*, bk. 2, pt. 16, chap. 3 (PL 176, col. 584):

> Quidam putant animas corporalibus poenis cruciari non posse, nisi per corpora et in corporibus manentes. Quapropter a corporibus exutas animas nullas alias poenas sustinere credunt. . . . Sed verissime auctoritate sacri eloquii et catholicae veritatis probatur testimonio, corporali et materiali igne animas etiam nunc ante susceptionem corporum cruciari.

"Quod anima separata nullo modo patiatur ab igne" is proposition 19, which was condemned in Paris in 1277. See Robert Klein, "L'enfer de Ficino," in *Umanesimo e esoterismo*, ed. Enrico Castelli (Padua: Cedam, 1960), 63; and Bynum, *The Resurrection of the Body*, 281.

49. The olfactory sense is highlighted in the second torment, which consists of the great stench surrounding the sinner (329–72); sight is stressed in the fifth punishment, which is the vision of the miserable faces of the other damned and of the devils' horrible and frightening figures (433–92); hearing is emphasized in the sixth pain, which consists of the doleful voices, the weeping and the uproar that the damned are unremittingly forced to bear (493–536). If taste is not mentioned explicitly, it seems nonetheless implied in the hunger and thirst of the eighth torment, where, instead of bread, the sinners eat burning coals, and, instead of water, they drink molten bronze (653–704). Other punishments deal with touch and with the physical pain that the sinner experiences when he is beaten and wounded. The fourth punishment, for instance, consists of venomous worms that "poison the sinner with the worst of bites" (405) and torment all his limbs. The ninth pain is the grievous roughness of garments, which are woven of thorn and brambles, and of bedding, which consists of burning irons, scorpions, adders, and sulfur (705–44).

50. In his commentary to *Volgari scelti*, Stefanini differentiates Bonvesin's souls from those inhabiting Dante's *Comedy* (Bonvesin, *Volgari scelti*, 129):

> Bonvesin's sinner . . . is still the "representative for his species," Everyman or Every-damned, and therefore capable of committing all crimes and suffering all punishments. Only Dante, fortified by his reading of the classics, will succeed in replacing this didactic mask with the individual and historical reality of his characters.

We will see in chapters 2 and 4 that the individuality of the souls of the *Comedy* is connected not only with Dante's knowledge of the classics but also with his philosophical background, which allows him to exploit the most updated Scholastic doctrines.

51. For a chart that contrasts them, see Bonvesin, *Volgari scelti*, 127–28.

52. See my article "From Decay to Splendor," 88–90.

53. The reference to the beginning of the poem is so explicit that the comparison between the two parts of the poem is virtually required of the audience. For instance, the "gran beltae del iusto   ke mai no dessomente" (the great beauty of the just man which never fails [601]) is the opposite of "beltae mondana" (the earthly beauty in *Black Scripture* 110). "Li membri tugi quangi   strabei e straformai" (all the very fair and well-formed limbs [616]) contrasts with the "membra flevre e lasse," the weak and slack limbs of man in *Black Scripture* 31. Lines 617–32 describe the balanced perfection of the blessed soul's body and explicitly represent a counterpart to *Black Scripture* 77–80. The affirmation that in heaven everybody is beautiful both inside and out (631) recalls the opposition between beautiful aspect and interior rottenness in *Black Scripture* 41–48. The detail of the fragrant breath of the blessed (632) contrasts with the image of the spittle and slime that come from the mouth of man in *Black Scripture* 50.

54. Theologians discussed at length the age at which we will resurrect and generally agreed that everyone's resurrected body will be that which he or she had or would have had at the age of thirty. Of course, the paradigm for everyone's resurrection is Christ. Peter Lombard, for instance, states that the resurrection body of the blessed will be not only young but also perfected and cured from its earthly defects (*Sententiae*, bk. 4, distinction 44, chap. 1, where the Lombard goes back to Augustine's *De civitate Dei* 2.15). One of the most interesting and influential discussions of the resurrected body is found in Augustine's *Enchiridion* (chaps. 85 and 87) and deals with the fate of abortive conceptions and monstrous births. But the passage that Bonvesin is translating into a more popular understanding is probably the end of Bonaventure's *Breviloquium* (part 7, chap. 5; in *The Works of Bonaventure*, trans. José de Vinck [Paterson, N.J.: St. Anthony Guild Press, 1963], 2:296–97):

> Now, perfect grace conforms us to Christ our Head, in whom there was no physical imperfection, but perfect age, due stature, and comely appearance. Therefore it is fitting that the good be raised in a state as perfect as possible, implying the removal of any imperfection and the fulfillment of natural integrity, any missing portion being restored, any excess growth eliminated, and any malfunctioning corrected. Those who died in childhood are to be raised by divine power at an age corresponding to that of Christ at His resurrection, although not "with exactly the same bodily size." The old and the wasted shall be restored to that same age. Giants and dwarfs shall be given proper stature. Thus all shall come forth, whole and perfect, to *perfect manhood, to the mature measure of the fullness of Christ.*

CHAPTER 2   Embryology and Aerial Bodies in Dante's *Comedy*

1. "Est ergo subiectum totius operis, litteraliter tantum accepti, status animarum post mortem simpliciter sumptus; nam de illo et circa illum totius operis versatur processus" (24), in Dante Alighieri, *Epistole*, in *Opere minori*, ed. Arsenio Frugoni and Giorgio Brugnoli (Milan: Ricciardi, 1989), 2:612.

2. Citations from the *Comedy* are from *"La Commedia" secondo l'antica vulgata*, ed. Giorgio Petrocchi (Milan: Mondadori, 1966–67).

3. While Bonvesin lingers on the deaths of the sinner and the just man because he aims at the immediate conversion of his audience, throughout the *Comedy* and especially in the first cantos of the *Purgatorio*, Dante stresses instead the possibility of repentance that everybody has until the very last moment of his or her earthly existence. Manfred, for instance, makes it clear that, no matter how abominable the crimes one might have committed, it is possible to repent at the very last minute of one's life and thereby be forgiven by God: "Poscia ch'io ebbi

rotta la persona / di due punte mortali, io mi rendei, / piangendo, a quei che volentier perdona. / Orribil furon li peccati miei; / ma la bontà infinita ha sì gran braccia, / che prende ciò che si rivolge a lei" (*Purg.* 3.118–22). Likewise, the possibility of repenting and thereby attaining salvation just before dying is stressed, among those who died a violent death, by Iacopo del Cassero: "Noi fummo tutti già per forza morti, / e peccatori infino a l'ultima ora; / quivi lume del ciel ne fece accorti, / sì che, pentendo e perdonando, fora / di vita uscimmo a Dio pacificati, / che del desio di sé veder n'accora" (*Purg.* 5.52–57).

4. Translations are, with occasional changes, from Dante Alighieri, *The Divine Comedy,* trans. Charles S. Singleton (Princeton: Princeton University Press, 1970–75; repr. 1977). For other passages mentioning Minos's judgment, see *Inf.* 13.94–96, where Pier de la Vigna tells what happens to the souls of those who have committed suicide: "Quando si parte l'anima feroce / dal corpo ond' ella stessa s'è divelta, / Minòs la manda a la settima foce"; and 27.124–29, where Guido da Montefeltro narrates his own encounter with the infernal judge: "A Minòs mi portò; e quelli attorse / otto volte la coda al dosso duro; / e poi che per gran rabbia la si morse, / disse: 'Questi è d'i' rei del foco furo'; / per ch'io là dove vedi son perduto, / e sì vestito, andando, mi rancuro." It seems that only the neutrals (who are punished outside of hell proper) and the souls condemned to limbo (which is the first circle of hell) go to their punishment without being judged by Minos.

5. See *Purg.* 2.104–5: "sempre quivi [alla foce del Tevere] si ricoglie / qual verso Acheronte non si cala."

6. This is Dante's typical strategy to have the reader suspend disbelief. See Teodolinda Barolini, *The Undivine "Comedy": Detheologizing Dante* (Princeton: Princton University Press, 1992), 3–20. On the discrepancy between Scholastic theologians and contemporary descriptions of the afterlife, see chap. 1, n. 26, above.

7. Etienne Gilson, "Qu'est-ce qu'une ombre? (Dante, Purg. XXV)," in *Dante et Béatrice: Études dantesques* (Paris: Vrin, 1974), 22–45 (previously published as the first part of "Trois études dantesques pour le VIIe centenaire de la naissance de Dante," *Archives d'histoire doctrinale et littéraire du moyen âge* 40 [1965]: 72–93); idem, "Ombre et luci dans la Divine Comédie," *in Dante et Béatrice,* 47–65 (previously published as the second part of "Trois études dantesques," *Archives d'histoire doctrinale et littéraire du moyen âge* 40 [1965]: 94–111); idem, "Dante's Notion of a Shade: *Purgatorio* XXV," *Mediaeval Studies* 29 (1967): 124–42. Marianne Shapiro further develops Gilson's ideas in "Dante's Twofold Representation of the Soul," *Lectura Dantis* 18–19 (Spring–Fall 1996): 49–90 (now the fourth chapter of Marianne Shapiro, *Dante and the Knot of Body and Soul* [New York: St. Martin's Press, 1998], 161–97).

8. Virgil can only remind the pilgrim of two facts—one from Ovid's *Metamorphoses* (8.260–65) and one from contemporary science—but is unable to give a

real explanation (*Purg.* 25.22–27). Once again, Dante is expressing his poetic debt to Vergil and, at the same time, his superiority to him. For the dialectical relationship between Dante and Vergil, see Teodolinda Barolini, *Dante's Poets: Textuality and Truth in the "Comedy"* (Princeton: Princeton University Press, 1984), 201–56.

9. Giovanni Busnelli's major works on the soul in Dante are: *Cosmogonia e antropogenesi secondo Dante Alighieri e le sue fonti* (Rome: Civiltà Cattolica, 1922), 97–297, and the tenth appendix ("L'origine dell'anima razionale") in Dante Alighieri, *Il Convivio ridotto a miglior lezione e commentato da G. Busnelli e G. Vandelli*, ed. Antonio E. Quaglio (Florence: Le Monnier, 1964; 1st ed. 1934), 392–404. Bruno Nardi's major writings on the soul are: "L'origine dell'anima umana secondo Dante," in *Studi di filosofia medievale* (Rome: Edizioni di storia e letteratura, 1960), 9–6 (first published in *Giornale critico della filosofia italiana* 12 [1931]: 433–56, and 13 [1932]: 45–56 and 81–102); "Il canto XXV del *Purgatorio*," in *Letture dantesche*, vol. 2, *Purgatorio*, ed. Giovanni Getto (Florence: Sansoni, 1966; 1st ed. 1964), 1173–91; "Raffronti fra alcuni luoghi di Alberto Magno e di Dante," in *Saggi di filosofia dantesca* (Florence: La Nuova Italia, 1967), 63–72 (1st ed. 1930, but the article first appeared in *Giornale storico della letteratura italiana* 80 [1922]: 295–303); "Il tomismo di Dante e il padre Busnelli S.J.," in ibid., 341–80 (first published in a slightly different form in *Giornale storico della letteratura italiana* 81 [1923]); "Sull'origine dell'anima umana," in *Dante e la cultura medievale*, ed. Paolo Mazzantini (Rome: Laterza, 1990), 207–24 (1st ed. 1942, but the article had already been published in *Giornale dantesco* 39 [1938]: 15–28).

10. See, for instance, the explicit formulation in "Meditantur sua stercora scarabei," *Nuovo giornale dantesco* 4 (1920): 62: "che l'unica anima umana sia forma sostanziale del corpo, Dante non asserisce e non nega in nessun luogo."

11. Gilson demolishes Busnelli's commentary to Dante's *Convivio* with the following words: "Il est difficile d'imaginer un commentaire mieux fait pour obscurcir le sens de son texte. Ce genre d'attentat historique devrait être interdit par une loi" (review of Bruno Nardi, *Dal "Convivio" alla "Commedia" [Sei saggi danteschi]*, *Giornale storico della letteratura italiana* 138 [1961]: 562–73 [quotation on 572]). He argues, however, that Statius's account in *Purg.* 25 is fully Thomistic ("Qu'est-ce qu'une ombre?" and "Dante's Notion of a Shade").

Foster's quotation is from "Tommaso d'Aquino," *Enciclopedia Dantesca* (Rome: Istituto della Enciclopedia Italiana G. Treccani, 1976), 5:645. Ernesto Travi has subsequently hinted at the possibility that Statius's explanation lies in between Bonaventure's hypothesis of plurality of forms and Aquinas's doctrine of unicity of form ("Il tema del corpo nella *Divina Commedia*," in *Il corpo in scena: La rappresentazione del corpo nella filosofia e nelle arti*, ed. Virgilio Melchiorre and Annamaria Cascetta [Milan: Vita e Pensiero, 1983], 199–203). Both Efrem Bettoni ("Anima," *Enciclopedia Dantesca*, 1970, 1:278–85) and Alfredo Maierù ("Forma," in *Enciclopedia Dantesca*, 1970, 2:969–75) follow Nardi. Other good readings of *Purg.* 25 that follow Nardi are: Fernando Figurelli, "Il canto XXV del *Purgatorio*," in *Nuove letture dantesche* (Florence: Le Monnier, 1972), 5:33–67; Giorgio Padoan, "Il canto XXV del *Purgatorio*," in *Purgatorio. Letture degli anni 1976–79* (Rome: Bonacci, 1981), 577–600; Tobia R. Toscano, "Il canto XXV del *Purgatorio*," in *La tragedia degli ipocriti e altre letture dantesche* (Naples: Liguori, 1988), 85–105; Elvio Guagnini, "Canto XXV," in *Purgatorio,* ed. Pompeo Giannantonio (Naples: Loffredo, 1989), 487–503.

Both Patrick Boyde (*Dante Philomythes and Philosopher: Man in the Cosmos* [Cambridge: Cambridge University Press, 1981], 271–80) and Stephen Bemrose ("'Come d'animal divegna fante': The Animation of the Human Embryo in Dante," in *The Human Embryo: Aristotle and the Arabic and European Tradition,* ed. G. R. Dunstan [Exeter: University of Exeter Press, 1990], 123–35) have commented on the passage of *Purgatorio* 25 with great knowledge and subtlety but have not referred to the debate between plurality and unicity of form, which I deem crucial for a thorough understanding of the passage and its implications. For a recent reading of Statius's account, see Marc Cogan, *The Design in the Wax* (Notre Dame, Ind.: University of Notre Dame Press, 1999), 129–40.

12. See J. M. Da Cruz Pontes, "Le problème de l'origine de l'âme de la patristique à la solution thomiste," *Recherches de théologie ancienne et médiévale* 31 (1964): 175–229, esp. 197–229.

13. See Daniel Callus, "The Problem of the Plurality of Forms in the Thirteenth Century: The Thomist Innovation," in *L'homme et son destin d'après les penseurs du moyen âge. Actes du premier congrès international de philosophie médiévale: Louvain-Bruxelles, 28 Aoûte–4 Septembre 1958* (Louvain: Nauwelaerts, 1960), 577–80; idem, "The Origin of the Problem of the Unity of Form," *The Thomist* 24 (1961): 258.

14. Richard C. Dales, *The Problem of the Rational Soul in the Thirteenth Century* (Leiden: E. J. Brill, 1995), 99. The principles of the two different positions and all their implications were progressively made clear through the philosophical debate that started during Thomas Aquinas's second regency in Paris (1269–72), became inflamed after his death (1274), and continued until the first decades of the fourteenth century. See Daniel Callus, "Forms, Unicity and Plurality of," *New Catholic Encyclopedia* (New York: McGraw-Hill, 1967), 5:1025.

For the controversy, I have used idem, "The Problem of the Plurality of Forms in the Thirteenth Century," 577–85; idem, "The Origins of the Problem of the Unity of Form," 257–85; A. Michel, "Forme du corps humain," *Dictionnaire de théologie catholique* (Paris: Letouzey et Ané, 1915), 6:546–88, esp. 569–78; Roberto Zavalloni, *Richard de Mediavilla et la controverse sur la pluralité des formes* (Louvain: Éditions de l'Institut Supérieur de Philosophie, 1951); Etienne Gilson, *History of Christian Philosophy in the Middle Ages* (New York: Random House, 1955), 416–20; Pasquale Mazzarella, *Controversie medievali: Unità e pluralità delle forme* (Naples: Giannini, 1978); Bernardo C. Bazán, "La corporalité selon saint Thomas," *Revue philosophique de Louvain* 4th ser., no. 51 (1983): 369–400; Francesco Santi, "Il cadavere e Bonifacio VIII, tra Stefano Tempier e Avicenna: Intorno a un saggio di Elisabeth Brown," *Studi medievali* ser. 3, 28, 2 (1987): 861–78; Edouard-Henri Weber,

La personne humaine au XIIIe siècle: L'avènement chez les maîtres parisiens de l'acception moderne de l'homme (Paris: J. Vrin, 1991), 74–198; Caroline Walker Bynum, *The Resurrection of the Body in Western Christianity, 200–1336* (New York: Columbia University Press, 1995), 256–65 and 269–76; Dales, *The Problem of the Rational Soul.*

15. Callus, "Forms, Unicity and Plurality of," 1024. See also Dales, *The Problem of the Rational Soul,* 1–2.

16. See Richard Heinzmann, *Die Unsterblichkeit der Seele und die Auferstehung des Leibes: Eine problemgeschichtliche Untersuchung der frühscholastischen Sentenzen- und Summenliteratur von Anselm von Laon bis Wilhelm von Auxerre* (Münster: Aschendorff, 1965); idem, "Was ist der Mensch? Zu einer Grundfrage des mittel-alterlichen Denkens," *Theologie und Philosophie* 49 (1974): 542–47; and Bynum, *The Resurrection of the Body,* 135–36 (and n. 59 on p. 135 for bibliography).

17. See Dorothea E. Sharp, *Franciscan Philosophy at Oxford in the Thirteenth Century* (London: Oxford University Press, 1930), 155–59 (for Bacon), 185–91 (for Peckham), and 234–48 (for Richard of Middleton). See also Dales, *The Problem of the Rational Soul,* 75–78 (for Bacon), 100–102 (for Bonaventure), and 128 (for Peckham).

18. See Etienne Gilson, *The Philosophy of St. Bonaventure,* 2nd ed. trans. Dom I. Trethowan (London: Sheed & Ward, 1949), 315–40. Gilson makes clear that, even though Bonaventure does not use the term "plurality of forms" ex-plicitly, his philosophical system follows all the principles of that doctrine. See also Philip L. Reynolds, *Food and the Body: Some Peculiar Questions in High Me-dieval Theology* (Leiden: Brill, 1999), 348; Sofia Vanni Rovighi, *San Bonaventura* (Milan: Vita e Pensiero, 1974), 67–81; Mazzarella, *Controversie medievali,* 63 and 277–87. Of course, the matter of the soul is spiritual matter. See Frederick Copleston, *A History of Philosophy,* vol. 2, *Medieval Philosophy: Augustine to Scotus* (Westmin-ster, Md.: Newman Press, 1950), 278–80. For the "controversial notion" of spiritual matter that most pluralists (have to) accept, see Robert Pasnau, "Olivi on the Metaphysics of the Soul," *Medieval Philosophy and Theology* 6 (1997): 122–26. For my understanding of the anthropological conceptions that were implied in the doc-trines of plurality and unicity, I have found most useful Bynum, *The Resurrection of the Body,* esp. 229–78; and Dales, *The Problem of the Rational Soul,* esp. 99–112.

19. Bonnie Kent, *Virtues of the Will: The Transformation of Ethics in the Late Thirteenth Century* (Washington, D.C.: Catholic University of America Press, 1995), 214–15.

20. For the attention that those who assume plurality of form show toward bodiliness, see Santi, "Il cadavere e Bonifacio VIII," esp. 869–72; and David L. d'Avray, "Some Franciscan Ideas about the Body," in *Modern Questions about Medieval Sermons: Essays on Marriage, Death, History and Society,* ed. Nicole Bérion and David L. d'Avray (Spoleto: Centro Italiano di Studi sull'alto Medioevo, 1994), 155–74.

21. One of the strongest concerns of those who assumed plurality of forms was to defend the unity of the soul. See Zavalloni, *Richard de Mediavilla,* 319–30;

Dales, *The Problem of the Rational Soul,* 195; Pasnau, "Olivi on the Metaphysics of the Soul," 129. For Aquinas's attacks on the doctrine of plurality on the basis that to assume several substantial forms in any compound—including the human being—would be irreconcilable with its unity, see Zavalloni, *Richard de Mediavilla,* 255 and 269; Callus, "The Problem of the Plurality of Forms," 583; Bazàn, "La corporalité selon saint Thomas," 395.

22. See Bynum, *The Resurrection of the Body,* 256–57.

23. "Deus in productione corpus animae alligavit, et naturali et mutuo appetitu invicem copulavit; . . . nec naturalis appetituts patitur, quod anima sit plene beata, nisi restituatur ei corpus, ad quod resumendum habet inclinationem naturaliter insertam" (in *Bonaventurae opera omnia,* ed. A. C. Peltier [Paris: Vivès, 1866], 7:340–41; my translation). As Richard Dales formulates about Bonaventure's conception of body and soul, "Each [i.e., soul and body] is composed of its own matter and form, but in neither case is the appetite of either one exhausted by its own matter and form; each has a remaining appetite to be joined to the other, the soul to perfect the body, the body to be perfected by the soul. It is in the composite that each one finds its highest development" (*The Problem of the Rational Soul,* 102). See also Bynum (*The Resurrection of the Body,* 248–51), who points out that Bonaventure does not always affirm or imply that the desire between body and soul is mutual. While he never questions the soul's desire for the body, he "remains unwilling to decide how far matter or body yearns for soul."

24. The fact that the separated soul of the blessed could enjoy the vision of God had been a commonplace since 1241, when the bishop of Paris, William of Auvergne, and the masters of the faculty of theology had explicitly affirmed: "Firmiter credimus et asserimus, quod Deus in sua essentia vel substantia videbitur ab angelis et omnibus sanctis et videtur ab animabus glorificatis." See X. Le Bachelet, "Benoit XII," *Dictionnaire de théologie catholique,* 2:691; and H.-F. Dondaine, "L'objet et le 'medium' de la vision béatifique chez les théologiens du XIIIᵉ siècle," *Recherches de théologie ancienne et médiévale* 19 (1952): 60–99.

25. See Bynum, *The Resurrection of the Body,* 248–55.

26. In the *De Genesi ad litteram,* Augustine wondered how it can be that the souls cannot enjoy the beatific vision without the body, as angels can: if the mind can enjoy beatitude on its own, why is the resurrection of the body necessary for the attainment of beatitude? Augustine argued that it is certain that the human mind, both with the earthly body and when it is separated from it, cannot see God the way angels do, either for some obscure cause or because the soul has within it the desire to administer its body, which distracts it from full beatitude until that desire is fulfilled. Only with the resumption of the resurrected body will the beatific vision be as perfect as the angels' (*De Genesi ad litteram* 12.35 [PL 34.483 f.]):

. . . dubium non est, et raptam a carnis sensibus hominis mentem, et post mortem ipsa carne deposita non sic videre posse incommutabilem substantiam, id est, Deum, sicut sancti angeli vident, sive alia latentiori causa, sive ideo quia inest ei naturalis quidam appetitus corpus administrandi, quo retardatur quodam modo, ne tota intentione pergat in illud summum coelum, donec ille appetitus conquiescat. Porro si tale sit corpus, cujus sit difficilis et gravis administratio, sicut haec caro, quae corrumpitur, multo magis avertitur mens ab illa visione summi coeli. Proinde cum hoc corpus jam non animale, sed spirituale receperit, aequata angelis habebit perfectum naturae suae modum, obediens et imperans, vivificata, et vivificans, tam ineffabili facilitate, ut sit ei gloriae, quod fuit sarcinae.

For Augustine's concept of *retardatio,* see Simon Tugwell, *Human Immortality and the Redemption of Death* (London: Darton, Longman and Todd, 1990), 116; and Bynum, *The Resurrection of the Body,* 97.

27. "Et beatitudo non esset consummata, nisi personaliter ibi esset, et persona non est anima, sed coniunctum: patet, quod secundum coniunctum, id est corpus et animam, ibi est; alioquin consummatam non haberet fruitionem, quia, secundum Augustinum, 'mentes sanctorum ex naturali inclinatione sui ad corpus retardantur quodam modo, ne totae ferantur in Deum'" (Martin Jugie, *La mort et l'assomption de la Sainte Vierge: Étude historico-doctrinale* [Vatican City: Biblioteca Apostolica Vaticana, 1944], 40). The English translation in the main text is from Bynum, "Material Continuity, Personal Survival and the Resurrection of the Body: A Scholastic Discussion in Its Medieval and Modern Context," in *Fragmentation and Redemption: Essays on Gender and the Human Body in Medieval Religion* (New York: Zone Books, 1992), 257.

For the positive vision of the body and the importance of the doctrine of the resurrection of the body in Franciscan sermons of the later Middle Ages, see d'Avray, "Some Franciscan Ideas about the Body."

28. "Concedendum est igitur, quod glorificatio corporis facit ad maius gaudium quantum ad extensionem; facit etiam quantum ad intensionem, non augendo habitum, sed removendo impedimentum" (*Sentence commentary,* bk. 4. dist. 49, pt.2, art. 1, sect. 1, q. 1 [in *Bonaventurae opera omnia,* ed. Peltier, 6: 579]). See Christian Trottmann, "Deux interprétations contradictoires de Saint Bernard: Les sermons de Jean XXII sur la vision béatifique et les traités inédits du cardinal Jacques Fournier," *Mélanges de l'École Française de Rome: Moyen Age* 105 (1993): 367–68.

29. Although some scholars, including Zavalloni, tend to consider Albert as expressing plurality, it seems now certain that Albert followed the doctrine of unicity of form, though not yet as forcefully or consistently as Aquinas. See Sofia Vanni Rovighi, "Alberto Magno e l'unità della forma sostanziale nell'uomo," in *Medioevo e Rinascimento: Studi in onore di Bruno Nardi* (Florence: Sansoni, 1955), 2:753–78; Mazzarella, *Controversie medievali,* 271–72; Weber, *La personne humaine,* 120–39; Callus, "The Problem of the Plurality of Forms"; Bynum, *The Resurrection of the Body,* 262–64.

30. "Dicendum est quod nulla alia forma substantialis est in homine nisi sola anima intellectiva; et quod ipsa, sicut virtute continet omnes inferiores formas, et facit ipsa sola quidquid imperfectiores formae in aliis faciunt." Citations of the Latin text are from the *Summa theologiae* (which will be indicated with the abbreviation "ST"), and their translations are from the Blackfriars edition (New York: McGraw-Hill, 1964–81).

31. "In hoc homine non est alia forma substantialis quam anima rationalis, et per eam homo non solum est homo, sed animal et vivum et corpus et substantia et ens" (in *Thomae Aquinatis opera omnia,* ed. S. Fretté [Paris: Vivès, 1875], 14:19); my translation.

32. The same idea that the soul contains the body is made explicit by Aquinas when he discusses whether all the limbs of the human body will be resurrected. Aquinas writes that the soul originally and implicitly contains everything that appears in the parts of the body, and that man cannot be perfect unless the body expresses externally what the soul contains implicitly:

> Et similiter quidquid in partibus corporis apparet, totum originaliter et quodammodo implicite in anima continetur. . . . nec homo posset esse perfectus nisi totum quod in anima implicite continetur, exterius in corpore explicaretur: nec enim corpus animae ad plenum proportionaliter responderet. Cum ergo oporteat in resurrectione corpus hominis esse animae totaliter correspondens, quia non resurget nisi secundum ordinem quem habet ad animam rationalem; oporteat etiam hominem perfectum resurgere, utpote qui ad ultimam perfectionem consequendam reparatur: oportet quod omnia membra quae nunc sunt in corpore, in resurrectione hominis reparentur.

> In like manner whatever appears in the parts of the body is all contained originally and, in a way, implicitly in the soul. . . . neither could man be perfect, unless the whole that is contained enfolded in the soul be outwardly unfolded in the body, nor would the body correspond in full proportion to the soul. Since then at the resurrection it behooves man's body to correspond entirely to the soul, for it will not rise again except according to the relation it bears to the rational soul, it follows that man must also rise again perfect, seeing that he is thereby repaired in order that he may obtain his ultimate perfection. Consequently all the members that are now in man's body must needs be restored at the resurrection.

Quoted from: *Supplementum,* q. 80, a. 1, resp.; in *Sancti Thomae Aquinatis doctoris angelici opera omnia iussu impensaque Leonis XIII p.m. edita* (Rome: S. C. de Propaganda Fide, 1906), 12:181 (this ed. henceforth "ed. Leonine"); and St. Thomas Aquinas, *Summa theologica,* trans. Fathers of the English Dominican Province

(New York: Benzinger Brothers, 1948), 3:2894. The *Supplementum* was put together by Aquinas's disciple Reginald of Piperno with material from the Sentence commentary after his master's death. See Bynum, *The Resurrection of the Body*, 234 n. 18.

33. "Che la *mens* fosse l'unica anima, che non ci fossero nell'uomo tre anime (vegetativa, sensitiva e intellettiva) era comunemente ammesso dai teologi del XIII secolo, ma tutti (salvo, credo, Alberto Magno) ammettevano che l'anima intellettiva si unisse a un corpo già formato, che nell'uomo ci fossero, precisamente, anima e corpo. Tommaso afferma invece che l'anima intellettiva è l'unica forma sostanziale nell'uomo, il che voleva dire che l'anima intellettiva non è solo il principio per cui l'uomo conosce intellettivamente, ma è anche ciò per cui l'uomo ha un determinato colore degli occhi; voleva dire sottolineare al massimo l'unità dell'uomo in tutti i suoi aspetti" (*Introduzione a Tommaso d'Aquino*, 6th ed. [Rome-Bari: Laterza, 1995; 1st ed. 1973], 94–95).

34. In *Opera omnia*, ed. Leonine (1930), 15:286.

35. "Manifestum est quod animae sanctorum separatae a corporibus ambulant per speciem, Dei essentiam videntes, in quo est vera beatitudo."

36. *Human Immortality*, 152–53; see also 149–51. Aquinas seems at ease when he emphasizes the perfection of the beatific vision of the saintly soul but less consistent when he speaks about its improvement at resurrection. See Tugwell, ibid., where he says that for Aquinas, "the resurrection . . . inevitably appears as rather an embarrassment"; Patrick Quinn, "Aquinas's Concept of the Body and Out of Body Situations," *Heythrop Journal* 34 (1993): 398; Bynum, *The Resurrection of the Body*, 266–68.

37. Aquinas's position regarding the increase of the beatific vision with the resurrection of the body fluctuates in the course of his life. In his early *Sentence* commentary, he does not argue for a "substantial" improvement but nonetheless speaks, like Bonaventure, of both an "extensive" and an "intensive" increase (bk. IV, d. 49, q. 1, a. 4). Progressively, however, Aquinas stresses that the saintly soul can enjoy perfect happiness even before the Resurrection. See John Weakland, "Pope John XXII and the Beatific Vision Controversy," *Annuale Mediaevale* 9 (1968): 79 n. 12; Marc Dykmans, *Pour et contre Jean XXII en 1333: Deux traités avignonnais sur la vision béatifique* (Vatican City: Biblioteca Apostolica Vaticana, 1975), 15 and 50; Trottmann, "Deux intérpretations," 368–69; Tugwell, *Human Immortality*, 149–53; Bynum, *The Resurrection of the Body*, 236. Moreover, as Bynum has pointed out, Aquinas states in some passages that the saintly soul is happier when it is reunited with its body. When he discusses epistemology, he furthermore seems to suggest that even in heaven humans need body for full knowledge, because without the body the soul would be able to understand the universal principles but would lack the capacity to grasp the particulars (*The Resurrection of the Body*, 266ff.). However, Aquinas does not develop what the resurrected body adds to the soul's knowledge, and in other passages he also contrasts intellectual knowledge on earth—which

passes through the senses and cannot grasp God's essence—and the separated soul's intuitive knowledge, which does not occur through the mediation of any image and does not need the senses fully to attain the beatific vision. See Christian Trottmann, "Sulla funzione dell'anima e del corpo nella beatitudine: Elementi di riflessione nella Scolastica," in *Anima e corpo nella cultura medievale. Atti del V Convegno di studi della Società italiana per lo Studio del Pensiero Medievale: Venezia, 25–28 settembre 1995,* ed. Carla Casagrande and Silvana Vecchio (Florence: Sismel–Edizioni del Galluzzo, 1999), 140–47.

38. See, for instance, Bruno Nardi, "Anima e corpo nel pensiero di San Tommaso," in *Studi di filosofia medievale* (Rome: Edizioni di storia e letteratura, 1960), 176: "La tesi tomistica [of unicity of form] ci appare il più originale tentativo di superare il dualismo platonico." On Aquinas's anthropology, see Sophia Vanni Rovighi, *L'antropologia filosofica di San Tommaso d'Aquino* (Milan: Vita e Pensiero, 1965), esp. 35–61; Horst Seidl, "Zur Leib-Seele-Einheit des Menschen bei Thomas von Aquin," *Theologie und Philosophie* 49 (1974): 548–53; Bazán, "La corporalité selon saint Thomas"; Bynum, *The Resurrection of the Body,* 256–71.

39. See Etienne Gilson, *La philosophie au moyen âge: Des origines patristiques à la fin du XIVᵉ siècle,* 2nd ed. (Paris: Payot, 1952), 541. By stressing the hylomorphic composition of both soul and body, on the contrary, the doctrine of plurality could easily defend the immortality of the soul. See Copleston, *A History of Philosophy,* 2:280.

40. See Dales, *The Problem of the Rational Soul,* 108–9; and Bynum, *The Resurrection of the Body,* 257 n. 113.

41. In *Opera omnia,* ed. Fretté (1876), 21:33–34; my translation. Thomas commented upon St. Paul's epistle twice, a first time leaving to his disciple Reginald the task of writing down the text, and a second time during his last sojourn in Naples (1272–73), and writing the exposition himself. When he died, he had arrived only at chapter 10. Reginald completed the work with his own previous transcripts. See Dominique Chenu, *Toward Understanding St. Thomas,* translated, with authorized corrections and bibliographical additions, by A.-M. Landry and D. Hughes (Chicago: Henry Regnery, 1964), 248.

42. ". . . nec tamen est verum quod aliquis actus sit hominis in vita praesenti in quo corpus non communicet" (*Quodlibet VII,* q. 5, art. 11, ad 3, in *Quaestiones quodlibeticas,* in *Opera omnia,* ed. Fretté [1875], 15:511). For a reference to passages in which Aquinas insists on the unity of man, see S. J. Von Heinz Schulte, "Johannes Duns Scotus: Der Mensch—Einheit in Differenz. Zur Auseinandersetzung des Duns Scotus mit der Anthropologie des Thomas von Aquin," *Theologie und Philosophie* 49 (1974): 554 n. 1. See also Umberto Degl'Innocenti, "La struttura ontologica della persona secondo S. Tommaso d'Aquino," in *L'homme et son destin d'après les penseurs du moyen âge: Actes du premier congrès international de philosophie médiévale: Louvain-Bruxelles, 28 Août–4 Septembre 1958* (Louvain: Nauwelaerts, 1960), 523–33; Vanni Rovighi, *L'antropologia filosofica di Tommaso d'Aquino,* 47–61; Weber, *La personne humaine au XIIIe siècle,* 143–87.

In a passage that confirms his adherence to the doctrine of unity of form, Albert the Great says that just as a dead man is a man only "equivocally," so the body without the soul is an organic body only "equivocally": "Dicendum quod corpus organicum non est actu nisi per animam. Cum autem non habet animam non est corpus organicum nisi aequivoce, ut homo mortuus dicitur homo" (*Summa de creaturis,* pars IIa, tr. I, q. 4, art. 5, ad 3um, in *Alberti Magni opera omnia,* ed. S. Borgnet [Paris: Vivès, 1896], 35:33).

43. "Sicut enim de ratione huius hominis est quod sit ex hac anima et his carnibus et his ossibus, ita de ratione hominis est quod sit anima et carnibus et ossibus . . . manifestum est quod homo non est anima tantum, sed est aliquid compositum ex anima et corpore." Then he even adds that just as a hand or a foot cannot be said to be the person, so the soul is not the person, because it is only a part of the "species humana": ". . . non quaelibet substantia particularis est hypostasis vel persona, sed quae habet completam naturam speciei. Unde manus vel pes non potest dici hypostasis vel persona, et similiter nec anima, cum sit pars speciei humanae" (ST 1a, q. 75, art. 4, reply to objection 2). Also, Giles of Rome emphasizes the unity of the human person, even asserting that one can say that Peter is in Paradise only by synecdoche, because only his soul is there, and that, in the same way, a dead man is said to be a man only by synecdoche, because only the body is in the tomb, and not the entire man: ". . . dicimus quod beatus Petrus in Paradiso est. Sed hoc est per synecdochen, quia est anima ibi eius. Et dicimus de aliquo homine mortuo quod est in sepulchro, sed hoc est per synecdochem, quod est ibi corpus eius" (*Quodlibet* 4, q. 4, quoted in Kieran Nolan, *The Immortality of the Soul and the Resurrection of the Body according to Giles of Rome: A Historical Study of a 13th Century Theological Problem* [Rome: Studium Theologicum "Augustinianum," 1967], 60 n. 47). For Giles's conception of the human being, see Nolan, *Giles,* 58–64.

44. For a thorough analysis of material continuity and its problems, see Bynum, *The Resurrection of the Body,* 21–225; and Tugwell, *Human Immortality,* 95–109.

45. For the concept of prime matter as mere potentiality that is implied by a consistent understanding of unicity of form, see Bazán, "La corporalité selon saint Thomas," 394–400, where he explains what he calls "les exigens métaphysiques" of hylomorphic doctrine:

> Pour arriver à la doctrine de l'unicité de la forme substantielle, on doit pouvoir identifier le «corps» avec la matière première, entendue comme pure puissance, et l'âme avec la forme substantielle, conçue comme le seul principe de toutes les déterminations, y compris la corporalité. Une seule forme substantielle doit être reconnue comme l'unique principe d'actualité qui établit le composé dans le genre plus général aussi bien que dans l'espèce. (394)

See also Zavalloni, *Richard de Mediavilla,* 249–50. The problem in conceiving prime matter as pure potentiality is that, in the human being, the soul does not actuate primary matter, but body. The doctrine of prime matter as pure potency created a number of problems for Thomas, and (particularly early in his career) he talked as if matter had some designation. Hence his reference to "materia signata." See Copleston, *A History of Philosophy*, 2:326–28. On Aquinas's "inconsistency" in suggesting some actuality in prime matter, see also Bynum, *The Resurrection of the Body*, 264; and Reynolds, *Food and the Body*, 397–99.

46. "Ad primum ergo dicendum quod res naturalis non est id quod est ex sua materia, sed ex sua forma. Unde, quamvis illud materiae quod quandoque fuit sub forma carnis bovinae, resurgat in homine sub forma carnis humanae, non sequitur quod resurgat caro bovis, sed caro hominis" (*Supplementum*, q. 80, a. 4, ad 1; ed. Leonine, 184).

47. "Nam quamdiu manet in re quod est formale, quantumque varietur secundum materiam, non tollitur numeralis identitas" (*Quaestiones de resurrectione mortuorum*, chap. 3, 175–77; in Nolan, *Giles*, 110). Numerical identity means retaining identity through spatio-temporal continuity. "Identity" can also mean similar appearance. For this distinction, see Bynum, *The Resurrection of the Body*, 2ff. Giles moved slowly toward unicity of form but then defended it with vigor and wrote the treatise *Contra gradus et pluralitatem formarum*. This is why in 1277 Tempier refused Giles a master's license and sent him down from the university. When he came back to Paris, probably in 1285, he had to be more moderate. See Anthony M. Hewson, *Giles of Rome and the Medieval Theory of Conception: A Study of the "De formatione corporis humani in utero"* (London: Athlone Press, 1975), 3–12.

48. Nolan, *Giles*, 120.

49. It is probably at this point that the idea of formal identity is fully understood.

50. See Bynum, *The Resurrection of the Body*, 259–60.

51. *In Sententias theologicas Petri Lombardi commentariorum libri quatuor* (Lyon: Apud Gasparem a Portinaris, 1556), dist. 44, q. 1, par. 6, fol. 341 r (quoted in Bynum, *The Resurrection of the Body*, 260).

52. See Bynum, *The Resurrection of the Body*, 264–65 and 270–71; and Reynolds, *Food and the Body*, 429–40.

53. In Henry's own words, he was asked to state clearly and overtly that in man there are several substantial forms: "Sit sollicitus ut clare et aperte determines plures formas substantiales esse in homine" (Henricus de Gandavo, *Quodlibet X*, in *Opera omnia*, ed. R. Macken [Leuven: Leuven University Press, 1981], 14:128). For Henry's own, original position, see Santi, "Il cadavere e Bonifacio VII"; and Zavalloni, *Richard de Mediavilla*, 287–95.

54. See Callus, "Forms, Unicity and Plurality," 1025–26; Zavalloni, *Richard de Mediavilla*, 219–21; Bynum, "Continuity, Survival, and Resurrection," 260–61; eadem, *The Resurrection of the Body*, 271–78.

55. "Exponitur autem quod predictum est de unitate formarum in hunc modum, quod ultima forma adveniente, que est perfectiva compositi, omnes alie

que precesserunt citra materiam corrumpuntur et ultima adveniens per se ipsam agit omnium actiones. Istud intolerabile est et impossibile et primum quoad sensum videmus. Videmus enim sensibiliter in homine carnem, os, nervum, sanguinem, oculum, pedem et talia, quorum nullum est sine vera et propria sua forma; unde aut omnia talia phantastice nobis aparent aut eorum vere forme sunt ibi. . . . Item sequitur, cum non sit corpus nisi per formam corpoream, nec vegetativum nisi per formam vegetativam, nec sensitivum nisi sensitivum per formam sensitivam, quod non esset in homine actio sentiendi vel vegetandi vel existentia corporis, et hoc idem dico de aliis innumerabilibus formis repertis in homine. Item tunc intellettiva potentia nude materie uniretur et non esset homo aliud, nisi quoddam compositum ex intelligibili et materia aliis formis nudata. Item tunc intellettiva potentia sentiret sensu proprie dictu et esset perfectio oculi ad videndum, auris ad audiendum et sic de aliis sensibus" (in Alexander Birkenmajer, "Der Brief R. Kilwardbys an Peter von Conflans und die Streitschrift des Ägidius von Lessines," in *Vermischte Untersuchungen zur Geschichte der mittelalterlichen Philosophie* [Münster: Aschendorff, 1922], 60–61).

56. See Bazán, "La corporalité selon saint Thomas"; Tugwell, *Human Immortality*, 149–55; Bynum, "Continuity, Survival, and Resurrection," and *The Resurrection of the Body*, 271–78. See also Quinn, "Aquinas's Concept of the Body."

57. Santi points out that in his rejection of unicity of form, Henry of Ghent remarks that the people of London had protested against the partisans of unicity because this doctrine would have made vain the cult of Thomas Becket's head, ("Il cadavere e Bonifacio VIII," 867). See also Elisabeth Brown, "Death and the Human Body in the Later Middle Ages: The Legislation of Boniface VIII on the Division of the Corpse," *Viator* 12 (1981): 221–70. For the importance of the corpse in the tomb both religiously and humanly, see Tugwell, *Human Immortality*, 129–31. The importance of the cadaver is such that Aquinas's position about it is one of his weakest points. While unicity of form implies that the body without the soul is not the same body because the form is different (and Aquinas says that the cadaver has another form, precisely the form of the cadaver), in his *Quodlibet II*, q. 1, a. 1 of Christmas 1269, he says that the body when it is alive and when it is dead cannot be said to be the same numerically in an absolute way ("non potest dici quod simpliciter fuerit idem numero"), but in a relative way, because form is not same but matter is. ("Dicendum est ergo quod fuit secundum quid idem: secundum materiam quidem idem, secundum formam vero non idem.") See Santi, "Il cadavere e Bonifacio VIII," 868.

58. The opponents of unicity argued that if in Christ, as in any other man, there is only one substantial form, Mary's divine maternity is negated. Because the rational soul is created directly by God and is the only form of the body, what Christ would have received from his mother is not flesh but simple primary matter. He would therefore not be Mary's true son. In Peter Olivi's words, "Videtur ex ea [positione unitatis] sequi quod Christus non susceperit ex Virgine nisi solum

materiam primam; administrare autem solum materiam primam non videtur esse administratio quae competit matri in generatione prolis, nam ita bene posset terra administrasse materiam primam corpori Christi sicut et Virgo" (*Quaestiones*, q. 50 [quoted in Zavalloni, *Richard de Mediavilla*, 319]). Moreover, if, as Robert Kilwardby formulated in his condemnation, "the living body and the dead body are body equivocally," then Christ's body during the *triduum* could be the same as the earthly and resurrection one only "equivocally." Such a position seems to threaten soteriology—that is, the doctrine that Christ's resurrection guarantees ours. See Bynum, *The Resurrection of the Body*, 273. Other heresies followed from this interpretation of unicity of form, such as that the bread on the altar is not Christ's body, and that there is no original sin in man. See also Zavalloni, *Richard de Mediavilla*, 317–18; and Michel, "Forme du corps humain," 575–79.

59. It is precisely the concern for the materiality of the body that either held the partisans of unicity from stressing its principles to its full extent or forced them to be inconsistent. See Bynum, *The Resurrection of the Body*, 269–78.

60. See Bynum, *The Resurrection of the Body*, 268–69.

61. Zavalloni, *Richard de Mediavilla*, 253–55; Bazán, "La corporalité selon saint Thomas," 390–94, who explains that these two principles imply that matter loses its single form each time it receives another one and that, therefore, a "resolutio usque ad materiam primam" is required.

62. "Et ideo dicendum est quod cum generatio unius semper sit corruptio alterius, necesse est dicere quod tam in homine quam in animalibus aliis, quando perfectior forma advenit fit corruptio prioris; ita tamen quod sequens forma habet quidquid habebat prima, et adhuc amplius. Et sic per multas generationes et corruptiones pervenitur ad ultimam formam substantialem, tam in homine quam in aliis animalibus."

63. "Sic igitur dicendum est quod anima intellectiva creatur a Deo in fine generationis humanae, quae simul est et sensitiva et nutritiva, corruptis formis praeexistentibus." See also *De potentia*, q. 3, a. 9, ad 9: "Per virtutem formativam quae a principio est in semine, abiecta forma spermatis, inducitur alia forma; qua abiecta, iterum inducitur alia: et sic primo inducitur anima vegetabilis; deinde ea abiecta, inducitur anima sensibilis et vegetabilis simul; qua abiecta, inducitur non per virtutem praedictam sed a creante, anima quae simul est rationalis, sensibilis et vegetabilis. Et sic dicendum est secundum hanc opinionem quod embryo, antequam habeat animam rationalem, vivit et habet animam, qua abiecta, inducitur anima rationalis" (in *Opera omnia*, ed. Fretté [1875], 13:72).

64. In *Supplementum*, q. 70, art. 1, resp., we find the idea that the sensitive powers of the separated soul, which remain only in a relative sense, will reactivate when the soul gets its body back: "Hence others say that the sensitive and other like powers do not remain in the separated soul except in a restricted sense, namely radically, in the same way as a result is in its principle: because there remains in the separated soul the ability to produce these powers if it should be reunited to its

body; nor is it necessary for this ability to be anything in addition to the essence of the soul, as stated above. This opinion appears to be the more reasonable."

See also ST 1a, q. 77 ("Whether all the powers of the soul remain in the soul when it is separated from the body"), art. 8: "All the soul's powers go back only to the soul as their source. But certain powers, namely understanding and will, are related to the soul taken on its own as their subject of inhesion, and powers of this kind have to remain in the soul after the death of the body. But some powers have the body-soul compound for subject; this is the case with all the powers of sensation and nutrition. Now when the subject goes the accident cannot stay. Hence when the compound corrupts such powers do not remain in actual existence. They survive in the soul in a virtual state only, as in their source or root."

65. See Zavalloni, *Richard de Mediavilla*, 312–16, who points out that those who defend plurality of forms move from empirical observation and reject unicity of form by stressing the absurdity of what they see as an implication that prime matter is pure potentiality and form is something that unites to it with no mediation. In the case of generation, they stress that, if the rational soul is the form of the body, it unites, therefore, to prime matter without the mediation of any other substantial form. But the essence of prime matter is present in the same way in any element. It might therefore happen that man is generated from either the elements or the semen, and that the rational soul unites to any matter with no mediation. But this is impossible in nature. It is the same argument that pluralists propose when they affirm that plurality of forms is also required for natural corruption. If rational soul is the only form of the body and unites with prime matter with no mediation, how can a man die, if the two elements that compose him—the soul and primary matter—are immortal? See also Boyde, *Dante Philomythes*, 274–75, who points out that the commonsense view of generation rebels against Aquinas's theory that necessitates what he defines as a "clumsy section and division of what is clearly a continuous process."

66. A. Michel ("Resurrection des Morts," in *Dictionnaire de théologie catholique*, 13.2:2560) explains that all the forms that are educed from matter (because they are potentally contained in primary matter) are liable to corruption and disappear at physical death:

> Subordonnées à la forme proprement substantielle qu'est l'âme intellective, les formes inférieures, par exemple, la forme de la chair, la forme des éléments premiers et mixtes, sont sujettes à corruption. Ces formes inférieures se trouvent à l'état de puissance dans la matière et c'est avec une forme de corporéité particulière que l'âme humaine individuelle s'unit pour constituer la substance d'un corps humain. De même donc que cette substance, avant la génération, était en puissance dans la matière qui a été prise pour former le corps de l'individu, de même après la mort elle retombe par la corruption dans cette même matière, pour y rester cachée à l'état de puissance—de *raisons séminales*, dit plus expressément encore saint Bonaventure en reprenant le terme con-

sacré par saint Augustin—jusqu'à ce qu'elle soit rappelée à l'existence par la voix du Dieu tout-puissant.

67. Dales, *The Problem of the Rational Soul*, 195; see also 107.

68. Boyde, *Dante Philomythes*, 271–73.

69. For the continuity of the development in Statius's account up to the formation of the sensitive soul, see Boyde, who also stresses that Statius's "phraseology, syntax and deliberate repetition of key-words do present the embryo's development as one continuous process" (*Dante Philomythes*, 275).

70. "Relinquitur intellectum solum deforis advenire, et divinum esse solum; nichil enim ipsius operationi communicat corporalis operatio" (*De generatione animalium* II, 3, 736b 27–28). See Boyde, *Dante Philomythes*, 276–78.

71. ". . . quest' è tal punto, / che più savio di te fé già errante, / sì che per sua dottrina fé disgiunto / da l'anima il possibile intelletto, / perché da lui non vide organo assunto" (*Purg.* 25.62–66). The consequence of Averroës's interpretation was the negation of the immortality of the individual soul. See: Boyde, *Dante Philomythes*, 277–78; Nardi, "Anima e corpo nel pensiero di San Tommaso," 174–76; and Fernand Van Steenberghen, *Thomas Aquinas and Radical Aristotelianism* (Washington, D.C.: Catholic University of America Press, 1980), 29–74.

72. Busnelli, *Cosmogonia e antropogenesi*, 248–74, and comment to Dante's *Convivio*, 2:399.

73. "Substantia illa quae est anima hominis partim est ab intrinseco et partim ab extrinseco ingrediens: quia licet vegetativum et sensitivum in homine de materia educantur mediante virtute formativa, quae est in gutta matris et patris, tamen haec formativa non educeret eas hoc modo prout sunt potentiae rationalis et intellectualis formae et substantiae, nisi secundum quod ipsa formativa movetur informata ab intellectu universaliter movente in opere generationis; et ideo complementum ultimum, quod est intellectualis formae et substantiae, non per instrumentum neque ex materia, sed per lucem suam influit intellectus primae causae purus et immixtus" (*Liber de natura et origine animae*, tr. I, chap. 5, ed. Bernhard Geyer [Münster: Aschendorff, 1955], 14).

74. "Unde alii dicunt quod anima vegetabilis est in potentia ad animam sensibilem, et sensibilis est actus eius; unde anima vegetabilis, quae primo est in semine, per actionem naturae perducitur ad complementum animae sensibilis; et ulterius anima rationalis est actus et complementum animae sensibilis; unde anima sensibilis perducitur ad suum complementum, scilicet ad animam rationalem, non per actione generantis, sed per actum creantis" (*De potentia*, q. 3, a. 9, ad 9).

"Neque enim dici potest, quod quidam dicunt . . . ipsam praedictam virtutem fieri animam vegetabilem; deinde, organis magis perfectis et multiplicatis, eandem perduci ut sit anima sensitiva; ulterius autem, forma organorum perfecta, eandem animam fieri rationalem, non quidem per actionem virtutem seminis, sed ex influxu exterioris agentis: propter quod suspicantur Aristotelem dixisse intellectum ab extrinseco esse" (*Summa contra gentiles*, II, c. 89).

"Et ideo alii dicunt quod illa eadem anima quae primo fuit vegetativa tantum, postmodum, per actionem virtutis quae est in semine, perducitur ad hoc ut ipsa eadem fiat sensitiva; et tandem ipsa eadem perducitur ad hoc ut ipsa eadem fiat intellectiva, non quidam per virtutem activam seminis, sed per virtutem superioris agentis, scilicet Dei deforis illustrantis" (ST, 1a, q. 118, a. 2, ad 2).

75. For a convincing distinction of Statius's account from the one offered by Albert, see Bemrose, "'Come d'animal,'" who shows that for Albert "the *inchoatio sensibilis* is in the vegetative soul, and indeed the *inchoatio rationalis* is in the sensitive," while "there is no such idea in Dante," according to whom the rational soul absorbs the sensitive (131). For the significance of the biblical references contained in lines 67–75, see Zygmunt Barański, "Canto XXV," in *Lectura Dantis Turicensis,* ed. Georges Güntert and Michelangelo Picone (Florence: Franco Cesati, 2001), 389–406, esp. 398–400. Barański's essay offers a clear analysis of the broad implications that Statius's embryological account has within the (meta)poetic discourse of the whole *Comedy,* especially with respect to the epistemological power that Dante attributes to poetry in general and to his own poem in particular.

76. Gilson, "Dante's Notion of a Shade," 128–29. See also "Qu'est-ce qu'une ombre?"; Gilson's well-known passion for Aquinas might have misled him on some points and pushed him toward certain exaggerations. Nonetheless, he has the important merit of restating the influence of Aquinas's philosophy in Dante's works after Bruno Nardi's fundamental, but sometimes too vigorous, attempt to distinguish Dante's positions from Aquinas's.

77. For Nardi's claim, see "L'origine dell'anima umana," 36.

78. "Item quod anima intellettiva introducta, corrumpitur sensitiva et vegetativa. . . . Item quod vegetativa, sensitiva et intellectiva sint una forma simplex" (H. Denifle and E. Chatelain, eds., *Chartularium Universitatis Parisiensis* [Paris: Delalain, 1889], 1:559).

79. Furthermore, when Dante thinks back to his ascent to heaven and recalls Saint Paul, he says that he does not know whether he was there in the body, or whether only his soul was there. I will discuss this passage at length in chapter 4, but what interests me now is that Dante defines the soul as that which is created last, implying therefore that the rational soul is the human soul: "S'i' era sol di me quel che creasti / novellamente, amor che 'l ciel governi, / tu 'l sai, che col tuo lume mi levasti" (*Par.* 1.73–75). The same identification of the human soul with the rational soul is also stressed when Dante contrasts the human soul to the soul of animals and plants precisely because it is created directly by God: "L'anima d'ogne bruto e de le piante / di complession potenzïata tira / lo raggio e 'l moto de le luci sante; / ma vostra vita sanza mezzo spira / la somma beninanza, e la innamora / di sé sì che poi sempre la disira" (*Par.* 7.139–44).

80. On Dante's syncretism, see especially: Zygmunt Barański, *Dante e i segni: Saggi per una storia intellettuale di Dante Alighieri* (Naples: Liguori, 2000); Giuseppe

Mazzotta, *Dante's Vision and the Circle of Knowledge* (Princeton: Princeton University Press, 1992); and Lino Pertile, *La puttana e il gigante. Dal "Cantico dei Cantici" al Paradiso terrestre di Dante* (Ravenna: Longo, 1998). On the diversity of medieval Aristotelianism (which in the Middle Ages, as we have seen, was not a homogenous doctrine but was interpreted in several, often discordant, ways) and on Dante's original use of it, see Simon Gilson, "Rimaneggiamenti danteschi di Aristotele: *Gravitas e levitas* nella *Commedia*," in *Le culture di Dante*, ed. Michelangelo Picone, Theodore J. Cachey, and Margherita Mesirca (Florence: Franco Angeli 2004), 157–77.

81. Thus, Statius's theory also manages to maintain the connection between body and soul that seems to be lost with Aquinas's discontinuous account.

82. While Singleton translates "in virtute" in line 80 as "in potency," I changed his translation with "as faculties," because, as Chiavacci Leonardi explains in her commentary to the passage, "l'espressione *in virtute* non può significare 'in potenza,' cioè 'non in atto,' come molti spiegano, perché nella terzina seguente è detto chiaramente che le facoltà intellettive *(il divino)* restano *in atto* anche più acutamente di prima. Si dovrà dunque intendere *virtute* come 'virtù sostanziale,' nel senso che la parola ha anche a XVIII 51. Tutte le potenze, 'umane e divine,' sono infatti radicate ('in radice,' come si esprime Tommaso) nell'essenza stessa dell'anima" (746).

83. Dante also speaks of the formation of the soul in *Convivio* 4.21.4–5, where he explains why human souls have different degrees of nobility:

> E però dico che quando l'umano seme cade nel suo recettaculo, cioè ne la matrice, esso porta seco la vertù de l'anima generativa e la vertù del cielo e la vertù de li elementi legati, cioè la complessione; e matura e dispone la materia a la vertù formativa, la quale diede l'anima del generante; e la vertù formativa prepara li organi a la vertù celestiale, che produce de la potenza del seme l'anima in vita. La quale, incontanente produtta, riceve da la vertù del motore del cielo lo intelletto possibile.

Usually scholars believe that the explanations in the *Convivio* and *Purgatorio* 25 follow the same principles. See Nardi, "L'origine dell'anima umana," 34–46. I would argue, however, that this is true only up to the point of the formation of the rational soul, and that the emphasis is different concerning the formation of the rational soul. In the *Convivio*, Dante simply says that the sensitive soul ("l'anima in vita") receives from God the rational soul ("lo intelletto possibile") but does not give any further specification. In the *Comedy*, on the contrary, where Dante is concerned with imagining a separated soul that is fully immortal, Dante is less ambiguous and stresses the discontinuity of the creation of the rational soul, which is the surviving agent and draws into its substance (and renders therefore immortal) the faculties that it gets from the fetus to which it unites. For the different agendas that the two embryological explanations have in the *Convivio* and

Purgatorio 25, see Bemrose, "'Come d'animal'"; and, most recently, Paul A. Dumol, "Soul," in *The Dante Encyclopedia*, ed. Richard Lansing (New York: Garland, 2000), 795–97.

84. While at line 95 Petrocchi reads "ch'è," I agree with Chiavacci Leonardi and Sapegno, following the other editors, who read "che."

85. On the individuality of the characters of the *Comedy*, see Morgan, *Dante and the Medieval Other World* (Cambridge: Cambridge University Press, 1990), 51–83. Morgan shows the gradual development in the presentation of the characters within medieval vision literature, from the "inclusion of the individual" to the "description of appearance" to the "description of circumstances," and finally to the "description of characters." She concludes her analysis by stating that "the presentation of characters reaches a climax in the *Comedy*" (73).

86. Piero Boitani, "*I Know the Signs of the Ancient Flame:* Dante's Recognitions," in *The Tragic and the Sublime in Medieval Literature* (Cambridge: Cambridge University Press, 1991), 150.

87. For an excellent explanation of Dante's concept of the will's freedom as connected with obedience to the judgment of reason, see Giorgio Stabile, "Volontà," in *Enciclopedia dantesca*, 5:1134–40, esp. 1135:

> Fondata com'è sul giudizio di ragione, la libertà in Dante non consiste né nel potere della volontà di sollecitare l'intelletto a giudicare in merito all'oggetto dell'appetizione, né nel potere di non volere appetire l'oggetto giudicato conforme al bene dell'intelletto, ma nel fatto che l'intelletto ha potestà— prevenendo l'appetito—di analizzare discorsivamente tale oggetto, in quanto ordinato a un fine e, sulla base dalla regola tratta da quel fine, intendere ciò che è meglio quanto alla volizione. Non quindi libertà della volontà "di" determinarsi rispetto agli oggetti appetibili, ma libertà della ragione "da" ogni appetito per determinare rettamente la volizione.

See also Bruno Bernabei, "Libertà," in *Enciclopedia dantesca*, 3:642: "La libertà si realizza nel perfetto costante equilibrio fra ragione e volontà nella piena chiarezza e osservanza del bene morale."

For a thorough analysis of the concept of love as the motive force of all our actions which needs to be governed by reason and will, see Barolini, *The Undivine "Comedy,"* 104–12; eadem, "Guittone's *Ora parrà*, Dante's *Doglia me reca*, and the *Commedia*'s Anatomy of Desire," in *Seminario Dantesco Internazionale. International Dante Seminar 1: Atti del primo convegno tenutosi al Chauncey Conference Center. Princeton, 21–23 ottobre 1994*, ed. Zygmunt Barański (Florence: Le Lettere, 1997), 3–23.

88. "L'anima umana . . . con la nobilitade de la potenza ultima, cioè ragione, partecipa de la divina natura a guisa di sempiterna intelligenza" (*Conv.* 3.2.14). As we have seen, the intellectual powers of memory, intellect, and will ("memoria, intelligenza e volontade") form what Statius calls the divine part ("'l divino") of

the soul (*Purg.* 25.81–83). On how the use of reason and will defines an action that can be properly called human, see *Convivio* 3.9.4: "E a vedere li termini de le nostre operazioni, è da sapere che solo quelle sono nostre operazioni che subiacciono a la ragione e a la volontade; che se in noi è l'operazione digestiva, questa non è umana ma naturale"; and 4.7.11: "Sì come dice Aristotile nel secondo de l'Anima, «vivere è de li esseri viventi»; e per ciò che vivere è per molti modi (sì come ne le piante vegetare, ne li animali vegetare e sentire e muovere, ne li uomini vegetare, sentire, muovere e ragionare, o vero intelligere), e le cose si deono denominare da la più nobile parte, manifesto è che vivere ne li animali è sentire—animali, dico, bruti—, vivere ne l'uomo è ragione usare."

89. See, for instance, Kenneth Gross, who shows that the pains of hell are more a manifestation of the damned souls' corruption than an antithetical retribution for their sin ("Infernal Metamorphoses: An Interpretation of Dante's 'Counterpass,'" *Modern Language Notes* 100 [1985]: 47ff.). The same point is made by Anthony Cassell, who says that in the *Inferno* not only does the punishment fit the crime, but the contrapasso "is, in all cases, more profoundly, a strict manifestation of the sin as guilt. . . . The souls are fixed in the guilt and pain of their ultimate, accrued, unrepented wickedness, as Christian orthodoxy insisted: immediately after death, the damned are punished by becoming unchangeable in their iniquity; the disorder of their wills, responsible for their damnation, remains in them throughout eternity; for them goodness is no longer possible" (*Dante's Fearful Art of Justice* [Toronto: University of Toronto Press, 1984], 9). See also Leonard Barkan, who points out that "the living sinner, through his death but more particularly through the fate of his special damnation, is transformed into an eternal objectification of his sin" (*The Gods Made Flesh: Metamorphosis and the Pursuit of Paganism* [New Haven: Yale University Press, 1986], 142).

90. Charles Singleton, "Justification," in *Dante Studies 2: Journey to Beatrice* (Cambridge: Harvard University Press, 1958), 57–71. Singleton shows that original justice is precisely what Thomas Aquinas defines as justice "metaphorice dicta":

> Alio modo dicitur iustitia, prout importat rectitudinem quandam ordinis in ipsa interiori dispositione hominis, prout scilicet supremum hominis subditur Deo, et inferiores vires animae subduntur supremae, scilicet rationi; et hanc etiam dispositionem vocat Philosophus, iustitiam metaphorice dictam. Haec autem iustitia in homine potest fieri dupliciter. Uno quidem modo, per motum simplicis generationis, qui est ex privatione ad formam. Et hoc modo iustificatio posset competere etiam ei qui non esset in peccato, dum huiusmodi iustitiam a Deo acciperet, sicut Adam dicitur accepisse originalem iustitiam.—Alio modo potest fieri huiusmodi iustitia in hominem secundum rationem motus qui est de contrario in contrarium. Et secundum hoc, iustificatio importat transmutationem quandam de statu iniustitiae ad statum iustitiae predicate. (ST 1a2ae, q. 113, a. 1, resp.)

Thomas then adds that any sin, so far as it implies some disorder in the mind that is not subject to God, can be called injustice: "dicendum quod omne peccatum secundum quod importat quamdam inordinationem mentis non subditae Deo, iniustitia potest dici predictae iustitiae contraria" (ST 1a2ae, q. 113, a. 1, ad primum). See also John Freccero, "The Sign of Satan," in *Dante: The Poetics of Conversion* (Cambridge: Harvard University Press, 1986), 167–79.

91. See especially Gross, "Infernal Metamorphoses," esp. 42–50; and Warren Ginsberg, *Dante's Aesthetics of Being* (Ann Arbor: University of Michigan Press, 1999). The phrase "motus a forma" is Ginsberg's (120). See also Cassell, *Dante's Fearful Art of Justice*, 3–10; and Barkan, *The Gods Made Flesh*, 137–70.

92. From *Purgatorio* 25.83 we know that the "divine" faculties of the human being are the intellective ones, i.e., "memoria, intelligenza e volontade." Through analysis of *Inferno* 10.100–108, Ginsberg suggests that not only are will and reason corrupted by sin but also the intellectual memory of the damned souls is impaired once they cross the Acheron (*Dante's Aesthetics of Being*, 119 and 127–29).

93. Virgil replies that his proud disposition, which does not change, is precisely what makes his punishment harsher (*Inf.* 14.63–66).

94. As Chiavacci Leonardi writes in the commentary to *Inferno* 14.51, "La dichiarazione contenuta in questo verso può essere considerata definitoria di tutti i dannati dell'inferno dantesco, la cui individualità non è altro che ciò che essi furono in vita." Like Capaneus, other souls of hell reveal their lack of understanding by perpetuating the same error that condemned them to hell. A few examples are Pier della Vigna (who still believes he has gained a good reputation through his suicide), Brunetto Latini (who still believes himself alive through literary achievements), and Guido da Montefeltro (who still builds very rational arguments on wrong premises).

95. Gross refers to Aquinas's definition of sin as the state wherein the soul is misdirected or halted in its movement toward its true form ("actus debito ordine privatus"), and, at the same time, points out that no being ever loses its inner drive to fullfill the form it was created to be. Even the damned soul does not lose this drive but is harmed and impaired by sin. This is why it remains a "worm in which full formation is failing," a hybrid being that still has its potential to express its true form but is forbidden to do it by sin ("Infernal Metamorphoses," 45). See also Ginsberg, *Dante's Aesthetics of Being*, 118–28.

96. For the association of sin with perverted or distorted bodily functions in the *Inferno*, see Robert Durling, "Deceit and Digestion in the Belly of Hell," in *Allegory and Representation*, ed. Stephen J. Greenblatt (Baltimore: Johns Hopkins University Press, 1980), 61–93.

97. For the deformation or dissolution of the "human image" in hell, see Barkan, *The Gods Made Flesh*, 142–45 and 158–60.

98. On the suicides, see Leo Spitzer, "Speech and Language in *Inferno* 13," in *Representative Essays*, ed. Alban K. Forcione, Herbert Lindenberger, and Madeline

Sutherland (Stanford: Stanford University Press, 1988), 153–71. Spitzer highlights the connection between the metamorphosed shape of the shades and their speech, which is also of a nonhuman order. On the thieves, see: Ginsberg, *Dante's Aesthetics of Being*, 115–59; Barkan, *The Gods Made Flesh*, 149–70; Gross, "Infernal Metamorphoses"; Joan Ferrante, *The Political Vision of the "Divine Comedy"* (Princeton: Princeton University Press, 1984), 180–82 and 348–51.

99. On the increasing corporeality of infernal shades, see Rachel Jacoff, "'Our Bodies, Our Selves': The Body in the *Commedia*," in *Sparks and Seeds: Medieval Literature and Its Afterlife*, ed. Dana E. Stewart and Alison Cornish (Turnhout: Brepols, 2000), 124–25.

100. On the association between sin and weight (which increases as one moves toward the bottom of hell), see Giuseppe Mazzotta, *Dante, Poet of the Desert: History and Allegory in the "Divine Comedy"* (Princeton: Princeton University Press, 1979), 161–64; and Ginsberg, *Dante's Aesthetics of Being*, 116.

101. In *Monarchia*, ed. Bruno Nardi, in *Opere minori* (Milan: Ricciardi, 1989), 2:346–48; *Monarchy and Three Political Letters*, trans. Donald Nicholl (New York: Garland, 1972), 19. The passage of the *Paradiso* that Dante is referring to is 5.19–24, where freedom of the will is defined as the greatest gift that God gave to all the intelligent creatures—angels and human beings: "Lo maggior don che Dio per sua larghezza / fesse creando, e a la sua bontate / più conformato, e quel ch'e' più apprezza, / fu de la volontà la libertate; / di che le creature intelligenti / e tutte e sole, fuoro e son dotate." Here Dante is speaking of "de la volontà la libertate," i.e., freedom of the will, while in the passage of the *Monarchia* he was referring to "libertas arbitrii," i.e., freedom of decision. For the distinction between the two, see Kent, *Virtues of the Will*, 98–99. Kent explains that, while Bonaventure and Aquinas discussed especially "liberum arbitrium," stressing the harmony between the will's preference and the intellect's judgment, philosophers of the late thirteenth century started discussing freedom of the will ("libertas voluntatis"), i.e., the will's freedom to act against reason's dictates (100–110). Even though he speaks of "freedom of the will" in *Paradiso* 5, it seems to me that this distinction is not so sharp for Dante, who is less interested in discussing the relationship between will and reason than in stressing man's freedom in making his choices (to the extent that in the passage of the *Monarchia* he is discussing "libertas arbitrii" and quotes a passage of the *Comedy* where he was referring to freedom of the will, "de la volontà la libertate").

What Dante is concerned to highlight is that freedom is the product of intellect and will working together. (See Patrick Boyde, *Perception and Passion in the "Divine Comedy"* [Cambridge: Cambridge University Press, 1993], 210–14.) In *Convivio* 4.9.8, Dante says that one can lose equity for two reasons, either because one does not know what it is or because one does not want to follow it: "e con ciò sia cosa che in tutte queste volontarie operazioni sia equitade alcuna da conservare e iniquitade da fuggire (la quale equitade per due cagioni si può perdere, o per non sapere quale essa sia o per non volere quella seguitare)." For the importance of reason in Dante's conception of "liberum arbitrium," see: Sofia Vanni Rovighi, "Arbitrio," in *Enciclopedia dantesca*, 1:345–48; and Giorgio Stabile, "Volontà," esp. 1137.

102. The motif is constantly repeated throughout the third cantica. See, for instance, 8.52–54: "La mia letizia mi ti tien celato / che mi raggia dintorno e mi nasconde / quasi animal di sua seta fasciato"; 15.52; 17.36 and 121–23; 18.76–77; and 21.55–56. See Boyde, *Dante Philomythes*, 167–69.

103. The "light of glory" is, as Thomas Aquinas explains, the supernatural light that is given by God to the saintly souls and that enables them to attain the beatific vision: "Cum autem aliquis intellectus creatus videt Deum per essentiam, ipsa essentia Dei fit forma intelligibilis intellectus. Unde oportet quod aliqua dispositione supernaturalis ei superaddatur, ad hoc ut elevetur in tantam sublimitatem. Cum igitur virtus naturalis intellectus creati non sufficiat ad Dei essentiam videndam, oportet quod ex divina gratia superaccrescatur ei virtus intelligendi. Et hoc augmentum virtutis intellectivae illuminationem intellectus vocamus, sicut et ipsum intelligibile vocatur lumen vel lux" (ST 1a, q. 12, a. 5, resp.; cf. also *Summa contra gentiles* 3, 53–54). See Singleton, "The Three Lights," in *Dante Studies 2*, 20–23; and Christian Trottmann, *La vision béatifique: Des disputes scolastiques à sa définition par Benoît XII* (Rome: École française de Rome, 1995), 302–21.

104. For the connection between the fact that a "Christian paradise requires the preservation of the individual's irreducible and essential self" and Dante's stress on the blessed souls' unique identity, see Barolini, *The Undivine "Comedy,"* 173.

CHAPTER 3 Productive Pain: The *Red Scripture*, the *Purgatorio*, and a New Hypothesis on the "Birth of Purgatory"

1. Giuliana Cavallini, ed., *Il dialogo della divina provvidenza ovvero libro della divina dottrina* (Siena: Cantagalli, 1995), 8–9. "I have shown you, dearest daughter, that in this life guilt is not atoned for by any suffering, but rather by suffering borne with desire, love, and contrition of heart. The value is not in the suffering but in the soul's desire. Likewise, neither desire nor any other virtue has value or life except through my only-begotten Son, Christ crucified, since the soul has drawn love from him and in virtue follows his footsteps. In this way and in no other is suffering of value. It satisfies for sin, then, with gentle unitive love born from the sweet knowledge of itself and its own sins" (Catherine of Siena, *The Dialogue*, trans. Suzanne Noffke [New York: Paulist Press, 1980], 29).

2. Le Goff has written that "Purgatory triumphed in the thirteenth century both in theology and in dogma. Doubts about its existence were silenced: it became a truth of faith and of the Church. In one form or another, concretely or in varying degrees of abstraction, it was accepted as a place. It took on an official character. . . . When the Church brought Purgatory down from the heights of theological

controversy into the realm of daily teaching and pastoral practice, mobilizing the resources of the imagination in the process, it apparently scored a tremendous success. By the end of the thirteenth century Purgatory is ubiquitous: we find it mentioned in sermons, in wills (still hesitantly), and in vernacular literature" (Jacques Le Goff, *The Birth of Purgatory*, trans. Arthur Goldhammer [Chicago: University of Chicago Press, 1984], 289).

For the 1274 definition, which was incorporated in an appendix to the constitution *Cum sacrosanta* of the council, see *The Birth of Purgatory*, 225–26. The first pontifical definition of purgatory dates to 1254, when Innocent IV wrote a letter to his legate to the Greeks in Cyprus to ask the Greeks to accept the definition of "purgatory" as the place where "the souls of those who die after receiving penance but without having had the time to complete it, or who die without mortal sin but guilty of venial (sins) or minor faults, are purged after death and may be helped by the suffrages of the Church." See Le Goff, *The Birth of Purgatory*, 283–84.

3. Ibid., 333.

4. Ibid.

5. "Centri di Cultura nel Medio Evo: L'Italia settentrionale," in *Storia della civiltà letteraria italiana*, directed by Giorgio Bárberi Squarotti, vol. 1, *Dalle Origini al Trecento* (Turin: UTET, 1990), part 2, 638–39.

6. "Nella seconda cantica richiami a Cristo ricorrono con un'insistenza quasi pressante, l'influenza e il ricordo di lui sono ovunque" ("Cristo," in *Enciclopedia dantesca* [Rome: Istituto della Enciclopedia Italiana G. Treccani, 1970], 2:267). The Christological significance of the second canticle is also emphasized, especially with regard to the episode of the gate of purgatory (but also with digressions concerning the whole realm), by Peter Armour, *The Door of Purgatory: A Study of Multiple Symbolism in Dante's "Purgatorio"* (Oxford: Clarendon Press, 1983).

7. Barbara Newman, "On the Threshold of the Dead: Purgatory, Hell, and Religious Women," in *From Virile Woman to Woman Christ: Studies in Medieval Religion and Literature* (Philadelphia: University of Pennsylvania Press, 1995), 108–36; quotation on 109. See also: Adriaan Bredero, "Le Moyen Âge et le Purgatoire," *Revue d'histoire ecclésiastique* 78 (1983): 429–52; Aron Gurevich, "Popular and Scholarly Medieval Cultural Traditions: Notes in the Margin of Jacques Le Goff's Book," *Journal of Medieval History* 9 (1983): 71–90; review by Alan Bernstein in *Speculum* 59 (1984): 179–83; Jean Pierre Massaut, "La vision de l'au-delà au moyen âge: A propos d'un ouvrage récent," *Le Moyen Âge* 91 (1985): 75–86; Graham Edwards, "Purgatory: Birth or Evolution?" *Journal of Ecclesiastical History* 36 (1985): 634–46; Brian McGuire, "Purgatory, the Communion of Saints, and Medieval Change," *Viator* 20 (1989): 61–84.

8. Quotations from Bonvesin's poems are from *Le opere volgari di Bonvesin da la Riva*, ed. Gianfranco Contini (Rome: Società Filologica Romana, 1941). Unless otherwise indicated, translations are from Bonvesin, *Volgari scelti*, trans. Patrick S. Diehl and Ruggero Stefanini (New York: Lang, 1987).

9. For the allegorical comparison between Christ's wounded body and a book inscribed in red as a means to engage the mind in sustained attention to the sufferings of Christ, see Richard Kieckhefer, *Unquiet Souls: Fourteenth-Century Saints and Their Religious Milieu* (Chicago: University of Chicago Press, 1984), 91.

10. For a detailed discussion of the rationale of the *Book of the Three Scriptures*, its emphasis on the body, and the role played by the *Red Scripture*, see my essay "From Decay to Splendor: Body and Pain in Bonvesin da la Riva's *Book of the Three Scriptures*," in *Last Things: Death and Apocalypse in the Middle Ages*, ed. Caroline Walker Bynum and Paul Freedman (Philadelphia: University of Pennsylvania Press, 1991), 83–97.

11. For a thorough and specific analysis of the way in which these new details were emphasized in literary works, see Frederick P. Pickering, "The Gothic Image of Christ: The Sources of Medieval Representations of the Crucifixion," in *Essays on Medieval German Literature and Iconography* (Cambridge: Cambridge University Press, 1980), 3–30. For a detailed development of Pickering's study which considers also contemporary artistic treatments, see James H. Marrow, *Passion Iconography in Northern European Art of the Late Middle Ages and Early Renaissance. A Study of the Transformation of Sacred Metaphor into Descriptive Narrative* (Kortrijk: Van Ghemmert, 1979). See also Thomas H. Bestul, *Texts of the Passion: Latin Devotional Literature and Medieval Society* (Philadelphia: University of Pennsylvania Press, 1996), 26–68.

12. Several scholars have underscored this shift in Christian spirituality and devotion. See: André Wilmart, *Auteurs spirituels et textes dévots du moyen âge latin: Études d'histoire littéraire* (Paris: Bloud et Gay, 1932); Richard W. Southern, *The Making of the Middle Ages* (New Haven: Yale University Press, 1959), 231–40; Colin Morris, *The Discovery of the Individual 1050–1200* (New York: Harper and Row, 1972), esp. 139–57; Kieckhefer, *Unquiet Souls*, 89–91; Marrow, *Passion Iconography*, 1–10; Jean Leclercq, *The Love of Learning and the Desire for God: A Study of Monastic Culture*, trans. C. Misrahi (New York: Fordham University Press, 1982), esp. 191–235 and 255–70; Ewert Cousins, "The Humanity and the Passion of Christ," in *Christian Spirituality: High Middle Ages and Reformation*, ed. J. Raitt (New York: Crossroad, 1987), 375–91; Caroline Walker Bynum, *Holy Feast and Holy Fast: The Religious Significance of Food to Medieval Women* (Berkeley: University of California Press, 1987), 251–59; eadem, "The Body of Christ in the Later Middle Ages: A Reply to Leo Steinberg," in *Fragmentation and Redemption: Essays on Gender and the Human Body in Medieval Religion* (New York: Zone Books, 1991), 79–117; Giles Constable, "The Ideal of the Imitation of Christ," in *Three Studies in Medieval Religion and Social Thought* (Cambridge: Cambridge University Press, 1995), 179–93; and, more recently, the essays contained in *Il Corpo Passionato: Modelli e rappresentazioni medievali dell'amore divino*, ed. Carla Bino and Manuele Gragnolati, *Comunicazioni Sociali* 25, n.s., 2 (2003).

13. For the possibility of suffering as the justification for the Incarnation, see Marie-Christine Pouchelle, "Représentations du corps dans la *Légende dorée*," *Eth-*

nologie française 6 (1976): 293–308, esp. 294. For the twelfth- and thirteenth-century emphasis on Christ's *impassibilitas* before the Incarnation and after the Resurrection, see also Erich Auerbach, "Excursus: *Gloria passionis*," in *Literary Language and Its Public in Late Latin Antiquity and in the Middle Ages,* trans. R. Manheim (Princeton: Princeton University Press, 1993), 89 n. 3.

14. For an analysis of the complexity of this symbol, see Bynum, "The Body of Christ in the Later Middle Ages," 86–92. On blood as suffering and on the intense devotion to Christ's blood which started in the twelfth century and increased in the centuries to follow, see Louis Gougaud, *Devotional and Ascetic Practices in the Middle Ages,* trans. G. C. Bateman (London: Burns Oates and Washbourne, 1927), 75–130; and Constable, "The Ideal of the Imitation of Christ," 209–17.

In addition to being associated with blood, Christ's suffering is often defined as difficult to imagine and as the harshest that any human being has ever experienced. To free humankind from the sins of the world, Christ had to suffer even more than any animal ever did: "No fu unca hom il mondo   ke tal desnor portasse, / Ni asno ni zumenta   ke tant passïonasse / Com fé 'l nostro Segnor   azò k'el ne scampasse / Da li peccai del mondo   e nu e quang ne nasce" (*Red Scripture* 125–28). Christ's physical agony evokes the picture of the damned and the description of their punishments in hell. (See Stefanini in Bonvesin da la Riva, *Volgari scelti,* 124.) Infernal pains and Christ's suffering are even referred to in the same way: though "passio" and "pena" are the terms that denote, respectively, Christ's suffering and the pain of hell most frequently, both terms can also indicate both concepts, in the same way as other expressions such as "marturio," "angustia," and "tormento." Moreover, the devils who persecute the damned and the Jews who torture Christ are described as having the same role and are both called "renegai" or "renegades." Stefanini (in Bonvesin da la Riva, *Volgari scelti,* 262 n. 57) thinks that these similarities are due to the "subconscious memory of the poet" and dismisses them. I suggest that these parallels convey an important message: in *Black Scripture* 113–20, it is said that the description of earthly miseries can help to give an idea of the much worse pains of hell; then, after the description of these torments, the fact that Christ's Passion is described as explicitly recalling them, appears to be a way to underline Christ's limitless suffering, an attempt to express it in words. In the *Red Scripture* there are several passages that focus on the description of Christ's sufferings, but here I refer only to those that are connected with blood.

15. See also lines 65–68. For the idea as expressed in Bonaventure's *Breviloquium* (part 4, chap. 10, par. 1), cf. Caroline Walker Bynum, *The Resurrection of the Body in Western Christianity, 200–1336* (New York: Columbia University Press, 1995), 251–52. For the Western equation of pain sensitivity with a higher degree of development, see Esther Cohen, "The Animated Pain of the Body," *American Historical Review* 105 (2000): 37–39.

16. For the ambivalence of the strong emotions that Christ's Passion evoked in the later Middle Ages, see Kieckhefer, *Unquiet Souls,* 92. Christ's Passion was

interpreted not only as enormous pain that must induce people to grief and tears, but also as incredible love—the generous sacrifice that saves the world and should induce people to consolation and hope. Auerbach points out that this ambivalence is expressed by the very term "passio": "Those who stress the distinction between the two meanings 'suffering' and 'passion' have not understood the dialectical relation between them in the Christian use of the word—for God's love, which moved him to take upon himself the sufferings of men, is itself a *motus animi* without measure or limit" (Auerbach, "Excursus: *Gloria passionis*," 70).

17. For the evolution of the doctrine of Mary's compassion, see: Wilmart, *Auteurs spirituels et textes dévots du moyen âge latin*, 505–14; O. Von Simson, *"Compassio* and *Co-redemptio* in Roger van der Weyden's *Descent from the Cross,"* *The Art Bulletin* 35 (1953): 9–16; Sandro Sticca, *The "Planctus Mariae" in the Dramatic Tradition of the Middle Ages*, trans. Joseph R. Berrigan (Athens: University of Georgia Press, 1988), 102–17. For bibliographical information, see Marrow, *Passion Iconography*, 252 n. 41. See also Mirella Levi d'Ancona, *The Iconography of the Immaculate Conception in the Middle Ages and Early Renaissance* (New York: College Art Association of America, in conjunction with *The Art Bulletin*, 1957); Hilda Graef, *Mary: A History of Doctrine and Devotion* (London: Sheed & Ward, 1963–65). I will discuss the doctrine of co-redemption at the end of this chapter.

18. For Mary's physical suffering during Christ's Passion in late medieval sermons, see Donna Spivey Ellington, "Impassioned Mother or Passive Icon: The Virgin's Role in Late Medieval and Early Modern Passion Sermons," *Renaissance Quarterly* 48:2 (Summer 1995): 227–41.

19. In the *Red Scripture*, Mary's suffering is so intense that it is presented as similar to infernal punishments, like Christ's. Her invocation to death as a way to end her agony in lines 309–12 is identical to the invocations of the damned continuously uttered in the *Black Scripture*. Her last words, "Per gran dolor delenguo e tuta me desvenio" (I droop in great suffering and pine away), repeat the words of a damned soul; see *Black Scripture* 883.

20. One of the most famous examples is the fifteenth-century *Descent from the Cross*, by Roger van der Weyden, now in the Prado (see appendix, fig. 1). As Mary swoons, her body assumes a position almost identical to that of the dead Christ. Thus Mary, in her compassion, becomes nearly as important to the composition as the figure of Christ. See Von Simson, *"Compassio* and *Co-redemptio,"* 10–11.

21. Bonaventure, *De assumptione B. Virginis Mariae*, sermo 2, in *Bonaventurae opera omnia* (Quaracchi: Collegium S. Bonaventurae, 1901), 9:161.

22. In A. C. Peltier, ed., *Bonaventurae opera omnia* (Paris: Vivès, 1868), 12:606; *Meditations on the Life of Christ: An Illustrated Manuscript of the Fourteenth Century*, ed. Isa Ragusa and Rosalie B. Green, trans. Isa Ragusa (Princeton: Princeton University Press, 1961), 335.

23. The idea of mutual compassion is also in Ubertino of Casale's *Arbor vitae crucifixae Iesu*, whose chapter 15 is entitled "Jesus matri compatiens" (Ubertino da

Casale, *Arbor vitae crucifixae,* ed. Charles T. Davis [Turin: Bottega d'Erasmo, 1961], 321 [quoted in Sticca, *The "Planctus Mariae,"* 110]):

> Quamvis bone Iesu posset exprimere quando compassionis feriebaris telo: quando materna viscera contuebaris omni amaritudine tue passionis repleta. Nec non et ipsam faciem pallidam et quasi sine morte mortuam: et tui sanguinis aspersione manibus et vestibus et faciem cruentam gemitibus anxiam: voce raucam: lachrymis perflusam: et totam in tuis doloribus inabysatam . . . et Iesu novam et magnam amaritudinis crucem ex tue matris tali consortio pro nobis peccatoribus assumpsisti: unde cum nulla creatura minor ipsa dolores cordis eius mensurare sufficiat: tu solus tue dilectissime matri pro te et pro nobis miseris et indignis filiis fuisti debita mensura compassus. Et hoc bone Iesu fuit ad tui doloris augmentum: quod non solum in te sed in altero hoc est in materno corde fuisti sic letaliter crucifixus.

24. "To take the discipline" meant to take part in self-flagellation. For the extensive diffusion of this practice among both lay and religious people in the late Middle Ages, see Émile Bertaud, "Discipline," in *Dictionnaire de spiritualité, ascétique et mystique, doctrine et histoire* (Paris: Beauchesne, 1957), vol. 3, cols. 1302–11. From the last decades of the twelfth century, the spirituality of the Humiliati was characterized by a strong emphasis on penitence, the practices of which celebrated the valor of physical suffering and humiliation. According to André Vauchez, "Plus profondément, la pénitence comme état de vie se traduit par la recherche de la nudité, du dépouillement et de la souffrance physique" ("Pénitents," in *Dictionnaire de spiritualité, ascétique et mystique, doctrine et histoire* [Paris: Beauchesne, 1984], vol. 12, part 1, cols. 1010–23; quotation on col. 1020).

25. For the doctrine of bodily assumption, see: Martin Jugie, *La mort et l'assomption de la Sainte Vierge: Etude historico-doctrinale* (Vatican City: Biblioteca Apostolica Vaticana, 1944); Rachel Fulton, "Mimetic Devotion, Marian Exegesis, and the Historical Sense of the Song of Songs," *Viator* 27 (1996): 85–116; eadem, *From Judgment to Passion: Devotion to Christ and the Virgin Mary, 800–1200* (New York: Columbia University Press, 2002). For Bonaventure's sermon, see Bynum, "Material Continuity, Personal Survival and the Resurrection of the Body," in *Fragmentation and Redemption,* 257.

26. The representation of the wounded body of Christ on the cross inspired love and pity in the public, but also stressed the reality of Christ's flesh and suffering, thereby connecting the body of Christ with the rest of humankind. See Constable, "The Ideal of the Imitation of Christ," 208–15. And contemporary devotion to Mary was a way to move toward Christ. See Rosemary Hale, "*Imitatio Mariae:* Motherhood Motifs in Late Medieval German Spirituality" (Ph.D. diss., Harvard University, 1992), 33. For Mary as *mediatrix* between God and man, see: Kieckhefer, *Unquiet Souls,* 92ff. and 106; Fulton, "Mimetic Devotion," 87–89; Spivey Ellington, "Impassioned Mother," 297.

27. See: Hans Belting, *Likeness and Presence: A History of the Image before the Era of Art*, trans. E. Jephcott (Chicago: University of Chicago Press, 1994), 208–24; and Jeffrey Hamburger, "Vision and the Veronica," in *The Visual and the Visionary: Art and Female Spirituality in Late Medieval Germany* (New York: Zone Books, 1998), 316–82. For the deep emotional relationship between devotional image and beholder in the later Middle Ages, see idem, "The Visual and the Visionary: The Image in Late Medieval Monastic Devotion," *Viator* 20 (1989): 161–82.

28. The Milanese text of the two passages is found in *Le opere volgari di Bonvesin da la Riva*, 52 and 233.

29. See, for instance, *Black Scripture* 25–27: "La nassïon de l'omo   sí è de tal color / K'el fi inzenerao   il brut interïor / De sangu' ked è mesgiao   de puza e de sozor"; and 152–56: "Oi De, oi carne misera,   com ste tu lassa e trista: / Com e't desfigurao,   com he tu soza vista. / No's pò trovar pro homo   ni medic ni legista / Ke possa le defende   ked ella no marcisca."

30. At the end of the several glories, the blessed say what made them gain their beatitude and therefore indicate correct behaviors to the listeners. Among them, Bonvesin stresses some practices that are also found in the final lines of the *Red Scripture*, such as penitence, fasting, and weeping at the end of the first glory: "Perzò k'in penitentia   in mïa vita stigi, / In plang e in zezunij   li mei cor fon affligi, / E ked eo me tign mondo   per fag e anc per digi, / Perzò sont eo in numero   dri sancti benedigi" (*Golden Scripture* 169–72). Penitence will be stressed in the twelfth glory; fasting and affliction of the body in the eighth; poverty, humility, and misery in the third and tenth. Bonvesin stresses that the tale of Christ's pain should induce us to great contrition and to sorrow throughout the *Red Scripture*. See, for instance, 89–92: "Mai no è hom il mondo   ke no devess ess molle / A suspirar e a planze   olzand coté parole, / Ni far pro ge devrave   li versi dre vïole, / De Iesù Crist olzando   la passïon sì folle"; and 421–24: "In vita e pos la vita   lo nostro grand Segnor / Sosten pur e miserie   e strag e grand desnor: / Il mond no è hom vivo   ni iust ni peccaor / Lo qual no se dovesse   comov a grand dolor."

31. Esther Cohen, "Towards a History of European Physical Sensibility: Pain in the Later Middle Ages," *Science in Context* 8 (1995): 47–74. See also Cohen's "The Animated Pain of the Body." On the philopassianism of the time, see, in addition to the works cited in note 12: Newman, "On the Threshold of the Dead," 119–22; Jeffrey Hamburger, *Nuns as Artists: The Visual Culture of a Medieval Convent* (Berkeley: University of California Press, 1997); and Mitchell Merback, *The Thief, the Cross and the Wheel: Pain and the Spectacle of Punishment in Medieval and Renaissance Europe* (Chicago: University of Chicago Press, 1999).

32. "Atonement came not from charitable work, nor from prayer, nor from enlightenment, but from pain . . . God seemed to attach more weight to love manifested in suffering than to love displayed in other ways" (Kieckhefer, *Unquiet Souls*, 89).

33. Quoted in Le Goff, *The Birth of Purgatory,* 285. As the text does not have the noun "purgatorium" (which is so important for his point) but the expression "poenis purgatoriis seu catharteriis" (where "purgatoriis" is an adjective), Le Goff suggests the hypothesis of another previous formula, since lost (286).

34. On the distinction between *culpa* and *poena,* and its relevance for the concept of purgatory, see Le Goff, *The Birth of Purgatory,* 214; and Thomas Tentler, *Sin and Confession on the Eve of the Reformation* (Princeton: Princeton University Press, 1977), 23–24.

35. See Le Goff, *The Birth of Purgatory,* 334.

36. See Charles Singleton, "Justification," in *Dante Studies 2: Journey to Beatrice* (Cambridge: Harvard University Press, 1958). The result of the purgatorial journey is therefore exemplified by the pilgrim's journey, whose initial search for freedom ("libertà va cercando" [*Purg.* 1.71]) ends significantly in the Garden of Eden, where Virgil's words describe the attainment of a condition in which the will cannot err anymore because it is always free. That is, the will always behaves according to the judgments of reason. At that point, one can follow pleasure because it is always "rational" and therefore right: "Tratto t'ho qui con ingegno e con arte; / lo tuo piacere omai prendi per duce; /. . . / Non aspettar mio dir più né mio cenno; / libero, dritto e sano è tuo arbitrio, / e fallo fora non fare a suo senno" (*Purg.* 27. 130–41). We are free when we follow the judgment of reason. In heaven we can't help but do it and we are therefore free to the highest degree. See the passage in *Monarchia* 1.12.4 quoted in chapter 2.

The concept that the freedom of the saved souls improves because they cannot sin anymore is from Augustine. Their freedom is better than mankind's original freedom because, while Adam's "liberum arbitrium" could avoid sinning but could also sin ("potuit non peccare sed potuit et peccare"), theirs cannot sin ("peccare non poterit"). Concerning the blessed, Augustine writes as follows: "Nec ideo liberum arbitrium non habebunt, quia delectare non potuerunt. Magis quippe erit liberum a delectatione peccandi usque ad delectationem non peccandi indeclinabilem liberatum. Nam primum liberum arbitrium, quod homini datum est, quando primus creatus est rectus, potuit non peccare, sed potuit et peccare; hoc autem novissimum eo potentius erit, quo peccare non poterit" (*Civitate Dei* XXII 30; quoted from Sofia Vanni Rovighi, "Arbitrio," in *Enciclopedia dantesca* [Rome: Istituto della Enciclopedia Italiana G. Treccani, 1970], 1:348). Dante seems to make this distinction, too: the soul's journey to purgatory is a return to Eden but in an improved fashion.

37. Teodolinda Barolini, *The Undivine "Comedy": Detheologizing Dante* (Princeton: Princeton University Press, 1992), 99–121 (quote on 107).

38. Marc Cogan, *The Design in the Wax* (Notre Dame, Ind.: University of Notre Dame Press, 1999), 77–147.

39. In their addresses to the purging souls, the pilgrim and Virgil often stress the souls' eventual salvation. See, for instance, *Purg.* 3.73–75: "O ben finiti, o già

spiriti eletti, . . . per quella pace / ch'i credo che per voi tutti s'aspetti"; 13.85–87: "O gente sicura / . . . di veder l'alto lume / che 'l disio vostro solo ha in sua cura"; 19.76–77: "O eletti di Dio, li cui soffriri / e giustizia e speranza fa men duri"; 26.53–54: "O anime sicure / d'aver, quando che sia, di pace stato."

40. See Bruno Nardi, "Il mito del'Eden," in *Saggi di filosofia dantesca,* 2nd ed. (Florence: La Nuova Italia, 1967; 1st ed. 1930), 311–40; and also Alison Morgan, *Dante and the Medieval Other World* (Cambridge: Cambridge University Press, 1990), 145–65.

41. "Il mito dell'Eden," 313–14. For a precise analysis of the geographical coordinates of the mountain of purgatory and of its height and subsequent meteorology, see Patrick Boyde, *Dante Philomythes and Philosopher: Man in the Cosmos* (Cambridge: Cambridge University Press, 1981), 109–10 and 84–87. Boyde, *Dante Philomythes* 109–10 and 84–87.

42. For the "figural relation" that the topography of purgatory establishes between the place of the Crucifixion, the soul's process of purification from sin through Christ's sacrifice, and the Garden of Eden, see Peter Armour, "Purgatory," in *The Dante Encyclopedia,* ed. Richard Lansing (New York: Garland, 2000), 728–31, esp. 731.

43. In the terrace of pride, where the punishment consists of being bent under the weight of a heavy rock, Omberto Aldobrandeschi makes clear that purgatorial pain is the continuation of the *poena,* which was not completed on earth: "E qui convien ch'io questo peso porti / per lei [la superbia], tanto che a Dio si soddisfaccia, / poi ch'io nol fe' tra ' vivi, qui tra ' morti" (*Purg.* 11.70–72).

44. The clearest examples of the power of a last-minute, sincere contrition are the emperor Manfred ("Poscia ch'io ebbi rotta la persona / di due punte mortali, io mi rendei, / piangendo, a quei che volentier perdona. / Orribil furon li peccati miei; / ma la bontà infinita ha sì gran braccia, / che prende ciò che si rivolge a lei" [*Purg.* 3.118–22]), and Buonconte da Montefeltro ('Quivi perdei la vista e la parola; / nel nome di Maria fini', e quivi / caddi, e rimase la mia carne sola. / Io dirò vero, e tu 'l ridì tra ' vivi: / l'angel di Dio mi prese, e quel d'inferno / gridava: 'O tu del ciel, perché mi privi? / Tu te ne porti di costui l'etterno / per una lagrimetta che 'l mi toglie; / ma io farò de l'altro altro governo!'" [*Purg.* 5.100–108]).

45. Manfred himself, who had celebrated God's mercy in accepting last-minute repentance for even the most horrible sins (*Purg.* 3.118–22), makes this concept clear: "Vero è che quale in contumacia more / di Santa Chiesa, ancor ch'al fin si penta, / star li convien da questa ripa in fore, / per ognun tempo ch'elli è stato, trenta, / in sua presunzïon, se tal decreto / più corto per buon prieghi non diventa" (*Purg.* 3.136–41).

46. The fact that prayers help the purging souls shorten their *poena* is a constant motif of the *Purgatorio.* For other cases of souls who have skipped part of their sojourn in ante-purgatory thanks to the prayers on their behalf, see Sapia (canto 13), Adrian V (canto 19), and Forese (canto 23). On the intercession of the

living, see especially *Purgatorio* 6.37–39, where Virgil explains that one's punishment can be substituted by someone else's love: "ché cima di giudicio non s'avvalla / perché foco d'amor compia in un punto / ciò che de' sodisfar chi qui s'astalla." In the case of late repentance, the wait of ante-purgatory can be shortened also by some action that the person did on earth, even before repentance. Such is the case of Provenzan Salvani, who repented at the edge of his life but could go to the terrace of pride before the fixed term because he humiliated himself to help a friend (*Purg.* 11.121–38).

47. See Antonio Piolanti, "Il dogma del Purgatorio," *Euntes Docete* 6 (1953): 287–311, esp. 307; and Robert Ombres, "The Doctrine of Purgatory According to St. Thomas Aquinas," *Downside Review* 99 (1981): 279–87, esp. 282–83.

48. Silvio Pasquazi argues that while the *reatus poenae* is paid for only through the *poena sensus* of purgatory proper, the souls relegated to ante-purgatory undergo some sort of evolution, in the sense that through their waiting they would extinguish the debt for some venial sin that they have not expiated yet ("Antipurgatorio," in *Enciclopedia dantesca*, 1:304–6). It seems to me, however, that through the invention of ante-purgatory Dante is placing emphasis on the concept that without the *poena sensus,* the souls of ante-purgatory do not change. I therefore agree with Kenelm Foster when he writes that "desiring intensely the sight of God, and conscious that there is that in them which gets in the way of that vision, they [the souls in ante-purgatory] are in fact being held back from the process of inward purification which alone can remove the obstacle. . . . Their suffering is all in this delay, this forced inactivity; aware as they are that meanwhile their characters remain unchanged, unreformed" ("Dante's Idea of Purgatory, with Special Reference to *Purgatorio* XXI, 58–66," in *Dies Illa: Death in the Middle Ages. Proceedings of the 1983 Manchester Colloquium,* ed. Jane H. M. Taylor [Liverpool: Francis Cairns, 1984], 99–100).

Cogan has argued that not unlike the souls in hell, the souls in ante-purgatory continue to "repeat the actions that reflect the state in which they died" (*The Design in the Wax,* 299–303, quote on 301). It is only through the experience of pain in the seven terraces of purgatory that the repented guilt is removed and salvation attained. Jacopo del Cassero makes it clear, when he asks for prayers that may allow him to shorten his wait in ante-purgatory and hasten his ascent to real purgatory, where he will purge his serious sins: "Ond'io, che solo innanzi a li altri parlo, / ti priego, se mai vedi quel paese / che siede tra Romagna e quel di Carlo, / che tu mi sie di tuoi prieghi cortese / in Fano, sì che ben per me s'adori / pur ch'i' possa purgar le gravi offese" (*Purg.* 5.67–72). In the terrace of envy, Sapia is even clearer when she says that had Pier Pettinaio's prayers not helped her, she would not have started to pay for her debt yet and would still be in ante-purgatory: "Pace volli con Dio in su lo stremo / de la mia vita; e ancora non sarebbe / lo mio dover per penitenza scemo, / se ciò non fosse, ch'a memoria m'ebbe / Pier Pettinaio in sue sante orazioni, / a cui di me per caritate increbbe" (*Purg.* 13.124–29).

49. The fact that the aerial body unfolded by infernal souls is often deformed and even susceptible to monstrous deformation or metamorphosis is a manifestation of their sin, which has not been repented and still impairs the right use of reason and will. The thickness of the aerial body—which increases progressively in the circles of hell—is almost a sign of the degree of the souls' perversion and of their unchangeable state.

50. The intensity of the neutrals' cries of despair is due to the fact that they do not have any hope of death. See for instance *Inferno* 3.46: "Questi non hanno speranza di morte." In the same way, Lapo da Siena invokes death while being slaughtered by dogs among the squanderers: "Or accorri, accorri, morte!" (*Inf.* 13.118). But death is not going to occur in hell, where annihilation is no longer possible, and we have to imagine that, after being torn apart by the famished dogs, which carry around their several pieces (127–29), the squanderers' bodies are going to be reassembled so that they can be slaughtered (and composed) again forever and ever. In the same way, we can imagine that the monstrous metamorphoses of the thieves are going to be repeated for the interminable duration of hell. Dante insists that hell and infernal pain are never-ending. When Charon takes the sinful souls into his boat to drive them toward the other shore of the Acheron, the first thing he tells them is that they must have no hope of ever escaping from hell and its eternal punishments: "Guai a voi, anime prave! / Non isperate mai veder lo cielo: / i' vegno per menarvi a l'altra riva / ne le tenebre etterne, in caldo e 'n gelo" (*Inf.* 3.84–87).

51. While speaking about Cavalcante falling supine into his grave (*Inf.* 10.72), the Ottimo commentary points out that, in hell, sinners are always supine and never prone (as in purgatory) because being supine is a sign of their lack of conversion and spite for God: "E dice supin ricadde; a denotare li suoi arroganti costumi. Cadere supino è peccare. . . . E bene dice che li dannati caggiono indietro, però ch'elli caggiono in quelle pene, alle quali nel presente secolo volgono il viso; onde Salamone nel libro de' Proverbi dice: la via delli malvagi è tenebrosa; non sanno dove caggiono. E cadere in faccia si è umiliarsi, e adorare Idio, sì come si legge d'Abram, lo quale parlando con Dio cadde nella faccia sua" (*L' Ottimo commento della "Divina Commedia." Testo inedito di un contemporaneo di Dante*, ed. Alessandro Torri [Bologna: Forni, 1995] 1:180).

52. Against the traditional "maturi," Petrocchi reads "marturi" in the sense that Capaneus would not seem to be tormented by the fiery rain. I believe that the traditional "maturi," which is allowed by the manuscript tradition, expresses the psychological condition of the soul better, as this will be described in the following lines. See the commentaries of Singleton and Chiavacci Leonardi, who both read "maturi."

53. For what Thomas Greene calls the "tragedy of rigidity" of Capaneus and other damned souls, see "Dramas of Selfhood in the *Comedy*," in *From Time to Eternity*, ed. Thomas Bergin (New Haven: Yale University Press, 1967), 103–36, esp. 106ff.

54. The Ottimo commentary writes that "l'Autore descrive il luogo dove sono puniti li eretici, e descrive sotto generali parole loro dolorosa contenenza, e loro forte tormento: il quale, in quanto si considera per rispetto della divina giustizia, si può dire buono; se per rispetto a colui che 'l sostiene, si può dire reo, però che non è a purgazione, ma è pena" (*L'Ottimo commento della "Divina Commedia,"* 1:106).

55. The same image of ripening tears is repeated by Hadrian in lines 139–41 of the same canto: "Vattene omai: non vo' che più t'arresti; / ché la tua stanza mio pianger disagia, / col qual maturo ciò che tu dicesti." It contrasts with both the "pianti vani" of *Inferno* 21.5 and, if the reading of "maturi" instead of "marturi" is correct, with Capaneus's lack of ripening (*Inf.* 14.48).

56. Christ's strong presence in the *Purgatorio* contrasts with his almost complete absence from the *Inferno*. See Foster, who writes that "la regione del peccato, il *cieco mondo* (IV 13) offre poche occasioni di citare Cristo . . . L'*Inferno* descrive il mondo escluso dalla salvazione di Cristo" ("Cristo," in *Enciclopedia dantesca* 1970, 2:266–67).

57. A reference to the suffering of Christ's feet on the cross is found in *Paradiso* 20.104–5 ("in ferma fede / quel d'i' passuri e quel d'i' passi piedi"), while other references to the salvific power of Christ's blood and pain (represented by the nails of the cross) are found in *Paradiso* 31.2–3 ("La milizia santa / che nel suo sangue Cristo fece sposa"), *Paradiso* 19.103–5 ("A questo regno / non salì mai chi non credette 'n Cristo, / né pria né poi ch'el si chiavasse al legno"), and *Paradiso* 32.128–29 ("la bella sposa / che s'acquistò con la lancia e coi clavi").

58. See *Convivio* 4.5.3: "Volendo la 'nmensurabile bontà divina l'umana creatura a sé riconformare, che per lo peccato della prevaricazione del primo uomo da Dio era partita e disformata, eletto fu in quello altissimo e congiuntissimo consistorio de la Trinitade, che 'l Figliuolo di Dio in terra discendesse a fare questa concordia."

59. On Anselm's doctrine and its radical innovations with respect to the old doctrine, see especially Southern, *The Making of the Middle Ages,* 234–37; but also Gerard S. Sloyan, *The Crucifixion of Jesus: History, Myth, Faith* (Minneapolis: Fortress Press, 1995), 116–20; and Sarah Beckwith, *Christ's Body: Identity, Culture and Society in Late Medieval Writings* (London: Routledge, 1993), 45ff.

As is often the case, Dante is eclectic and mixes the Anselmian argument with an emphasis on God's charity taken from Aquinas and with an original stress on Christ's humility as the most significant sign of his greatness. For Dante and Anselm, see Franciscus S. Schmitt, "Anselmo d'Aosta, santo," in *Enciclopedia dantesca,* 1:293–94. For Dante's connections with Aquinas, see Giancarlo Rati, "L'alto e magnifico processo (Canto VII del *Paradiso*)," in *Saggi danteschi e altri studi* (Rome: Bulzoni, 1988), 57–80 (in which it is also pointed out that, like Aquinas, Dante emphasizes appropriateness—rather than necessity—of God's action). For Dante's departure from his sources in stressing Christ's humility, see Gabriele Muresu, "Le 'vie' della redenzione (*Paradiso* VII)," *Rassegna della letteratura italiana* 98 (1994): 5–19. .

60. "L'uomo è dunque la creatura che Dio ha voluto più somigliante a sé . . . Il genere umano gode *Di tutte queste doti,* immortalità, libertà dall'influenza delle cause seconde, somiglianza con Dio, ed esse lo mettono in una condizione di 'vantaggio,' cioè, con linguaggio feudale, di superiorità rispetto alle altre creature. Ma basta che una sola di queste qualità venga a mancare, che l'uomo decade . . . e perde la sua posizione di privilegio. Ciò è accaduto ai progenitori dell'umanità, Adamo ed Eva, e anche a tutti i loro discendenti, ogni volta che commettono peccato."

The ambivalence of the passage is exemplified by the problems that the critical tradition had in defining who or what is the human creature of line 77. Bosco is silent but seems to imply that it is the human soul. Chiavacci Leonardi does not explain it and seems to mean either the human soul or man. Singleton means man.

61. The passage from *Paradiso* 5:19–24 quoted in ch. 2, note 101 shows that the freedom that the human soul loses through sin is the freedom of the will, "de la volontà la libertate," which is God's greatest gift to the intelligent creatures (i.e., angels and human beings. For Dante's concept of freedom, see Stabile, "Volontà." In the *Comedy,* this freedom—which Beatrice in *Paradiso* 7 defines as the fact of being unconstrained by the influence of secondary causes (70–72)—is explained by Marco Lombardo's speech on "libero arbitrio" in *Purgatorio* 16.67ff.

62. A passage from the *Convivio* explains that returning to its creator is the soul's greatest desire: ". . . lo sommo desiderio di ciascuna cosa, e prima da la natura dato, è lo ritornare a lo suo principio. E però che Dio è principio de le nostre anime e fattore di quelle simili a sé (sì come è scritto: 'Facciamo l'uomo ad imagine e similitudine nostra'), essa anima massimamente desidera di tornare a quello" (*Conv.* 4.12.14).

63. Aquinas is responding to the objection that "no one can deliver from a sin not yet committed, but to be committed later" and says that "Christus sua passione nos a peccatis liberavit causaliter, idest instituens causam nostrae liberationis, ex quo possent quaecumque peccata quandoque remitti, vel praesentia vel passata vel futura" (ST 3a, q. 49, a. 1, ad 3). Dante seems to refer to the same concept in the heaven of the Sun, where the soul of Thomas Aquinas defines Christ as the one whose chest was transfixed by the lance and who redeemed all the past and future sins: "e in quel che, forato da la lancia, / e prima e poscia tanto sodisfece, / che d'ogne colpa vince la bilancia" (and into that [breast] which, pierced by the lance, made such satisfaction, both after and before, that it turns the scale against all fault [*Par.* 13.40–42]). While the old commentators tended to interpret "prima e poscia" as "before and after Christ's piercing," in the sense that his life and passion paid for Adam's sins, modern commentators agree that the expression refers to the fact that Christ redeemed past and future sins. (See Sapegno: "Con la sua passione il Cristo soddisfece il debito delle colpe passate e future, redense l'uomo dal peccato originale e gli porse il modo di redimere ogni altro peccato che potesse commettere nel

corso dei tempi.") I agree with the latter interpretation and suggest that, in the *Divine Comedy*, Aquinas's soul refers to the idea that Christ's Passion is always working for our atonement—the same idea that the "real" Aquinas had expressed in the *Summa theologiae*. Dante's image of Christ's Passion as redeeming "before and after" refers not only to the deliverance from original sin but also to the possibility of expiating one's own personal sins by conforming to the suffering Christ.

64. "Dicendum quod per Passionem Christi liberati sumus a reatu poenae dupliciter. Uno modo directe, inquantum scilicet passio Christi fuit sufficiens et superabundans satisfactio pro peccatis totius humani generis; exhibita autem satisfactione sufficienti, tollitur reatus poenae. Alio modo indirecte, inquantum scilicet passio Christi est causa remissionis peccati, in quo fundatur reatus poenae" (ST 3a, q. 49, a. 3, resp.).

65. "Dicendum quod, sicut supra dictum est, ad hoc quod consequamur effectum Passionis Christi, oportet nos ei configurari. Configuramur autem ei in baptismo sacramentaliter secundum illud *Rom., Consepulti sumus ei per baptismum in mortem*. Unde baptizatis nulla poena satisfactoria imponitur, quia sunt totaliter liberati per satisfactionem Christi. Quia vero *Christus semel tantum pro peccatis nostris mortuus est*, ut dicitur I *Pet.*, ideo non potest homo secundario configurari morti Christi per sacramentum baptismi. Unde oportet quod illi qui post baptismum peccant configurentur Christo patienti per aliquid poenalitatis vel passionis quam in seipsis sustineant; quae tamen multo minor sufficit quam esset condigna peccato, cooperante satisfactione Christi" (ST 3a, q. 49, a. 3, ad 2).

Two articles later, Aquinas explains that "two kinds of sin prevent us from entering the heavenly kingdom"—the sin common to the whole human race and the special sin of every man, "that is, the sin he commits by himself"—and reaffirms then that not only did Christ's Passion deliver the human race from original sin, but it also delivers the individual Christians from their personal sins: "Per passionem autem Christi liberati sumus, non solum a peccato communi totius naturae, et quantum ad culpam et quantum ad reatum poenae, ipso solvente pretium pro nobis, sed etiam a peccatis propriis singulorum, qui communicant ejus passioni per fidem, et charitatem, et fidei sacramenta. Et ideo per passionem Christi aperta est nobis janua regni coelestis" (ST 3a, q. 49, a. 5, resp.).

66. The Latin text is found in PP. Collegii S. Bonaventurae, ed., *Bonaventurae opera omnia* (Quaracchi: Collegium S. Bonaventurae, 1898), 8:171. The translation is found in *The Works of Bonaventure*, vol. 1, *Mystical Opuscula*, trans. José de Vinck (Paterson, N.J.: St. Anthony Guild, 1960), 167–68.

67. *Opera omnia*, ed. Quaracchi, 1898, 8:189; trans. de Vinck, 205. From the very first words of its preface, the *Lignum vitae* aims to enkindle the reader with love for the crucified Christ so that he may conform with him and join him on the cross: "*Christo confixus sum cruci*, ad Galatas secundo. Verus Dei cultor Christique discipulus, qui Salvatori omnium pro se crucifixo perfecte configurari desiderat, ad

hoc potissimum attento mentis conatu debet intendere, ut Christi Jesu crucem circumferat iugiter tam mente, quam carne, quatenus praefatum Apostoli verbum veraciter valeat in semetipso sentire" (in *Opera omnia*, ed. Quaracchi, 8:68; trans. de Vinck, 97). For Franciscan devotion to the suffering humanity of Christ in the thirteenth century, see Bestul, *Texts of the Passion*, 43–56.

68. Barolini, *The Undivine "Comedy,"* 99.

69. For a detailed analysis of the structure of the seven terraces and their variations, see Enrico De' Negri, "Temi e iconografia del *Purgatorio*," *Romanic Review* 49 (1958): 81–104; and three classic and still very useful works: Francesco D'Ovidio, *Nuovi studii danteschi: Il Purgatorio e il suo preludio* (Milan: Hoepli, 1906); Giovanni Busnelli, *La concezione del Purgatorio dantesco* (Rome: Civiltà Cattolica, 1906); and idem, *L'ordinamento morale del purgatorio dantesco*, 2nd ed. (Rome: Civiltà Cattolica, 1908). For the hymns and the psalms that the souls sing, see Erminia Ardissino, "I canti liturgici nel *Purgatorio* dantesco," *Dante Studies* 108 (1990): 39–65.

70. The same angel erases the *P* from the forehead of the pilgrim and, presumably, from all the purging souls. It is debated whether the pilgrim alone or all the souls have the *P* inscribed on the forehead. From *Purgatorio* 21.22–24 ("Se tu riguardi a' segni / che questi porta e che l'angel profila, / ben vedrai che coi buon convien ch'e' regni"), where Virgil shows the remaining three *P*s on the pilgrim's forehead to Statius as something common in purgatory, it is possible to infer that all the purging souls undergo the same process as the pilgrim: the guardian angel at the threshold of purgatory inscribes seven *P*s (for *Peccata*) on the souls' foreheads, each of which is erased by an angel when they move from one terrace to the next, that is, when the expiation for that sin has been completed. While Singleton thinks that only the pilgrim has the seven *P*s inscribed on his forehead, the majority of the commentaries—including those of Sapegno, Bosco, Chiavacci Leonardi, and Garavelli—seem to agree with Barbi's interpretation that they are written on the forehead of all the souls:

> Ma se non era quello dei segni profilati dall'angelo l'indizio normale, per tutti, d'essere ammessi alla purgazione, come avrebbe potuto Stazio da quei segni arguir tosto *(ben vedrai)* che Dante è destinato a regnare coi buoni? E l'espressione *che l'angel profila* può aver altro valore che "l'angelo suole profilare"? Dante, è vero, non fa mai notare i P sulla fronte degli spiriti che si purgano; gli basta che il lettore indovini dal suo caso che li hanno. E qui conferma la cosa indirettamente. (Quoted by Bosco)

71. For an analysis of the way Dante rewrites or translates the beatitudes from Matthew, see Federigo Tollemache, "Beatitudini evangeliche," in *Enciclopedia dantesca*, 1:540–41.

72. In his commentary, Charles Singleton highlights the richness of Dante's text and the ambiguity of line 154, which can mean "either hungering as much as is right (observing temperance in eating) or hungering after all that is just, i.e., after

justice, as the beatitude has it." In her commentary, Chiavacci Leonardi convincingly argues that the latter meaning is the most important one. The text from Matthew is "Beati qui esuriunt et sitiunt iustitiam: quoniam ipsi saturabuntur." Dante divides the beatitudes in two and uses the image of thirst for the avaricious (*Purg.* 22.4–5) and the image of hunger for the gluttonous. For the ambivalence of line 154, see Singleton's commentary to the passage.

73. Anna Maria Chiavacci Leonardi, "Introduzione," in her commentary to the *Purgatorio*, xviii:

> Delle antiche virtù, persino la giustizia—cardine dell'etica antica e massima delle quattro virtù cardinali cristiane—è assente da questa tavola. Le virtù delle Beatitudini, o virtù spirituali . . . vanno infatti tutte molto al di là della giustizia. I pacifici non sono qui quelli che non eccedono nell'ira, ma coloro che perdonano le offese, anche mortali (l'esempio principe sarà quello del martire Stefano, che prega per i suoi persecutori); la virtù opposta all'avarizia non è la sobrietà, ma la povertà estrema della stalla di Betlemme; i misericordiosi non sono quelli che danno "con pronta liberalitate" (*Conv.* I, viii 2), ma coloro che danno anche la vita per gli amici, come Pilade, o per i nemici, come il Cristo. Ogni virtù del purgatorio ha questo segno di oltranza; qui siamo nel regno del gratuito, che non misura, che non dà "a ciascuno il suo," ma molto di più.

See also, by the same author, "Le beatitudini e la struttura poetica del *Purgatorio*," *Giornale storico della letteratura italiana* 161 (1984): 1–29. Foster has suggested but not developed the same point: "Risultato di questo accurato disegno di esempi ed esortazioni è la completa cristianizzazione dell'etica del *Purgatorio*, cosicché in questo, è resa del tutto diversa da quella dell'*Inferno*, il cui fondamento era aristotelico" ("Cristo," 267). Tollemache, "Beatitudini evangeliche," underlines Dante's agreement with Thomas Aquinas, who thought that the beatitudes are seven and not eight, because the last one is a summary of all the others: "Beati qui persecutionem patiuntur propter iustitiam: quoniam ipsorum est regum coelorum." This is precisely the ultimate model of purgatory. Of the remaining seven, Dante splits the fourth in two parts and uses it for both the avaricious and the gluttonous. I would suggest that Dante does not use the second one—"Beati mites: quoniam ipsi possidebunt terram"—precisely because patience characterizes all the purging souls in accepting and experiencing their punishment.

74. On the use of the *exemplum* in the *Comedy*, see Carlo Delcorno, "Dante e l'*exemplum*' medievale," *Lettere italiane* 35 (1983): 3–28, who speaks of "carattere pragmatico dell'*exemplum*" and defines it as a "genere letterario agitatorio" (8). On the pragmatic value of the *exemplum*, see Jacques Berlioz, "Le récit efficace: L'exemplum au service de la prédication (XIIIe–XVe siècles)," *Mélanges de l'École française de Rome. Moyen Âge–Temps Modernes* 92 (1980): 113–46.

75. Conrad of Saxony, *Speculum seu salutatio Beatae Mariae Virginis ac Sermones mariani,* ed. Petrus de Alcantara Martinez (Grottaferrata: Editiones Collegii S. Bonaventurae ad Claras Aquas, 1975), 203–4:

> Ipsa enim est Maria, quae et omni vitio caruit et omni virtute claruit. Ipsa, inquam, est Maria, quae a septem vitiis capitalibus fuit immunissima et virtutibus eis contrariis fuit munitissima: Maria enim contra superbiam profundissima per humilitatem; Maria contra invidiam affectuosissima per charitatem; Maria contra ira mansuetissima per lenitatem; Maria contra accidiam indefessissima per sedulitatem; Maria contra avaritiam tenuissima per paupertatem; Maria contra gulam temperatissima per sobrietatem; Maria contra luxuriam castissima per virginitatem fuit. Haec omnia ex illis Scripturis colligere possumus, in quibus nomen Mariae expressum invenimus.

Quotations from the *Speculum* will be from this edition. The English translation attributes the text to Bonaventure: Bonaventure, *The Mirror of the Blessed Virgin Mary (Speculum Beatae Mariae Virginis) and The Psalter of Our Lady (Psalterium Beatae Mariae Virginis),* trans. Mary Emmanuel (St. Louis: B. Herder, 1932), 28. See also lectio 13:

> Maledictionem per septem vitia capitalia mundus incurrit, benedictionem autem per virtutes contrarias Maria obtinuit. *Benedicta* ergo *tu in mulieribus,* o Maria! Benedicta utique pro humilitate contra superbiam, benedicta pro charitate contra invidiam, benedicta pro lenitate contra iracundiam, benedicta pro strenuitate contra accidiam, benedicta pro liberalitate contra avaritiam, benedicta pro sobrietatem contra gulam, benedicta pro castitate contra luxuriam. (419–20)

The influence of the *Speculum* (which was for a long time attributed to Bonaventure) on the *Comedy* was already recognized by: Paolo Perez, *I sette cerchi del Purgatorio di Dante. Saggio di studi,* 2nd ed. (Verona: Libreria della Minerva, 1867), 266 n. 1; Edward Moore, *Studies in Dante, Second Series: Miscellaneous Essays* (Oxford: Clarendon Press, 1899), *passim* and esp. 194–95; and D'Ovidio, *Nuovi studii danteschi,* 237–38. Recently, see Chiavacci Leonardi, "Le beatitudini e la struttura poetica del *Purgatorio,*" 26: "Quest'opera [Conrad's *Speculum*], di grande diffusione nei conventi francescani di tutta Europa, può ritenersi con sufficiente sicurezza nota a Dante, frequentatore di Santa Croce e appassionato lettore; e comunque la precisione del riscontro è tale che anche con tutta la cautela necessaria in questo tipo di ricerche sembra non si possa fare a meno di ammettere una conoscenza, se non proprio di questo testo, di un suo derivato o affine."

76. Samuele Girotto, *Corrado di Sassonia predicatore e mariologo del sec. XIII* (Florence: Studi francescani, 1952), 202–16. It is the only essay that to my knowledge analyzes the relationship between Conrad's and Dante's texts. Sergio Cristaldi

acknowledges the derivation of Dante's choice from the *Speculum* but dismisses it: "Meno interessante è in tal senso lo *Speculum* di Corrado di Sassonia: la sua mariologia, tutta intesa alla celebrazione della *regina virtutum* come paradigma unico, non ha molto da offrirci, e tutto sommato, nonostante le accertate corrispondenze con il *Purgatorio,* di cui è quasi certamente una fonte, finisce col risultarne non poco distante nello spirito" ("Dalle beatitudini all' 'Apocalisse.' Il Nuovo Testamento nella *Commedia,*" *Letture classensi* 17 [1988]: 27).

77. In the following section on Conrad's spirituality, I am indebted to Girotto, *Corrado di Sassonia,* esp. 75–104 for Christ and 132–202 for Mary. See also de Alcantara Martinez's "Introduction" to Conrad of Saxony, *Speculum seu salutatio Beatae Mariae Virginis ac Sermones mariani,* 5–137, esp. 66–95; and A. Teetaert, "Saxe (Conrade de)," *Dictionnaire de théologie catholique* (Paris: Letouzey et Ané, 1939), vol. 14, cols. 1234–35.

78. "Di questo mistero [Christ's Passion] Corrado ne parla così spesso e con tali accenti d'un appassionato ardore, che noi siamo costretti a riconoscere in lui un vero innamorato del divin Crocifisso. Interprete fedele della pietà francescana, egli ci rappresenta il Cristo come l'uomo dei dolori, l'umiliato, che soffre e muore per l'umanità, come il Salvatore sceso fra gli uomini che sente tutte le amarezze del dolore umano, sia nell'anima che nel corpo: è l'uomo che prega e si sacrifica per l'uomo. Ed è per questo che i suoi sermoni destano in noi una devota e pietosa commozione verso il Crocifisso" (Girotto, *Corrado di Sassonia,* 87–88).

79. Ibid., 91–92.

80. Ibid., 93. The passage is from the first sermon on the Sunday of the Passion, which Girotto defines as "un vero panegirico sul sangue di Cristo" (92).

81. Christ's Passion and opposition to the seven deadly sins is also what characterizes his presence in the *Purgatorio:* "Nel Purgatorio due aspetti di Cristo traspaiono in particolare: il maestro di un'etica assolutamente contraria ai sette vizi capitali, e il crocifisso" (Foster, "Cristo," 267). For Christ's blood in the *Speculum,* see for instance lectio 12: "[Christus] servus noster factus est, serviens nobis miseris usque ad sanguinem. Propter nos enim servus, propter nos quoque sanguineus factus est Christus: sanguineus in dorso per flagella, sanguineus in capite per spinas, sanguineus in latere per lanceam, sanguineus in manibus et pedibus per clavos" (398–99). For Christ as a model of virtue against the seven capital sins, see the whole lectio 15, which is summarized in the beginning as follows: "Christus enim fructus est mentis non vitiosae, sed virtuosae, non vitiosae per septem vitia capitalia, sed virtuosae contra septem vitia capitalia. Fructus ergo iste est: Fructus humilium contra superbiam, fructus amantium contra invidiam, fructus mitium contra iram, fructus laborantium contra accidiam, fructus liberalium contra avaritiam, fructus abstinentium contra gulam, fructus continentium contra luxuriam" (463–64).

82. In his second Sermon on the Annunciation, Conrad writes that the Son of God "ad modum . . . roris suaviter, subtiliter, utiliter descendit in uterum

virginis, qui per vellus significatur. Ps. 71, 6: *Descendet sicut pluvia in vello.* De hoc vellere uteri virginalis facta est tunica tam pretiosa, quae pro debitis totius mundi fuit impignorata, videlicet, caro Christi" (in Conrad of Saxony, *Speculum seu salutatio,* 518). See also *Speculum Beatae Virginis Mariae,* lectio 6: "Quintum Mariae privilegium est quod ipsa super omnem creaturam Deo etiam corporaliter familiarissima fuit. Nam, quod numquam creaturae concessum fuit nec concedetur in aeternum, ipsa Deum novem mensibus in utero portavit, ipsa Deum 'ubere de coelo pleno' lactavit, ipsa Deum multis annis dulciter educavit, ipsa Deum sibi subditum habuit, ipsa Deum purum in amplexibus et osculis familiarissime contrectavit" (250–51). For the identity of Christ's and Mary's flesh and the subsequent resurrection of Mary, see Girotto, *Corrado di Sassonia,* 150–52 and 169–71.

83. *Speculum Beatae Virginis Mariae,* lectio 3, 175–78; *The Mirror of the Blessed Virgin Mary,* 16. For the doctrine of Mary's compassion in Conrad of Saxony and its importance in other contemporary Franciscan authors, see *Speculum,* n. 9 on 178–80, where de Alcantara Martinez quotes passages from Bonaventure: "Dolores namque, plagas et opprobria Filii in se retorquens, in suam propriam personam recipiebat, sentiens *quod et in Christo Iesu* (Phil. 2, 5). In animo enim illi martyri commartyr astabat, vulnerato convulnerata, crucifixo concrucifixa, gladiato congladiata" *(Sermo 1 dom. infra oct. Epiph.).* See also *Vitis mystica,* chap. 9, James of Milan's *Stimulus amoris,* the *Meditationes passionis Christi,* and Ubertino da Casale's *Arbor vitae crucifixae.*

84. On the dowries of Mary's glorified body, see *Speculum,* lectio 4: "Quodlibet enim corpus glorificatum habet quatuor dotes gloriosas, videlicet dotem mirae claritatis, dotem mirae subtilitatis, dotem mirae agilitatis, dotem mirae impassibilitatis. Et si omnium sanctorum corpora his quatuor dotibus Deus glorificabit, quanto magis corpus illud, quod ipsum glorificatorem omnium corporum genuit?" (256–57).

85. *Corrado di Sassonia,* 167. For Mary's mediation in the *Speculum,* see lectio 9: "Securum iam habet homo accessum ad Deum, ubi mediatorem causae suae Filium habet ante Patrem et ante Filium matrem. Christus, nudato corpore Patri ostendit latus et vulnera; Maria filio pectus et ubera. Non potest ullo modo fieri repulsa, ubi concurrunt et perorant omni lingua disertius haec clementiae monumenta et charitatis insigna" (342–43).

86. In the encounter between the pilgrim and St. John in the heaven of the Fixed Stars, Dante simultaneously rejects John's bodily assumption to heaven and supports that of Mary (*Par.* 25.121–29). I will return to this episode in the next chapter.

87. As Bernard will say at the end of *Paradiso,* Mary is "umile e alta più che creatura" (33.2). She is the best example of the generous love that characterizes the ethics of the *Purgatorio:* "La tua benignità non pur soccorre / a chi domanda, ma molte fïate / liberamente al dimandar precorre. / In te misericordia, in te pietate, /

in te magnificenza, in te s'aduna / quantunque in creatura è di bontate" (*Par.* 33.16–21). On Mary as the perfect embodiment of the gratuitous love that is expressed by the beatitudes, see Chiavacci Leonardi, "Le beatitudini e la struttura poetica del *Purgatorio*," esp. 20–29.

88. The contrapasso in hell is often by analogy ("per analogia") in the sense that it corresponds to the sin that is punished, while in purgatory it is usually by contrast to the sin to be purged ("per contrasto"). See D'Ovidio, *Nuovi studii danteschi*, 198; and Silvio Pasquazi, "Contrapasso," in *Enciclopedia dantesca*, 1970, 2:181.

89. The text of the entire line that the souls sing is as follows: "Domine, labia mea aperies, et os meum adnuntiabit laudem tuam." While on earth they had used their lips to indulge in gluttony, now they use them to praise God.

90. "(Exivit ergo Iesus portans coronam spineam, et purpureum vestimentum.) Et dicit: Ecce homo" (19:5).

91. For the image of Christ's body on the cross as a book inscribed with his own sufferings, see also Caesarius of Heisterbach's *Dialogus miracolorum:* "Librum hunc Christum ipse scripsit; quia propria voluntate passus est. In pelle siquidem corporis eius scriptae erant litterae minores et nigrae, per lividas plagas flagellorum; litterae rubeae et capitales, per infixiones clavorum; puncta etiam et virgulae, per punctiones spinarum. Bene pellis eadem prius fuerat multiplici percussione pumicata, colaphis et sputis cretata, arundine limata" (distinctio VIII, c. 35; in Caesarius of Heisterbach, *Dialogus miracolorum*, ed. Josephus Strange [Cologne: Heberle, 1851], 2:108–9); and Iacopone's *lauda* "Oi dolze amore," 49–56: "Vocce currendo / en Croce legendo, / ennel Liver che c'è ensanguenato, / cà issa scriptura / me fa en natura / e 'n filosafia conventato. / O libro signato, / che dentro è 'nnaurato, / ch'è tutto florito d'Amore!" (Iacopone da Todi, *Laude,* ed. Franco Mancini [Rome and Bari: Laterza, 1974], 200).

92. Gertrud Schiller, *Iconography of Christian Art*, vol. 2, *The Passion of Jesus Christ,* trans. Janet Seligman (Greenwich, Conn.: New York Graphic Society, 1972), 74.

93. See A. Legner, "Ecce homo," in *Lexikon der Christlichen Iconographie*, ed. Engelbert Kirschbaum et al. (Rome: Herder, 1968), 1:558–61, esp. 558. Duccio painted two scenes connected with the Ecce Homo theme. The first one is properly a Flagellation with Pilate indicating Christ, while in the second one, Christ is crowned and mocked in front of Pilate (see appendix, figs. 2 and 3). Duccio's paintings, and similar, quite common scenes painted on Tuscan Romanesque crucifixes, could represent the beginning of what becomes widespread Ecce Homo iconography. In fact, this particular association of Pilate and the tormented Christ was very popular in medieval Tuscany. Several popular examples of this kind of painting—which Dante must have known well—include the Crucifix no. 434 at the Uffizi Gallery (mid-thirteenth century) by an anonymous Florentine master, and another one by Enrico di Tedice in the Church of S. Martino in Pisa. Quite interesting may

also be the scene by an anonymous Gothic artist from Northern Italy (Bologna), where the Flagellation and the Mocked Christ are in the same scene (altarpiece in the Pinacoteca of Bologna, early fourteenth century).

94. The pilgrim has no problem recognizing "Giudice Nin" (*Purg.* 8.52–54), while he needs some time to recognize Casella and Belacqua, but not because their features are different or torn by the punishment, which is not physical in ante-purgatory. In the case of Casella, the pilgrim did not expect to find him on the shore of the mountain but further in the process of purification (*Purg.* 2.76–93); in the case of Belacqua, the pilgrim could not see his face, but as soon as he perceives it, he recognizes his old friend (*Purg.* 4.106–15). The only case of failed recognition in the second realm occurs with Manfred because the pilgrim has never met him and not because he is not recognizable.

95. I think that the best reading of this passage is given by Foster, "Dante's Idea of Purgatory." But see also Giorgio Padoan, "Il canto XXI del *Purgatorio*," in *Nuove letture dantesche* (Florence: Le Monnier, 1970), 4:327–54, esp. 342–44; and, for a more technical reading of the terms employed by Dante, Stabile, "Volontà."

96. In her study of the psalms sung or mentioned in the *Purgatorio,* Ardissino points out that they are connected with the motifs of exodus (i.e., liberation from sin) and Christ's sacrifice ("I canti liturgici nel *Purgatorio* dantesco").

97. The doctrine of co-redemption is connected with the idea that Mary participated in the Redemption not only by giving birth to Christ but also by sharing his sufferings on Calvary in a unique sacrifice:

> Movebat enim eum Matris affectio, et omnino tunc erat una Christi et Mariae voluntas, unumque holocaustum ambo pariter offerebant Deo: haec in sanguine cordis, hic in sanguine carnis. . . . Una est Mariae et Christi caro, unus spiritus, una charitas . . . Unitas divisionem non recepit, non secatur in partes, et si ex duobus factum sit unum, illud tamen ultra scindi non potest, et Filii gloriam cum matre non tam communem judico quam eandem. (Arnauld, *De laudibus B. Mariae Virginis*, PL 189, cols. 1726–31; quotation on c. 1727)

For the doctrine of co-redemption, see: Von Simson, *"Compassio* and *co-redemptio";* and Sticca, *The "Planctus Mariae,"* 19–30.

98. After describing the intensity of Mary's compassion and its connection with her love for Christ, Marcel-Marie Desmarais explains the principle that her sorrow would have been "douleur suprême mais douleur inutile, douleur vaine, douleur perdue, si elle n'avait pas eu à son principe une foi inébranlable. Car à elle seule, les souffrances endurés avec Jésus ne suffisent pas à constituer ce privilège qu'est la communion au Christ souffrant, la 'communicatio passionis'" (*S. Albert le Grand docteur de la médiation mariale* [Paris: Institut d'études médiévales, 1935], 73).

99. "Sicut Dominus omnium simul habuit summum gaudium et summum dolorem, sic Domina nostra simul habuit summam compassionem et summam congratulationem. . . . Vel dicatur quod summum tristabile in tali genere est

dupliciter accipere: uno modo ut summe contrarium appetitui, et sic summum infert dolorem; alio modo prout est via et medium ad summum gaudium" (*De laude Beatae Mariae Virginis,* resp. ad qq. 148–50, quoted in Bruno Korosak, "De cooperatione B. Virginis Mariae ad salutem mundi," in *Mariologia S. Alberti Magni eiusque coequalium* [Rome: Academia Mariana Internationalis, 1954], 491–587, quotation on 522 [quoted also in Sticca, *The "Planctus Mariae,"* 26]). The idea of Mary's agreement to her son's sacrifice is already in Bonaventure: "Secundo, *persolvit* istud pretium ut mulier *fortis et pia,* scilicet quando Christus passus est in cruce ad persolvendum pretium istud, ut nos purgaret, lavaret et redimeret; tunc beata Virgo fuit praesens, acceptans et concordans voluntati divinae. Et placuit ei, quod pretium uteri sui offerretur in cruce pro nobis" (*De septem donis Spiritus Sancti. Collatio VI,* in *Opera omnia,* ed. Quaracchi [1891], 5:486). Hence the coexistence of sorrow and agreement/pleasure: "Beata Virgo compatiebatur ei maxime, sed ex altera parte placebat ei, quod pro nobis [Christus] traderetur" (487).

100. "Quando consensit, sensit se per suum consensum dedicari et iungi praefatis humilitatibus et humilibus officiis Redemptoris . . . Quando magis Virgo cum Christo crucifixa est in hora conceptionis" (quoted in Sticca, *The "Planctus Mariae,"* 27).

101. "Licet Virgo perfectissima voluntate et caritate voluerit Christum pati, secundum quod ipsa passio erat a Deo et Christo homine volita, non tamen creditur de Filii passione tunc gavisa fuisse, immo summe doluisse"; quoted in Sticca, *The "Planctus Mariae,"* 27. See 27–29 for the Catalonian Raymund Lull, another Franciscan theologian whose doctrine is very similar to Olivi's.

102. Dante indirectly refers to the doctrine of compassion at the end of *Purgatorio* when, while describing Beatrice's reaction at the sight of what happens to the chariot, he refers to Mary's sorrow under the cross as the greatest ever experienced: "E Bëatrice, sospirosa e pia, / quelle ascoltava sì fatta, che poco / più a la croce si cambiò Maria" (*Purg.* 33.4–6). In this brief reference to Mary's sorrow, the verb "cambiarsi," to change, is important because it points out Mary's transformation through compassion. A possible reference to the doctrine of co-redemption may be found at the end of *Paradiso,* when Mary is indicated as the one who healed the wound opened by Eve: "La piaga che Maria richiuse e unse, / quella ch'è tanto bella da' suoi piedi / è colei che l'aperse e che la punse" (*Par.* 32.4–6).

103. "Noi eravam partiti già da esso, / e brigavam di soverchiar la strada / tanto quanto al poder n'era permesso, / quand' io senti', come cosa che cada, / tremar lo monte; onde mi prese un gelo / qual prender suol colui ch'a morte vada" (*Purg.* 20.124–29).

104. "Poi cominciò da tutte parti un grido / tal, che 'l maestro inverso me si feo, / dicendo: 'Non dubbiar mentr' io ti guido.' / 'Gloria in excelsis' tutti 'Deo' / dicean, per quel ch'io da' vicin compresi, / onde intender lo grido si poteo. / No' istavamo immobili e sospesi / come i pastor che prima udir quel canto, / fin che 'l tremar cessò ed el compiési" (*Purg.* 20.133–41).

105. The earthquake in Jerusalem is connected with the one in purgatory also by the feelings of fear to which they give rise: "Et ecce velum templi scissum est in duas partes a summo usque deorsum: et terra mota est, et monumenta aperta sunt. . . . Centurio autem, et qui cum eo erant, custodientes Iesum, viso terraemotu et his quae fiebant, timuerunt valde, dicentes: Vere Filius Dei erat iste" (Matthew 27:51–54).

106. For the connection between Christ's Incarnation and *passibilitas*, that is, the possibility of experiencing pain, see note 13 above.

107. See my discussion in chapter 2 above.

CHAPTER 4 Now, Then, and Beyond: Air, Flesh, and Fullness in the *Comedy*

1. John Bruce-Jones, "L'importanza della materia prima (Why Does Primary Matter Matter?): Aspetti della materia nella poesia e nel pensiero di Dante," in *Dante e la scienza*, ed. Patrick Boyde and Vittorio Russo (Ravenna: Longo, 1995), 221: "Non è forse neanche esagerato affermare che la posizione di Dante sulla materia prima (dalla parte dei tomisti se pure molto individuale) è una delle ragioni per cui si continua a leggere la *Divina Commedia*. . . . Il potere della *Commedia* è che in una serie di incontri con anime umane che sono le forme sostanziali di vere persone, il lettore deve affrontare dure e difficili verità sulla condizione umana. La cultura filosofica che rese possibile lo scrivere di questa *Commedia*, è una dove l'anima umana è l'unica forma sostanziale dell'uomo."

2. Francesco Santi, "Un nome di persona al corpo e la massa dei corpi gloriosi," *Micrologus* 1 (1993): 288: "Prendiamo per cominciare un caso molto chiaro di tomismo nell'illustrazione della resurrezione dei corpi. Esso ci è offerto da Dante nel suo racconto dell'aldilà; egli presenta i suoi personaggi come anime che hanno in sé, molto prima del giudizio, la sostanza del loro corpo."

3. For a detailed analysis of the interpretations that have been given to line 63, see Antonino Pagliaro, *Ulisse: Ricerche semantiche sulla "Divina Commedia"* (Messina-Florence: D'Anna, 1967), 25–42; and, more recently, Robert Hollander, *Il Virgilio dantesco: Tragedia nella "Commedia"* (Florence: Olschki, 1983), 23–79. In his commentary to *Inferno* 1.63, Singleton suggests that the verse is deliberately ambiguous.

4. Singleton translates "omo certo" as "living man." I have changed his translation to "real man"—an expression that not only translates the Italian literally but also points to the difference between a person and a shade.

5. These lines refer to the moment in which the Sibyl keeps Aeneas from trying to use his sword against the shades because it would be useless: "Et, ni docta comes tenuis sine corpora vitas / Admoneat volitare cava sub imagine formae, / Inruat et frustra ferro diverberat umbras" (292–94). The same term "vita" is used throughout the *Comedy* to define the human soul.

6. *In epistolam I ad Corinthios Commentaria,* chap. 15, lectio 2, in *Opera omnia,* ed. Fretté (1876), 21:33. See chap. 2, n. 41 above.

7. See Teodolinda Barolini, *The Undivine "Comedy": Detheologizing Dante* (Princeton: Princeton University Press, 1992), 42–43.

8. In *Opera omnia,* ed. Leonine (1930), 15:249; *Summa contra gentiles,* 2nd ed. (Notre Dame, Ind.: University of Notre Dame Press, 1975), 4:299.

9. Only the blessed will attain "true perfection," i.e., the union of a perfect soul and a perfect flesh (which, as we will see, will be "gloriosa e santa" [*Par.* 14.43], which is to say, endowed with the four gifts of impassibility, clarity, subtlety, and agility). The damned will never attain true perfection because their souls will remain contaminated by sin, and their bodies, as theologians explained, will be dark, heavy, and infinitely passible. See Caroline Walker Bynum, *The Resurrection of the Body in Western Christianity, 200–1336* (New York: Columbia University Press, 1995), 265ff. Another possible interpretation of line 110 is that even though the damned will not attain true perfection with the resurrection of the body, they nonetheless desire to be after the Last Judgment rather than before. What Virgil's statement would imply, in this case, is that the anxiety of being separated from the body is so strong that the damned souls are looking forward to being reunited with their bodies, even though they know that at that point their suffering will increase.

10. While the episode of the avaricious only hints at these changes (*Inf.* 7.55–57), the pilgrim's encounter with the heretics underlines again the increase in pain of the damned at the end of time: not only will the fiery sepulchers tormenting the shades be shut down when the souls return from the Jehoshaphat Valley with the bodies they have left on earth ("Tutti seran serrati / quando di Iosafàt qui torneanno / coi corpi che la sù hanno lasciati" [*Inf.* 10.10–12]), but as time ends and the damned can only know what is remote from them, they will remain in a perpetual state of complete ignorance (*Inf.* 10.100–108).

11. Singleton translates "ma non però ch'alcuna sen rivesta" (104) as "but not, however, that any may inhabit it again." I have modified the translation and kept the image of the body as clothing—an image that, as we will see, is very meaningful.

12. Several phrases in the *Comedy* indicate the psychosomatic wholeness of the person and highlight the imperfect condition of the separated soul. When the pilgrim recognizes the shade of Brunetto Latini among the sodomites and expresses the wish that his old master were still alive, he uses an expression that implies that the soul without its body is "exiled" from human nature: "'Se fosse tutto pieno il mio dimando,' / rispuos' io lui, 'voi non sareste ancora / de l'umana natura posto in bando'" (*Inf.* 15.79–81). Like Virgil's answer, this passage suggests that the soul alone is not the whole human being but only a part of it.

The psychosomatic unity of the human being is reflected also in the fact that usually physical death is not referred to as the moment in which the soul finally rids itself of the body, but as the temporary separation from it. The soul of Master Adam, for instance, says that it left its body after it was burned ("il corpo sù arso lasciai" [*Inf.* 30.75]); Pier de la Broccia's soul was divided from its body by hate and envy: "Vidi conte Orso e l'anima divisa / dal corpo suo per astio e per inveggia / com' e' dicea, non per colpa commisa" (*Purg.* 6.19–21); in the heaven of the Sun, Thomas Aquinas points to the soul of Boethius and says that the body from which it was expelled lies in Pavia: "Lo corpo ond' ella fu cacciata giace / giuso in Cieldauro" (*Par.* 10.127–29). The prayer that the pilgrim addresses to Beatrice in the Empyrean expresses the belief that body and soul are knotted together: "La tua magnificenza in me custodi, / sì che l'anima mia, che fatt' hai sana, / piacente a te dal corpo si disnodi" (*Par.* 31.88–90). The same sense of separation is also echoed in the images of the body's loneliness, nakedness, and emptiness, once it has been abandoned by its soul. Virgil refers to his death as the moment in which the flesh was divested of the soul ("Di poco era di me [anima] la carne nuda" [*Inf.* 9.25]); when mentioning Manto's death, he says that her body was left empty ("e visse, e vi lasciò suo corpo vano" [*Inf.* 20.87]); and, while describing his own death, Bonconte da Montefeltro's soul says that his flesh remained alone ("e quivi / caddi, e rimase la mia carne sola" [*Purg.* 5.101–2]).

13. See, for instance, 3.88–93; 5.4–6 and 25–27; 6.57; 9.9–10; 11.43–45; 13.130–32; 16.24; 20.40–42; 23.112–14; 24.5–6; 26.7–8.

14. The following line ("Se per veder la sua ombra restaro") shows that it is real precisely because it produces a shadow.

15. The same souls ask the pilgrim how he can have an aerial body as though he were not dead yet (*Purg.* 26.16–24). The pilgrim's answer highlights the difference between the shades' "corpo fittizio" and his "corpo uman," which is made of flesh and blood: "non son rimase acerbe né mature / le membra mia di là, ma son qui meco / col sangue suo e con le sue giunture" (55–57).

16. In *Aeneid* 2.792–94, 6.700–702; and *Georgics* 4.500–502. In Western literature, the failed embraces expressing the tragedy of loss have a long tradition, including the *Iliad* (Achilles' attempt to embrace Patroclus's ghost in book 23.99–102), the *Odyssey* (Odysseus' attempt to embrace his mother in book 11.204–8).

17. When the pilgrim tells Statius that the soul in front of him is Virgil, Statius bows down in order to embrace Virgil's feet, leading Virgil to remind him of the uselessness of that action given that both of them are simple shades: "Frate, / non far, ché tu se' ombra e ombra vedi" (*Purg.* 21.131–32). Statius acknowledges his mistake and says that his great love for Virgil made him forget the corporeal inconsistency of the shades: "Ed ei surgendo: 'Or puoi la quantitate / comprender de l'amor ch'a te mi scalda, / quand' io dismento nostra vanitate, / trattando l'ombre come cosa salda'" (*Purg.* 21.133–36). This passage, which recalls the failed embrace between the pilgrim and Casella and also underscores the distinction between shades and real people, contrasts with the passage from *Purgatorio* 6 where the shades of Virgil and Sordello are able to embrace each other (75). At the same

time, however, I would argue that the reason for the possibility of the embraces between Virgil and Sordello is that in constructing this episode, Dante is so concerned with political issues that the need for embraces is stronger than the consistency about the shades' incorporeality. On the embraces in Dante's poem, see "Nostalgia in Heaven: Embraces, Affection and Identity in Dante's Comedy," in *Dante and the Human Body*, ed. John Barnes (Dublin: Irish Academic Press, forthcoming).

18. See Rachel Jacoff, "'Our Bodies, Our Selves': The Body in the *Commedia*," in *Sparks and Seeds: Medieval Literature and Its Afterlife*, ed. Dana E. Stewart and Alison Cornish (Turnhout: Brepols, 2000), 128.

19. See, for instance, Anna Maria Chiavacci Leonardi, "'Le bianche stole': Il tema della resurrezione nel *Paradiso*," in *Dante e la Bibbia. Atti del Convegno Internazionale promosso da "Biblia": Firenze, 26–27–28 settembre 1986*, ed. Giovanni Barblan (Florence: Olschki, 1988), 259–60; and Jacoff, "'Our Bodies, Our Selves': The Body in the *Commedia*," 128–29.

20. Manfred died at the battle of Benevento in 1266, one year after Dante's birth. This is why the pilgrim cannot recognize him.

21. The same attention to what happened to the corpse is expressed by Bonconte da Montefeltro among those who died by violence (*Purg.* 5.104–29).

22. See especially the discussion of what Barolini defines as the "Augustinian basis" of purgatory in *The Undivine "Comedy,"* 99–121 (quote on 102).

23. As Singleton explains through the philosophy of Thomas Aquinas, intellect has primacy with respect to the beatific vision, while the will has primacy in regard to moral action. But any operation of the mind implies the combined use of both: "The two faculties of the rational soul are coordinated in their respective operations. Each has a function complementary to the other and together they make up one total act. Indeed, they are so closely conjoined in their movements that we speak of them as two rather than one only because we find that we must think of them so, as faculties separate and distinct one from the other—or so St. Thomas instructs us: 'The mind is moved to God both through intellect and through love, and these two movements of the mind can *be* at the same time, although they cannot be *thought* at the same time'" (*In IV Sent.*, d. 17, q. 1, a. 3, sol. 3; Singleton's emphasis; quotation from "The Allegorical Journey," in *Dante Studies 2: Journey to Beatrice* [Cambridge: Harvard University Press, 1958], 11; see pages 9–12 for the relation between intellect and will, reason and love). Also Giovanni Fallani, in "Visio beatifica," in *Enciclopedia dantesca* (Rome: Istituto della Enciclopedia Italiana G. Treccani, 1976), 5:1070–71, points out that Dante is following Thomas Aquinas (according to whom the main constituent element of the beatific vision is knowledge) rather than Bonaventure (who attributed the greatest importance to love). On the significance that Aquinas grants to the role of the intellect in the attainment of the beatific vision with respect to the will, see Christian Trottmann, *La vision béatifique: Des disputes scolastiques à sa définition par Benoît XII* (Rome: École française de Rome, 1995), 319.

24. Marc Cogan, *The Design in the Wax* (Notre Dame, Ind.: University of Notre Dame Press, 1999), 158–59, where Cogan explains that all the souls in heaven receive as much glory as they are both entitled to and capable of.

25. The same concept is expressed throughout the *Paradiso*. See, for instance, 6.112–20:

> Questa picciola stella si correda
> d'i buoni spirti che son stati attivi
> perché onore e fama li succeda:
> e quando li disiri poggian quivi,
> sì disvïando, pur convien che i raggi
> del vero amore in sù poggin men vivi.
> Ma nel commensurar d'i nostri gaggi
> col merto è parte di nostra letizia,
> perché non li vedem minor né maggi.

See also *Paradiso* 19.88, and 20.133–38.

26. As Lino Pertile has pointed out, often Dante distances himself from the theologians' idea of beatitude as absence of desire and, like some mystics, imagines that desire continues to remain in heaven as a force that renews itself while being constantly fulfilled. It is clear, however, that even when desire remains in heaven, it is never experienced as a hindrance to bliss. See: Lino Pertile, "'La punta del disio': Storia di una metafora dantesca," *Lectura Dantis* 7 (1990): 3–28; idem, "*Paradiso:* A Drama of Desire," in *Word and Drama in Dante: Essays on the "Divina Commedia,"* ed. John C. Barnes and Jennifer Petrie (Dublin: Irish Academic Press, 1993), 143–80; and idem, "A Desire of Paradise and a Paradise of Desire: Dante and Mysticism," in *Dante. Contemporary Perspectives,* ed. Amilcare Iannucci (Toronto: University of Toronto Press, 1997), 148–66. See also Bynum, *The Resurrection of the Body,* 304–5.

27. For the connection between the two passages in *Inferno* 6 and *Paradiso* 14, see: Umberto Bosco, "Domesticità del *Paradiso* (Lettura del XIV canto)," in *Studi in onore di Alberto Chiari* (Brescia: Paideia, 1973), 1:217–34; Patrick Boyde, *Perception and Passion in the "Divine Comedy"* (Cambridge: Cambridge University Press, 1993), 167–68.

28. Gabriele Muresu, "La 'gloria della carne': Disfacimento e trasfigurazione (*Par.* XIV)," *Rassegna della letteratura italiana* 91 (1987): 253–68. He begins his article by emphasizing the importance of the question but then gives a reading that completely differs from mine both in the aspects that are considered and in conclusions. For an interpretation that dismisses resurrection as a dogma that Dante has to follow but which does not touch his personal faith and devotion, see Armand Carraccio, "Quelques considérations sur le dogme de la résurrection de la chair, sur le 'lyrisme de l'ineffable' et sur le mécanisme de la révélation dans le 'Paradis' dan-

tesque," in *Studi di varia umanità in onore di Francesco Flora* (Milan: Mondadori, 1963), 302–21, esp. 301–8. Other articles that on the contrary stress the importance of resurrection in the *Commedia* are: Romano Guardini, "Corpo e corporeità nella *Commedia*," in *Studi su Dante*, 3rd ed. (Brescia: Morcelliana, 1986), 221–43; Giovanni Fallani, "Il canto XIV del *Paradiso*," in *Nuove letture dantesche* (Florence: Le Monnier, 1973), 6:147–62; Chiavacci Leonardi, "'Le bianche stole': Il tema della resurrezione nel *Paradiso*"; Nancy Lindheim, "Body, Soul, and Immortality: Some Readings in Dante's *Commedia*," *Modern Language Notes* 105 (1990): 1–32; Robin Kirkpatrick, "Dante and the Body," in *Framing Medieval Bodies*, ed. Sarah Kay and Miri Rubin (Manchester: Manchester University Press, 1994), 243–45; and Caroline Walker Bynum, "Faith Imagining the Self: Somatomorphic Soul and Resurrection Body in Dante's *Divine Comedy*," in *Faithful Imagining: Essays in Honor of Richard R. Niebuhr*, ed. Sang Hyun Lee, Wayne Proudfoot, and Albert Blackwell (Atlanta, Ga.: Scholars Press, 1995), 81–104.

29. See chap. 2, in the section "Competing Anthropological Models."

30. For the earthly body, see, for instance, *Inferno* 33.31–63: "Padre, assai ci fia men doglia / se tu mangi di noi: tu ne vestisti / queste misere carni, e tu le spoglia"; *Purgatorio* 11.44: "la carne d'Adamo onde si veste"; 16.37–38: "quella fascia / che la morte dissolve." The same sense of body as something distinct from soul is expressed in *Paradiso* 20.102–17, where the eagle explains that the soul of Trajan went back to its body so that it could believe in Christ and be saved. Regarding the resurrected body, we have seen a few passages that suggest that the resurrected body is a separate entity from the soul: the suicides go to Jehoshaphat Valley to get their bodies back but will not wear them and drag them to hell where they will hang on the bush forever (*Inf.* 13.103–8), while the heretics will go to the same valley, get the body back, and be enclosed with it in their tomb (*Inf.* 10.10–12). The image of the resurrected body as clothing appears also in *Purgatorio* 1.75 ("la vesta ch'al gran dì sarà sì chiara"), 30.13–15 ("Quali i beati al novissimo bando / surgeran presti ognun di sua caverna, / la revestita voce alleluiando"), *Paradiso* 25.95 (where the resurrected bodies are "bianche stole"), and 31.60 (where Bernard is "vestito con le genti glorïose").

31. See chap. 1, n. 32.

32. The resurrected body will therefore have the same appearance as Christ's resurrected body, which the pilgrim sees in the heaven of the Fixed Stars: "e per la viva luce trasparea / la lucente sustanza tanto chiara / nel viso mio, che non la sostenea" (*Par.* 23.31–33).

33. "Sicut etiam carbo per suam naturam alicuius coloris est, adveniente autem igne efficitur luminosus, et tamen est coloratus, quia est ibi lux materiae terrestri incorporata; sic in proposito intelligendum, quod corpus resurgens per naturam suam habebit colorem, et claritas luminis superinduet ipsum sicut ignis carbonem" (bk. 4, dist. 49, pt. 2, art. 2, sect. 2, q. 1, in *Opera omnia*, ed. Peltier [1886], 6:592).

34. Chiavacci Leonardi, "'Le bianche stole': Il tema della resurrezione nel *Paradiso*," 261, where she quotes Aquinas's *Sentence* commentary, bk. 4, d. 44, q. 2, a. 4, solutio 1:

> Claritas illa [of the resurrection bodies] causabitur ex redundantia gloriae animae in corpus. Quod enim recipitur in aliquo, non recipitur per modum influentis, sed per modum recipientis; et ita claritas, quae est in anima ut spiritualis, recipitur in corpore ut corporalis. Et ideo, secundum quod anima maioris claritatis secundum maius meritum, item etiam erit differentia claritatis in corpore; ut patet per Apostolum I Corinth XV; et ita in corpore glorioso cognoscetur gloria animae, sicut in vitro cognoscitur color corporis quod continetur in vase vitreo.

Luigi Blasucci even points out that while Bonaventure simply stresses that the body retains its own color, Dante also emphasizes that the clarity of the body will surpass the brightness produced by the soul ("Discorso teologico e visione sensibile nel canto XIV del *Paradiso*," *Rassegna della letteratura italiana* 95:3 [Sept.–Dec. 1991]: 12).

35. While Thomas Aquinas considers the qualities of the resurrection body as a spillover from the soul into the body and, concerning the four gifts of the resurrected body, makes them therefore dependent on the soul, Bonaventure gives more importance to the body in itself and makes a distinction between "dispositio" (which belongs to the body per se and depends on God) and "consummatio" (which depends on the soul that activates them). See Nikolaus Wicki, *Die Lehre von der himmlischen Seligkeit in der mittelalterlichen Scholastik von Petrus Lombardus bis Thomas von Aquin* (Freiburg: Universitätsverlag, 1954), 287–88.

36. See Colleen McDannell and Bernhard Lang, *Heaven: A History* (New Haven: Yale University Press, 1988), 90–94.

37. ". . . quod tantum gaudet de bono proximi, quantum de suo, dicendum quod verum est: unde Petrus plus gaudet de bono Lini, quam ipse Linus" (bk. 4, dist. 49, pt. 1, art. 1, q. 6, in *Opera omnia*, ed. Peltier [1866], 6:578).

38. The use of the word "mamme," typical of *sermo humilis*, within such theological language is the sign of a switch into tenderness and intimacy. As Barolini comments, "These souls are happily celebrating the future resurrection of their flesh, that most irreducible husk of selfhood, because only in the flesh will they fully experience their love for 'those who were dear to them *before* they were eternal flames.' In other words, their desire for their dead bodies is an expression of their desire to love fully in heaven what they loved in earth: their 'mamme,' their 'padri,' and the 'altri che fuor cari.' The rhyme of *mamme* with *fiamme*, the flesh with the spirit, is one of Dante's most poignant envisionings of a paradise where earthly ties are not renounced but enhanced" (*The Undivine "Comedy*," 138). Barolini also points out that the conception of heaven as a place of reunion with our

dear ones is still very popular. While stressing the intimacy of this passage, Ettore Bonora points out, "La gentilezza della parola *mamme* che fa pensare al legame inscindibile della creatura con colei che le ha dato vita, come non saprebbe il termine più nobile *madri*" ("Struttura e linguaggio nel XIV del *Paradiso*," *Giornale storico della letteratura italiana* 86 [1969]: 6).

39. "Communion des saints et jugement dernier: Dans les chant XIX–XX du *Paradis*," in *Pour Dante: Dante et l'Apocalypse. Lectures humanistes de Dante*, ed. Bruno Pinchard (Paris: Honoré Champion, 2001), 181–98, esp. 189–97.

40. See Rachel Jacoff, "Dante and the Legend(s) of St. John," *Dante Studies* 117 (1999): 45–57.

41. See Chiavacci Leonardi, "'Le bianche stole': Il tema della resurrezione nel *Paradiso*," 260, and Piero Boitani, "*I Know the Signs of the Ancient Flame:* Dante's Recognitions," in *The Tragic and the Sublime in Medieval Literature* (Cambridge: Cambridge University Press, 1991), 174.

42. Boitani, "*I Know the Signs*," 174–76.

43. While theologians usually agreed that people would resurrect at the age of thirty, it seems that the pilgrim sees the blessed with the features they had when they died.

44. See: Leo Spitzer, "Note on the Poetic and Empirical 'I' in Medieval Authors," in *Romanische Literaturstudien 1936–1956* (Tübingen: Max Niemeyer Verlag, 1959), 100–112, esp. 103–6; and Singleton, "The Allegorical Journey," in *Dante Studies 2*, 3–14.

45. For the *Commedia* as an *itinerarium mentis*, see Singleton, "The Allegorical Journey," esp. 4–6.

46. On Beatrice's argument, see Bruno Nardi, "Il concetto dell'Impero," in *Saggi di filosofia dantesca*, 2nd ed. (Florence: La Nuova Italia, 1967, 1st ed. 1930), 215–28, esp. 225–27; and the "Nota integrativa" that Chiavacci Leonardi writes at the end of her commentary on *Paradiso 7*.

47. See "Il concetto dell'Impero"; "Il mito dell'Eden," 329; and "L'arco della vita," in *Saggi di filosofia dantesca*, 137–38.

48. "And I believe if Christ had not been crucified, and had lived out the span of years for which nature had fitted him, it would have been in his eighty-first year that he would have exchanged the mortal body for the eternal" (*The Banquet*, trans. Christopher Ryan [Saratoga, Calif.: Anma Libri, 1989], 184). Nardi also says that while theologians usually argued that Adam's body would have become immortal if he had not sinned, they did not specify at what age this transformation would have occurred ("L'arco della vita," 137–38).

49. For Augustine, see Bynum, *The Resurrection of the Body*, 96–97. For the improvement of the redeemed condition with respect to the prelapsarian one, see also Giuseppe Mazzotta, *Dante, Poet of the Desert: History and Allegory in the "Divine Comedy"* (Princeton: Princeton University Press, 1979), 14–65, esp. 18–20.

50. See, for instance, John Freccero, "The Prologue Scene," in *Dante: The Poetics of Conversion* (Cambridge: Harvard University Press, 1986), 1–28; idem, "The Firm Foot on a Journey without a Guide," in *Dante: The Poetics of Conversion*, 29–54; Robert Hollander, *Allegory in Dante's "Commedia"* (Princeton: Princeton University Press, 1969), 260.

51. See the thorough study by Simona Bargetto, "Il 'battesimo di fuoco': Memorie liturgiche nel XXVII canto del *Purgatorio*," *Lettere Italiane* 49:2 (April/June 1997): 185–247; and, for the Christological atmosphere, see also Freccero, "The Sign of Satan," in *Dante: The Poetics of Conversion*, 176–78.

52. As Chiavacci Leonardi puts it in the commentary to this passage: "Si deve intendere che i sensi dell'uomo (vista, udito ecc.) sono in questo luogo affinati e esaltati rispetto alle capacità che hanno normalmente sulla terra; come se l'uomo, uscendo dall'Eden, avesse offuscate le sue qualità primigenie, e tornandovi le recuperasse. Dante si ritrova dunque come Adamo, nella purezza e perfezione dell'umanità innocente." See also Boyde, *Perception and Passion*, 86–87.

53. The issue of whether the pilgrim enters heaven in his body has been widely debated but not settled by Dante critics. For a recent discussion of the passage, see Michelangelo Picone, "Il corpo della/nella luna: Sul canto II del *Paradiso*," *L'Alighieri* 51 (2000): 7–25. See also: Kevin Brownlee, "Pauline Vision and Ovidian Speech in *Paradiso* I," in *The Poetry of Allusion: Virgil and Ovid in Dante's "Commedia,"* ed. Jeffrey Schnapp and Rachel Jacoff (Stanford: Stanford University Press, 1991), 202–13; Zygmunt G. Barański, *Dante e i segni: Saggi per una storia intellettuale di Dante Alighieri* (Naples: Liguori, 2000), 72 n. 61 (who has recently suggested that the pilgrim is necessarily journeying through heaven in his body because human communication must occur through signs necessitating the body).

54. I quote both the Latin text and the English translation from Ovid, *Metamorphoses*, 2nd ed., trans. Frank J. Miller (Cambridge: Harvard University Press, 1984), 2:294–95. Quotations from the *Metamorphoses* are from this edition.

55. See also *Paradiso* 4.139–42, 5.1–6, 14.76–84, 18.55–69.

56. Kevin Brownlee, "Ovid's Semele and Dante's Metamorphosis: *Paradiso* 21–22," in *The Poetry of Allusion*, 224–95.

57. See, for instance, 26.1–12 and 70–81, 27.4–15 and 88–99, 28.13–18.

58. On the significance of the Incarnation as the culmination of Dante's vision, see Peter Dronke, "The Conclusion of Dante's *Commedia*," *Italian Studies* 49 (1994): 21–39, esp. 35; and Christopher Ryan, "The Theology of Dante," in *The Cambridge Companion to Dante*, ed. Rachel Jacoff (Cambridge: Cambridge University Press, 1993), 136–52.

Bibliography

Primary Sources

Albert the Great. *Alberti Magni opera omnia.* Edited by S. Borgnet. 38 vols. Paris: Vivès, 1890–99.

Augustine. *De Genesi ad litteram.* In *Patrologia latina,* vol. 34. Edited by J. P. Migne. Paris: Garnier, 1841.

Bonaventure. *Bonaventurae opera omnia.* Edited by A. C. Peltier. 15 vols. Paris: Vivès, 1864–71.

———. *Bonaventurae opera omnia.* Edited by PP. Collegii S. Bonaventurae. 11 vols. Quaracchi: Collegium S. Bonaventurae, 1882–1902.

———. *The Mirror of the Blessed Virgin Mary (Speculum Beatae Mariae Virginis) and The Psalter of Our Lady (Psalterium Beatae Mariae Virginis).* Translated by Mary Emmanuel. St. Louis: B. Herder, 1932.

———. *The Works of Bonaventure.* Translated by José de Vinck. 5 vols. Paterson, N.J.: St. Anthony Guild Press, c.1960–70.

Bonvesin da la Riva. *Il Libro delle Tre Scritture e il Volgare delle vanità.* Edited by Vincenzo De Bartholomaeis. Rome: Società Filologica Romana, 1901.

———. *Il Libro delle Tre Scritture e i Volgari delle false scuse e delle vanità.* Edited by Leandro Biadene. Pisa: E. Spoerri, 1902.

———. *Le opere volgari di Bonvesin da la Riva.* Edited by Gianfranco Contini. Rome: Società Filologica Romana, 1941.

———. *De Cruce. Testo frammentario inedito.* Edited by Silvia Brusamolino Isella. Milan: Scheiwiller, 1979.

———. *Volgari scelti.* Edited and translated by Patrick S. Diehl and Ruggero Stefanini. New York: Lang, 1987.

Caesarius of Heisterbach. *Dialogus miracolorum.* Edited by Josephus Strange. 2 vols. Cologne: Heberle, 1851.

Catherine of Siena. *The Dialogue.* Translated by Suzanne Noffke. New York: Paulist Press, 1980.

———. *Il dialogo della divina provvidenza ovvero libro della divina dottrina.* Edited by Giuliana Cavallini. Siena: Cantagalli, 1995.

Concordanze della lingua poetica italiana delle Origini. Edited by D'Arco Silvio Avalle. Milan: Ricciardi, 1992.

Conrad of Saxony. *Speculum seu salutatio Beatae Mariae Virginis ac Sermones mariani.* Edited by P. de Alcantara Martinez. Grottaferrata: Editiones Collegii S. Bonaventurae ad Claras Aquas, 1975.

Dante Alighieri. *"Il Convivio" ridotto a miglior lezione e commentato da G. Busnelli e G. Vandelli,* 2nd ed. Edited by Antonio E. Quaglio. 2 vols. 1934; Florence: Le Monnier, 1964.

———. *"La Commedia" secondo l'antica vulgata.* Edited by Giorgio Petrocchi. 4 vols. Milan: Mondadori, 1966–67.

———. *La Divina Commedia.* 2nd ed. Edited by Natalino Sapegno. 3 vols. Florence: La Nuova Italia, 1968.

———. *The Divine Comedy.* Translated by Charles S. Singleton. 6 vols. 1970–75. Reprint, Princeton: Princeton University Press, 1977.

———. *Monarchy and Three Political Letters.* Translated by Donald Nicholl. New York: Garland, 1972.

———. *La Divina Commedia.* Edited by Umberto Bosco and Giovanni Reggio. 3 vols. Florence: Le Monnier, 1979.

———. *Opere minori.* 2 vols. Milan and Naples: Ricciardi, 1984–89.

———. *The Banquet.* Translated by Christopher Ryan. Saratoga, Calif.: Anma Libri, 1989.

———. *Commedia.* Edited by Anna Maria Chiavacci Leonardi. 3 vols. Milan: Mondadori, 1991–97.

———. *La Commedia.* Edited by Bianca Garavelli. 3 vols. Milan: Bompiani, 1993.

"The Desputisoun bitwen the Bodi and the Soule, herausgegeben von Wilhelm Linow. Nebst der ältesten altfranzösischen Bearbeitung des Streites zwischen Leib und Seele, herausgegeben von Hermann Varnhagen." *Erlanger Beiträge zur englischen Philologie* 1 (1889): 113–96.

Documents inédits pour servir à l'histoire littéraire de l'Italie, depuis le VIIIe siècle jusqu'au XIIIe, avec des recherches sur le moyen âge italien. Edited by Frédéric Ozanam. Paris: Jacques Lecoffre, 1850.

Durand of St. Pourçain. *In Sententias theologicas Petri Lombardi commentariorum libri quatuor.* Lyon: Apud Gasparem a Portinaris, 1556.

Giacomino da Verona. *La Gerusalemme celeste e la Babilonia infernale.* Edited by Emilio Barana. Verona: La Tipografica Veronese, 1921.

Heningham, Eleonor, ed. *An Early Latin Debate of the Body and the Soul Preserved in MS Royal 7 A III in the British Museum.* New York: privately printed, 1939.

Henry of Ghent. *Henrici de Gandavo opera omnia.* Edited by R. Macken. 29 vols. Leuven: Leuven University Press, 1979–.

Lotario dei Segni. *De miseria condicionis humanae.* Edited by Robert E. Lewis. Athens: University of Georgia Press, 1978.

Meditations on the Life of Christ: An Illustrated Manuscript of the Fourteenth Century. Edited by Isa Ragusa and Rosalie B. Green. Translated by Isa Ragusa. Princeton: Princeton University Press, 1961.

"Monumenti antichi di dialetti italiani." Edited by Adolfo Mussafia. *Sitzungsberichte der Kaiserlichen Akademie der Wissenschaften. Philosophisch-Historische Classe* 46 (1864): 113–235. Anastatic facsimile reprint, Bologna: Forni, 1980.

Ovid. *Metamorphoses.* Translated by Frank J. Miller. 2nd ed. 2 vols. Cambridge: Harvard University Press, 1984.

Pietro da Barsegapè. *Die Reimpredigt des Pietro da Barsegapè. Kritischer Text mit Einleitung, Grammatik und Glossar.* Edited by Emil Keller. Frauenfeld: Huber, 1901.

Poésies populaires latines antérieures au douzième siècle. Edited by Edelstand P. du Méril. Paris: Brockhaus et Avenarius, 1843.

Poeti del Duecento. Edited by Gianfranco Contini. 2 vols. Milan and Naples: Ricciardi, 1960.

Thomas Aquinas. *Thomae Aquinatis opera omnia.* Edited by S. Fretté. 34 vols. Paris: Vivès, 1871–80.

———. *Sancti Thomae Aquinatis doctoris angelici opera omnia iussu impensaque Leonis XIII p.m. edita.* 47 vols. Rome: S. C. de Propaganda Fide, 1882–1969.

———. *Summa theologica.* Translated by Fathers of the English Dominican Province. 3 vols. New York: Benzinger Brothers, 1946–48.

———. *On Spiritual Creatures.* Translated by M. C. Fitzpatrick. Milwaukee: Marquette University Press, 1951. Also in Thomas Aquinas, *Works.* CD-ROM. Pittsboro, N.C.: Intelex, 1992.

———. *Summa theologiae.* Edited by Blackfriars. 61 vols. New York: McGraw-Hill, 1964–81.

———. *Summa contra gentiles.* 2nd ed. 4 vols. Notre Dame, Ind.: University of Notre Dame Press, 1975.

———. *Questions on the Soul.* Translated by James H. Robb. Milwaukee: Marquette University Press, 1984.

Ubertino da Casale. *Arbor vitae crucifixae.* Edited by Charles T. Davis. Turin: Bottega d'Erasmo, 1961.

Uguccione da Lodi. "Das Buch des Uguçon da Laodho." Edited by Adolf Tobler. *Abhandlungen der Preussischen Akademie der Wissenschaften zu Berlin* 18 (1884): 1–95.

———. "L'opera di Uguccione da Lodi." Edited by Romano Broggini. *Studi Romanzi* 32 (1956).

Secondary Sources

Ackerman, Robert. "The Debate of the Body and the Soul and Parochial Christianity." *Speculum* 37 (1962): 541–65.

Ardissino, Erminia. "I canti liturgici nel *Purgatorio* dantesco." *Dante Studies* 108 (1990): 39–65.

Ariès, Philippe. *Western Attitudes toward Death: From the Middle Ages to the Present.* Translated by Patricia Ranum. Baltimore: Johns Hopkins University Press, 1974.
———. *L'homme devant la mort.* Paris: Editions du Seuil, 1977.
Armour, Peter. *The Door of Purgatory: A Study of Multiple Symbolism in Dante's "Purgatorio."* Oxford: Clarendon Press, 1983.
———. "Purgatory." In *The Dante Encyclopedia,* edited by Richard Lansing, 728–31. New York: Garland, 2000.
Auerbach, Erich. *Dante, Poet of the Secular World.* Chicago: University of Chicago Press, 1961.
———. *Literary Language and Its Public in Late Latin Antiquity and in the Middle Ages.* Translated by Ralph Manheim. Princeton: Princeton University Press, 1993.
Avalle, D'Arco Silvio. "L'origine della quartina monorima di alessandrini." In *Saggi e ricerche in onore di Ettore Li Gotti,* 119–60. Palermo: Centro di studi filologici e linguistici siciliani, 1962.
———. "Bonvesin da la Riva." In *Dizionario biografico degli Italiani,* 12:465–69. Rome: Istituto della Enciclopedia Italiana, 1970.
Baldassaro, Lawrence. "Dante the Pilgrim: Everyman as Sinner." *Dante Studies* 102 (1974): 63–76.
Barański, Zygmunt G. *Dante e i segni: Saggi per una storia intellettuale di Dante Alighieri.* Naples: Liguori, 2000.
———. "Canto XXV." In *Lectura Dantis Turicensis,* edited by Georges Güntert and Michelangelo Picone, 389–406. Florence: Franco Cesati, 2001.
Bárberi Squarotti, Giorgio, Francesco Bruni and Ugo Dotti. "Centri di Cultura nel Medio Evo: L'Italia settentrionale." In *Storia della civiltà letteraria italiana,* vol. 1, *Dalle Origini al Trecento,* part 2, directed by Giorgio Bárberi Squarotti, 549–761. Turin: UTET, 1990.
Bargetto, Simona. "Il 'battesimo di fuoco': Memorie liturgiche nel XXVII canto del *Purgatorio.*" *Lettere Italiane* 49:2 (April/June 1997): 185–247.
Barkan, Leonard. *The Gods Made Flesh: Metamorphosis and the Pursuit of Paganism.* New Haven: Yale University Press, 1986.
Barolini, Teodolinda. *Dante's Poets: Textuality and Truth in the "Comedy."* Princeton: Princeton University Press, 1984.
———. *The Undivine "Comedy": Detheologizing Dante.* Princeton: Princeton University Press, 1992.
———. "Guittone's *Ora parrà,* Dante's *Doglia me reca,* and the *Commedia*'s Anatomy of Desire." In *Seminario Dantesco Internazionale. International Dante Seminar 1: Atti del primo convegno tenutosi al Chauncey Conference Center. Princeton, 21–23 ottobre 1994,* edited by Zygmunt Barański, 3–23. Florence: Le Lettere, 1997.
Baschet, Jérôme. "Jugement de l'âme, jugement dernier: Contradiction, complémentarité, chevauchement?" *Revue Mabillon* n.s. 6 (1995): 159–92.

Batiouchkof, Theodore. "Le débat de l'âme et du corps." *Romania* 20 (1891): 1–55 and 513–78.

Battaglia, Salvatore. *La poesia dottrinale del Purgatorio.* Naples: Liguori, 1964.

Bazán, Bernardo C. "La corporalité selon saint Thomas." *Revue philosophique de Louvain* 4th ser., no. 51 (1983): 369–400.

Beckwith, Sarah. *Christ's Body: Identity, Culture and Society in Late Medieval Writings.* London: Routledge, 1993.

Belting, Hans. *Likeness and Presence: A History of the Image Before the Era of Art.* Translated by Edmund Jephcott. Chicago: University of Chicago Press, 1994.

Bemrose, Stephen. "'Come d'animal divegna fante': The Animation of the Human Embryo in Dante." In *The Human Embryo: Aristotle and the Arabic and European Tradition,* edited by G. R. Dunstan, 123–35. Exeter: University of Exeter Press, 1990.

Berlioz, Jacques. "Le récit efficace: L'exemplum au service de la prédication (XIIIe–XVe siècles)." *Mélanges de l'Ecole française de Rome. Moyen Âge–Temps Modernes* 92 (1980): 113–46.

Bernabei, Bruno. "Libertà." In *Enciclopedia dantesca,* 3:641–43. Rome: Istituto della Enciclopedia Italiana G. Treccani, 1971.

Bernardo, Aldo S. "Flesh, Spirit, and Rebirth at the Center of Dante's *Comedy.*" *Symposium* 19 (1965): 335–51.

Bernstein, Alan. "Review of Jacques Le Goff's *Birth of Purgatory.*" *Speculum* 59 (1984): 179–83.

Bertaud, Émile. "Discipline." In *Dictionnaire de spiritualité, ascétique et mystique, doctrine et histoire,* vol. 3, cols. 1302–11. Paris: Beauchesne, 1957.

Bertoni, Giulio. "Un rimaneggiamento toscano del *Libro* di Uguçon da Laodho." *Studi medievali* 1 (1904–5): 235–62. Published with some changes as "Un rimaneggiamento fiorentino del *Libro* di Uguçon da Laodho." *Rendiconti della Reale Accademia dei Lincei* serie V, 21 (1912): 607–85.

———. "Una redazione tosco-veneta di un sermone in rima sul giudizio universale." In *Poeti e poesie del Medio Evo e del Rinascimento,* 213–26. Modena: Orlandini, 1922.

———. "Intorno alla cosiddetta *Contemplazione della morte* attribuita a Uguccione." *Giornale storico della letteratura italiana* 94 (1929): 197–200.

Bestul, Thomas H. *Texts of the Passion: Latin Devotional Literature and Medieval Society.* Philadelphia: University of Pennsylvania Press, 1996.

Bettoni, Efrem. "Anima." In *Enciclopedia dantesca,* 1:278–85. Rome: Istituto della Enciclopedia Italiana G. Treccani, 1970.

Bino, Carla, and Manuele Gragnolati, eds. *Il Corpo Passionato: Modelli e rappresentazioni Medievali dell' amore divino. Comunicazioni Sociali* 25, n.s. 2 (2003).

Birkenmajer, Alexander. "Der Brief R. Kilwardbys an Peter von Conflans und die Streitschrift des Ägidius von Lessines." In *Vermischte Untersuchungen zur Geschichte der mittelalterlichen Philosophie,* 36–69. Münster: Aschendorff, 1922.

Blasucci, Luigi. "Discorso teologico e visione sensibile nel canto XIV del *Paradiso.*" *Rassegna della letteratura italiana* 95:3 (Sept.–Dec. 1991): 5–19.

Boitani, Piero. *The Tragic and the Sublime in Medieval Literature.* Cambridge: Cambridge University Press, 1991.

Bologna, Corrado. "La letteratura dell'Italia settentrionale nel Duecento." In *Letteratura italiana: Storia e geografia,* vol. 1, *L'età medievale,* directed by Alberto Asor Rosa, 101–88. Turin: Einaudi, 1987.

Bonora, Ettore. "Struttura e linguaggio nel XIV del *Paradiso.*" *Giornale storico della letteratura italiana* 86 (1969): 1–17.

Bosco, Umberto. "Domesticità del *Paradiso* (Lettura del XIV) canto." In *Studi in onore di Alberto Chiari,* 1:217–34. Brescia: Paideia, 1973.

Bossy, Michel-André. "Medieval Debates of Body and Soul." *Comparative Literature* 28 (1976): 144–63.

Boyde, Patrick. *Dante Philomythes and Philosopher: Man in the Cosmos.* Cambridge: Cambridge University Press, 1981.

———. *Perception and Passion in the "Divine Comedy."* Cambridge: Cambridge University Press, 1993.

Bredero, Adriaan. "Le Moyen Âge et le Purgatoire." *Revue d'histoire ecclésiastique* 78 (1983): 429–52.

Brown, Elisabeth. "Death and the Human Body in the Later Middle Ages: The Legislation of Boniface VIII on the Division of the Corpse." *Viator* 12 (1981): 221–70.

Brownlee, Kevin. "Ovid's Semele and Dante's Metamorphosis: *Paradiso* 21–22." In *The Poetry of Allusion: Virgil and Ovid in Dante's "Commedia,"* edited by Rachel Jacoff and Jeffrey Schnapp, 224–95. Stanford: Stanford University Press, 1991.

———. "Pauline Vision and Ovidian Speech in *Paradiso* I." In *The Poetry of Allusion: Virgil and Ovid in Dante's "Commedia,"* edited by Rachel Jacoff and Jeffrey Schnapp, 202–13. Stanford: Stanford University Press, 1991.

Bruce-Jones, John. "L'importanza della materia prima (Why Does Primary Matter Matter?): Aspetti della materia nella poesia e nel pensiero di Dante." In *Dante e la scienza,* edited by Patrick Boyde and Vittorio Russo, 213–19. Ravenna: Longo, 1995.

Bultot, Robert. *Christianisme et valeurs humaines: La doctrine du mépris du monde en Occident, de S. Ambroise à Innocent III.* Louvain: Éditions Nauwelaerts; Paris: Béatrice-Nauwelaerts, 1963–64.

Busnelli, Giovanni. *La concezione del Purgatorio dantesco.* Rome: Civiltà Cattolica, 1906.

———. *L'ordinamento morale del purgatorio dantesco.* 2nd ed. Rome: Civiltà Cattolica, 1908.

———. *Cosmogonia e antropogenesi secondo Dante Alighieri e le sue fonti.* Rome: Civiltà Cattolica, 1922.

Bynum, Caroline Walker. *Holy Feast and Holy Fast: The Religious Significance of Food to Medieval Women*. Berkeley: University of California Press, 1987.

———. *Fragmentation and Redemption: Essays on Gender and the Human Body in Medieval Religion*. New York: Zone Books, 1991.

———. "Faith Imagining the Self: Somatomorphic Soul and Resurrection Body in Dante's *Divine Comedy*." In *Faithful Imagining: Essays in Honor of Richard R. Niebuhr*, edited by Sang Hyun Lee, Wayne Proudfoot, and Albert Blackwell, 81–104. Atlanta, Ga.: Scholars Press, 1995.

———. *The Resurrection of the Body in Western Christianity, 200–1336*. New York: Columbia University Press, 1995.

———. "Why All the Fuss about the Body? A Medievalist's Perspective." *Critical Inquiry* 22 (Autumn 1995): 1–33.

Bynum, Caroline Walker, and Paul Freedman, eds. *Last Things: Death and Apocalypse in the Middle Ages*. Philadelphia: University of Pennsylvania Press, 1999.

Callus, Daniel A. "The Problem of the Plurality of Forms in the Thirteenth Century: The Thomist Innovation." In *L'homme et son destin d'après les penseurs du moyen âge. Actes du premier congrès international de philosophie médiévale: Louvain-Bruxelles, 28 Août–4 Septembre 1958*, 577–85. Louvain: Nauwelaerts, 1960.

———. "The Origins of the Problem of the Unity of Form." *The Thomist* 24 (1961): 257–85.

———. "Forms, Unicity and Plurality of." In *New Catholic Encyclopedia*, 5:1024–27. New York: McGraw-Hill, 1967.

Carozzi, Claude. "Structure et fonction de la vision de Tnugdal." In *Faire Croire: Modalités de la diffusion et de la réception des messages réligieux du XIIe au XVe siècle: Table Ronde organisée par l'École française de Rome, en collaboration avec l'Institut d'Histoire Médiévale de l'Université de Padoue (Rome, 22–23 juin 1979)*, 223–34. Rome: École française de Rome; Turin: Bottega d'Erasmo, 1981.

———. *Le voyage de l'âme dans l'au-delà d'après la littérature latine*. Rome: École française de Rome; Paris: Diffusion de Boccard, 1994.

Carraccio, Armand. "Quelques considérations sur le dogme de la résurrection de la chair, sur le 'lyrisme de l'ineffable' et sur le mécanisme de la révélation dans le 'Paradis' dantesque." In *Studi di varia umanità in onore di Francesco Flora*, 302–21. Milan: Mondadori, 1963.

Cassell, Anthony K. *Dante's Fearful Art of Justice*. Toronto: University of Toronto Press, 1984.

Cecchetto, Vittorina. "The Language of Giacomino da Verona and a Concordance of His Works." Ph.D. diss., University of Toronto, 1982.

Cerroni, Monica. "Tipologia dell'allegoria e dinamiche del vero in Giacomino da Verona e Bonvesin da la Riva." *Strumenti critici* 92 (2000): 53–74.

Cestaro, Gary. *Dante and the Grammar of the Nursing Body*. Notre Dame, Ind.: University of Notre Dame Press, 2002.

Chenu, Dominique. *Toward Understanding St. Thomas.* Translated by A.-M. Landry and D. Hughes. Chicago: Henry Regnery, 1964.

Chiavacci Leonardi, Anna Maria. "Le beatitudini e la struttura poetica del *Purgatorio.*" *Giornale storico della letteratura italiana* 161 (1984): 1–29.

———. "'Le bianche stole': Il tema della resurrezione nel *Paradiso.*" In *Dante e la Bibbia. Atti del Convegno Internazionale promosso da "Biblia": Firenze, 26–27–28 settembre 1986,* edited by Giovanni Barblan, 249–71. Florence: Olschki, 1988.

Cianciolo, Umberto. "Contributo allo studio dei cantari di argomento sacro." *Archivium Romanicum* 30 (1938): 163–241.

Ciccone, Giacinto. "Un poemetto lombardo del secolo XIV inedito sul contrasto fra l'anima e il corpo." *Rivista Abruzzese di scienze, lettere ed arti* 23 (1908): 223–33.

Ciociola, Claudio. "Nominare gli anonimi (Per Uguccione)." *Filologia e critica* 15:2–3 (May–Dec. 1990): 419–33.

Cogan, Marc. *The Design in the Wax.* Notre Dame, Ind.: University of Notre Dame Press, 1999.

Cohen, Esther. "Towards a History of European Physical Sensibility: Pain in the Later Middle Ages." *Science in Context* 8 (1995): 47–74.

———. "The Animated Pain of the Body." *American Historical Review* 105 (2000): 36–68.

Colussi, Giorgio, ed. *Glossario degli antichi volgari italiani.* Foligno: Editoriale Umbra, 1983–.

Constable, Giles. *Three Studies in Medieval Religion and Social Thought.* Cambridge: Cambridge University Press, 1995.

Copleston, Frederick. *A History of Philosophy.* 9 vols. Westminster, Md.: Newman Press, 1946–75.

Cousins, Ewert. "The Humanity and the Passion of Christ." In *Christian Spirituality: High Middle Ages and Reformation,* edited by J. Raitt, 375–91. New York: Crossroad, 1987.

Cristaldi, Sergio. "Dalle beatitudini all' 'Apocalisse.' Il Nuovo Testamento nella *Commedia,*" *Letture classensi* 17 (1988): 23–67.

Curtius, Ernst R. *European Literature and the Middle Ages.* Translated by W. R. Task. 1948; New York: Pantheon Books, 1953.

Da Cruz Pontes, J. M. "Le problème de l'origine de l'âme de la patristique à la solution thomiste." *Recherches de théologie ancienne et médiévale* 31 (1964): 175–229.

Dales, Richard C. *The Problem of the Rational Soul in the Thirteenth Century.* Leiden: E. J. Brill, 1995.

Dauphiné, James. "'Il Libro delle tre scritture' de Bonvesin da la Riva ou du pouvoir de l'écriture." In *Mélanges de langue et littérature médiévales offerts à Alice Planche,* edited by Maurice Accarie and Ambrose Queffelec, 137–48. Paris: Belles Letrres, 1984.

D'Avray, David L. "Some Franciscan Ideas about the Body." In *Modern Questions about Medieval Sermons: Essays on Marriage, Death, History and Society,* edited by Nicole Bérion and David L. d'Avray, 155–74. Spoleto: Centro Italiano di Studi sull'alto Medioevo, 1994.

De Bartholomaeis, Vincenzo. "Due testi latini e una versione ritmica italiana della *Visio Philiberti*." *Studi medievali* n.s. 1 (1928): 228–309.

Degl'Innocenti, Umberto. "La struttura ontologica della persona secondo S. Tommaso d'Aquino." In *L'homme et son destin d'après les penseurs du moyen âge: Actes du premier congrès international de philosophie médiévale: Louvain-Bruxelles, 28 Août–4 Septembre 1958*, 523–33. Louvain: Nauwelaerts, 1960.

Delcorno, Carlo. "Dante e l'"exemplum" medievale." *Lettere italiane* 35 (1983): 3–28.

Delumeau, Jean. *Sin and Fear: The Emergence of a Western Guilt Culture, 13th–18th Centuries*. Translated by Eric Nicholson. New York: St. Martin's Press, 1990.

De' Negri, Enrico. "Temi e iconografia del *Purgatorio*." *Romanic Review* 49 (1958): 81–104.

Denifle, Heinrich, and Emile Chatelain, eds. *Chartularium Universitatis Parisiensis*. 2 vols. Paris: Delalain, 1889.

De Sanctis, Francesco. *Storia della letteratura italiana dai primi secoli agli albori del Trecento*. Edited by G. Lazzeri. Milan: Hoepli, 1950.

Desmarais, M.-M. *S. Albert le Grand docteur de la médiation mariale*. Paris: Institut d'études médiévales, 1935.

Dinzelbacher, Peter. "Il corpo nelle visioni dell'aldilà." *Micrologus: Natura, scienze e società medievali* 1 (1993): 301–26.

Dondaine, H.-F. "L'objet et le 'medium' de la vision béatifique chez les théologiens du XIIIᵉ siècle." *Recherches de théologie ancienne et médiévale* 19 (1952): 60–99.

Douie, Decima. "John XXII and the Beatific Vision." *Dominican Studies* 3:2 (1950): 154–74.

D'Ovidio, Francesco. *Nuovi studii danteschi: Il Purgatorio e il suo preludio*. Milan: Hoepli, 1906.

Dronke, Peter. "The Conclusion of Dante's *Commedia*." *Italian Studies* 49 (1994): 21–39.

Dumol, Paul A. "Soul." In *The Dante Encyclopedia*, edited by Richard Lansing, 795–97. New York: Garland, 2000.

Durling, Robert. "Deceit and Digestion in the Belly of Hell." In *Allegory and Representation*, edited by Stephen J. Greenblatt, 61–93. Baltimore: Johns Hopkins University Press, 1980.

Dykmans, Mark. *Les sermons de Jean XXII sur la vision béatifique*. Rome: Presse de l'Université Gregorienne, 1973.

———. *Pour et contre Jean XXII en 1333: Deux traités avignonnais sur la vision béatifique*. Vatican City: Biblioteca Apostolica Vaticana, 1975.

Edwards, Graham. "Purgatory: Birth or Evolution?" *Journal of Ecclesiastical History* 36 (1985): 634–46.

Emmerson, Richard K. *Antichrist in the Middle Ages: A Study of Medieval Apocalypticism, Art, and Literature*. Seattle: University of Washington Press, 1981.

Fallani, Giovanni. "Il canto XIV del Paradiso." In *Nuove letture dantesche*, 6:147–62. Florence: Le Monnier, 1973.

———. "Visio beatifica." In *Enciclopedia dantesca*, 5:1070–71. Rome: Istituto della Enciclopedia Italiana G. Treccani, 1976.

Ferguson, Mary Heyward. "The Debate between the Body and the Soul: A Study in the Relationship between Form and Content." Ph.D. diss., Ohio State University, 1965.

Ferrante, Joan. *The Political Vision of the "Divine Comedy."* Princeton: Princeton University Press, 1984.

———. "Good Thieves and Bad Thieves: A Reading of *Inferno* XXIV." *Dante Studies* 104 (1986): 83–98.

Figurelli, Fernando. "Il canto XXV del *Purgatorio*." In *Nuove letture dantesche*, 5:33–67. Florence: Le Monnier, 1972.

Finucane, Ronald. *Appearances of the Dead: A Cultural History of Ghosts*. London: Junction Books, 1982.

Foster, Kenelm. "Cristo." In *Enciclopedia dantesca*, 2:262–69. Rome: Istituto della Enciclopedia Italiana G. Treccani, 1970.

———. "Tommaso d'Aquino." In *Enciclopedia dantesca*, 5:626–49. Rome: Istituto della Enciclopedia Italiana G. Treccani, 1976.

———. "Dante's Idea of Purgatory, with Special Reference to *Purgatorio* XXI, 58–66." In *Dies Illa: Death in the Middle Ages. Proceedings of the 1983 Manchester Colloquium*, edited by Jane H. M. Taylor, 99–100. Liverpool: Francis Cairns, 1984.

Freccero, John. *Dante: The Poetics of Conversion*. Cambridge: Harvard University Press, 1986.

Fulton, Rachel. "The Virgin Mary and the Song of Songs in the High Middle Ages." Ph.D. diss., Columbia University, 1994.

———. "Mimetic Devotion, Marian Exegesis, and the Historical Sense of the Song of Songs." *Viator* 27 (1996): 85–116.

———. *From Judgment to Passion: Devotion to Christ and the Virgin Mary, 800–1200*. New York: Columbia University Press, 2002.

Gallardo, Pietro. "Bonvesin da la Riva." In *Letteratura Italiana. I minori*, 1:171–83. Milan: Marzorati, 1961.

Gilson, Etienne. *The Philosophy of St. Bonaventure*. 2nd ed. Translated by Dom I. Trethowan. London: Sheed & Ward, 1949.

———. *La philosophie au moyen âge: Des origines patristiques à la fin du XIVe siècle*. 2nd ed. Paris: Payot, 1952.

———. *History of Christian Philosophy in the Middle Ages*. New York: Random House, 1955.

———. Review of Bruno Nardi, *Dal "Convivio" alla "Commedia" (Sei saggi danteschi)*. *Giornale storico della letteratura italiana* 138 (1961): 562–73.

————. "Dante's Notion of a Shade: *Purgatorio* XXV." *Mediaeval Studies* 29 (1967): 124–42.

————. *Dante et Béatrice: Études dantesques*. Paris: Vrin, 1974.

Gilson, Simon. "Rimaneggiamenti danteschi di Aristotele: *Gravitas e levitas* nella *Commedia*." In *Le culture di Dante*, edited by Michelangelo Picone, Theodore J. Cachey, and Margherita Mesirca, 151–77. Florence: Franco Angeli, 2004.

Ginsberg, Warren. "Dante, Ovid, and the Transformation of Metamorphosis." *Traditio* 46 (1991): 205–23.

————. *Dante's Aesthetics of Being*. Ann Arbor: University of Michigan Press, 1999.

Girotto, Samuele. *Corrado di Sassonia predicatore e mariologo del sec. XIII*. Florence: Studi francescani, 1952.

Goering, Joseph. "The *De dotibus* of Robert Grosseteste." *Mediaeval Studies* 44 (1982): 83–101.

Gougaud, Louis. *Devotional and Ascetic Practices in the Middle Ages*. Translated by G. C. Bateman. London: Burns Oates and Washbourne, 1927.

Graef, Hilda. *Mary: A History of Doctrine and Devotion*. 2 vols. London: Sheed & Ward, 1963–65.

Gragnolati, Manuele. "From Decay to Splendor: Body and Pain in Bonvesin da la Riva's *Book of the Three Scriptures*." In *Last Things: Death and Apocalypse in the Middle Ages*, edited by Caroline Walker Bynum and Paul Freedman, 83–97. Philadelphia: University of Pennsylvania Press, 1991.

————. "Bonvesin da la Riva." In *Italian Literature of the Thirteenth Century*, edited by Zygmunt Barański and Theodore J. Cachey. Columbia, S.C.: Bruccoli Clark Layman, forthcoming.

————. "Nostalgia in Heaven: Embraces, Affection and Identity in Dante's Comedy," In *Dante and the Human Body*, edited by John Barnes. Dublin: Irish Academic Press, forthcoming.

Greene, Thomas. "Dramas of Selfhood in the *Comedy*." In *From Time to Eternity*, edited by Thomas Bergin, 103–36. New Haven: Yale University Press, 1967.

Gross, Kenneth. "Infernal Metamorphoses: An Interpretation of Dante's 'Counterpass.'" *Modern Language Notes* 100 (1985): 42–69.

Guagnini, Elvio. "Canto XXV." In *Purgatorio*, edited by Pompeo Giannantonio, 487–503. Naples: Loffredo, 1989.

Guardini, Romano. *Studi su Dante*. 3rd ed. Brescia: Morcelliana, 1986.

Gurevich, Aron. "Au Moyen Âge: Conscience individuelle et image de l'au-delà." *Annales* 37 (1982): 255–73.

————. "Popular and Scholarly Medieval Cultural Traditions: Notes in the Margin of Jacques Le Goff's Book." *Journal of Medieval History* 9 (1983): 71–90.

————. *Medieval Popular Culture: Problems of Belief and Perception*. Translated by János M. Bak and Paul A. Hollingsworth. Cambridge: Cambridge University Press, 1988.

———. "Perceptions of the Individual and the Hereafter in the Middle Ages." In *Historical Anthropology of the Middle Ages,* edited by Jana Howlett, 65–89. Cambridge: Polity Press, 1992.

Hale, Rosemary. "*Imitatio Mariae:* Motherhood Motifs in Late Medieval German Spirituality." Ph.D. diss., Harvard University, 1992.

Hamburger, Jeffrey. "The Visual and the Visionary: The Image in Late Medieval Monastic Devotion." *Viator* 20 (1989): 161–82.

———. *Nuns as Artists: The Visual Culture of a Medieval Convent.* Berkeley: University of California Press, 1997.

———. *The Visual and the Visionary: Art and Female Spirituality in Late Medieval Germany.* New York: Zone Books, 1998.

Harrison, Anna. "Community Among the Saints in Heaven in Bernard of Clairvaux's *Sermons for the Feasts of All Saints.*" In *Last Things: Death and Apocalypse in the Middle Ages,* edited by Caroline Walker Bynum and Paul Freedman, 191–204. Philadelphia: University of Pennsylvania Press, 1991.

Heinzmann, Richard. *Die Unsterblichkeit der Seele und die Auferstehung des Leibes: Eine problemgeschichtliche Untersuchung der frühscholastischen Sentenzen- und Summenliteratur von Anselm von Laon bis Wilhelm von Auxerre.* Münster: Aschendorff, 1965.

———. "Was ist der Mensch? Zu einer Grundfrage des mittelalterlichen Denkens." *Theologie und Philosophie* 49 (1974): 542–47.

Hewson, Anthony M. *Giles of Rome and the Medieval Theory of Conception: A Study of the "De formatione corporis humani in utero."* London: Athlone Press, 1975.

Hollander, Robert. *Allegory in Dante's "Commedia."* Princeton: Princeton University Press, 1969.

———. *Il Virgilio dantesco: Tragedia nella "Commedia."* Florence: Olschki, 1983.

Huizinga, Johan. *The Waning of the Middle Ages: A Study of the Forms of Life, Thought, and Art in France and the Netherlands in the XIV and XV Centuries.* Translated by F. Hopman. London: Arnold, 1924; reprint, Garden City, N.Y.: Doubleday, 1956.

Jacoff, Rachel. "Dante and the Legend(s) of St. John." *Dante Studies* 117 (1999): 45–57.

———. "'Our Bodies, Our Selves': The Body in the *Commedia.*" In *Sparks and Seeds: Medieval Literature and Its Afterlife,* edited by Dana E. Stewart and Alison Cornish, 119–37. Turnhout: Brepols, 2000.

Jugie, Martin. *La mort et l'assomption de la Sainte Vierge: Etude historico-doctrinale.* Vatican City: Biblioteca Apostolica Vaticana, 1944.

Kent, Bonnie. *Virtues of the Will: The Transformation of Ethics in the Late Thirteenth Century.* Washington, D.C.: Catholic University of America Press, 1995.

Kieckhefer, Richard. *Unquiet Souls: Fourteenth-Century Saints and Their Religious Milieu.* Chicago: University of Chicago Press, 1984.

Kirkpatrick, Robin. "Dante and the Body." In *Framing Medieval Bodies,* edited by Sarah Kay and Miri Rubin, 236–53. Manchester: Manchester University Press, 1994.

Klein, Robert. "L'enfer de Ficino." In *Umanesimo e esoterismo,* edited by Enrico Castelli, 47–84. Padua: Cedam, 1960.

Korosak, Bruno. *Mariologia S. Alberti Magni eiusque coequalium.* Rome: Academia Mariana Internationalis, 1954.

Lazzari, Francesco. *Mistica e ideologia tra XI e XIII secolo.* Milan and Naples: Ricciardi, 1972.

Le Bachelet, X. "Benoit XII." In *Dictionnaire de théologie catholique,* 2:653–704. Paris: Letouzey et Ané, 1910.

Leclercq, Jean. *The Love of Learning and the Desire for God: A Study of Monastic Culture.* Translated by C. Misrahi. New York: Fordham University Press, 1982.

Legner, A. "Ecce homo." In *Lexikon der Christlichen Iconographie,* edited by Engelbert Kirschbaum et al., 1:558–61. Rome: Herder, 1968.

Le Goff, Jacques. *The Birth of Purgatory.* Translated by Arthur Goldhammer. Chicago: University of Chicago Press, 1984.

———. *L'immaginario medievale.* Milan: Mondadori, 1993.

Leonardi, Lino, and Francesco Santi. "La letteratura religiosa." In *Storia della letteratura italiana,* vol. 1, *Dalle origini a Dante,* directed by Enrico Malato, 339–404. Rome: Salerno, 1995.

Lerner, Robert. "Millennialism." In *The Encyclopedia of Apocalypticism,* edited by Bernard McGinn, 2:326–60. New York: Continuum, 1998.

Levi, Ezio. *I poeti antichi lombardi.* Milan: Cogliati, 1921. Anastatic facsimile reprint, Bologna: Forni, 1979.

———. *Uguccione da Lodi e i primordi della poesia italiana.* 2nd ed. Florence: La Nuova Italia, 1928.

Levi d'Ancona, Mirella. *The Iconography of the Immaculate Conception in the Middle Ages and Early Renaissance.* New York: College Art Association of America, in conjunction with *The Art Bulletin,* 1957.

Lindheim, Nancy. "Body, Soul, and Immortality: Some Readings in Dante's *Commedia.*" *Modern Language Notes* 105 (1990): 1–32.

Maierù, Alfredo. "Forma." In *Enciclopedia dantesca,* 2:969–75. Rome: Istituto della Enciclopedia Italiana G. Treccani, 1970.

Manselli, Raoul. "Italie. Haut Moyen Âge: Mouvements spirituels orthodoxes et hétérodoxes (11ᵉ et 12ᵉ siècles)." In *Dictionnaire de spiritualité, ascétique et mystique, doctrine et histoire,* vol. 7, part 2, cols. 2184–93. Paris: Beauchesne, 1971.

Marri, Fabio. *Glossario al milanese di Bonvesin.* Bologna: Patron, 1977.

Marrow, James H. *Passion Iconography in Northern European Art of the Late Middle Ages and Early Renaissance. A Study of the Transformation of Sacred Metaphor into Descriptive Narrative.* Kortrijk: Van Ghemmert, 1979.

Massaut, Jean Pierre. "La vision de l'au-delà au moyen âge: A propos d'un ouvrage recent." *Le Moyen Âge* 91 (1985): 75–86.

Matsuda, Takami. *Death and Purgatory in Middle English Didactic Poetry.* Rochester, N.Y.: Brewer, 1997.

May, Esther I. *The "De Jerusalem celesti" and the "De Babilonia infernali" of Fra Giacomino da Verona.* Florence: Le Monnier, 1930.

Mazzarella, Pasquale. *Controversie medievali: Unità e pluralità delle forme.* Naples: Giannini, 1978.

Mazzotta, Giuseppe. *Dante, Poet of the Desert: History and Allegory in the "Divine Comedy."* Princeton: Princeton University Press, 1979.

———. *Dante's Vision and the Circle of Knowledge.* Princeton: Princeton University Press, 1992.

McDannell, Colleen, and Bernhard Lang. *Heaven: A History.* New Haven: Yale University Press, 1988.

McGinn, Bernard. "Introduction: Apocalyptic Spirituality." In *Apocalyptic Spirituality: Treatises and Letters of Lactantius, Adso of Montier-en-Der, Joachim of Fiore, the Franciscan Spirituals, Savonarola,* edited by Bernard McGinn, 1–16. New York: Paulist Press, 1979.

———. *Visions of the End: Apocalyptic Traditions in the Middle Ages.* New York: Columbia University Press, 1979.

———. *Antichrist: Two Thousand Years of the Human Fascination with Evil.* San Francisco: Harper, 1994.

———. "The Last Judgment in the Christian Tradition." In *The Encyclopedia of Apocalypticism,* edited by Bernard McGinn, 2:361–401. New York: Continuum, 1998.

McGuire, Brian. "Purgatory, the Communion of Saints, and Medieval Change." *Viator* 20 (1989): 61–84.

Medin, Antonio. "L'opera poetica di Uguccione da Lodi." *Atti del Reale Istituto Veneto di scienze, lettere ed arti* 81 (1921–22): 185–209.

Merback, Mitchell. *The Thief, the Cross and the Wheel: Pain and the Spectacle of Punishment in Medieval and Renaissance Europe.* Chicago: University of Chicago Press, 1999.

Michel, A. "Forme du corps humain." In *Dictionnaire de théologie catholique,* vol. 6, cols. 546–88. Paris: Letouzey et Ané, 1915.

———. "Résurrection des morts." In *Dictionnaire de théologie catholique,* vol. 13, part. 2, cols. 2501–71. Paris: Letouzey et Ané, 1937.

Moore, Edward. *Studies in Dante, Second Series: Miscellaneous Essays.* Oxford: Clarendon Press, 1899.

Morgan, Alison. *Dante and the Medieval Other World.* Cambridge: Cambridge University Press, 1990.

Morris, Colin. *The Discovery of the Individual, 1050–1200.* New York: Harper and Row, 1972.

Muresu, Gabriele. "La 'gloria della carne': Disfacimento e trasfigurazione (*Par.* XIV)." *Rassegna della letteratura italiana* 91 (1987): 253–68.

———. "Le 'vie' della redenzione (*Paradiso* VII)." *Rassegna della letteratura italiana* 98 (1994): 5–19.

Nardi, Bruno. "Meditantur sua stercora scarabei." *Nuovo giornale dantesco* 4 (1920): 56–62.

———. *Saggi di filosofia dantesca.* 2nd ed. 1930; Florence: La Nuova Italia, 1967.

———. *Studi di filosofia medievale.* Rome: Edizioni di storia e letteratura, 1960.

———. "Il canto XXV del *Purgatorio.*" In *Letture dantesche,* vol. 2, *Purgatorio,* 2nd ed. edited by Giovanni Getto, 1173–91. 1964; Florence: Sansoni, 1966.

———. *Dante e la cultura medievale.* 2nd ed. Edited by Paolo Mazzantini. Rome: Laterza, 1990.

Newman, Barbara. *From Virile Woman to Woman Christ: Studies in Medieval Religion and Literature.* Philadelphia: University of Pennsylvania Press, 1995.

Nolan, Kieran. *The Immortality of the Soul and the Resurrection of the Body according to Giles of Rome: A Historical Study of a 13th Century Theological Problem.* Rome: Studium Theologicum "Augustinianum," 1967.

Ombres, Robert. "The Doctrine of Purgatory according to St. Thomas Aquinas." *Downside Review* 99 (1981): 279–87.

Padoan, Giorgio. "Il canto XXI del *Purgatorio.*" In *Nuove letture dantesche,* 4:327–54. Florence: Le Monnier, 1970.

———. "Il canto XXV del *Purgatorio.*" In *Purgatorio. Letture degli anni 1976–79,* 577–600. Rome: Bonacci, 1981.

Pagliaro, Antonino. *Ulisse: Ricerche semantiche sulla "Divina Commedia."* Messina-Florence: D'Anna, 1967.

Pasnau, Robert. "Olivi on the Metaphysics of the Soul." *Medieval Philosophy and Theology* 6 (1997): 122–26.

Pasquazi, Silvio. "Antipurgatorio." In *Enciclopedia dantesca,* 1:304–6. Rome: Istituto della Enciclopedia Italiana G. Treccani, 1970.

———. "Contrapasso." In *Enciclopedia dantesca,* 2:181–83. Rome: Istituto della Enciclopedia Italiana G. Treccani, 1970.

Pasquini, Emilio. "La letteratura didattica e allegorica." In *La letteratura italiana. Storia e testi,* vol. 1, *Il Duecento,* edited by Carlo Muscetta, part 2, 3–111. Bari: Laterza, 1970.

Pecchiai, Pio. "I documenti sulla biografia di Bonvicino della Riva." *Giornale storico della letteratura italiana* 78 (1921): 96–127.

Perez, Paolo. *I sette cerchi del Purgatorio di Dante. Saggio di studi.* 2nd ed. Verona: Libreria della Minerva, 1867.

Pertile, Lino. "'La punta del disio': Storia di una metafora dantesca." *Lectura Dantis* 7 (1990): 3–28.

———. "*Paradiso:* A Drama of Desire." In *Word and Drama in Dante: Essays on the "Divina Commedia,"* edited by John C. Barnes and Jennifer Petrie, 143–80. Dublin: Irish Academic Press, 1993.

———. "A Desire of Paradise and a Paradise of Desire: Dante and Mysticism." In *Dante. Contemporary Perspectives,* edited by Amilcare Iannucci, 148–66. Toronto: University of Toronto Press, 1997.

———. *La puttana e il gigante. Dal "Cantico dei Cantici" al Paradiso terrestre di Dante.* Ravenna: Longo, 1998.

Pickering, Frederick P. *Essays on Medieval German Literature and Iconography.* Cambridge: Cambridge University Press, 1980.

Picone, Michelangelo. "Il corpo della/nella luna: Sul canto II del *Paradiso.*" *L'Alighieri* 51 (2000): 7–25.

Piolanti, Antonio. "Il dogma del Purgatorio." *Euntes Docete* 6 (1953): 287–311.

Pouchelle, Marie-Christine. "Représentations du corps dans la *Légende dorée.*" *Ethnologie française* 6 (1976): 293–308.

Quinn, Patrick. "Aquinas's Concept of the Body and Out of Body Situations." *Heythrop Journal* 34 (1993): 387–400.

Rati, Giancarlo. *Saggi danteschi e altri studi.* Rome: Bulzoni, 1988.

Reeves, Marjorie. *The Influence of Prophecy in the Later Middle Ages: A Study in Joachinism.* Oxford: Clarendon Press, 1969.

———. "History and Prophecy in Medieval Thought." *Medievalia et Humanistica* n.s. 5 (1974): 51–75.

Reynolds, Philip L. *Food and the Body: Some Peculiar Questions in High Medieval Theology.* Leiden: Brill, 1999.

Ricci, Pier Giorgio. *Rari ed inediti.* Edited by Alberto Chiari. Rome: Edizioni di storia e letteratura, 1981.

Ringbom, Sixten. *Icon to Narrative: The Rise of the Dramatic Close-up in Fifteenth-Century Devotional Painting.* Åbo: Åbo Akademi, 1965.

Rossi, Aldo. "Poesia didattica del Nord." In *Storia della letteratura italiana,* directed by Emilio Cecchi and Natalino Sapegno, 1:470–86. Milan: Garzanti, 1965.

Rusconi, Roberto. "Antichrist and Antichrists." In *The Encyclopedia of Apocalypticism,* edited by Bernard McGinn, 2:287–325. New York: Continuum, 1998.

Ryan, Christopher. "The Theology of Dante." In *The Cambridge Companion to Dante,* edited by Rachel Jacoff, 136–52. Cambridge: Cambridge University Press, 1993.

Santi, Francesco. "Il cadavere e Bonifacio VIII, tra Stefano Tempier e Avicenna: Intorno a un saggio di Elisabeth Brown." *Studi medievali* ser. 3, 28, 2 (1987): 861–78.

———. "Un nome di persona al corpo e la massa dei corpi gloriosi." *Micrologus* 1 (1993): 273–300.

Schiller, Gertrud. *Iconography of Christian Art.* Translated by Janet Seligman. 2 vols. Greenwich, Conn.: New York Graphic Society, 1971–72.

Schmitt, Franciscus S. "Anselmo d'Aosta, santo." In *Enciclopedia dantesca,* 1:293–94. Rome: Istituto della Enciclopedia Italiana G. Treccani, 1970.

Schmitt, Jean-Claude. *Les Revenants: Les vivants et les morts dans la société médiévale.* Paris: Gallimard, 1994.

Schrage, Marco. *Giacomino da Verona: Himmel und Hölle in der frühen italienischen Literatur.* Frankfurt am Main: Lang, 2003.

Schulte, Heinz. "Johannes Duns Scotus: Der Mensch—Einheit in Differenz. Zur Auseinandersetzung des Duns Scotus mit der Anthropologie des Thomas von Aquin." *Theologie und Philosophie* 49 (1974): 554–60.

Segre, Cesare. "Le forme e le tradizioni didattiche." In *Grundriss der romanischen Literaturen des Mittelalters,* vol. 6, *La littérature didactique, allégorique et satirique,* part 1, directed by Hans Robert Jauss, 60–66. Heidelberg: Carl Winter and Universitätsverlag, 1968.

———. L'*itinerarium animae* nel Duecento e Dante." *Letture classensi* 13 (1984): 9–32.

Seidl, Horst. "Zur Leib-Seele-Einheit des Menschen bei Thomas von Aquin." *Theologie und Philosophie* 49 (1974): 548–53.

Shapiro, Marianne. "Dante's Twofold Representation of the Soul." *Lectura Dantis* 18–19 (Spring–Fall 1996): 49–90.

———. *Dante and the Knot of Body and Soul.* New York: St. Martin's Press, 1998.

Sharp, Dorothea E. *Franciscan Philosophy at Oxford in the Thirteenth Century.* London: Oxford University Press, 1930.

Singleton, Charles. *Dante Studies 2: Journey to Beatrice.* Cambridge: Harvard University Press, 1958.

Sloyan, Gerard S. *The Crucifixion of Jesus: History, Myth, Faith.* Minneapolis: Fortress Press, 1995.

Southern, Richard W. *The Making of the Middle Ages.* New Haven: Yale University Press, 1959.

Spitzer, Leo. *Romanische Literaturstudien 1936–1956.* Tübingen: Max Niemeyer Verlag, 1959.

———. "Speech and Language in *Inferno* 13." In *Representative Essays,* edited by Alban K. Forcione, Herbert Lindenberger, and Madeline Sutherland, 153–71. Stanford: Stanford University Press, 1988.

Spivey Ellington, Donna. "Impassioned Mother or Passive Icon: The Virgin's Role in Late Medieval and Early Modern Passion Sermons." *Renaissance Quarterly* 48:2 (Summer 1995): 227–41.

Stabile, Giorgio. "Volontà." In *Enciclopedia dantesca,* 5:1134–40. Rome: Istituto della Enciclopedia Italiana G. Treccani, 1976.

Sticca, Sandro. *The "Planctus Mariae" in the Dramatic Tradition of the Middle Ages.* Translated by Joseph R. Berrigan. Athens: University of Georgia Press, 1988.

Teetaert, A. "Saxe (Conrade de)." In *Dictionnaire de théologie catholique,* vol. 14, cols. 1234–35. Paris: Letouzey et Ané, 1939.

Tenenti, Alberto. *Il senso della morte e l'amore della vita nel Rinascimento.* Turin: Einaudi, 1957.

Tentler, Thomas. *Sin and Confession on the Eve of the Reformation.* Princeton: Princeton University Press, 1977.

Tibiletti, Carlo. "Le anime dopo la morte: Stato intermedio o visione di Dio? (Dalla Patristica al sec. XIV)." *Augustinianum* 28 (1988): 631–59.

Tollemache, Federigo. "Beatitudini evangeliche." In *Enciclopedia dantesca,* 1:540–41. Rome: Istituto della Enciclopedia Italiana G. Treccani, 1970.

Toscano, Tobia R. *La tragedia degli ipocriti e altre letture dantesche.* Naples: Liguori, 1988.

Travi, Ernesto. "Il tema del corpo nella *Divina Commedia.*" In *Il corpo in scena: La rappresentazione del corpo nella filosofia e nelle arti,* edited by Virgilio Melchiorre and Annamaria Cascetta, 197–223. Milan: Vita e Pensiero, 1983.

Trottmann, Christian. *La vision béatifique: Des disputes scolastiques à sa définition par Benoît XII.* Rome: École française de Rome, 1995.

———. "Sulla funzione dell'anima e del corpo nella beatitudine: Elementi di riflessione nella Scolastica." In *Anima e corpo nella cultura medievale. Atti del V Convegno di studi della Società Italiana per lo Studio del Pensiero Medievale: Venezia, 25–28 settembre 1995,* edited by Carla Casagrande and Silvana Vecchio, 140–47. Florence: Sismel-Edizioni del Galluzzo, 1999.

———. "Communion des saints et jugement dernier: Dans les chant XIX–XX du *Paradis.*" In *Pour Dante: Dante et l'Apocalypse. Lecture humanistes de Dante,* edited by Bruno Pinchard, 181–98. Paris: Honoré Champion, 2001.

Tugwell, Simon. *Human Immortality and the Redemption of Death.* London: Darton, Longman and Todd, 1990.

Vanni Rovighi, Sofia. "Alberto Magno e l'unità della forma sostanziale nell'uomo." In *Medioevo e Rinascimento: Studi in onore di Bruno Nardi,* 2:753–78. Florence: Sansoni, 1955.

———. *L'antropologia filosofica di San Tommaso d'Aquino.* Milan: Vita e Pensiero, 1965.

———. "Arbitrio." In *Enciclopedia dantesca,* 1:345–48. Rome: Istituto della Enciclopedia Italiana G. Treccani, 1970.

———. *San Bonaventura.* Milan: Vita e Pensiero, 1974.

———. *Introduzione a Tommaso d'Aquino.* 6th ed. Rome: Laterza, 1995.

Van Os, Arnold Barel. *Religious Visions: The Development of the Eschatological Elements in Mediaeval English Religious Literature.* Amsterdam: H. J. Paris, 1932.

Van Steenberghen, Fernand. *Maître Siger de Brabant.* Louvain: Publications Universitaires, 1977.

———. *Thomas Aquinas and Radical Aristotelianism.* Washington, D.C.: Catholic University of America Press, 1980.

———. *La philosophie au XIIIᵉ siècle.* 2nd ed. Louvain-La-Neuve: Éditions de l'Institut Supérieur de Philosophie, 1991.

Vauchez, André. "Pénitents." In *Dictionnaire de spiritualité, ascétique et mystique, doctrine et histoire,* vol. 12, part 1, cols. 1010–23. Paris: Beauchesne, 1984.

Viola, Colomon. "Jugements de Dieu et jugement dernier: Saint Augustin et la scolastique naissante (fin XIᶜ–milieu XIIIᶜ siècles)." In *The Use and Abuse of Eschatology in the Middle Ages,* edited by Werner Verbeke, Daniel Verhelst, and Andries Welkenhuysen, 242–98. Leuven: Leuven University Press, 1988.

Von Simson, Otto. *"Compassio* and *Co-redemptio* in Roger van der Weyden's *Descent from the Cross." The Art Bulletin* 35 (1953): 9–16.

Vovelle, Michel. *La mort et l'Occident: De 1300 à nos jours.* Paris: Gallimard, 1983.

Walther, Hans. *Das Streitgedicht in der lateinischen Literatur des Mittelalters.* Munich: Beck, 1920.

Warner, Marina. *Alone of All Her Sex: The Myth and the Cult of the Virgin Mary.* New York: Vintage Books, 1983.

Weakland, John. "Pope John XXII and the Beatific Vision Controversy." *Annuale Mediaevale* 9 (1968): 76–84.

Weber, Edouard-Henri. *La personne humaine au XIIIᶜ siècle: L'avènement chez les maîtres parisiens de l'acception moderne de l'homme.* Paris: Vrin, 1991.

Wicki, Nikolaus. *Die Lehre von der himmlischen Seligkeit in der mittelalterlichen Scholastik von Petrus Lombardus bis Thomas von Aquin.* Freiburg: Universitätsverlag, 1954.

Wilmart, André. *Auteurs spirituels et textes dévots du moyen âge latin: Études d'histoire littéraire.* Paris: Bloud et Gay, 1932.

Zaleski, Carol. *Otherworld Journeys: Accounts of Near-Death Experience in Medieval and Modern Times.* New York: Oxford University Press, 1987.

Zambon, Francesco. "Tradizione latina e tradizione romanza." In *Manuale di letteratura italiana: Storia per generi e problemi,* vol. 1, *Dalle origini alla fine del Quattrocento,* edited by Franco Brioschi and Costanzo Di Girolamo, 463–91. Turin: Bollati Boringhieri, 1993.

Zanoni, Luigi. "Fra Bonvesin della Riva fu Umiliato o Terziario Francescano?" *Il Libro e la Stampa* 8 (1914): 141–48.

Zavalloni, Roberto. *Richard de Mediavilla et la controverse sur la pluralité des formes.* Louvain: Éditions de l'Institut Supérieur de Philosophie, 1951.

General Index

Acheron, 54–55

Adam, xvii, 9, 79, 97, 110, 113, 117, 119, 169–70

Aeneas, 57, 148

Albert the Great, 59, 61, 71, 133–34

Anchises, 148

anger (wrath), 41, 72, 124, 127

Anselm of Bec, 93, 119

Anthony of Padua, 22, 28

ante-purgatory, 113, 115–16, 122, 129, 151

Antichrist, 9

Apocalypticism, 22, 26

Apollo, 135

Ariès, P., xii, 14

Aristotelianism, 59, 62, 64, 73, 144

Aristotle, 69–70

Arnauld of Bonneval, 133

assumption (of Christ and Mary), 104, of Mary, 60, 103, 125–26; of John, 166

Auerbach, E., xi

Augustine, 60, 92, 110, 159, 169–70

avarice, 116, 124, 134, 149

Averroës, 70

Avicenna, 69

Azzolino da Romano, 77

Babylon (infernal), 20–22

Bacon, R., 59

Balçabù. See Satan

baptism, 109–10, 112, 120, 163

Bárberi Squarotti, G., 90

Barolini, T., xiv, 110, 160

Bazán, B., 68

beatitude (bliss/joy in heaven), xii, xvii, 5, 11, 15, 17, 19, 23–25, 27, 29, 30–35, 44–46, 48–50, 53, 60–63, 66, 71, 84–86, 92–93, 96, 123, 128, 132–34, 137, 144, 151–56, 158–60, 163–67. *See also* glory

Beatitudes (Sermon on the Mount), 123–24, 126

Beatrice, xvii, 78, 82, 113, 117, 119, 122, 154, 157, 166–76

Belacqua, 113, 129

Benedict, 163–65, 167

Benedict XIII (Pope), xii

Bernard of Clairvaux, 159, 167–68, 176–77

Bible
  Matthew, 123
  Luke, 135
  John, 120, 129
  2 Corinthians, 172

blood, 69–70, 92, 105, 109; of Christ, 94–96, 99, 104–5, 117, 120, 125, 132, 136–37

body (aerial), xv–xvi, 55–58, 67, 74–77, 80, 82, 85–86, 111–12, 115, 122, 127, 130, 135, 137, 139, 141–43, 145–51, 156–57, 160, 162, 167; dead, 1, 3, 6–7, 15, 17, 33, 38, 41, 66, 151–67 (*see also* decay; desire); resurrected (*see* Resurrection)

Boitani, P., 77, 168

Bonaventure, 58–62, 66, 98, 100, 103, 120, 122, 154, 156, 158–59; pseudo-Bonaventure, 101

Index of Passages from Dante's Works

Divine Comedy

Inferno

MANUELE GRAGNOLATI

is Fellow and Tutor in Italian
at Somerville College, Oxford.